TEXT

Contributing Editor, Volume 13

Hans Walter Gabler
University of Munich

TEXT

An Interdisciplinary Annual

of Textual Studies

13

W. SPEED HILL

EDWARD M. BURNS

Co-Editors

PETER L. SHILLINGSBURG

Review Editor

Ann Arbor

THE UNIVERSITY OF MICHIGAN PRESS

2000

T E X T

An Interdisciplinary Annual
of Textual Studies

Volume 13

Copyright © 2000 by the University of Michigan

INTERNATIONAL STANDARD BOOK NUMBER
Set: 0-404-62550-9
Volume 13: 0-472-11194-9

INTERNATIONAL STANDARD SERIALS NUMBER
0736-3974

THE UNIVERSITY OF MICHIGAN PRESS
839 Greene Street
P.O. Box 1104
Ann Arbor, Michigan 48106-1104

Manufactured in the United States of America

⊗Printed on acid-free paper

2003 2002 2001 2000   4 3 2 1

Contents

Reviews

Preface and Acknowledgments

WITH THIS VOLUME OF *TEXT* the editors continue a policy of modestly internationalizing the journal. Hans Walter Gabler recommended to us Klaus Hurlebusch's substantial essay, "Understanding the Author's Compositional Method: Prolegomenon to a Hermeneutics of Genetic Writing," originally published in volume 10 of *editio: International Yearbook of Scholarly Editing* (1998), and assisted the editors in translating it for English-speaking readers. And two essays by the Dutch scholarly editors H. T. M. van Vliet and Annemarie Kets–Vree exemplify vigorous and active editorial work centered at the Constantijn Huygens Institute for Text Editions and Intellectual History in The Hague. Both were given at the 1999 meeting of the Society. The editors welcome suggestions of articles for translation and of books for review in future volumes of *TEXT*.

*   *   *

The editors wish to thank the following for their support of the Society for Textual Scholarship and of *TEXT*: Marlene Gottlieb, Dean of Arts and Humanities, Lehman College, CUNY, for her support of the work of the Co-Editor of *TEXT*, Speed Hill; Chernoh M. Sesay, Provost and Executive Vice President of William Paterson University, for support of the work of the Co-Editor, Edward Burns; the English Department, University of North Texas for its support of Peter Shillingsburg, Book Review Editor and our typesetter; and the following administrators at the Graduate School and University Center, CUNY, for their support of the Society: President, Frances Degen Horowitz; Provost and Vice President for Academic Affairs, William Kelly; Executive Officer of the Ph.D. Program in English, Joan Richardson; and Joseph Margolis for his assistance to Edward Burns.

We wish to thank as well the following, members of the Advisory Board, of the Graduate Faculty of the English Program at CUNY, and others, whose careful reviews of submissions have helped to shape the contents of this volume: Stephen Blum, Stanley Boorman, George Bornstein, Maureen M. B. Boulton, Ronald Broude, William E. Coleman, Don L. Cook, Gregory M. Downing, Hoyt Duggan, A. S. G. Edwards, Paul Eggert, Daniel Eisenberg, Joseph Grigely, Michael Groden, Jay Halio, Richard Harrier, Andrea Harris, T. H. Howard–Hill, James M. Hutchisson, David Kastan, Geert Lernout, Richard McCoy, Joseph R. McElrath, Jr., Jerome J. McGann, Clarence Miller, Fred Nichols, Derek Pearsall, Bodo Plachta, Cheryl J. Plumb, Peter Robinson, Ludo Rocher, Christa Sammons, David Sider, Peter Simpson, Paul Stanwood, Margaret E. Winters, and David Yerkes. In addition, the following were of material assistance to the editors in preparing Klaus Hurlebusch's article for publication in English: Hans Walter Gabler, Uta Nitschke–Stumpf, Ogden Goelet, Henry Heuser, and Helene Erlichson Kloehn.

Edward M. Burns
W. Speed Hill
Peter L. Shillingsburg

Where Would Anglo–American Textual Criticism Be If Shakespeare Had Died of the Plague in 1593?

W. SPEED HILL

"**W**HAT IF?" EVOKES A WELL-KNOWN deconstructive turn: what if up were down, the margin were the center? There is a mathematical version: what if parallel lines did meet at infinity (as they do in non-Euclidian geometry)? It is also a recognized historical exercise, as when one poses a "counterfactual" question: what would have happened if England had not entered into the first war against Germany?[1] In the present instance, the question is both historical and deconstructive: what if Shakespeare *had* died of the plague in 1593? What would textual criticism in the Anglo–American tradition be if England's national poet had been Spenser, or Milton, or Jonson? Or Chaucer, as Tim William Machan discusses below. Or, to go outside Shakespeare's early modern milieu, Wordsworth (as Jim Mays suggested[2])?

If we stay in the early modern period, the first hurdle a non-Shakespearean textual criticism would have to clear is the split between dramatic (Shakespeare and his theatrical colleagues) and non-dramatic (everybody else) texts. Nowhere is this divide more entrenched than in the editing of these two sub-groups. Editors of

---

[1] See Niall Ferguson, *The Pity of War: Explaining World War I* (New York: Basic Books, 1999).

[2] In the paper Mays gave at S.T.S. in April, 1999.

Spenser, Milton (or Hooker) are seldom recruited to edit a play by Shakespeare, Jonson, or Middleton, and reciprocally, Shakespearean editors do not ordinarily harvest grapes in the textual vineyards of Sir Philip Sidney's pastoral romances, Edmund Spenser's epics, odes, or sonnets, or Donne's lyrics, epicedes, or Anniversaries. It follows that guidelines for editing plays will necessarily differ from those for editing works of prose or verse.

However, when it comes to deriving a *theory* of editing, a textual criticism as distinct from (though derived from) the practice of editing, the binary of dramatic/non-dramatic disappears. The problems of editing Shakespeare's authorially orphaned plays simply overwhelm adjacent authors and texts, whether they were connected to the theater or not. It is this historical fact that gave rise to the panel in which the following two essays were given as talks.

We all know that Shakespeare was a late-bloomer. In 1593, by which time he was twenty-nine, he had written the following plays (I use the Oxford Shakespeare chronology): *The Two Gentlemen of Verona, The Taming of the Shrew, The First Part of the Contention* [=*2 Henry VI*], *Richard Duke of York* [= *3 Henry VI*], *1 Henry VI, Titus Andronicus,* and *Richard III*—a substantial achievement, to be sure, but not a draft on literary immortality. Two months Shakespeare's elder and himself dead by 30 May 1593, Christopher Marlowe had also written seven plays: *Dido Queen of Carthage, 1 and 2 Tamburlaine, The Jew of Malta, The Massacre at Paris, Edward the Second,* and *Doctor Faustus*. Most of us would concede that by the time of his death, Marlowe had the better of it. But if Marlowe's plays were not collected until the early nineteenth century, it is unlikely that Shakespeare's seven pre-1593 plays would have been, either.

Which leads to the question, if Shakespeare *had* died of the plague in the spring of 1593 (which closed the theaters for the rest of the year), where would a native textual criticism have gotten a foothold? Editing the works of Spenser, Shakespeare's elder by twelve years or so? No. Spenser's texts—as texts—are unproblematic. Whether Spenser saw *The Faerie Queene* through the press himself or deputized someone else to do it, it presents no problems (or opportunities) to the textual scholar. When A. C. Hamilton edited *The Faerie Queene* for Longman in 1977, he simply photo-reprinted J. S. Smith's Oxford English Text text of 1909. Sidney? No—or at least not until the various Sidney circle manuscripts had been identified and collected—and this did not take place until the twentieth century. In the absence of the relevant manuscripts, the 1598 Folio edited by his sister Mary supplied carefully prepared texts that invited careful reprinting, not aggressive editorial intervention.

Ben Jonson? A better case, but still, no. Jonson's own meticulous care with the preparation and printing of his 1616 Folio effectively pre-empted later textual criticism. Given the author-centered ideology of editing early modern writers dominant until quite recently, Jonson's burly authorial presence in his own folio elbows the would-be helpful editor out of the print shop. True, there is the great Herford and Simpson Oxford *Ben Jonson*. But its momumentality broke no new ground textually, its texts honored Jonson's own choices in the Folio when two versions were available (as in *Every Man in his Humour*), and its auspices were more nineteenth-century and classical than twentieth-century and vernacular. Only now is it being reconceived as a new "Complete Works of Ben Jonson," co-edited by Ian Donaldson and David Bevington.[3]

Beaumont and Fletcher? Well, their plays were collected in the 1647 folio, and students of Fredson Bowers have scrupulously re-edited the entire *Beaumont and Fletcher Canon*,[4] whose title recognizes that attribution of theatrical scripts to particular authors of the time remains a major issue. But, again, there is no advancement of textual criticism here, only the careful execution of the orthodox copy-text editing of the Greg-Bowers persuasion, demonstrated earlier by Bowers himself in his edition of the works of Thomas Dekker.[5]

Middleton? Well, yes, if you are Gary Taylor, but there was no contemporary attempt to collect Middleton by Middleton (as Jonson collected Jonson) or by his friends and colleagues (as Heminges and Condell collected Shakespeare). Taylor argues that Middleton rightly belongs with the triumvirate of Jonson, Shakespeare, and Beaumont and Fletcher, whose folios carried forward the Tudor–Stuart theatrical canon into the seventeenth century,[6] but it is not clear that, had Shakespeare *not* been collected in the 1623 Folio, Middleton's advocates would have stepped into the breach. Throughout the seventeenth century, it was Beaumont and Fletcher and Jonson who were esteemed over Shakespeare. Not until Dryden's rehabilitation in the 1680s does Shakespeare begin to overtake his rivals on his way to becoming the

---

3 See Ian Donaldson, "The Cambridge Edition of the Works of Ben Jonson," *The Ben Jonson Journal* 5 (1998), 257–69.

4 *The Dramatic Works in the Beaumont and Fletcher Canon*, gen. ed. Fredson Bowers (Cambridge: Cambridge UP, 1966–).

5 *The Dramatic Works of Thomas Dekker*, ed. Fredson Bowers, 4 vols. (Cambridge: Cambridge UP, 1953–61).

6 "The Renaissance and the End of Editing," *Palimpsest: Editorial Theory in the Humanities*, ed. George Bornstein and Ralph G. Williams (Ann Arbor: The U of Michigan P), 121–49, esp. 133–34. Taylor explicitly asks: "How might our editorial paradigms . . . be different, if they were founded on the evidence of Middleton's texts, rather than Shakespeare's?" (134).

universal genius we know him as.[7] And if Shakespeare was in the shadows of Jonson and Beaumont and Fletcher for almost six decades, would Middleton have fared any better? It seems unlikely. Even now (some would say) Middleton is an acquired taste.

Granted, Bowers and his students must be credited with the one innovation in the field that European editors occasionally do exploit, namely, analytical bibliography, especially when used as an aid in detecting multiple issues of editions ostensibly identical through the use of a Hinman Collator (or its equivalent).[8] The demonstration editions deriving from this school are Bowers's own *Dekker*, *Marlowe* and *The Beaumont and Fletcher Canon*, to be followed by the mighty editorial enterprise of editing nineteenth-century American authors according to Greg–Bowers copy-text principles that followed from the founding of the Center for Editions of American Authors (CEAA), which evolved into the Committee on Scholarly Editions (CSE), both under the aegis of the Modern Language Association.[9] But the dramatic texts Bowers (and his students) edited were seen as prefatory to the Everest of editorial challenges, the preparation of a critical old-spelling text of all of Shakespeare's plays. This remains a goal, but an increasingly elusive one. Had only seven of his plays survived, it is difficult to imagine the justification for such full-scale editions of Shakespeare's peers. Stanley Wells and Gary Taylor have edited a complete works "in Original Spelling" (Oxford: Clarendon P, 1986), but it has not received universal acclaim, and the very concept of a "critical" edition, if by that we mean an eclectically constructed edition, no longer commands uncritical assent. Paul Werstine's account below helpfully problematizes the early twentieth-century history of Shakespearean editing.

If we look farther afield, we might assume that Chaucer, "the father of English poetry," would, in Shakespeare's absence, have attracted ambitious would-be textual critics. The extent to which that happened—or more accurately—did *not* happen is the focus of Tim Machan's essay below. Moving forward in time, Milton or Wordsworth were suggested by Jim Mays. To be sure, Milton's texts are various

---

7 Gerald E. Bentley, *Shakespeare and Jonson: Their Reputations in the Seventeenth Century Compared*, 2 vols. (U of Chicago P; Cambridge UP, 1945).

8 See Annemarie Kets–Vree, "Dutch Scholarly Editing: The Historical–Critical Edition in Practice," 134–35, below. For the reluctance of other traditions of scholarly editing to exploit the evidence analytical bibliography turns up, see Conor Fahy, "Preaching to the Half-Converted: The Bowers Legacy in Italian Studies," and Wallace Kirsop, "Fredson Bowers and the French Connection," *TEXT* 8 (1995), 37–52, 53–66.

9 See "The Center for Scholarly Editions: An Introductory Statement" (New York: MLA, 1977).

enough to challenge one's editorial skills,[10] and Milton is canonical enough to warrant the effort. But no Milton editor historically contributed to the field apart from Richard Bentley, whose textual interventions in Milton's texts have not proven persuasive. As with Spenser, it is in the preparation of a commentary rather than the establishment of the text that most editors of Milton have worked. As for Wordsworth, certainly the *Cornell Wordsworth* is both theoretically and practically an enormously influential achievement. But will it be found, a century hence, to have advanced the field of textual criticism *per se?* The answer is, perhaps, especially if its perceived bias toward the early rather than the late Wordsworth and its versionist editorial implications come to be endorsed and absorbed by readers and critics.

That leaves John Donne. Here Shakespeare's counterfactual absence from the canon is, for the editor of Donne, of little consequence. That is because the vast majority of Donne's verse was circulated in manuscript, not print. Each author orphaned his works, leaving their care to others, both before and after their deaths.[11] But whereas Shakespeare arguably left us only his share in *The Book of Thomas More* as a sample of his handwriting (another "perhaps": Werstine is skeptical; see below, 31 and n.12), so that the editing of Shakespeare remains quintessentially the editing of printed books, Donne left us (for the most part) nothing but manuscripts of his poetry, and these are, with one exception, scribal, not holograph. This has required the editors of the *Donne Variorum* to reconfigure contemporary textual theory—be it copy-text theory, best-text theory, or Lachmannian stemmatics—as it applies to such a huge corpus of extant manuscripts circulating without their author's control and interest. Here, indeed, is an editorial task that challenges us to rethink our paradigms, which is precisely what Gary Stringer, Ted–Larry Pebworth, and Ernest Sullivan have done in the *Donne Variorum*.[12]

---

[10] See John T. Shawcross, "Scholary Editions: Composite Editorial Principles of Single Copy-Texts, Multiple Copy-Texts, Edited Copy-Texts," *TEXT* 4 (1988), 297–317.

[11] Ernst Honigmann points out to me that Heminges and Condell, in their letter "To the great Variety of Readers" in the front matter of the First Folio, say that "It had bene a thing ... worthie to haue bene wished, that the Author himselfe had liu'd to haue set forth, and ouerseen his owne writings; ... ," which implies that Shakespeare was intending to "set [them] forth" and to oversee them, implying his presence at the press. Still, the printing of the earlier quartos conspicuously lacked authorial authorization or supervision, as implied by the well known references in the same letter to "diuerse stolne, and surreptitious copies, maimed and deformed by the frauds and stealthes of iniurious imposters, that expos'd them: .... "

[12] *The Variorum Edition of the Poetry of John Donne*, vols. 6 and 8, gen. ed. Gary Stringer (Bloomington and Indianapolis: Indiana UP, 1995). For an overview of the surviving texts of Donne's poetry, see General Introduction (6: xliii-xlviii; 8: xlviii-liv);

Nothing of what the *Donne Variorum* editors do has not been done before. Their stated goal is to isolate the single version closest to the lost holograph ("what Donne wrote") through Lachmannian stemmatic analysis and to reprint it with the absolute minimum of emendation (McKerrow's best-text theory, for which see Werstine below). However, the aim of copy-text critical editing, to recover the accidentals as well as the substantives of the author's missing manuscript, is rejected as impossible of realization. Staggering as the amount of material that survives from the seventeenth century is, none of it—with the exception of Donne's verse letter to Lady Carey and Mrs. Essex Rich—comes from Donne's own hand, and his authorial practices in accidentals are permanently inaccessible to the modern editor.

In this, as Paul Werstine's essay makes abundantly clear, the editing of Donne is not so very different from the editing of Shakespeare's plays. In both cases, the sought-for evidence of authorial usage lies barricaded behind second-order authorities: the printed quartos and the Folio in the case of Shakespeare, the extensive manuscript archive of Donne's verse compiled by friends and various scribes.[13] Editorial success, Werstine suggests, below, lies in our abandoning the myth that we can reliably identify the nature of the copy that lies behind the surviving printed artifacts.

Still, there is a difference between the paradigm governing the editing of the texts of Donne's poetry in the *Donne Variorum* and its predecessors. It is twofold. First, the *Donne Variorum* editors recognized that the operative textual unit was the poem—or sequence of poems—not the manuscript in which it or they appear, as such manuscript collections will inevitably contain individual poems of widely differing authority. Second, with the writing of a computer program that automates the collation of individual poems (though not their transcription from source documents), it became technologically feasible to collate *all* the surviving textual evidence, poem by poem. Sensing the scale of the task, earlier editors shied away from the editorial implications of such an abundance of the surviving manuscript evidence. Part of the elegance of Lachmannian stemmatic analysis is its ability to winnow a mass of manuscript evidence so as to identify the texts closest to missing archetype, allowing one quite legitimately to ignore derivative manuscripts, a process called *eliminatio codicum descriptorum*. Certainly Helen Gardner and Wesley Milgate did not deliberately ignore

---

for the theoretical underpinnings of the edition, see Ted–Larry Pebworth, "Manuscript Transmission and the Selection of Copy-Text in Renaissance Coterie Poetry," *TEXT* 7 (1994), 243–61.

[13] Critical to the whole *Donne Variorum* enterprise is the listing of surviving manuscript copies of Donne's verse compiled by Peter Beal: *Index of English Literary Manuscripts*, vol. 1, pt. 1 (London: Mansell, 1980).

relevant textual evidence, but for them the operative unit was the manuscript not the texts in the manuscript. Familiar as they were with the surviving families of Donne manuscripts, Shakespeare's shade still haunted their editorial practice, for the 1633 (and 1635) printed texts continued to serve as copy-texts, even though stemmatic analysis showed clearly enough that the texts used as printer's copy for these posthumous editions were (1) of mixed character and (2) well down the stemmata that Grierson had first begun to construct and to which Gardner and Milgate in their Oxford English Texts editions added. Thus did un- (or less) authoritative printed texts typically become the copy-texts of choice. Such was the authority of the printed artifact to Anglo–American editors accustomed to working within a (Shakespearean) textual tradition in which *only* printed texts have survived.

The following two essays take up these and other issues in greater detail.

"I endowed thy purposes": Shakespeare, Editing, and Middle English Literature

TIM WILLIAM MACHAN

'Tis much he dares;
And to that dauntless temper of his mind
He hath a wisdom that doth guide his valor
To act in safety. There is none but he
Whose being I do fear; and under him
My genius is rebuked, as it is said
Mark Antony's was by Caesar.

—*Macbeth*, III.i.51–57

"Well, what I try to show," said Persse, "is that we can't avoid reading Shakespeare through the lens of T.S. Eliot's poetry. I mean, who can read *Hamlet* today without thinking of "Prufrock"? Who can hear the speeches of Ferdinand in *The Tempest* without being reminded of "The Fire Sermon" section of *The Waste Land?*"

—*Small World*

C HAUCER MAY BE THE FIGURE that the early modern period designated the "father of English poetry," but it is Shakespeare who has generated the defining features of Anglo–American textual criticism. To Shakespeare's era we trace the development of collation and reconstruction techniques still used today, and in Shakespeare's texts lie the inspirations for the New Bibliography, the New Historicism, and much of the even newer, socially oriented textual criticism. More than any other author's, Shakespeare's works have been the litmus test of editorial theories, works to be appropriated and used to validate criticism and critic alike, with the result that Hamlet's flesh and Lear's fool have provoked enough text-critical rancor to make even Scaliger or Poliziano blush.

Chaucer—and medieval literature more generally—is another matter. Chaucer, Lydgate, Gower, and Langland preceded Shakespeare into print, of course, and medieval literature has occasioned its own editorial vitriol. But it certainly has not inspired any ambitious text-critical theories and programs comparable to those developed by Greg and Bowers and focused on Shakespeare and early drama. In their monumental eight-volume edition of the *Canterbury Tales*, John Matthews Manly and Edith Rickert sought primarily to edit one poem, not to construct a widely applicable editorial theory, and the same is true of George Kane and E. Talbot Donaldson in their edition of Langland's *Piers Plowman*. More influential than either of these editions are the publications of the English Early Text Society. Initiated in 1864 as a series at once serving nationalistic impulses and providing texts for the readers of the New English Dictionary, EETS has produced editions of medieval English works that are often the only ones available and that, even when this is not the case, sometimes remain the standard ones for scholarly use. While EETS has cast a wider editorial net than either Manly–Rickert or Kane–Donaldson, however, its largely diplomatic approach has nonetheless ensnared few non-medieval works.

The situation today is that whatever Renaissance readers like Foxe, Spenser, and Shakespeare himself may have thought of Chaucer and his writings,[1] Shakespeare's text-critical prominence has rendered him a daunting figure not just for scholars of medieval literature but in effect, in a weird way, for the literature as well. As much as Macbeth fears Banquo's wisdom, valor, and caution, so might medieval writers fear Shakespeare, whose genius has continually rebuked their own among textual critics and (consequently) readers as well. Macbeth manages to create and summon the very ghost that haunts him to his doom. My ambitions in this paper are rather more limited and, I hope, less spectral. I wish to understand why Shakespeare and not Chaucer, Hoccleve, or Henryson became, if not the father of Anglo–American textual criticism, then its favorite son. And having explored the cultural, literary, and bibliographical reasons underlying Shakespeare's prominence at the expense of his medieval ancestors, I want

---

[1] A convenient record of early responses can be found in Caroline F.E. Spurgeon's *Five Hundred Years of Chaucer Criticism and Allusion (1357–1900)*, 3 vols. (London: Kegan Paul, 1914–25).

to consider how such a prominent son has affected the presentation of these literary forebears. To put matters in another, distinctively post-modern way, I am interested in Shakespeare's influence on the Middle Ages.

Before Shakespeare could become the favorite son of textual criticism, of course, his literary prominence had first to surpass that of his predecessors and contemporaries, and this seems to have happened very rapidly after his death. Harold Bloom would attribute this achievement simply to Shakespeare's transcendent genius, and up to a point I would agree with him.[2] But since textual criticism is a cultural institution serving cultural ambitions, I think Bloom himself might grant the relevance of its social impulses in the formation of literary reputation. Even as early modern audiences were calling Chaucer the father of English poetry, various ideas and concerns coalesced to render Shakespeare the more culturally representative and celebrated figure. Shakespeare brought with him, for instance, none of the theological ambiguity that accompanied Chaucer, Langland, or other medieval writers, for coming from pre-Reformation times, the religious sentiments of these writers had to be ignored, tolerated, or appropriated for a Protestant ethic. Even if in some cases, like those of Chaucer and Langland, such appropriation was accomplished to great effect, Shakespeare, who could in no way be identified with Rome and whose plays bore no resemblance to those of the Corpus Christi cycle, offered fewer complications for readers and critics alike. His inescapably Protestant background rendered him a figure who more easily mirrored the sentiments of seventeenth- and eighteenth-century audiences than did his medieval predecessors. For all his quickly acknowledged literary pre-eminence, he was in many ways more approachable than his rivals of the Middle Ages.[3] With small Latin and less Greek, Shakespeare's learning generates far more empathy than does that of Gower or Richard Rolle or William Dunbar, all of whom were still being read well into the sixteenth century and all of whom affect a style and outlook that foregrounds their education,

---

[2] *Shakespeare: The Invention of the Human* (New York: Riverhead Books, 1998).

[3] In the seventeenth century Richard Davies did claim that Shakespeare "died a papist," but this claim is not corroborated historically nor did it have a significant impact on the reception of Shakespeare and his works (S. Schoenbaum, *Shakespeare's Lives*, 2d ed. [Oxford: Clarendon P, 1991], 122–24). On the cultural appropriation of Shakespeare in the early modern period, see, in addition to *Shakespeare's Lives*, Gary Taylor, *Reinventing Shakespeare: A Cultural History, from the Restoration to the Present* (New York: Weidenfeld and Nicolson, 1989; New York and Oxford, Oxford UP, 1991). On the efforts of early editors, see Jonna Gondris, ed., *Reading Readings: Essays on Shakespeare Editing in the Eighteenth Century* (Madison, NJ: Fairleigh Dickinson UP, 1998); Marcus Walsh, *Shakespeare, Milton, and Eighteenth-Century Literary Editing: The Beginnings of Interpretative Scholarship* (Cambridge: Cambridge UP, 1997).

sometimes rather ostentatiously. Dr. Johnson in fact considers this empathetic quality to be one of Shakespeare's greatest accomplishments. "Shakespeare," he says, "is above all writers, at least above all modern writers, the poet of nature; the poet that holds up to his readers a faithful mirrour of manners and of life. His characters . . . are the genuine progeny of common humanity, such as the world will always supply, and observation will always find."[4] To Dr. Johnson, Shakespeare sees a king as a man before he sees him as a king, and Shakespeare's kings therefore display human foibles like drunkenness in a way that kings of many a medieval romance do not.[5]

Excluding Chaucer, no other pre-modern writer generated such cultural empathy or inspired such critical admiration. In his edition of the poems of Laurence Minot, for example, Joseph Ritson notes that "the creative imagination and poetical fancy which distinguish Chaucer, who, considering the general barbarism of his age and country, may be regarded as a prodigy, admit, it must be acknowledged, of no competition."[6] Rather more vividly, Thomas Warton conceives literary history in a seasonal metaphor:

> I consider Chaucer as a genial day in an English spring. A brilliant sun enlivens the face of nature with an unusual lustre: the sudden appearance of cloudless skies, and the unexpected warmth of a tepid atmosphere, after the gloom and the inclemencies of a tedious winter, fill our hearts with the visionary prospect of a speedy summer: and we fondly anticipate a long continuance of gentle gales and vernal serenity. But winter returns with redoubled horrors: the clouds condense more formidably than before: and those tender buds, and early blossoms, which were called forth by the transient gleam of a temporary sunshine, are nipped by frosts and torn by tempests.[7]

---

4 Preface to 1765 edition, quoted from Brian Vickers, ed., *Shakespeare: The Critical Heritage*, 6 vols. (London: Routledge, 1974), 5: 57.

5 Preface, *Shakespeare: The Critical Heritage*, 5: 60.

6 *Poems Written Anno MCCCLII by Laurence Minot* (London: J. H. Burn, 1825), xiii.

7 *The History of English Poetry, from the Eleventh to the Seventeenth Century* (1778; rpt. London: Ward, Lock, and Co., 1870), 348. Also see George Ellis, ed., *Specimens of the Early English Poets*, 2nd ed., 3 vols. (London: W. Bulmer, 1801), 1: 212: "the poetical beauties with which it [the *Canterbury Tales*] abounds have insured to its author, the first rank among the English poets, anterior to Shakspeare." At about this same time, David Laing does mention Dunbar in the same breath as Chaucer: "Although the poets who preceded him were neither few in number, nor inconsiderable in point of genius, there was concentrated in him such a rare association of talents as had not, in Britain at least, been known, except in Chaucer" (*The Poems of William Dunbar*, 2 vols. [Edinburgh: Ballantyne, 1834; Supplement, 1865], 1: 36). Inasmuch as this comment occurs in Laing's edition of Dunbar's poems, however, it might best be regarded as an example of special pleading rather than a widely shared sentiment. A similarly vested

Before Chaucer, by this seasonal metaphor, were the gloomy lyrics, cold romances, and cloudy treatises of the twelfth and thirteenth centuries; after him came the winter of Hoccleve, Lydgate, and Ashby. For many early modern readers, this was a winter that produced more anxiety and outright horror than mere discontent—as for an anonymous writer in 1791. In an "Address to the Reader" prefacing a translation of the "Miller's Tale," the writer declares Chaucer's achievement particularly remarkable given the literary crudity of his age. At the same time, Chaucer's claim to originality is undermined by this very crudity, which necessarily makes other writing look good by comparison:

> Their language is as uncouth, compared to his, as the Canterbury Tales are inferior in harmony to the numbers of Pope and Dryden: their versification, if it deserve that name, is bald and poor: and the most fervent admirer of antiquated poetry will confess, that a miserable dearth of genius and invention, as well as a total want of judgment and propriety, marks every composition except the poems of Chaucer, during that cloudy period.[8]

Ritson demonstrates with particular effect the disparity perceived between Shakespeare and his medieval predecessors, for in the same volume in which he infamously labels Lydgate a "voluminous, prosaick, and driveling monk," he describes Shakespeare as "the wonder and ornament of the Engleish [sic] drama."[9] If publication of Shakespeare was thus justified by his distinctive literary artistry, linguistic utility, and national value, and of Chaucer by his literary status and historical significance, early modern publication of non-Chaucerian Middle English depended largely on the apologies of antiquarianism.

And apologize antiquarians did. With their formulaic diction, episodic plots, non-representational style, obtrusive allegory, and general authorial and stylistic anonymity, few Middle English works met the

---

interest is presumably operative when an anonymous editor of Hoccleve's poems rejects Warton's dismissal of the poet as harsh and based on inadequate knowledge of the manuscript here edited for the first time. Even this writer, however, claims only that Hoccleve has poetic moments, not greatness, and his editorial motivation remains thoroughly antiquarian: "Private anecdotes in the least degree characteristical are always amusing; and when they bring us acquainted with peculiar habits and manners after the intervention of centuries, can hardly fail of interesting readers of curiosity" (*Poems by Thomas Hoccleve, Never before Printed: Selected from a MS. in the Possession of George Mason* [London: C. Roworth, 1796], 4–5).

[8] Betsy Bowden, ed., *Eighteenth-Century Modernizations from the Canterbury Tales* (Woodbridge: D. S. Brewer, 1991), 167–68.

[9] *Bibliographia Poetica: A Catalogue of Engleish* [sic] *Poets of the Twelfth, Thirteenth, Fourteenth, Fifteenth, and Sixteenth Centurys, with a Short Account of Their Works* (London: C. Roworth, 1802), 87 and 329.

aesthetic criteria valued among early modern readers and thought to be epitomized in much of Shakespeare's writing. The rationale for editing and reading such works therefore lay in their quaint charm or in the insights they offered on an earlier, proverbially simpler time. It was the antique charm of his *Reliques*, for example, that Bishop Percy offered as the source of their potential interest to an eighteenth-century audience: "In a polished age, like the present, I am sensible that many of these reliques of antiquity will require great allowances to be made for them. Yet have they, for the most part, a pleasing simplicity, and many artless graces, which in the opinion of no mean critics have been thought to compensate for the want of higher beauties, and, if they do not dazzle the imagination, are frequently found to interest the heart."[10] Evidently, even the heart's interests, unlike the putative universality of Shakespeare's characters, provided insufficient justification for pre-modern literature, for, having apologized for the literary merits of his *Reliques*, Percy proceeds to apologize for editing them at all: "the editor hopes he need not be ashamed of having bestowed some of his idle hours on the ancient literature of our own country, or in rescuing from oblivion some pieces (though but the amusements of our ancestors) which tend to place in a striking light their taste, genius, sentiments, or manners" (*Reliques*, 1: 15). Though he disagreed with him on nearly everything else, Percy's nemesis, Ritson, did share the bishop's apologetic attitude. In his monumental *English Anthology*, Ritson admits that "the nicety of the present age" is "ill disposed to make the necessary allowances for the uncouth diction and homely sentiments of former times,"[11] and his extended efforts on ballads, minstrels, and popular entertainments bespeak this same sense that the literary achievement of the merry old England of the Middle Ages lay in its charm, curiosity, and distance from the present.[12]

There is something fundamentally defensive about this posture, suggesting that already by the late eighteenth century medieval literature lay well outside the major concerns of literary and textual studies, that far from representing and speaking to the qualities shared by all humanity, it appealed only to a select few of the population who were in fact embarrassed to admit this appeal. Henry Weber, for instance, displayed little enthusiasm for the metrical romances he edited

10 Thomas Percy, ed., *Reliques of Ancient English Poetry*, 4th ed., ed. Henry B. Wheatley, 3 vols. (London: Swan Sonnenschein, 1889), 1: 8.

11 *The English Anthology*, 3 vols. (London: C. Clarke, 1793–94), 1: v. Also see Charlotte Brewer, *Editing "Piers Plowman": The Evolution of the Text* (Cambridge: Cambridge UP, 1996), 33.

12 See also Ritson, *Ancient Songs and Ballads*, 3d ed., rev. W. Carew Hazlitt (London: Reeves and Turner, 1877 [1790]), xxii; and *Northern Garlands* (London: Harding and Wright, 1810).

in 1810 when he judged them "as amusing as the prolix and wire-drawn moralities and second-hand narrations" of Gower, Hoccleve, and Lydgate. Judging a work to be as amusing as Lydgate's verbosity is damning with faint praise indeed, but Weber displayed even less respect for the romances' artistic merits when he saw them validated not by their own achievement or even quaintness but by the fact that other antiquaries had been interested in them: "It is undoubtedly an evidence, that these tales, though dressed in the most homely garb, contain something very attractive, when we consider that they formed the favourite study of Warton, and that they have been collected and illustrated by some of the most polite scholars of the present day."[13] In this formulation, the editing and study of medieval literature is an activity almost hermetically sealed off from the present, one practiced by antiquaries for antiquaries and their interest in the past as such. For Thomas Wright, similarly, *Piers Plowman* is worth editing and reading not because of any literary merits or any representation it might make of what Dr. Johnson calls "common humanity" but because it is a "national work" that illuminates England's political, linguistic, and literary past. Langland's poem

> is a pure specimen of the English language at a period when it had sus-tained few of the corruptions which have disfigured it since we have had writers of "Grammars;" and in it we may study with advantage many of the difficulties of the language which these writers have misunderstood. It is, moreover, the finest example left of the kind of versification which was purely English, inasmuch as it had been the only one in use among our Anglo–Saxon progenitors, in common with the other people of the North.[14]

Such attitudes represented medieval poems as museum pieces to be studied for the light they shed on primitive, unadulterated stages of the language or on native but abandoned poetic forms. From them emerged the many nineteenth-century literary organizations like the Roxburghe Club, the Bannatyne Club, the Maitland Club, the Surtees Society, the Ælfric Society, and the Camden Society.[15] Often publish-ing in small press runs only for their members, such organizations

---

[13] *Metrical Romances of the Thirteenth, Fourteenth, and Fifteenth Centuries*, 3 vols. (Edinburgh: George Ramsay, 1810), 1: ix–x.

[14] Thomas Wright, ed., *The Vision and Creed of Piers Ploughman* (London: John Russell Smith, 1856), xxvii–xxviii.

[15] Brewer, *Editing "Piers Plowman,"* 50. The Early English Texts Society can also be mentioned in this regard, though its size and twin emphases on patriotism and philology distances it a bit from contemporary antiquarian enterprises. On the history of editing medieval English literature, see A. S. G. Edwards, "Observations on the History of Middle English Editing," in *Manuscripts and Texts: Editorial Problems in Later Middle English*, ed. Derek Pearsall (Cambridge: D.S. Brewer, 1987), 34–48.

solidified the reception of medieval literary works as antiquarian and philological curiosities—the concern of select, learned coteries—even as Shakespeare, in the monumental Cambridge edition of 1863–66, was solidified as the premier English poet for the ages.[16]

As English text-critical discussions evolved in the early modern period, they did so in ways that inevitably reflected the cultural, literary, and bibliographical differences between Shakespeare's works and medieval literature. For the latter, the most prominent—perhaps only— issue that concerned textual critics was that of an editor's negotiation between the demands of textual accuracy imposed by antiquarianism and those of intelligibility imposed by a modern reading audience. Efforts by Dryden, Pope, Ellis and others effected one solution by simply abandoning historical impulses and offering medieval literature in modern renderings. Percy achieved another, less radical though perhaps ultimately more contested, solution by emending what he regarded as "wretched readings" displaying "unintelligible nonsense" but also by including the original readings in the margins.[17] Ritson, of course, vigorously rejected such a compromise between antiquarianism and intelligibility, implying its results were not only inaccurate but unethical: "This mode of publishing ancient poetry displays, it must be confess'd, considerable talent and genius, but savours strongly, at the same time, of unfairness and dishonesty. Here are numerous stanzas inserted which are not in the original, and others omitted which are there. The purchasers and perusers of such a collection are deceive'd and impose'd upon; the pleasure they receive is derive'd from the idea of antiquity, which, in fact, is perfect illusion."[18] Ritson continues in this righteously indignant vein by advocating a policy of selective emendation that bears similarities to modern text-critical practice,[19] but the truly striking feature of the editorial discussion emblemized by Percy and Ritson is not the rancor as such but the narrowness of the issues that inspired the rancor. Like Percy and Ritson, most early

---

[16] *The Works of William Shakespeare*, 9 vols., ed. William George Clark and William Aldis Wright (Cambridge: Macmillan, 1863–1866).

[17] Percy, *Reliques*, 11.

[18] *Ancient English Metrical Romances*, 3 vols. (London: W. Bulmer, 1802), 1: cxli–cxlii.

[19] "If the ingenious editour had publish'd all his imperfect poems by correcting the blunders of puerility or inattention, and supplying the defects of barbarian ignorance, with proper distinction of type (as, in one instance, he actually has done), it would not onely have gratify'd the austerrest antiquary, but allso provided refine'd entertainment 'for every reader of taste and genius.' He would have acted fairly and honorablely, and given every sort of reader complete satisfaction. Authenticity would have been united with improvement, and all would have gone wel; whereas, in the present editions, it is firmly believe'd, not one article has been ingenuously, or faithfully printed from the beginning to the end."

editors of medieval literature concerned themselves with only two practical and theoretical variables: reproductive accuracy and textual intelligibility. Further, these variables constitute a kind of zero-sum editorial game, for attention devoted to one is necessarily attention taken away from the other. In such circumstances, editorial decisions may be difficult, but they are also clear by nature and limited in consequence.

Text-critical discussions of Shakespeare's works, by contrast, expatiate across a range of literary issues, in the process leaving Shakespeare's image stamped on modern editorial conceptions of critic, reader, and criticism as well as author. Most generally, as the discipline of modern textual criticism emerged from the early modern period, it did so out of the dispute between what are traditionally called the gentlemen and scholars who contended over Shakespeare— between the presumptive aristocrats who, appreciative of large social and artistic issues, understood themselves to seek the larger picture of literature's genius, and the putatively low-rank pedants whose narrow intellectual vision, focused on historical meanings and developments, allegedly damaged its achievement. The most trenchant and sophisticated commentary on this dispute occurs, significantly, in Pope's *Dunciad*, where the Shakespearian editor Theobald, who had severely criticized Pope's own efforts at editing Shakespeare, is pilloried for the substance and manner of scholarly criticism alike:

> There, dim in clouds, the poreing Scholiasts mark,
> Wits, who like Owls see only in the dark,
> A Lumberhouse of Books in ev'ry head,
> For ever reading, never to be read.

Pope's biting explication of this passage further develops the connection I have been tracing between Shakespeare and the rise of English textual criticism: "These few lines exactly describe the right verbal Critick: He is to his author as a Quack to his Patients, the more they suffer and complain, the better he is pleas'd."[20] In an early modern context that conceives the infirmity of a text as validating—even creating—the textual critic, it comes as no surprise that the texts of Shakespeare, widely acknowledged as the pre-eminent English poet, should also be widely acknowledged as not simply infirm but moribund. In his 1756 "Proposals for an Edition of Shakespeare," Dr. Johnson maintains, "To have a text corrupt in many places and in many doubtful is, among the authours that have written since the use of types, almost peculiar

---

[20] The *Dunciad* quotation comes from the 1729 text, III.187–90. For this text and Pope's note, see *The Dunciad*, ed. James Sutherland, 2nd ed. (London: Methuen, 1953), 172.

to Shakespeare."[21] What saves the reader from such numerous and gross corruptions, of course, is the critic, who in the act of saving the Shakespearian text from obscurity also points the reader towards a new, more profitable habit of reading, one that draws on the *art* of textual criticism in order to appreciate the artistry of a work.[22]

For Pope, Johnson, and other early modern editors, then, Shakespeare enabled a powerful heuristic for organizing the production, transmission, and reception of literary works. With his unique genius and ability to represent shared humanity, Shakespeare had become regarded, by the early eighteenth century, as both the foremost English writer and (therefore) the model for aspiring poets, playwrights, and novelists alike. Just as his example in effect helped to create a new generation of writers, however, so did the putative corruption of his texts help to create textual critics, whose very existence depended on textual objects debased enough to require editorial ministration. Such ministrations, in turn, not only saved the textual patient but brought to life a new, sophisticated reader.

By this literary book of *Genesis*, Shakespeare begat textual critics, who begat readers, leaving one to propose that had he in fact died in the plague of 1593, there could have been no editing of at least medieval works in the Anglo–American tradition. And I think this genealogy is largely true, to the extent that many of the central theoretical propositions and practical concerns of textual criticism—at least up to the last twenty years or so—have furthered the traditions that emerged from early modern classical and biblical scholarship and that in the editing of English works crystallized around (or, perhaps, into) the figure of Shakespeare. These are propositions and concerns like the equation of the authoritative text with the authorial one, the idealist conception of a work as primarily lexical, the moral underpinning of textual criticism, an ambivalent sense of historicity, and strongly totalizing impulses about the applicability of the same text-critical principles to all literary works, regardless of date or provenance. For critics of medieval literature, the result has been a situation fraught with anachronism, rather like the curious one proposed by Persse McGarrigal in David Lodge's *Small World*, when he maintains that we can't read Shakespeare except through the lens of T. S. Eliot. Both Persse and Lodge have their tongues firmly planted in their cheeks, I presume, but at the same time there is something striking in Persse's argument. We do use the present to read the past, and for our readings

---

21 Johnson, "Proposals," *Shakespeare: The Critical Heritage*, 4: 268. Cf. Johnson, "Preface," 5: 83.

22 Johnson, "Preface," *Shakespeare: The Critical Heritage*, 5: 96, 99. Also see Taylor, *Reinventing Shakespeare*, 73; and Margreta de Grazia, *Shakespeare Verbatim: The Reproduction of Authenticity and the 1790 Apparatus* (Oxford: Clarendon P, 1991).

we are dependent on strong readers, not simply poets like Eliot but also textual critics like Pollard, McKerrow, Greg, and Bowers. And while recollection of Prufrock's timidity may be of little consequence for our reading of *Hamlet*—McGarrigal and Lodge notwithstanding— the Anglo–American tradition of textual criticism centered on Shakespeare has had a profound and often invisible effect on the editing and criticism of Middle English literature.

From a strictly bibliographic point of view, a textual criticism focused on Shakespeare has influenced—even predetermined—the presentation of medieval literary remains in several ways. With some well-known and much discussed exceptions like *King Lear*, most of Shakespeare's plays have been transmitted in a resolutely unilinear fashion, monogenetically descending from either the first folio or one of the early quartos. While the second, third, and fourth folios do embody textual variation from each other, all ultimately derive from the first folio, and none can claim descent from an independent authority like a Shakespearian holograph. Eighteenth-century transmission of the plays extends this same unilinear descent, for all the text-critical machinations of Rowe, Pope, Theobald, and the rest manifest editorial acuity and not consultation of new manuscript witnesses.[23]

Editions of Chaucer's collected *Works* effectively followed much the same principle, since each of the editions after Thynne's *editio princeps* of 1532 essentially reprinted and supplemented the most recent edition. But this procedure was an editorial choice, not a necessity imposed by the documentary remains. Indeed, the preeminent textual difference between Middle English writers (including Chaucer) and Shakespeare lies in the fact that potentially competing authorities are available for the earlier writers, as early modern editors acknowledged when their title pages claimed (often inaccurately) that their editions depended on newly discovered and never before consulted manuscripts. With the nineteenth-century advent of philology, editors of medieval works genuinely did begin to consult manuscript witnesses. In so doing, they confronted local and structural variation

---

[23] This monogenetic descent occasioned an irony in the history of textual criticism. Early editors of Shakespeare were trained as classical scholars and typically attempted to approach the various folios as if each were like a manuscript with independent authority, drawing readings from one or another without evidently realizing that in the monogenesis of Shakespeare's texts, none of the later editions had authority superior to that of the first folio. Ironically, then, when editors of medieval works approached their materials, they did encounter polygenetic traditions like those of classical literature, which they proceeded to understand and edit as if they were like the monogenetic texts of print culture. See further Ronald B. McKerrow, *The Treatment of Shakespeare's Texts by His Earlier Editors 1709–1768*, Annual Shakespeare Lecture of the British Academy (London: Humphrey Milford, 1933), 19–21; and Fredson Bowers, *On Editing Shakespeare* (Charlottesville: UP of Virginia, 1966), 83–86.

of an order far greater than even that between the quarto and folio versions of *King Lear*. At the level of individual lections, manuscript copies of romances like *Beves of Hamtoun* vary widely—even wildly—from one another, while larger, compositional variation occurs in tale arrangements of the *Canterbury Tales* and Henryson's *Moral Fables* or in the codicological contexts of lyrics and romances.

Unlike the unilinear transmission of Shakespeare's plays, these kinds of variation bespeak textual polygenesis of multiple texts, versions, and works. Nonetheless, the theoretical and practical expectations of the Anglo–American tradition have been so strong in medieval studies that reducing these multiple forms to a single reading text like that of Shakespeare's plays has been the persistent if intractable task of textual criticism since at least the middle part of the nineteenth century. That it can be achieved—that divergent authorities can be reduced to a clean text—has been demonstrated many times over and has sustained many more readings of medieval literature and culture in general. But this achievement does not demonstrate the suitability of such an approach to medieval materials. Like the evidence produced by any heuristic, single reading texts of medieval works can testify only that they are as they are because a powerful explication has conceptualized them this way. In literary criticism, as opposed to natural science, the results of an interpretive system are necessarily consistent with that system and cannot therefore validate it to the exclusion of other systems. Or, to put the matter another way, a text-critical theory can be internally consistent—it can assign notions of author, work, and text in mutually compatible ways—without necessarily displaying any consistency with the external world, in this case the external world of literary production and transmission.[24]

In rare instances, some of the implications of the multiple descent of medieval works have been acknowledged. Since Walter Skeat's 1866 conceptualization of the *Piers Plowman* materials, for example, the poem's existence in multiple versions has been a given in medieval studies. As responsive to the peculiarities of pre-Shakespearian literature as Skeat's conceptualization may be, however, in reducing the textual dynamics of the *Piers* manuscripts to just three versions and in attributing these versions to a single historical author—William Langland—even it demonstrates the influence of the Anglo–American tradition, in which the cult of Shakespearian personality developed by early modern editors became a model mandating that both textual and literary critics concentrate their efforts on the single, transcendent voice of the author. I leave others to evaluate the validity of such

---

24 See, more generally, Douglas R. Hofstadter, *Gödel, Escher, Bach: An Eternal Golden Braid* (New York: Vintage Books, 1980), esp. 82–102.

a mandate for post-Shakespearian literature; for pre-Shakespearian literature its impact has been pervasive, profound, and, to the extent that Anglo–American criticism has been defined by Shakespeare studies, under-appreciated if not simply unrecognized. This impact emerges perhaps most clearly when critics point to medieval writers' self-evident and characteristic artistry as an editorial rationale for resolving variation,[25] but it is also evident in editions organized on the principle of a single, controlling author, even for works like metrical romances, whose style and transmission do not involve distinctive authorial voices, or for resolutely anonymous works of theological consolation.

What renders Anglo–American textual criticism almost ideological in medieval studies, however, is the way its principles are reproduced even in projects that attempt to transcend them. For example, ongoing electronic editions of the *Canterbury Tales* and *Piers Plowman* utilize hypertext technology in order to make available multiple copies of these poems and to enable multiple kinds of collation and study among them. Both projects in part endeavor to do this with a view towards circumventing traditional text-critical concentrations on the words of only recognized authors, towards providing readers with a kind of textual raw material from which they might construct their own authoritative texts. Ultimately, however, both projects also use modern technology to further early modern objectives and to realize works and authors in ways that are entirely consistent with Anglo–American textual criticism. The *Canterbury Tales* project, that is, understands that the "principal reason" for its "exploration of the textual tradition of the *Canterbury Tales* is to try to discover what Chaucer actually wrote," while the ultimate goal of the *Piers Plowman* Electronic Archive is "the creation of a multi-level, hyper-textually linked electronic archive of the textual tradition" of the three Langlandian versions of the poem.[26] Similar affirmations of traditional conceptions of authorship can paradoxically emerge from manuscript studies. When read from the vantage of the literal margins of medieval manuscripts or of the metaphoric margins of medieval culture, the pages of medieval culture have taken on new appearances. Indeed, scholarly inquiry of late has transcended the received texts and canons of a few individuals, like

---

[25] See for example, George Kane, *Piers Plowman: The Evidence for Authorship* (London: Athlone P, 1965), 24, and "The 'Z Version' of *Piers Plowman*," *Speculum* 60 (1985): 910–30; also see Kane and E. Talbot Donaldson, eds., *Piers Plowman: The B Version*, rev. ed. (Berkeley and Los Angeles: The U of California P, 1988), 73.

[26] *The "Canterbury Tales" Project*, Newsletter no.1, p.3 (also see *The "Canterbury Tales" Project Occasional Papers*, vol.1, ed. Norman Blake and Peter Robinson [Oxford: Office for Humanities Communication, 1993]); "The Piers Plowman Electronic Archive," http://www.jefferson.village.virginia.edu/piers/ archive.goals.html.

Chaucer and Langland, to include bilingual sermons, neglected poets like Laȝamon, and the multiple voices of vernacular culture. While all this represents an advance in historical sensitivity, such readings nonetheless require and effectively sustain the very subjects they seek to destabilize, for without these situated subjects, there can be no margins.[27] Without the presumption of a stable author or a dominant medieval culture, that is, there can be no subjectivity to deconstruct, no canon to expand, and no hegemony to overturn.

One way for medievalists to exorcize Shakespeare's ghost is to play a what-if game: What if Shakespeare *had* died in 1593? What would textual criticism of medieval literature then be like? Would there have been a nineteenth-century resurgence of interest in the Middle Ages, and would it have produced editions as resolutely author-centered and lexically defined as it did? Would a new and newer bibliography have developed in recognition of the specifics of medieval manuscript culture, rather than of early modern print production? Would we be reading medieval works less retrospectively, less the way Persse McGarrigal wants to read Shakespeare, and more the way Macbeth circumspectly reads the man in front of him?

Outside of the editorial paradigms that have shaped its presentation and reception in the modern period, medieval literature might then be presented as a literature that descended not unilinearly but multivalently, pointing back to a multiplicity of related but distinct works and not to a single text, however constructed. It would be a literature produced by authors, though not by authors easily accommodated in an Anglo–American model, which is an important and, I think, much misunderstood point. As Peter Shillingsburg has recently argued, some sense of agency is a prerequisite for the editing and reading of any literary work:[28] Editors need to conceptualize some controlling and organizing principle for a work's production, just as readers need to imagine some controlling and organizing voice for the propagation of its meanings, even when the work proceeds by giving voice to divergent viewpoints and perspectives. From this theoretical vantage, medieval literature is no exception. Where it does differ from the literature of other epochs is in its operative definition of authorship.

Medieval authorship—especially medieval vernacular authorship—derived not from the nexus of subjectivity, print culture, nationalism,

---

27 The paradox I describe runs through a number of recent and valuable studies. See, for example, Ralph Hanna, *Pursuing History: Middle English Manuscripts and Their Texts* (Stanford: Stanford UP, 1996); Seth Lerer, ed., *Reading from the Margins: Textual Studies, Chaucer, and Medieval Literature* (San Marino: Huntington Library, 1996); and Stephen G. Nichols and Siegfried Wenzel, eds., *The Whole Book: Cultural Perspectives on the Medieval Miscellany* (Ann Arbor: U of Michigan P, 1996).

28 Peter L. Shillingsburg, *Resisting Texts: Authority and Submission in Constructions of Meaning* (Ann Arbor: U of Michigan P, 1997), 151–64.

and literary self-consciousness that rendered Shakespeare the pre-eminent early modern author. Rather, its generation lay in material facts like the perpetually open-ended character of manuscript production by booklets; in social issues like the changing status of the English language within late-medieval England's diglossia; and in literary discourses like the substantially oral poetics of alliterative poems or the aesthetic and academic traditions that framed Latin over English as the language of artistry, insight, and prestige. These are the facts, issues, and discourses that motivate much late-medieval vernacular literature, and what the imposition of an early modern view of authorship does is to undermine this motivation, to accept as a given for editorial theory and practice the very indeterminacy that underwrote medieval English literature and gave it its distinctive character. In this way, the claim that Chaucer is the "father of English poetry" becomes even more attenuated, since such a title presumes an early modern notion of authorship and thus reveals more about the literary children making the claim of paternity than about Chaucer or medieval literature. That Chaucer and Langland (at least) did in fact demonstrate an authorial consciousness that Shakespeare might have recognized does not by itself validate the retroactive transference of early modern notions of authorship to them. Unlike Shakespeare, Chaucer and Langland identified themselves in opposition to the prevailing standards of their day; they sought to exercise authorial consciousness *because* medieval culture denied it so broadly to vernacular writers. Moreover, whether medieval or modern, writers do not autonomously create authorship, for this is a cultural construction, a sense of agency that emerges from a variety of discourses, institutions, and social practices that individual writers participate in but do not themselves define. A modern writer who plagiarized all or part of a copyrighted work, for example, would not be considered a legitimate illustration of contemporary notions of authorship, however artistically successful the plagiarism might be or whatever theoretical justifications the writer might provide for it. There is thus a disquieting implication to all I have just argued. The poetry that modern editorial practice assigns to Chaucer may be charming, astute, and, simply, beautiful, but the stable Chaucer whose agency determines this achievement—the Chaucer who serves as a canonical center against whom the marginal voices of vernacular culture have been defined—is more the creation of a Shakespearian-focused textual criticism than a historical medieval reality.

Focusing on issues like the cultural status of vernacular writers, the malleable character of medieval book production, and the anonymity and adaptability of specific phrases and stanzas, several recent critics have in fact interrogated Anglo–American textual criticism's conception of authorship and its implications for the editing of Middle English literature.[29] Interrogations like these have typically been met by equating them with the theoretical challenges to authorship originating among what Bloom memorably calls "recent Parisian speculators," or by affirmations of authorial integrity as a prerequisite for editing.[30] Such responses confuse the issues, however. The Parisian speculators concern themselves with a theoretical proposition about subjectivity that lies at the heart of certain conceptions of literary and cultural production; in undermining this proposition, they undermine the very idea of the integrity of a literary work or, indeed, of those who write or read it. A non-Shakespearian textual criticism, on the other hand, would resist not subjectivity but the transcendence of any one conception of authorship, seeing this instead as a fundamentally historicized concept.

The point of interrogating the text-critical conception of authorship emblemized by Shakespeare is not to assassinate the author. Nor is it to deny the validity of isolating and studying an individual medieval writer's words or to eliminate textual criticism in general. The purpose behind raising topics like the ones I have here and others have

---

[29] Some representative studies are: Julia Boffey, "The Reputation and Circulation of Chaucer's Lyrics in the Fifteenth Century," *Chaucer Review* 28 (1993): 23–40; A.S.G. Edwards, "Middle English Editing: The Limits of Editing, the Limits of Criticism," in *Medieval Literature: Texts and Interpretation*, ed. T.W. Machan (Binghamton: Medieval & Renaissance Texts & Studies, 1991), 91–104; Boffey and Edwards, " 'Chaucer's Chronicle,' John Shirley, and the Canon of Chaucer's Shorter Poems," *Studies in the Age of Chaucer* 20 (1998): 201–18; David Greetham, "Phylum–Tree–Rhizome," in *Reading from the Margins*, ed. Lerer, 99–126; Machan, *Textual Criticism and Middle English Texts* (Charlottesville: UP of Virginia, 1994); and Derek Pearsall, "Editing Medieval Texts: Some Developments and Some Problems," in *Textual Criticism and Literary Interpretation*, ed. Jerome J. McGann (Chicago: U of Chicago P, 1985), 92–106, and "Texts, Textual Criticism, and Fifteenth Century Manuscript Production," in *Fifteenth-Century Studies, Recent Essays*, ed. Robert F. Yeager (Hamden: Archon Books, 1984), 121–36.

[30] See, for example, Hoyt N. Duggan, "Some Unrevolutionary Aspects of Computer Editing," in *The Literary Text in the Digital Age*, ed. Richard J. Finneran (Ann Arbor: U of Michigan P, 1996), 77–98; Anne Hudson, "The Variable Text," in *Crux and Controversy in Middle English Textual Criticism*, eds. A.J. Minnis and Charlotte Brewer (Cambridge: Boydell and Brewer, 1992), 49–60; Nicholas Jacobs, "Kindly Light or Foxfire? The Authorial Text Reconsidered," in Vincent P. McCarren and Douglas Moffat, eds., *A Guide to Editing Middle English* (Ann Arbor: U of Michigan P, 1998), 3–14; and George Kane, " 'Good' and 'Bad' Manuscripts: Texts and Critics," in *Studies in the Age of Chaucer, Proceedings No. 2*, ed. Thomas J. Heffernan (Knoxville: New Chaucer Society, 1987), 137–45. For an example of the compounded consequences such confusion can create for literary criticism, see Kathryn Kerby–Fulton, "Langland and the Bibliographic Ego," in *Written Work: Langland, Labor, and Authorship*, ed. Steven Justice and Kerby–Fulton (Philadelphia: U of Pennsylvania P, 1997), 67–143. The "bibliographical ego" that Kerby–Fulton describes, that is, elides all distinctions between rhetorical voice in a literary work and the *text* of that work as it participates in literary processes.

elsewhere, rather, is to examine issues like the historicity of textual criticism and the historical character of essential concepts like "author," "work," and "text"; to investigate the relations between individuals' and their societies' representations of literary authority; to explore the inherent but fundamentally contingent connections between literary and textual criticism; to understand the interdependence between material bibliography and literary history; and to summon flexible methods in response to the flexibility of historicity, the historical record, and historicized activity. Given the literary genealogy centered on Shakespeare, these issues stand at the nexus between literary work, critic, and reader. A reorientation of them, consequently, is a reorientation in critical approach to medieval literary remains. To conceive (and then contest) these issues as if they constitute relativism, post-modernism, and other perceived threats to the integrity of the subject, whether that of the author, the critic, or the society, is to engage in a rear guard action against a straw army, an army that has been fashioned, like Prospero's wedding revels, out of thin air.

Like Prospero, indeed, Shakespeare has endowed the purposes not only of those who willingly enter into his influence but also of those unwittingly overcome by it and even of those who attempt to resist it, as I have here. Understood to depict and speak for what Dr. Johnson calls "common humanity," Shakespeare perhaps inevitably has represented a view of authorship and inspired a conceptualization of textual criticism that have been judged applicable to the writers and writings of all time periods, thereby constituting the Anglo–American tradition of editing. Yet as Shillingsburg reminds us,[31] to questions about the intentions determining a work's production, or to more general questions about text-critical theory and practice, there are optional answers. To the question of how to edit medieval literature, the tradition of Shakespearian editing offers one, entirely valid, and successfully attested answer. The literature itself offers others.

---

[31] *Resisting Texts*, 45–46. I would like to thank W. Speed Hill, Michael McCanles, and Albert Rivero for their encouragement and helpful comments on early drafts of this paper.

Editing Shakespeare and Editing Without Shakespeare: Wilson, McKerrow, Greg, Bowers, Tanselle, and Copy-Text Editing

PAUL WERSTINE

i.

WHEN W. W. GREG WROTE HIS FAMOUS ESSAY "The Rationale of Copy-Text" in 1949, he indicated that he was "concerned chiefly with works of the sixteenth and seventeenth centuries."[1] His "Rationale" grew out of observations he had made over a long career as a student of manuscripts and printed books from this period. These texts, he remarked, resist the notion that their accidentals, as Greg chose to term their spelling, punctuation, word-division, and so forth, follow any system. He recommended that editors of texts from this period, and this period alone, therefore "choose whatever extant text may be supposed to represent most nearly what the author wrote and ... follow it ... *in the matter of accidentals*" (21–22; italics mine). His recommendation was a pragmatic response to what he regarded as the impossibility of establishing, within the centuries in question, standard accidentals "for a particular period or district or author" (21). Greg chose his examples for "The Rationale" only from Ben Jonson, Christopher Marlowe, Thomas Nashe, and William Shakespeare (his

---

[1] *Studies in Bibliography* 3 (1950–51): 19–36, esp. 21 n3.

principal focus). He refused to extend his theory beyond the centuries he named, denying his ability to judge the success of editorial normalization of Old and Middle English texts, and ignoring altogether eighteenth-, nineteenth-, and twentieth-century writing in England and elsewhere.

In view of the strict temporal boundaries that Greg drew around his theory, it was perhaps remarkable that Fredson Bowers should have invoked it in developing "Some Principles for Scholarly Editions of Nineteenth-Century American Authors."[2] Yet, without regard to country or century, Bowers declared that "the theory of copy-text proposed by Sir Walter Greg rules supreme" (224), and went on to exhort "scholars editing American literature" to "bring to their task the careful effort that has been established as necessary for English Renaissance texts" (228). Thanks to Bowers, Greg's "Rationale," designed though it was to guide editors principally of Shakespeare and his contemporaries, began to be extended far beyond the time and place to which Greg had explicitly limited it. While Bowers's efforts were staunchly resisted by such well-informed scholars as, for example, James Thorpe and Morse Peckham, nonetheless, in the absence of claims about the virtually universal applicability of any other editorial theories, the editorial scene, to the extent to which it was centered at all, became centered upon Greg's copy-text editing and thus upon Shakespeare.[3]

Oddly enough, in the period in which Greg's theory "rule[d] supreme" there appeared no edition of the Shakespeare canon, however defined, presented according to Greg's principles.[4] Instead, Shakespeare's writings continued to be offered almost invariably in the dress of modernized spelling and punctuation, rather than in the "accidentals" of their early printings. Nevertheless, key assumptions that undergird Greg's theory of copy-text—especially the assumption that we can determine the probable nature and history of manuscripts underlying the printed texts—are to be found in a great many of the textual introductions or notes on the text in Shakespeare editions from the latter half of this century, including some quite recent ones. So are Greg's applications of these assumptions and terms to the textual

---

2 *Studies in Bibliography* 17 (1964): 223–28.

3 James Thorpe, "The Ideal of Textual Criticism," in Thorpe and Claude M. Simpson, Jr., eds., *The Task of the Editor* (Los Angeles: Clark Library, 1969), 3–27; Morse Peckham, "Reflections on the Foundation of Modern Textual Editing," *Proof: The Yearbook of American Bibliographical and Textual Studies* 1 (1971): 122–55.

4 The demonstration edition, what Jerome McGann calls a "polemical" edition ("The Monks and the Giants: Textual and Bibliographical Studies and the Interpretation of Literary Works," *Textual Criticism and Literary Interpretation*, ed. Jerome J. McGann [Chicago: U of Chicago P, 1985], 194), was Bowers's edition of *The Dramatic Works of Thomas Dekker*, 4 vols. (Cambridge: Cambridge UP, 1953–61).

problematics of specific Shakespeare plays. Greg recommended that an editor "choose whatever extant text may be supposed to represent most nearly what the author wrote" as the basis for an edition; in the case of a Shakespeare play, this text would be the one printed from the manuscript that Greg figured as "Shakespeare's foul papers." A great many Shakespeare editors since 1950 not only have followed Greg's dictum, but also have simply reproduced the arguments from his *The Editorial Problem in Shakespeare* (1942)[5] or from his *The Shakespeare First Folio* (1955)[6] with which he purported to identify which early printed texts were printed from "Shakespeare's foul papers," as opposed to a theatrical "prompt-book." (Of course, since these editors were preparing modernized editions, they were guided by "whatever extant text may be supposed to represent most nearly what the author wrote" for their choice of [most of] their text's substantives, rather than its accidentals, as Greg had advised.) In "The Rationale of Copy-Text," Greg also advised editors not simply to reproduce the "foul papers" text but to sift any other substantive texts for readings and passages and to incorporate into their editions any of these that they judged to be authorial. While Shakespeare editors working after Greg have naturally differed in their judgements about which readings and passages to regard as authorial, they have nonetheless again followed Greg's advice—some to a greater, others to a lesser extent—in attempting to make such judgements. Thus, although there is no copy-text edition of the Shakespeare canon, there have been plenty of Shakespeare editions in the last fifty years in which the text has been established according to Greg's general and particular assumptions about relations of the early printed texts to Shakespeare.[7]

In more recent years, however, the editing of Shakespeare has been doubly decentered—decentered both from its privileged position vis-à-vis the editing of other writers, and from its own narrow dependence upon Greg's assumptions. Although the term "decenter" is unmistakably post-structuralist in its origin, the decentering of Shakespeare is only incidentally related to that movement. It was the Oxford *Complete Works of William Shakespeare*,[8] edited without reference to post-structuralism by Stanley Wells and Gary Taylor (et al.), that displaced

---

[5] *The Editorial Problem in Shakespeare: A Survey of the Foundations of the Text* (Oxford: Clarendon P); cited below as *EPS*.

[6] *The Shakespeare First Folio: Its Bibliographical and Textual History* (Oxford: Clarendon P); cited below as *SFF*.

[7] I am grateful to David Nordloh for this distinction between, on the one hand, a copy-text edition of the Shakespeare canon and, on the other, editions in which the text has been established according to Greg's general and particular assumptions about relations of the early printed texts to Shakespeare.

[8] Oxford: Clarendon P, 1986 (modern spelling); 1988 ("original" spelling).

Shakespeare from the center of the editorial scene. This claim of mine may seem paradoxical since Wells and Taylor followed many of Greg's Shakespeare-centered general assumptions and much of his terminology in establishing their texts, as well as many of Greg's judgements about the origins of particular texts, although Wells and Taylor showed greater independence of mind concerning the latter than had many of their predecessors. Wells and Taylor also closely followed Greg in offering an old-spelling edition in which they preserved the accidentals of the early printed versions that they judged to be closest to the "foul papers." Also following Greg they introduced into the context of these accidentals readings from other early printed texts.

But in the choice of these readings Wells and Taylor departed strikingly from Greg's "Rationale" and from the Shakespeare editorial practice that followed in its wake, for rather than admitting from other early printed texts only readings deemed to be authorial in origin, Wells and Taylor admitted all readings and made all cuts to their copy-texts that they judged to represent the plays as they were staged, without regard to whether or not such readings and cuts were, in their opinion, authorial in origin. They did not, however, identify this departure from Greg's "Rationale" as their own innovation, or even as one that, like the "Rationale" itself, could be claimed to be guided only by the specific historical circumstances that attended the production and reproduction in manuscript and print of sixteenth- and seventeenth-century texts. Instead, in preferring the readings of the early printed texts that, according to Greg's assumptions for establishing the texts, could be judged to be those that had been performed, Wells and Taylor were following a strategy first outlined by Jerome McGann in *A Critique of Modern Textual Criticism*.[9] There McGann had argued that Greg's "Rationale" was ill-suited to the task of editing certain Romantic poets for reasons peculiar to their specific relations to their publishers, and that editors of these poets would be well advised to prefer as "copy-texts" the published texts in which these poets were first read—their "social texts"—rather than extant authorial manuscripts never before presented to a reading public and never designed to be so by their writers. Wells and Taylor judged it appropriate to construct an analogy between McGann's Romantic poets and Shakespeare, argued that "dramatic texts are necessarily the most socialized of all literary forms," and properly cited McGann for their conception of the "socialization of the text."[10] Now Byron, say, rather than Shakespeare, had come, at least on this occasion, to occupy the center of the editorial scene, as

9 (Chicago: Chicago UP, 1983; rpt., Charlottesville: UP of Virginia, 1992).

10 *William Shakespeare: A Textual Companion* (Oxford: Clarendon P, 1987; rpt. New York: Norton, 1997), 15, 63 n34.

Shakespeare was being edited by reference to him. My own account of Wells and Taylor's decentering of Shakespeare on the editorial scene is not to be read as negative criticism of their edition if only because I cannot imagine why Shakespeare, rather than Byron or any other writer, alone has the right to centrality.[11]

Far more radical an innovation has been the second decentering of Shakespeare, this time from editions of the Shakespeare plays, where Greg's "Rationale" had located him. Greg felt confident about orienting his editorial principles toward the author in part because he had apparently come to believe by the end of 1927 that he knew what Shakespeare's manuscripts looked like. In his "Shakespeare's Hand Once More," Greg joined J. Dover Wilson and A. W. Pollard in championing the cause of attributing to Shakespeare three so-called Hand-D pages in *The Booke of Sir Thomas Moore*.[12] When Greg later developed his ideas of "the various types of written and printed copy that we know or *may suppose*" to have served in the houses where Shakespeare plays were printed, he depended upon his identification of Shakespeare as Hand D in his attempts to ground one of his types, at least to some extent, in documentary evidence (italics mine). He acknowledged that his "types . . . are in a sense ideals that we construct in our imagination, but," he argued, "we are fortunate in being able at many points to check conjecture by comparison with actually surviving manuscripts or prints as the case may be." In constructing one of his two primary types of "written . . . copy," so-called author's "foul papers," Greg sought to check conjecture against the Hand-D pages.[13]

While he later admitted into his discussion the possibility that at least some of Shakespeare's plays may have been printed from extra-theatrical scribal transcripts, Greg bracketed this option until he had

---

[11] An anonymous reader of this essay is of an opinion entirely contrary to mine. For this reader, Wells and Taylor did not decenter Shakespeare on the editorial scene; "if anything [their] effort to do so, if that's what it was, gave the centrality of Shakespeare editing a renewed prominence that McGann *et al.* had challenged."

[12] "Shakespeare's Hand Once More," *TLS* (24 November and 1 December 1927), 871 and 908. A.W. Pollard collected essays by W. W. Greg, E. Maunde Thompson, R. W. Chambers, and J. Dover Wilson in *Shakespeare's Hand in the Play of Sir Thomas More* (Cambridge: Cambridge UP, 1923); Greg was alone among the contributors and the editor in keeping silent about whether he believed any pages in *More* were Shakespeare's. He joined the "cause," as Pollard called it in his book (32), only in 1927. The belief in Shakespeare as Hand D was still strong in some editorial quarters only a decade or so ago. Wells and Taylor offer in their *Textual Companion* an excerpt from *Hamlet* as they judge Shakespeare allegedly inscribed it. The passage is drawn from the Second Quarto and adapted slightly to conventions evident in the three pages of *More* (*Textual Companion*, 5).

[13] *SFF*, 106, 109, 144. Although I quote Greg's 1955 book, he was already writing substantially the same argument in his 1942 book, *EPS;* compare 27–29.

completed his narrative of the two primary types of written copy, "foul papers" and "prompt-books."[14] He began by taking for granted that a Shakespeare play would first have come into material existence in an exclusively authorial inscription that he called "foul papers." This type of written copy, he conjectured, would have as its chief feature inconsistency—i.e., "loose ends and false starts and unresolved confusions in the text," "inconsistency in the designation of characters in directions and prefixes alike," and "the appearance of indefinite and permissive stage-directions" (*SFF*, 142). Because, according to Greg, these papers might be needed again if the "prompt-book" went missing and because the players allegedly feared the double sale of plays to other companies or to publishers, normally these "foul papers" were deposited in the playhouse for safe-keeping (*SFF*, 106; *EPS*, 31). There the "foul papers" *may* have been cursorily annotated by theatrical personnel; and there the "foul papers" were transcribed, the transcription becoming the second primary type of written copy imagined by Greg—the "prompt-book." For Greg, such transcription was necessary by definition, for he defined "foul papers" as too untidy for theatrical use.[15]

But Greg's conception of the features that distinguish his "prompt-book" from his "foul papers" is unstable. On the one hand, when he addressed the difference between his two types of written copy in general terms, he was careful to allow that there may not be much difference between them: "owing to the casual ways of book-keepers [i.e., the theatrical personnel who annotated and transcribed manuscripts] . . . characteristics [of "foul papers"] may persist, to some extent at least, in the prompt-book."[16] On the other hand, when he employed his types in the identification of printer's copy for particular Shakespeare printed plays, his habit was to insist that the features he attributed to "foul papers" would simply not be tolerated in a "prompt-book," in which they would have been tidied away. In these particular cases, like

---

[14] In *SFF*, Greg compares and contrasts "foul papers" and "prompt–books" from 106 to 152 and then takes up "private transcripts" from 152 to 154. In *EPS*, 27–41 are devoted to the first two types, and 44–45 to the third.

[15] See *SFF*, 107–8, for Greg's speculations on these matters.

[16] *SFF*, 142. As John Jowett points out in his "*Richard III* and the Perplexities of Editing," *TEXT* 11 (1998), 234–35 n23, Greg can write lyrically of the indeterminacy of the nature of the manuscripts underlying Shakespeare's printed plays: "when we . . . ask what sort of manuscript was handed to the Folio printer, . . . we enter an altogether different field of criticism, a misty mid region of Weir, a land of shadowy shapes and melting outlines, where not even the most patient inquiry and the most penetrating analysis can hope to arrive at any but tentative and proximate conclusions" (*SFF*, 105). Yet this tone of Greg's has not been influential on his followers; nor is it evident in his judgements about the printer's copy for particular plays, as what I am about to quote will show.

that of *The Comedy of Errors*, he listed inconsistencies in the naming of characters, and then wound up his identification of printer's copy by enforcing a binary opposition of his two primary types of written copy: "since it is difficult to believe that the confusion in character names and prefixes would have been tolerated in a prompt-book, it would seem that the manuscript was most likely foul papers" (*SFF*, 201–2). His conclusion about the manuscript used to print the First Quarto of *Titus Andronicus* is even more reductively binary in its elimination of the possibility that there could be any other types of written copy but the two that he imagined: "In the absence, then, of any definite indication of prompter's notes, we may assume that the copy was foul papers" (*SFF*, 203). Because Greg believed that a company would be most reluctant to part with its "prompt-book," which may have been the document containing the license of the Master of the Revels that alone could authorize performance, Greg assumed that when the company chose to sell a play to a stationer for publication, the company would sell the "foul papers"—"foul papers" being the only other kind of written copy imaginable for Greg. Thus in the author-centered narrative that enables Greg's author-centered editorial theory, we are fortunate to be able normally to read Shakespeare's plays very much as he wrote them, with only the clutter of occasional book-keeper's notes and the errors of the press imagined as standing between us and the author.

That there are severe problems with Greg's narrative and the terms in which it is written has been recognized for a long time. Fredson Bowers could observe in 1955 that "There is no evidence whatever . . . in Henslowe [i.e., in the records of theater-owner Philip Henslowe, to which Greg had turned for support] that an author ever submitted for payment anything but a fair copy, or that a company required a dramatist to turn over his original foul sheets along with the fair copy."[17] And, as Bowers further observed, if the textual theorist were simply to speculate about types of printed and written copy for published plays without rigorously grounding these types in extant documents from the period, there was no call to stop one's imagination at "foul papers" and "prompt-books"; Bowers could imagine thirteen types of possible copy.[18] Stephen Orgel has since called attention to the inappropriateness of imagining plays in the exclusively authorial form of "foul papers": "the creation of a play was a collaborative process, with the author by no means at the center of the collaboration. . . . The text thus produced was a working model, which the company then revised as deemed appropriate. The author had little or no say in these

---

17 *On Editing Shakespeare* (Charlottesville: UP of Virginia, 1966), 15.

18 Listing these on 11–12 of *On Editing Shakespeare*, Bowers himself says that "some of them [are] speculative."

revisions."[19]   Like his conceptions, Greg's terms "foul papers" and "prompt-books" have been shown not to be rooted in early modern theatrical culture in anything like the senses he accorded them. Since in that culture, "foul papers" were sometimes so called because they were incomplete, the term is not at all suited to Greg's notion of a complete authorial manuscript.[20] Greg himself knew that that culture did not use the term "prompt-book"; indeed its use is not recorded until the nineteenth century. Yet Greg argued that in the early modern theater the term "book" was reserved only for the kind of manuscript that he called a "prompt-book"; such was not the case, with the result that Greg's crucial distinction between "foul papers" and "prompt-books" loses any claim to historical validity.[21] Even if there were just the two types of manuscripts that Greg imagined, subsequent research into the theatrical manuscripts that Greg called "prompt-books" has borne out his view that "owing to the casual ways of book-keepers . . . characteristics [of "foul papers"] may persist, to some extent at least, in the prompt-book," rather than his practice in rigidly distinguishing between features of the two types.[22] Indeed, sometimes the extant manuscripts that he called "prompt-books" actually multiply the features that he thought peculiar to "foul papers."[23]

There is also no consensus today regarding the identification of Shakespeare as the Hand D of the manuscript Booke of Sir Thomas Moore, and therefore no agreement about what Shakespeare's manuscripts must have looked like. In the most recent collection of essays on the topic, all that could be said by way of a consensus among the contributors is contained in this extremely guarded and contorted statement: "none of them believes that the case for Shakespeare's presence in the More manuscript is less strong than that which could be made to deny it or to identify another playwright."[24] A survey of

[19] "What is a Text?" Research Opportunities in Renaissance Drama 14 (1981): 3–6, esp. 3.

[20] Paul Werstine, "Narratives about Printed Shakespeare Texts: 'Foul Papers' and 'Bad Quartos'," Shakespeare Quarterly 41 (1990): 65–86, esp. 72; "Post-Theory Problems in Editing," Yearbook of English Studies 29 (1999): 103–17, esp. 106 and 106–7 n9.

[21] Greg, Dramatic Documents From the Elizabethan Playhouses, 2 vols. (Oxford: Clarendon P, 1931), 192–93; Paul Werstine, "Plays in Manuscript" in A New History of Early English Drama, ed. John D. Cox and David Scott Kastan (New York: Columbia UP, 1997), 481–97, esp. 484.

[22] William B. Long, "Stage–Directions: A Misinterpreted Factor in Determining Textual Provenance," TEXT 2 (1985): 121–37.

[23] Paul Werstine, "McKerrow's 'Suggestion' and Twentieth-Century Shakespeare Textual Criticism," Renaissance Drama 19 (1989): 149–73.

[24] T. H. Howard–Hill, ed., Shakespeare and Sir Thomas More: Essays on the Play and its Shakespearian Interest (Cambridge: Cambridge UP, 1989), 2.

Shakespeareans' reception of the Hand D–Shakespeare identification indicates that its advocates have paradoxically acknowledged the inconclusiveness of each kind of evidence that has been advanced for it.[25]

As a consequence, a number of editors today have abandoned Greg's narrative and his claims that it is possible to determine the kinds of manuscripts that underlie Shakespeare's printed plays and to assess the relation of such printer's copy to Shakespeare himself. As H. R. Woudhuysen writes in his recent edition of *Love's Labour's Lost*,

> Since there are no certain surviving specimens of Shakespeare's manuscripts, it is impossible to know what his practice in writing his plays was–even with the fragment of *Sir Thomas More*, if it is in his hand, there is no certainty as to whether he was composing new material or making a fair copy of material already drafted elsewhere. Of the surviving theatrical manuscripts of the period, none exactly conforms to the generally established definition of 'foul papers'. . . . Furthermore, if compositors were capable of setting in type 'foul-paper' features . . ., scribes were equally capable of copying and reproducing them by hand. The only way by which scholars could be absolutely certain that a text was set from some kind of an authorial draft or fair copy would be if the printer's copy and the resulting print were both to survive. Unfortunately, no scribal let alone authorial manuscript copy for a printed play survives from this period.[26]

Thus, unlike many editions of *Love's Labour's Lost* published in the latter half of this century, Woudhuysen's Third Arden edition is not founded on a belief that the editor has located an authorial presence just behind the early printed text. In a similar vein, Jill Levenson's edition of *Romeo and Juliet* for the Oxford series will not, in contrast to many recent editions, assert a knowledge that the Second Quarto was printed from "foul papers" and that the First Quarto text is a memorial reconstruction. Nor will it offer to combine the two in some fashion to produce some putatively original "authorial" or "theatrical" version of the play; instead it will offer editions of both quartos. Anthony B. Dawson's New Cambridge edition of *Troilus and Cressida* will combine readings and passages from the Quarto and Folio printings of the play, but only for the reader's convenience, not in an announced attempt thereby to recover Shakespeare's final intention from the existing documents. Indeed, when a number of editions, including not only the New Folger that I am editing with

25 Paul Werstine, "Shakespeare *More* or Less: A. W. Pollard and Twentieth-Century Shakespeare Editing," *Florilegium* 16 (1999): 125–45.

26 The Arden Shakespeare, Third Series (London: Nelson, 1998), 320.

Barbara A. Mowat[27] but also the Third Arden *King Lear* edited by R. A. Foakes (1997), combine readings and passages from different early printed versions, such editions typographically distinguish such readings and passages to call their readers' attention to these combinations as editorial constructions. In this way Shakespeare editions have come to be centered on the early printed texts themselves rather than on editorial constructions of the author. And in this way "Shakespeare" has been decentered from the editing of Shakespeare texts.

ii.

Now that "the theory of copy-text proposed by Sir Walter Greg [no longer] rules supreme," the consensus Bowers imagined to obtain during the '60s, if it ever did exist at an intellectual rather than just at an institutional level, has been lost. From this situation arises the question on which the rest of this essay will focus: is the absence of consensus a new or an old editorial state of affairs? My answer will be that it is an old one, an answer that puts me at odds with G. Thomas Tanselle's account of the genesis of copy-text editing as issuing out of a consensus that slowly formed in the first half of this century. Tanselle writes that the theory of copy-text editing was long in the making, and that its gradual development, "growing [as it did] out of [R. B.] McKerrow's" earlier principles, was the work of more than the single man, Greg, who finally gave it full articulation.[28] "Greg's position," Tanselle continues,

> derived ... from the attitudes that were evolving among the leading textual scholars of Elizabethan and Jacobean drama. ... McKerrow, by the time of his death in 1940, had cautiously modified his earlier aversion to eclecticism; as his *Prolegomena for the Oxford Shakespeare* (1939) shows, he was by then willing to emend an early text with the variants in a later authoritative edition, if all those variants were accepted as a unit. Greg's "Rationale" (foreshadowed by his *The Editorial Problem in Shakespeare* [1942]) took the natural next step by removing that conditional requirement and allowing editorial judgment to operate on each variant individually.[29]

Tanselle's account of the origins of copy-text editing is grounded in Greg's own representation of his thinking, which Greg rhetorically

---

27 New York: Simon and Schuster, 1992–.

28 "Classical, Biblical and Medieval Textual Criticism and Modern Editing," in Tanselle's *Textual Criticism and Scholarly Editing* (Charlottesville: UP of Virginia, 1990), 274–321, esp. 303.

29 "The Varieties of Scholarly Editing," in *Scholarly Editing: A Guide to Research*, ed. D. C. Greetham (New York: MLA, 1995), 22.

casts, both in *The Editorial Problem in Shakespeare* and later in "The Rationale of Copy-text," as simply a modification of positions taken by McKerrow in *Prolegomena*[30] from which, in both cases, Greg lavishly quotes.

Yet Greg and Tanselle's representation of a chronological and logical continuum from McKerrow to Greg obscures the fact that McKerrow and Greg were engaged in debate; that McKerrow was concerned to differentiate his own thinking, sometimes rather sharply, from Greg's on a number of issues crucial to the "Rationale"; and that Greg was thus, in turn, forced to state his disagreements with McKerrow. McKerrow tells us in his December 22, 1938, Preface to *Prolegomena* that he has a debt "to my friend Dr. W. W. Greg, who very kindly read this introduction in its first form as long ago as 1933 or 1934, and with whom I have since discussed many of the matters of editorial practice with which it is concerned" (x). Greg presented his own views on these matters in the form of the Clark Lectures in the Lent term of 1939 only a couple of months after McKerrow wrote what I have just quoted. Greg's Clark Lectures were published in 1942 as *The Editorial Problem in Shakespeare*. Between delivering the lectures in 1939 and publishing them in 1942, Greg prefixed to them the section, which he entitled his "Prolegomena" (vii–lv), in which he quoted extensively from and modified McKerrow's *Prolegomena*. The relevance of the latter to Greg's Clark Lectures is attested by Greg's decision to preface the published lectures with a commentary on McKerrow's book. Nor is there any mystery in Greg's decision to understate the extent of McKerrow's disagreement with him. McKerrow had died just a couple of years before in January of 1940, and the two had been friends since their student days at Trinity College, Cambridge.[31]

It is important however that Greg's generosity toward his dead friend not obscure for later scholars the extent to which the two friends' opinions diverged. Some long overdue attention to the printed record of the debate between them will serve a number of purposes. It will show that Tanselle's attempt to backdate a consensus on issues essential to the theory of copy-text editing (especially for Shakespeare) cannot be sustained. It will show that the attitudes that were evolving among the leading textual scholars of Elizabethan and Jacobean drama, who included not only McKerrow and Greg but also J. Dover Wilson (about whom Tanselle is curiously silent), were every bit as diverse in the early part of the century as they are now. The extent of this diversity seems to become less legible as McKerrow's readers

---

[30] Ronald B. McKerrow, *Prolegomena for the Oxford Shakespeare: A Study in Editorial Method* (Oxford: Clarendon P, 1939).

[31] "Greg, Sir Walter Wilson, 1875–1959," DNB.

grow ever further removed from the occasion of his writing, perhaps because his style in representing the scholars with whom he disagrees is rather casual; he does not quote these scholars or even attach their names to his characterization of their positions. Nonetheless, as I hope to show, McKerrow is precise enough to make identification of his opponents possible; and this identification may make legible again McKerrow's strong difference of opinion with both Wilson and Greg.

The first matter on which McKerrow sought clearly to differentiate his views from Greg's and from Wilson's (in the latter's work on *Hamlet*) was "foul papers."[32] McKerrow keenly understood from the dramatic manuscripts he had studied that it was unlikely that Shakespeare's fellow actors would have left unannotated and unaltered the playwright's manuscripts in their possession so that later editors might possess printed versions based on Shakespeare's so-called "foul papers," in the technical sense that Greg imposed on this expression. And McKerrow seems to have been well aware, presumably from the discussions of "many of the matters of editorial practice" that he acknowledged having had with Greg, of the specific definition that, in the 1942 *Editorial Problem in Shakespeare*, Greg would give to "foul papers" as a holograph copy of a "play substantially in its final form" (32), for McKerrow unmistakably alluded to it and took issue with it:

> It is very doubtful [McKerrow writes] whether, especially in the case of the earlier plays, there ever existed any written 'final form'. Shakespeare as an active member of a theatrical company would, at any rate in his younger days, have been concerned with producing, not plays for the study, but material for his company to perform on the stage, and there can be little doubt that his lines would be subject to modification in the light of actual performance, as well as to later revision when, for example, a change in the constitution of the company necessitated a redistribution of the roles, or a desire was felt to introduce some topical allusion or to parody or improve upon some rival show. Such alterations may have been made by the author himself or, if he was not available, they may have been made by others. He may, or may not, have regarded them as improvements: he probably merely accepted them as necessary changes, and it is quite likely that he never bothered about whether they introduced inconsistencies into what was originally conceived as a consistent whole. We must not expect to find a definitive text in the sense in which the published version of the plays of a modern dramatist is definitive. And even in those plays which do seem to us to be finished

---

[32] According to Wilson "in the Second Quarto [of *Hamlet*] we possess what may . . . be described as a typographical facsimile . . . of the autograph manuscript of the greatest play in the world" (*The Manuscript of Shakespeare's 'Hamlet'*, 2 vols. [Cambridge: Cambridge UP, 1934], 1: xiii). As will become evident, Greg translates Wilson's term for printer's copy for *Hamlet* Q2 "autograph manuscript" into his own "foul papers" in characterizing Wilson's position.

wholes, written at one time with a single impulse of the creative spirit, and which show no signs of tampering or revision whether by the original author or by another, we cannot be certain of any close approach to the author's manuscript. (*Prolegomena*, 6–7)

One reason McKerrow refused to endorse Greg's speculations that many early printed texts were based directly on Shakespeare's "foul papers" was because, unlike Wilson and Greg, he had never been convinced of the attribution of an addition in the *More* manuscript to Shakespeare, and so he did not imagine that he knew what a Shakespeare holograph might look like. His skepticism on the question is repeated in *Prolegomena*, in which he initially classifies *More* among "doubtful plays in which some believe Shakespeare had a hand" (4 n1). Unlike many editors who have labored under Greg's influence in the last fifty years, McKerrow is quite unwilling to erect any further hypotheses upon what he recognizes is at best only a possibility that a fragment of the *More* manuscript is Shakespeare's:

Seeing that, with the exception of one possible fragment, we have neither any autograph manuscript of Shakespeare, nor even any manuscript copy of such a manuscript, and are compelled to rely, for any idea that we can form of a Shakespearian original, on printed texts of uncertain but undoubtedly varied provenance, we cannot hope to infer with any approach to certainty Shakespeare's own practice as regards such details as spelling, capitalization, the use of italics, or punctuation. (7)

In regard to the *More* manuscript, McKerrow's position had not evolved or changed in any other way since he had reviewed the 1923 book *Shakespeare's Hand in the Play of 'Sir Thomas More,'* in which A. W. Pollard had collected the arguments by the paleographer Edward Maunde Thompson, and by J. Dover Wilson and R. W. Chambers in favor of Shakespeare's authorship of a three-page addition to this manuscript play. In his 1924 review, McKerrow had expressed a strong sense of the inconclusiveness of the book's case: "I confess that in reading these chapters I have at times felt, even more than how much has been done, how much remains to do."[33]

McKerrow's tone in *Prolegomena* is almost always as gentle as it is in this earlier negative review, but it becomes slightly harsher when he seeks to separate himself from those among his contemporaries who purported to discover in features of the early printed texts the provenance or history of the manuscripts from which these texts were printed. When he first addresses this kind of scholarship, it is clear from his description that he is referring to J. Dover Wilson's highly speculative textual criticism both in the New Shakespeare edition that

---

[33] "Reviews," *The Library,* 4th series, 4 (1924): 238–42, esp. 239.

Wilson had begun in 1921[34] and in Wilson's two-volume monograph, *The Manuscript of Shakespeare's 'Hamlet'*:

> attempts have been made to explain the manifest or presumed defects in Shakespearian texts by means of theories often involving the assumption of an extremely complicated history. We are asked to suppose the incorporation of parts of lost plays, revision by several different hands for different theatrical or other purposes, that the text was copied by one person, the stage directions by another, and so on, until we sometimes feel that while the theory would no doubt explain well enough the disturbances to which the text appears to have been subjected, it would equally well serve to explain a far greater amount of disturbance than seems actually to have occurred. (9)

Although McKerrow does not document this passage with reference to Wilson's published work and does not even mention him by name, McKerrow characterizes Wilson's theories about the origin of printer's copy for a number of Shakespeare plays with enough precision so as to make his allusion to Wilson unmistakable. All three of the notions that McKerrow lists, "incorporation of lost plays," "the text ... copied by one person, the stage directions by another," and "revision by several different hands for different theatrical or other purposes," are to be found in work Wilson published in the two decades before McKerrow's *Prolegomena* appeared. The idea that the early printings of Shakespeare's plays incorporated "parts of lost plays" was a favorite of Wilson's, and was shared by Wilson's collaborator on The New Shakespeare series, Arthur Quiller–Couch. It appears in the series' first volume, *The Tempest* (1921); Wilson discovers in the Folio text of that play alleged traces of rhymed couplets that point, for him, to a version of the play in an earlier style and suggest to him that Shakespeare "had an old manuscript to go upon, possibly an early play of his own" (79). The idea turns up again in his edition of *The Merry Wives of Windsor* (also 1921), the Folio text of which, Wilson says, is "a revision of the same manuscript which lies, at whatever remove and however garbled and abridged, at the back of the Quarto version"; this revision is not quite complete, as evidenced for Wilson by, among other things, loose ends in the plot and what he regarded as an irrational mixture of verse and prose in some scenes (98–100). As Wilson's series continued throughout the '20s, the idea virtually became his signature, appearing in his editions of *Measure for Measure* (1922; 106), *The Comedy of Errors* (1922; 69), *Much Ado About Nothing* (1923; 93–94), *A Midsummer Night's Dream* (1924; 86–92), *The Merchant of Venice* (1926;

---

34 *The New Shakespeare*, ed. Arthur Quiller–Couch and J. Dover Wilson (Cambridge: Cambridge UP, 1921–66).

112), *The Taming of the Shrew* (1928; 125), and *All's Well That Ends Well* (1929; 113).

But McKerrow did not characterize Wilson's work only in terms of this *idée fixe*, but also with reference to speculations Wilson developed only occasionally. As to the printer's copy, for only two plays had Wilson inferred that "the text was copied by one person, the stage directions by another"; these were the Folio's *The Comedy of Errors* (69–73) and the 1600 Quarto of *The Merchant of Venice* (100). McKerrow's remaining allusion to Wilson's theories, namely, "revision by several different hands for different theatrical or other purposes," is the one that has the most important consequences for McKerrow's relation to Greg and to the principles underlying copy-text editing, for this allusion has possible reference to Wilson's work on *Hamlet*. In emphasizing *Hamlet*, I must at the same time acknowledge that Wilson *usually* imagined behind a printed Shakespeare play a manuscript containing "revisions by several different hands." Sometimes he even attempted to specify the hands. For example, the Folio's *Measure for Measure* Wilson represented as adapted by Shakespeare from an earlier play, then abridged by another hand for court performance, and then transcribed (from actors' parts) as a so-called "prompt-book" and, at the same time, expanded by a third hand (112–13). Wilson narrated such script-doctoring, both for *Measure for Measure* and for most other plays, as a theatrical project—as his narremes "court performance" and " 'prompt-book' " indicate.

With Folio *Hamlet*, however, Wilson speculated about a scribe, "Scribe C," who revised the play "for other purposes" (to use McKerrow's terms) after it had been adapted for "theatrical purposes" by "Scribe P." Both these hypothetical scribes are crucial to Wilson's construction of the Folio text of *Hamlet* as, at least at one stage of its history, a so-called "prompt-book": Scribe P because he is imagined to have transformed Shakespeare's manuscript into the "prompt-book," and Scribe C because to him, as a scribe "capable of anything," Wilson can attribute all of the many features of the Folio text that are as uncharacteristic of Wilson's conception of a "prompt-book" as are features to be found in the text printed in the Second Quarto of the play, which Wilson wants to imagine as having been printed from Shakespeare's own manuscript (*Manuscript*, 1: 32, 2: 316). It is important, I think, to recognize that McKerrow, in distancing himself from Wilson's wild speculations, made no distinction between Wilson's work in *The Manuscript of Shakespeare's 'Hamlet'* and the accounts of other plays Wilson had provided in his early volumes of the New Shakespeare series. Greg, as I shall show, did make such a distinction; indeed Greg's theory of copy-text rests to a large extent on his confidence in Wilson's work on *Hamlet*.

As McKerrow's argument in *Prolegomena* proceeds, it soon becomes clear that, in the matter of inferring the origin of manuscript copy for printed plays, he is putting as much distance as he can not only between himself and Wilson but also between himself and Greg.[35] McKerrow writes,

> If we find a text containing, say, certain errors or inconsistencies which we feel convinced that no intelligent author could have deliberately intended to stand, we shall as a rule find that such errors may be explained in a number of very different ways and that there is no criterion by which we can ascertain which explanation is correct. To mention a few of the more obvious possibilities, there may have been mere carelessness or indifference on the part of the author, who may have been handing over his manuscript sheet by sheet to the theatre as he wrote and have never bothered about any final revision, trusting to put right any too glaring inconsistencies at the time of the rehearsal; the play may have been revised on one or more occasions and the manuscript which was used for printing may have represented some kind of incomplete revision; or an imperfect manuscript may have been the only one available to the printer and this may have been completed by guess-work. As a rule there is no means of determining what actually did happen.... It seems to me in most cases impossible to arrive at any certainty—or even at any reasonable probability—in such matters, and I have therefore made no attempt to argue them. (9–10)

As was the case in McKerrow's discussion of Wilson's views without explicit reference to their author, so again in this engagement with Greg's position, McKerrow does not mention Greg by name. Yet the arguments to which he alluded are nonetheless available to be read in Greg's publication of his Clark Lectures, and so McKerrow's allusion to Greg is demonstrable.

As McKerrow begins to list "a number of different ways" in which "certain errors or inconsistencies which we feel convinced that no intelligent author could have deliberately intended to stand" might have made their way into a printed text, he gives pride of place to the only way, as I have already shown, that Greg imagined such inconsistencies

---

35 After the sentence in which he opens discussion of "attempts ... made to explain the manifest or presumed defects in Shakespearian texts by means of theories often involving the assumption of an extremely complicated history," McKerrow inserts a footnote naming Greg as one "of the principal scholars who have interested themselves in such research." Then McKerrow goes on in his main text to discuss first Wilson's theories and then Greg's. From the place in which McKerrow inserts his explicit reference to Greg, it is clear that McKerrow makes no distinction between the credibility of Greg's work on this topic and Wilson's. As I will show, McKerrow is right not to make any distinction because Greg's work cannot be disentangled from Wilson's. Greg himself understood as much when he began his *Editorial Problem in Shakespeare* with praise for the "advancement of our knowledge" achieved by Wilson (1).

could have seen print: "mere carelessness or indifference on the part of the author, who may have been handing over his manuscript sheet by sheet to the theatre as he wrote and have never bothered about any final revision, trusting to put right any too glaring inconsistencies at the time of the rehearsal." Specifically, McKerrow is alluding to the single document that Greg was ever able to cite in support of his belief that playwrights handed over to their companies "foul papers" of plays.[36] This is the dramatist Robert Daborne's letter to Philip Henslowe detailing the circumstances under which a single "foule sheete" got into a theater:

> Mr Hinchlow you accuse me with the breach of promise, trew it is J promysd to bring you the last scean which yt [i.e., that] you may see finished[,] J send you the foule sheet & ye [i.e., the] fayr J was wrighting as your man can testify[,] which if great busines had not prevented J had this night fynished[.] sir you meat me by ye common measuer of poets[.] if J could not liv by it & be honest J would giv it over[,] for rather then J would be vnthankfull to you J would famish[.] thearfor accuse me not till you hav cause[.] if you pleas to perform my request J shall think my self beholding to you for it[.] howsoever J will not fayle to write this fayr and perfit the book which shall not ly one your hands.[37]

Daborne emphasizes how unusual it is to be giving Henslowe even a single "foule sheete" and how he feels obligated to provide better copy. But McKerrow does not choose to criticize Greg for taking as a norm regarding "foul papers" for whole plays what Daborne says is an anomaly involving one "foule sheete."

Instead, McKerrow chooses to contest Greg's position by providing some "very different ways" through which "errors or inconsistencies" could have seen print. Neither of McKerrow's "different ways" is the least bit far-fetched. Indeed, both can be documented in the known practice of scribes and printers. Among the dramatic manuscripts that survive from Shakespeare's period it would be hard to find one that is free from error and inconsistency arising as a consequence of such incomplete revision as McKerrow assumes may have disfigured a printer's copy for a play. The most famous of such incompletely revised manuscripts are *The Booke of Sir Thomas Moore* and *Sir John*

---

[36] *EPS*, 28. Greg also tried to cite Edward Knight's reference to the use of "foul papers" in order to make his transcription of *Bonduca* evidence that playwrights turned these over to companies, but, as Greg had to admit, Knight says nothing about where he acquired the papers he used, and so his reference does nothing to support Greg's position that "foul papers" would have been found in an acting company's archives. See *Bonduca by John Fletcher,* Malone Society Reprint, ed. W. W. Greg (London: The Malone Society, 1951), xi n3.

[37] *Henslowe's Papers*, ed. W. W. Greg (London: Bullen, 1907), 78.

van Olden Barnavelt, but even *The Lady Mother*, by the obscure Henry Glapthorne, contains examples of revisions only partially carried through.[38] McKerrow's third alternative explanation for error and inconsistency in a printed playtext, the use as printer's copy of "an imperfect manuscript . . . completed by guess-work," may have been grounded in his own experience with the Second Quarto of *Titus Andronicus*. This quarto was not printed from manuscript, of course, but from printed copy—a copy of the First Quarto; yet McKerrow had been proven right in pointing out that the copy of the First Quarto used to print the Second must have been imperfect and that its deficiencies, we have every reason to believe, were repaired through no other agency than the "guesswork" to which he alludes as yet another alternative source of error in printed plays.[39]

However, the quality of McKerrow's objections to Greg's identification of lost manuscript copy behind playtexts should not be determined only by the plausibility of his own particular suggestions about how errors and inconsistencies may have got into print; instead, the force of McKerrow's objection lies simply in his recognizing, in contrast to Greg, that one must allow for alternatives. The crude binarism of Greg's method for identifying printer's copy as "foul papers" or "prompt-book" cannot admit any alternatives without collapsing.

Greg himself recognized that his—and not just Dover Wilson's—were views from which McKerrow was departing, and Greg acknowledged as much in a tone that was less than completely generous to his dead friend. In "McKerrow's 'Prolegomena' Reconsidered," Greg's first response to McKerrow's *Prolegomena*, published a little over a year after McKerrow's death, Greg addressed the passage from McKerrow I've just been analyzing.[40] While Greg held that McKerrow was right to reject "far-reaching speculations as to the evolution of the manuscripts of [Shakespeare's] plays," Greg charged that McKerrow's refusal to endorse "investigations into the relationship of extant texts to one another and into the nature of their immediate sources" and "to carry through [such] critical analysis to its legitimate conclusion, with its textual consequences, must be regarded as a blemish in McKerrow's work" (144).

Greg failed to acknowledge here that in *Prolegomena* McKerrow had carried his own critical analysis to its legitimate conclusion in editorial principles grounded in the early printed texts themselves, rather than in narratives of their origins. Because McKerrow had no confidence that he could come to know, through internal evidence

---

38 For a discussion of *The Lady Mother*, see note 23 above.

39 McKerrow, "A Note on *Titus Andronicus*," *The Library*, 4th series, 15 (1934): 49–53.

40 *Review of English Studies* 17 (1941): 139–49.

alòne, the relation to each other (and to the author and the theater) of substantive early printed texts, the choice of copy-text had to be based, for him, on the quality of the early printed texts themselves. The following passage represents his thoughts on this matter:

> Obviously if a work has been transmitted to us in several manuscripts or printed editions, none of which appears to have been copied or printed from another, and all of which may have originated during the lifetime of the author, it will, in the absence of any external evidence as to the relationship of the texts, be the duty of an editor to select for the basis of a new edition that text which in his judgement is most representative of the author and most nearly in accord with what, in view of his other works, we should have expected from him at the date to which the work in question is assigned. In the majority of cases this will mean simply that the editor must select the text which appeals most to his critical judgement, and this, in its turn, will as a rule be the one which appears to be the most careful copy of its original and the most free from obvious errors. (13–14)

Like Greg, McKerrow here used the terms "author" and "work," but, unlike Greg, he did so only along his way towards articulation of criteria of choice that are independent of both "author" and "work" as metaphysical categories. McKerrow chose his copy-text according to features—carefulness and freedom of obvious errors—that are available to critical judgement in the early printed texts themselves, rather than following Greg's model and choosing a copy-text according to features of the early printed texts that are meaningful only when they are embedded in uncertain narratives about the relation of these texts to author and theater.

When McKerrow presents his notion of authority, it becomes clear that he vests it primarily in the text of a particular document, even though, I freely admit, McKerrow continues to employ the term "author" in his discussion. So strong is McKerrow's identification of authority with the document in which a text is preserved, rather than with the transcendent "work," that McKerrow even toys with the possibility of calling the document's misprints authoritative:

> I shall use then 'authoritative reading' for any reading which may be presumed to derive by direct descent from the manuscript of the author. Thus all readings in whatever text appears to stand in the closest relation of all extant texts to the author's manuscript will be termed 'authoritative', with the exception of such readings as are on the face of them mis-copyings or misprints. In a sense, even these are authoritative, or at least we may say that they have more authority than the corrections of later editions, even when we may feel that we can accept such corrections as restoring what must have stood in the author's manuscript. It would, however, be rather absurd to term simple and obvious misprints in an earliest edition 'authoritative' when we know that it is much more likely

that they are due to the printer of the edition than to the manuscript from which he worked, and that they would certainly have been rejected by the author if they had come under his notice. (12–13)

Because McKerrow's understanding of authority is documentary rather than metaphysical, he is rather less sanguine than Greg about the power of an editor's critical judgement to identify authorial revision in what are otherwise later reprints of substantive texts in the absence of external, documentary evidence of authorial intervention:

> If we had external evidence that a particular text of any work had been revised throughout *by its author*, such a text should undoubtedly be made the basis of a modern edition—but such cases are rare and, so far as I am aware, it has never been suggested that there is such external evidence of correction in the case of any Shakespearian play. In the great majority of instances of 'correction' in later editions we have no external evidence whatever as to the source of the changes, and are therefore compelled to consider whether in themselves they show any signs of being made by the author of the work, or, on the other hand, are such as might be due to a corrector of the press or editor. . . . Unfortunately, however, in the great majority of cases, there is no means of deciding whether they are authentic or not, and though there may be a few readings of which we can say with some approach to certainty that they are not Shakespeare's, there are few, if any, of which we can safely make the opposite assertion. (14–17)

Although terms employed by McKerrow in developing his editorial strategy are often radically different in their logocentricity from those that some Shakespeare editors might use today, the strategy that emerged from his deliberations is uncannily close to strategies adopted today—provided that we remember to translate McKerrow's shorthand references to authority into his own documentary terms. He summed up his editorial strategy succinctly: "the only possible course is to determine for each play separately the most authoritative text of those which have come down to us from early times, and to reprint this as exactly as possible save for manifest and indubitable errors" (7).

iii.

Since the purpose of this paper is to sharpen appreciation of the enormously diverse principles for editing Shakespeare on offer in the early part of this century—a diversity later shut down through the widespread imposition of copy-text editing—it is not my object to idealize McKerrow or his *Prolegomena* at the expense of Greg or of Bowers and their apologies for copy-text editing. As early as 1941 Greg rightly pointed out that there is in *Prolegomena* "some want of correlation in the different parts," and this charge of incoherence can be borne out in even the very brief analysis that follows of McKerrow's presentation of his views on the possible determination of the nature and character of the manuscripts underlying Shakespeare's plays.[41] But there is also no basis for idealizing either Greg's or Bowers's positions when first Greg and then Bowers attack McKerrow for lack of coherence and then suggest that the only way in which McKerrow could have achieved coherence was through the adoption of their views;[42] neither attack is any more coherent than McKerrow's initial position simply because copy-text editing of Shakespeare was not itself a coherent theory. Greg's confidence in an editor's ability to determine the nature and/or history of the manuscripts behind collateral substantive texts is in large part grounded in his implicit belief in the success of Wilson's investigation of the Second Quarto and Folio *Hamlet* texts, but the coherence of Greg's own position becomes questionable when he investigates these *Hamlet*s for himself and casts doubt on Wilson's findings. In the story that Bowers narrates about the successful accumulation of knowledge concerning manuscript printer's copy for Shakespeare's plays, he grants all the credit to Greg, ignoring Greg's dependence on Wilson, from whom, defining himself as a follower of Greg's, Bowers tries entirely to separate himself.

Both Greg and Bowers find McKerrow contradicting himself in *Prolegomena* when McKerrow expresses disbelief about arriving "at any certainty—or even at any reasonable probability—" concerning the "possible history of the copy used in printing any of the extant 'substantive' texts of Shakespeare" (9, 10) after he has just written:

> The general character of the copy from which the substantive text (or texts) of a work was set up can often be determined with some degree of probability, and when this is possible it is of concern to an editor, as it naturally has a bearing on the degree of credence which he should give to the readings of the substantive texts in question. I have therefore discussed the general character of the various texts in the appropriate introductions [to his projected Oxford Shakespeare].... For example, I have attempted to show that a certain kind of variation in the speakers' names indicates derivation from the author's original manuscript, rather than from a fair copy prepared by a theatrical copyist. (8–9 and 9 n1)

The article to which McKerrow alludes in the last sentence I've quoted is "A Suggestion Regarding Shakespeare's Manuscripts," which he had published in 1935. Then he had presented himself as throwing "a light on the genesis of the MS. used by the printer as copy"

---

41 "McKerrow's 'Prolegomena' Reconsidered," 139.

42 Greg, "McKerrow's 'Prolegomena' Reconsidered," 143; Bowers, "McKerrow's Editorial Principles for Shakespeare Reconsidered," *Shakespeare Quarterly* 6 (1955), 309–24, esp. 311.

for Shakespeare's plays.[43] No matter how sympathetically one reads McKerrow, it is hard to see any difference between his construction of "a certain kind of variation in speakers' names" as a distinctive sign of an authorial manuscript and Greg's construction of, in McKerrow's terms, "certain errors or inconsistencies which we feel convinced that no intelligent author could have deliberately intended to stand" as a distinctive sign of "mere carelessness or indifference on the part of the author." Indeed, in practice, Greg incorporated McKerrow's "variations" among his own "inconsistencies" (*EPS*, 103). Greg and Bowers interpreted McKerrow's self-contradiction as evidence that he really did not disagree with them as severely as some of his writing I've quoted would indicate.[44] There is an invitation in McKerrow's *Prolegomena* to speculate, as Greg did, about incomplete revision, but nothing with which decisively to resolve McKerrow's self-contradiction.[45]

Yet McKerrow could hardly have achieved coherence if he had anticipated Greg's line of argument in the latter's "Prolegomena" in *The Editorial Problem in Shakespeare*. These are no less fraught with incoherence than McKerrow's, and again what is at issue is the question of how much can be known about printer's copy. According to Greg's "Prolegomena," a Shakespeare editor can acquire a knowledge of the history of the manuscripts that served as printer's copy for what Greg construes as collateral substantive playtexts. The editor can know which of these manuscripts was the author's "foul papers" and which "the prompt-book"; and *Hamlet* constitutes the particular case where such knowledge is already available and where it can be employed by an editor in the selection of a copy-text:

> The textual conditions that we perceive more or less clearly adumbrated behind the earliest editions are these: if a play was printed from the author's original draft—his 'foul papers' as they were called in the theatre—we may expect to find in it contradictions and uncertainties of action and unresolved textual tangles; if, on the other hand, a play was printed from a theatrical fair copy, we may indeed expect to find such contradictions and tangles smoothed out, but we have no assurance that this was done by the author himself—at best we may hope that it was done with his approval or at least his acquiescence. It is possible that in one instance (*Hamlet* Q2 and F) we are able to place the two types of text side by side, and are faced with a choice between the roughnesses and inconsequences of the author and the ordered levelling of the book-keeper. (ix)

---

43 *Review of English Studies* 11 (1935): 459–65, esp. 460.

44 Greg, *EPS*, xxiii–xxiv n1; Bowers, "McKerrow's Editorial Principles," 312.

45 "McKerrow's 'Prolegomena' Reconsidered," 139.

Greg does not here indicate where the knowledge that he claims we possess about *Hamlet* is to be found, and he does qualify his acceptance of this alleged knowledge, which he is willing to grant no higher status than "possible."

But when he returns to discussion of our knowledge of printer's copy for the *Hamlet* Q2 and F texts, it becomes clear that he regards these as the only so-called collateral substantive Shakespeare texts about which we have any such knowledge: "In the others there is, so far as I am aware, no obvious clue to the relative authority of the editions, but this may of course only be due to their having been less closely studied" (xxiv–xxv n2). While Greg is usually guarded in his references to the degree of certainty that can be attached to our "knowledge" of printer's copy for Q2 and F *Hamlet*, on at least one occasion, he appears—perhaps because of the brevity of his reference to the matter—to grant such "knowledge" the status of fact: with "*Hamlet*, . . . the choice lies between a careless but naïve print from the autograph [Q2] and an edited text derived ultimately from the same original [F]" (xxxv n1).

When later in *The Editorial Problem in Shakespeare* and well after his "Prolegomena,"[46] Greg returns to the issue of *Hamlet*, he indicates the source of our alleged knowledge of printer's copy for *Hamlet* Q2 and F and says why he privileges these among so-called collateral substantive Shakespeare texts as having been so "closely studied": "Dover Wilson['s] . . . monograph on *The Manuscript of Shakespeare's 'Hamlet'* . . . is by far the most exhaustive and penetrating study of the authoritative texts" (64). Yet the implicit faith in the success of Wilson's study that Greg shows in his "Prolegomena" simply does not cohere with his own findings about the relation of Q2 and F *Hamlet* from a study of their stage directions. Although in "Prolegomena" Greg simply reproduces Wilson's claim that Q2 is printed "from the autograph," Greg finds in Q2's stage directions what he takes to be signs of the prompter: "The demand for flourishes is generally more characteristic of the prompter." He may of course have added some of them when reading through the foul papers. As Wilson observes, there is certainly duplication in "Drum, trumpets, and shot. Flourish, a piece goes off" (166).[47] At the same time, while Greg in his "Prolegomena" can rely on Wilson's findings that F was printed from "theatrical fair copy, . . .

---

[46] Of course Greg's "Prolegomena" were actually written after the lectures that constitute the bulk of Greg's book.

[47] For Greg, duplication in stage directions is taken, quite reasonably I might add, as an indication of theatrical annotation of a manuscript. There are a number of extant dramatic manuscripts, the most famous being *The Booke of Sir Thomas Moore*, in which stage directions are duplicated in an annotator's hand. In the passage I have just quoted from Greg he refers to the stage direction that I have included in the quotation only by

an edited text derived ultimately from the same original" as Q2, when Greg examines the texts themselves, he judges that

> it is very difficult to derive the directions of F from those of Q2. . . . [F]lourishes are generally absent [from F, although as Greg has just noted, these are "generally more characteristic of the prompter"], and [F's] 'Exit Hamlet tugging in Polonius' [where Q2 reads simply "Exit"] would naturally be put down as a typical author's direction. [E.K.] Chambers remarks that indefiniteness has been cleared up; so it has in [four cases]; on the other hand in 'Enter four or five Players' and 'Enter Hamlet, and two or three of the Players' [where in contrast Q2 reads "Enter the Players" and "Enter Hamlet, and three of the Players"] indefiniteness is rather on the side of F. One can understand a prompt-book failing to make a number definite; it is less easy to see how it could introduce an unspecified number. . . . On the whole there seems to be something not explained in the relation of the directions that leaves an uncomfortable feeling of uncertainty. (166–67)

Thus Greg deconstructs the binary opposition—taken over so uncritically from Wilson's *Manuscript* in Greg's own "Prolegomena"—of Q2 as a "foul papers" text and F as a "prompt-book" one. Greg discovers "prompt-book" features in Q2 and "foul papers" features in F.

Greg's analysis of these texts is very different from Wilson's and from those of a number of recent editors of *Hamlet*. Wilson and his followers construct the binary opposition by bracketing selected variants in F to contrast to the readings in Q2; only by such selection can they argue that F must be a "prompt-book" text (made, for Wilson, by Scribe P) and Q2 the "foul papers" version. Then after F has been established as a "prompt-book" by this means, Wilson and his followers present the features of F that cannot be those of a "prompt-book" and go on to claim that F must have been printed from a transcript of a "prompt-book" by a non-theatrical scribe (Wilson's Scribe C).[48] However, Greg is far more rigorous. In order to regard F as a "prompt-book," he requires that, when F departs from Q2, F exhibit only features he associates with such a document; and he also demands that, if Q2 is to be considered a "foul papers" text, it contain, in comparison to F, only marks that Greg regards as distinctive of "foul papers." As a

---

the number he has attached to it in his list of stage directions that precedes what I have quoted. The same is true of the other stage directions I've included in quotations from Greg that follow.

48 Compare, for example, Philip Edwards's discussion on 8–32 of his New Cambridge edition of *Hamlet* (Cambridge: Cambridge UP, 1985); or George Hibbard's "identification" of Q2 as a "foul papers" text and F as a "prompt–book" in his edition of *Hamlet* (Oxford: Clarendon P, 1987), 89–130, although, for Hibbard, Wilson's Scribe C becomes "Shakespeare"; or Harold Jenkins's in his Arden edition of the play (London: Methuen, 1982), 36–64.

consequence, Greg finds himself casting doubt on Wilson's construction of printer's copy for the *Hamlet* texts, even though in "Prolegomena" this construction is his sole example of existing knowledge of the manuscripts behind so-called collateral substantive texts. Thus Greg puts into question the possibility of editors ever attaining the knowledge they need in order to choose a copy-text from such texts on the basis of the history of the printer's copy for them. So Greg's "Prolegomena," and "The Rationale of Copy-Text" that derives from them, are, as far as the editing of Shakespeare is concerned, just as bedeviled by contradiction as are McKerrow's *Prolegomena*.

The same goes for Bowers's attack on McKerrow, in which contradiction is much more obtrusive. According to Bowers, McKerrow erred in *Prolegomena* by reacting so strongly against Wilson's speculations about printer's copy that he failed to see the value and potential of research on the topic. Bowers altogether agrees with McKerrow that Wilson's work lacks any value and joins McKerrow in repudiating it. In doing so Bowers is far harsher towards Wilson than McKerrow was:

> I am not romancing when I offer the opinion that Wilson's shadow hangs heavily over *Prolegomena*. We must remember that the years in which McKerrow was experimenting with editorial method and evolving his principles were just those in which Wilson's eminence was greatest, when his ingenious and exciting textual criticism was sweeping all before it, especially in its influence on the younger generation of scholars. . . . Pollard had defected to Wilson's side; Greg was silent and neither openly opposed Wilson nor analyzed his want of bibliographical judgment. The hollowness of Wilson's claims to scientific method had not been perceived . . . , nor had his perversion of bibliography been exposed. . . . In my opinion McKerrow saw clearly the unsound foundations on which Wilson reared his towers of conjecture; but either he did not have the time to make the necessary investigations, or else (what I think is more probable) lacking the time he did not grasp the method by which he could demolish Wilson's glittering fabric. As a consequence, it would appear that his normal conservatism reacted excessively, and, because he could see no other choice, his reaction led him into a corresponding series of untenable positions and even to attack bibliography and scientific method as having no necessary connection with the editorial process.[49]

Thus, says Bowers, McKerrow was "blinded . . . to the fact that there were possibilities that other . . . methods [than Wilson's] might live up the road that he had just closed off" (312). As his example of the kind of knowledge that both is important to a Shakespeare editor and is denied to an editor by McKerrow's conservative over-reaction to Wilson, Bowers offers the following:

---

[49] "McKerrow's Editorial Principles," 310–11.

[I]n *Hamlet*, for instance, whereas it is important for an editor to know that the second quarto was probably set from Shakespeare's autograph, and the Folio not from autograph, editorial problems arise that cannot be solved on such a simple basis, problems that must depend upon the working hypothesis the editor draws for the transmission of the text up to the Folio print. And somewhere in this process an editor must positively make up his mind about one important question: did Shakespeare or did he not alter the text of *Hamlet* in any way after writing the manuscript that was used by the printer of the second quarto [sic]. (312–13)

Apparently, Bowers has forgotten that his construction of the *Hamlet* texts—"the second quarto ... probably set from Shakespeare's autograph, and the Folio not from autograph"—is part of Wilson's "glittering fabric" that Bowers wanted to "demolish." What's more, Greg was hardly silent about this particular speculation of Wilson's; instead, as has been shown, Greg enthusiastically endorsed it in his own "Prolegomena." While it is evident that McKerrow's *Prolegomena* are flawed by incoherence, as Greg and Bowers charged, it is also evident that Greg and Bowers had difficulty arriving at a coherent position from which to expose McKerrow's errors.

Other charges leveled at McKerrow seem to me to have less validity than that of incoherence. As Greg indicated in his 1941 article "McKerrow's 'Prolegomena' Reconsidered," it is easy to devise a Housmanian riposte to McKerrow's principles and charge that they might lead him to prefer as copy-text "a carefully edited 'report', accurately printed" to "a careless print of difficult 'foul papers'" (147). Yet since both these kinds of manuscripts are Greg's idealizations, there is virtually no chance that even the discovery of printer's copies for Shakespeare's plays could ever expose such a shortcoming in McKerrow's principles. While *Prolegomena* represent a pragmatic strategy for editing, rather than a theoretically rigorous and hence utterly impracticable agenda, and while *Prolegomena* therefore have many shortcomings, the same can evidently be said of any form of Greg's theory of copy-text. That theory has been presented by its advocates in attractive terms as a model for the liberation of critical judgement from mechanical rules. No doubt this is true of the many cases in which there is certain knowledge of the textual documents' provenance. But such is not the case with Shakespeare's plays. There Greg's theory of copy-text and its subsequent derivatives, as is now again becoming as clear as it once was to McKerrow, require an editor to associate with Shakespeare as author early printed versions of uncertain yet undoubtedly varied provenance. Greg's copy-text editing thus binds critical judgement to speculations that were intellectually repugnant to McKerrow when they were first advanced and that have again become so for a number of Shakespeare editors.

iv.

This review of a handful of texts by Wilson, McKerrow, Greg, and Bowers indicates some of what is excluded by a narrative of the gradual emergence of a consensus in the editorial community regarding the theory of copy-text editing. Such a narrative posits Shakespeare scholars from the first half of this century as arriving at agreement on their principles; then the application of these principles is extended to other fields, with the result that an author-centered editing of Shakespeare functions to center a wider editorial community. This is an attractively rational narrative of an allegedly rational process, but the texts upon which this story is fashioned do not bear it out. Suppressed in this narrative is McKerrow's determination to use the last of his energies before he died in order to publish *Prolegomena* that utterly repudiated Wilson's speculations about the genesis of the manuscripts from which *Hamlet* and other Shakespeare plays were allegedly printed, as well as Greg's selection of Wilson's conjectures about *Hamlet* to be the basis of his own editorial theory. Also suppressed is Greg's attack on McKerrow's *Prolegomena* in the 1941 article "McKerrow's 'Prolegomena' Reconsidered," an attack renewed by Bowers in 1955.[50] Right now we need a fuller history of the rise of copy-text editing than is provided by Tanselle's narrative of consensus. As long as such a narrative remains in place, today's Shakespeare editors who set themselves apart from Greg appear to be utterly rejecting the past in some fantasy of liberating themselves from it. But if McKerrow's dissent from Wilson and Greg is included in accounts of twentieth-century Shakespeare editorial history, today's editors who leave Greg behind need not be misunderstood as cutting themselves off from the past that enables their practice. When not reduced through the figure of consensus, history does in fact model the diversity of the present.

---

[50] In using the word "suppressed" in these sentences, I am leveling no accusation against Greg or Bowers or Tanselle of plotting against McKerrow. Indeed both Greg's 1941 answer to McKerrow and Bowers's 1955 examination of *Prolegomena* were in their frank and sharp confrontational styles anything but conspiratorial.

Understanding the Author's Compositional Method: Prolegomenon to a Hermeneutics of Genetic Writing

KLAUS HURLEBUSCH

Translated by Uta Nitschke–Stumpf
and Hans Walter Gabler

> Erst wenn man schreibt, weiss man am besten,
> was man selbst haben will.
> Auch beim dem Schreiben mus man sich nirgends
> anzukommen vorsezen.
> —Jean Paul[1]

i. The Dominance of the Author's Producing Subjectivity

a. Nulla dies sine linea:
Writing Between Toil and Pleasure

"THERE'S A GOOD DEAL OF INTEREST NOW in the process of writing" said Donald Hall in his interview with T. S. Eliot, which, together with others, was published in 1963 in *Writers at Work: The "Paris Review" Interviews.*[2] The volume was the successor to a collection

---

[1] "It is only when writing that one best knows what one intends. Even in writing, one must never will a goal beforehand."

[2] Second Series, ed. George Plimpton (London, 1963), 86 ff.

under the same title published in 1958.[3] Hall's statement apparently met an existing interest in connecting authors with their readers. A selection of these interviews was translated into German and published as a paperback in 1969.[4] The equivalent for fifteen German-speaking authors had already come out in 1962: Horst Bienek's collection, *Werkstattgespräche mit Schriftstellern* (*Workshop Talks with Authors*).[5] And of course, French authors have occasionally answered questions about their compositional methods; for example, in a radio series from 1982 to 1984. In 1986 those questions and answers were published by André Rollin under the title, *Ils écrivent. Où? Quand? Comment?*[6]

Naturally, interest in methods of literary composition, understood as the compound of material actions going into the drafting and inscribing of texts, is differently motivated in readers and authors. Readers are primarily drawn to the non-calculable and the inexplicable, to the operation of genius in literary creation, the mystical and extraordinary in the creative subject, whereas authors will tend to bask less in the divine gift and will focus instead on artistic technique and on the moral virtues of writing. Readers expect from authors' pronouncements on their art the expression of the incommensurable and of an inexhaustible, completely authentic individuality, whereas authors, in giving account of their activities, will rather emphasize the commensurable, "prosaic" aspects of their craft and its existential significance, even though they will not wholly disregard its creative, unanalyzable momentum. The resulting picture is often one of an "activité saugrenue soumise aux contraintes les plus materielles."[7]

Underlying these workshop talks is the situation that the authors not only answer the questions of their interviewers but also use them as occasions to ponder their own writing—an unmistakable indicator that the authors' interest in reflecting on their own compositional methods is genuine and not simply induced by others. What the writers communicate is characteristic of modern writers who turn to reflecting on the origins of their work to the extent that their creative work becomes disengaged from its orientation towards the trans-individual forces of creation, such as the traditions of ideas, genre,

---

3 First Series, ed. Malcolm Cowley (New York, 1958).

4 *Wie sie schreiben: Acht Gespräche mit Autoren der Gegenwart* (*How They Write: Eight Conversations with Contemporary Authors*; München, 1969). Hall's quote can be found on 56.

5 München, 1965 (dtv Nr. 291).

6 Préface de Bernard Frank (Paris, 1986).

7 "absurd activity subjected to the most material constraints," André Rollin, *Ils écrivent*, 11.

and form.[8] This gravitation towards subjectivity means that between the author's twinned orientation of reception and production, the productive impulse gains the upper hand and the perspective of the creatively composing author prevails. The heritage of writing shifts from the domain of reception into that of production. The most significant characteristics of this change are: a decrease in the use of traditional generic terminology (novel, lyric, epic, etc.) in whose place the term "text" (with all its derivatives, including the term "écriture" in France) increasingly enters.[9] Furthermore, the idea of the work is problematized and stripped of its receptional attributes of perfection, conclusiveness, finality, and permanence and receives instead production-related attributes, such as "finished" and "completed." The modern topos of the text's changeability actually belongs in the domain of the creatively working author, not in that of the reader, who considers the text as inviolable, assumes its perfection and sees it as "a tablet fallen from heaven,"[10] a perfect whole, an original text: "Readers always believe that what they read in one breath was created in one as well."[11] Fredson Bowers, one of the founders of analytical bibliography, had this privileged reader access to the author in mind when castigating the literary critic for believing that "texts are discovered under cabbage plants (or in bulrushes)."[12] As the transmission-conscious

---

[8] For Friedrich von Hagedorn the use of the term "labor" was still incompatible with the writing of poetry: "Même pour un Poëte, comme pour tout homme pensant, *travailler* et écrire ne sont pas des termes synonymes [...] Remarqués [...] que le Génie poëtique n'est pas celui qui brille le plus par la *quantité* des son Travail: le *Laboremus* ètant plûtôt pour Messieurs les Compilateurs, Glossateurs et les Auteurs en *aphes*"; ("Even for a Poet, as for any thinking man, working and writing are not synomymous terms [...] Note that [...] the poetic Genius is not the one that shines the most due to the *quantity* of his Work: the *Laboremus* being rather for our Gentlemen Compilers, Glossarizers and Authors 'en aphes' ['having ulcerated mouths']"). Hagedorn to Georg Ludwig von Bar, 23.3.1753; see also Friedrich von Hagedorn, *Briefe*, ed. Horst Gronemeyer, vol.1 (New York, 1997), 352.

[9] See, for example, Roland Barthes, "From Work to Text," in *Image Music Text*, trans. Stephen Heath (New York, 1977), 156: "Over against the traditional notion of the *work*, for long—and still—conceived of in a, so to speak, Newtonian way, there is now the requirement of a new object, obtained by the sliding or overturning of former categories. That object is the *Text*"; *Le bruissement de la langue: Essais critiques IV* (Paris, 1984), 61–77, esp. 70.

[10] Hilde Domin, "Über das Interpretieren von Gedichten" ("On the Interpretation of Poems") in *Doppelinterpretationen: Das zeitgenössische Gedicht zwischen Autor und Leser*, ed. Hilde Domin, Fischer Taschenbuch 1060 (Frankfurt a.M., 1969), 37.

[11] Jean Paul, *Ideen-Gewimmel: Texte und Aufzeichnungen aus dem unveröffentlichten Nachlass (Turmoil of Ideas: Texts and Notes from the Unpublished Literary Remains)*, ed. Thomas Wirtz and Kurt Wölfel (Frankfurt a.M., 1996), 50.

[12] *Textual and Literary Criticism* (Cambridge, 1959), 3.

advocate of the author, however, Bowers overlooked (because it was outside his field of interest) the fact that this widespread illusion of perfection is a prerequisite for the aesthetic effect of any literary text. Yet in contrast to the reader, the author relativizes himself and his text, "sees the completed, the realized, the in one way or another finished, as a possibility, and as something so to speak still under discussion [...] he does not regard the text as pre-ordained, but as construed throughout as an artefact [...]."[13]

Under the now dominant perspective of creative subjectivity "the" work loses the receptional appearance of an absolute and becomes something relative, a fixed but provisional result of the process of literary production, an "intertext," as one would call it today.

There are—if there be need for them—a number of witnesses to testify to this point:

> Maurice Blanchot: "What the author is drawn to, [...] is not the work as such but the search for it, the movement that gets him there, the approach towards something that makes the work possible: the art [...]. This is the reason why the writer is so often reluctant to finish and leaves a hundred stories in their fragmentary initial stages which are only interesting so far as they lead him to a certain point and to his attempting to reach beyond this point. [...] It is confusing to see an ever growing number of texts replace the so called literary work, texts that by the name of 'documents' or in the form of almost raw word material seem to deny any literary intention."[14]

> Roland Barthes: "The trap of complacency: to make believe that he is ready to regard what he has written as a 'work,' to turn it from the fortuitousness of all written words to the transcendence of a single sacred product. The word 'work' is already imaginary."[15]

> Max Frisch: "Anything completed ceases to be a dwelling-place for our spirit; but the developing is exquisite, what ever it may be—here one sees the warm breath of those working as a silvery tinge evermore fading away [...]."[16]

---

[13] See Domin (note 10), 40. Barthes (note 9) allows for a converging of the authorial and the readerly stance in structurally analogous acts of signification: "[T]he Text requires that one try to abolish (or at the very least to diminish) the distance between writing and reading, in no way by intensifying the projection of the reader into the work but by joining them in a single signifying practice" (75); "De l'oeuvre au texte," 162.

[14] *Le livre à venir.* Englished from the German translation by Karl August Horst: *Der Gesang der Sirenen: Essays zur modernen Literatur.* Ullstein-Buch, 35139 (Vienna, 1982), 270–71.

[15] *Roland Barthes par Roland Barthes* (Paris, 1975). German translation by Jürgen Hoch: *Roland Barthes: Über mich selbst* (München, 1978), 148.

[16] *Tagebuch* [Diary] *1946–1949* (Frankfurt a.M., 1958), 332.

And, finally, Hilde Domin, who through her own contributions confirmed the truth of her statement that in regard to the crucial "new definitions about the creative process, this century's theory of lyric poetry is altogether owed to the lyric poets themselves":[17]

> And what can be more interesting to him than the métier, the work process—except for the writing itself, of course. The métier has become increasingly interesting in the measure that the encounter with reality has become more problematic. It is not by accident that we have such a large number of contemporary poems about writing, because it is precisely the writing that has become the writer's medium to grapple with reality.[18]

In the course of the disillusioning of the receptional attitude to the work—a process that accompanies the progressive aestheticizing of literature at the expense of the representation of ideas—writing itself becomes revalued; it severs its ties of servitude to the work, even as the work comes to be seen as a mere transitional stage in the writing process. As the work recedes into genetic relativity, the process of literary writing tends to become correspondingly *existentialized* and, as such, to grow important to the author. For him or her it is more than just a mood-dependent temporarily practiced artistry of "setting-forth." It is an art—exercised regularly and day by day—of self-experience and self-realization.[19] It is not surprising, therefore, that contemporary writers willingly talk about their "craft," for it affects, to varying degrees, the very core of their sense of themselves. For Martin Walser literary writing has become, not a form of existence in which one merely endures life, but rather one in which the writer can achieve a harmonic development of his powers and can experience happiness, at least for the moment. It brings together what normally can only be experienced separately in daily life—intentionality and the reality of events. Writing is, for him, an organized spontaneity, the only activity

---

[17] See Domin (note 10), 44. Beda Allemann has compiled an anthology of essays on the poetics of modern lyrics: *Ars poetica: Texte von Dichtern des 20. Jahrhunderts zur Poetik* (Darmstadt, 1971). See also L. Hays's statement that the study of literature "has looked much later into the question of the nature of literary writing than the poets themselves. The writers' conscious reflection on the process of writing constitutes the beginning of 'Modernism' and has shaped it until today"; *Die dritte Dimension der Literatur: Notizen zu einer "critique génétique" (The Third Dimension of Literature: Notes on* critique génétique), in *Poetica: Zeitschrift für Sprach-und Literaturwissenschaft* 16 (1984), 308.

[18] See Domin (note 10), 39, and Domin's note 36.

[19] See Bienek (note 5): 99 (Nossak), 116 (Johnson), 149 (Andersch), and 249 (Walser).

that makes sense in itself: even if it may be only because he cannot *say* what it is that he *writes*.[20]

Literary writing is understood by Walser as an activity that makes sense in and of itself and can only partly be considered toilsome: what derives from this activity, the work, appears secondary. Musil too was attracted by the possibility, innate to writing, of experiencing it as more than labor—as an actively induced passivity, as a freely produced receptiveness. In one of his diaries (Heft no. 28), he entered on 5 January 1929: "I am looking to create a situation outside of myself. All my efforts of fallibly writing are that way directed. At that moment, I am no longer the one who speaks, the sentences exist outside of me, like a material substance, and I must manipulate them. This situation I wish to create."[21] Writing was for Musil—a man who admittedly did not enjoy writing, "although he did it passionately" (ibid., 943)—his "home,"[22] as it was in a different way for Martin Walser and in yet another way for Walter Benjamin ("Nulla dies sine linea—though certainly weeks"[23]) or Giacomo

---

20 "Enfin de compte, c'est devenu une manière de vivre. Mais j'allais vers elle dès le début: vers une compensation, une protection, un secours, un apaisement. [...] Tant qu'on écrit, on peut tout supporter. Tant qu'on écrit, on est sauvé. C'est lorsqu'on cesse d'écrire que revient le règne de la faiblesse. [...] Tous les préparatifs ne sont que des échafaudages: l'écriture est une spontanéité organisé. Pour un écrivain, c'est l'unique activité qui ait un sens, ne serait-ce que parce qu'il ne peut pas *dire* ce qu'il *écrit*"; ("In the end, it has become a way of life. But this was my aim from the very beginning: aiming for a compensation, a security, a safeguard, a relief. [...] As long as one writes, one is saved. It is only when one stops writing that the dominance of weakness returns. [...] All the forethoughts are mere scaffolding: writing is spontaneously organized. For a writer, it is the only action that makes sense, if only because he cannot *voice* what he *writes*."); Martin Walser, "Écrire," in Louis Hay, ed., *La naissance du texte* (Paris, 1989), 221–23.

21 *Tagebücher* [*Diaries*], ed. Adolf Frisé (Reinbek, 1976), 682.

22 Peter Härtling, "Federleicht oder doch etwas schwerer: Dichter und ihre Schreibgeräte" ("Featherweight or Somewhat Heavier: Writers and Their Writing Implements"), in *Vom Schreiben* (*On Writing*) 2: *Marbacher Magazin* 69 (1994), 11: "Im Schreiben haben sie (die rastlosen Dichter) ihren Ort, ihr Haus, ihr Zuhause" ("In writing, they [the restless writers] have their local habitation, their house, their home").

23 "Einbahnstrasse: Die Technik des Schriftstellers in dreizehn Thesen" ("One Way Street: The Writer's Technique in Thirteen Propositions"); for example, "VII. Höre niemals mit Schreiben auf, weil dir nichts mehr einfällt. Es ist ein Gebot der literarischen Ehre, nur dann abzubrechen, wenn ein Termin (eine Mahlzeit, eine Verabredung) einzuhalten oder das Werk beendet ist. VIII. Das Aussetzen der Eingebung fülle aus mit der sauberen Abschrift des Geleisteten. Die Intuition wird darüber erwachen [...]"; ("VII. Never cease to write because nothing happens to come to your mind. It is a point of literary honor to break off only for a date (a meal, an appointment) or when the work is finished. VIII. Bridge the slack of inspiration with fair-copying what you have achieved. Intuition will be rekindled thereby."). In Walter Benjamin, *Schriften*, ed. Theodor W. Adorno and Gretel Adorno, with Friedrich Podszus, vol. 1 (Frankfurt a.M., 1955), 536–38, esp. 537.

Leopardi.[24] Yet on their sense of finding a home within the writing process, authors prefer to remark more in private than in public. For it is true that writing as a form of self-intensification and realization of the self relates primarily to the authors themselves and only secondarily to the work and its potential readers. Such an egocentric attitude might be embarrassing, since it positively begs the question of the work's meaning to other readers. Consequently, authors will rather steer interest in these "Workshop Talks" towards external aspects of their work (the how, the where, the when, the why). By emphasizing the production-related attributes of their writing, they can represent themselves as members of a working society.

In terms of the traditional binomial formula, author and work (l'homme et l'oeuvre), as it is employed in literary studies, the workshop talks are author-centered studies. They are—if one takes as a base the disjunctive pair of terms commonly used in the eighteenth century, "character-writing" and "criticism"—the authors' own contributions to "character-writing" about themselves—even in those cases when their statements, led by a theoretical interest in self-searching, do not always reflect their own work habits. In all events, it is important to realize that genetic writing as such is being granted personal significance by authors.

b. Genetics of Authorial Writing:
Hermeneutic and Structural Genetic Criticism

Germanistic literary historians and, with a few exceptions, scholarly editors as well have thus far been unable to relate to this revalued literary writing that *in actu* inspires the author–writer and in this sense becomes generative of itself. Werner Mahnholz interpreted the writing activity solely as a purposeful production of a literary work, classifying inscription only as the reproduction of something previously conceived, as recording or copying. "The true author works,

---

24 "Felicità da me provata nel tempo del comporre, il miglior tempo ch'io abbia passato in mia vita, e nel quale mi contenterei di durare finch'io vivo. Passar le giornate senza accorgemene, paremi le ore cortissime, e maravigliarmi sovente io medesimo di tanta facilità di passarle"; ("Happiness experienced by me at the time of composing—the best time that I spent in my life, and where I would be happy to abide as long as I live. To spend days without my being aware of it—hours, it seems to me, quite short—and to often marvel, I myself, at how easy it was to spend them."). With reference to this note Leopardi later writes "Anche qui, come in tante altre cose della nostra vita, *i mezzi vagliono più che i fini*," 29 Marzo 1829 ("Here too, as in so many other things of our life, 'the means are worth more than the ends.'"). Giacomo Leopardi, *Opere*, vol.2, ed. Sergio and Raffella Solmi (Milano, Napoli, n.d.; La Letteratura italiana, vol.52, tomo 2), 870–71.

apart from the necessary breaks of production between individual larger works, almost constantly. It is true that one sees only a little of this activity because it takes place purely within his conscious and subconscious mind. The penning itself is, as any experienced writer can attest, the least labor, everything essential proceeds internally."[25] This *finalistic interpretation* of literary writing—which, incidentally, is closely prose-related, as the very term "labor" already suggests—has hitherto been predominant. For scholarly editors, an author's writing activity is only indirectly relevant, and only with regard to the choice of techniques for the representation of manuscript texts and their development. The author's "compositional method" is for them a matter of analysis, perhaps as well of description, but not of interpretation. The cardinal reference point of their description is always the text, not the author. External or paratextual manuscript characteristics are taken into account only as "author-related factors."[26] This limited understanding is the correlate of an attitude that favors production, and is geared to the editorial task of reproducing texts and their drafts. The biased concentration on the texts in turn can be explained by the dependency of scholarly editors on literary hermeneutics, which is a textual hermeneutics or, more precisely, a hermeneutics of *communicated texts*, not a hermeneutics of *pre-* or *extra-communicative texts* or of *private writing processes.*[27]

I try in the following to characterize Germanistic scholarly editing's largely constrained attitude to the author as writer and towards his genetic manuscripts. In particular I analyze how these editorial approaches succeed, and have succeeded, by auxiliary ploys to appropriate such genetic material and to bring into the domain of literary hermeneutics a type of material that—according to its very raison d'être—stands outside it. The result is, roughly speaking, *a reader's genesis of the text*. However, the example of *critique génétique* shows

---

25 "Die Wesenszüge des schriftstellerischen Schaffensprozesses" ("Characteristics of the Creative Process in Literary Writing"), in *Die geistigen Arbeiter*, Part 1, ed. Ludwig Sinzheimer, Verein für Sozialpolitik (München; Leipzig, 1922), 68.

26 Gerhard Seidel, *Die Funktions- und Gegenstandsbedingtheit der Edition, untersucht an poetischen Werken Bertholt Brechts (The Function and Object Determinants of Critical Editing, Studied in Relation to Bertolt Brecht's Literary Oeuvre)*. Deutsche Akademie der Wissenschaften zu Berlin. Veröffentlichungen des Instituts für deutsche Sprache und Literatur 46 (Berlin, 1970), Reihe E, 44 ff.

27 "Hermeneutics" here means "theory of understanding." It does not refer to the understanding or interpretation itself. On the ambiguities of the terms "hermeneutic" and "hermeneutics," see Klaus Weimar, *Historische Einleitung zur literaturwissenschaftlichen Hermeneutik* (Tübingen, 1975), 1.

that approaching the manuscript evidence of the author's work does not always have to be oriented towards the book-reader alone.[28] What really separates *critique génétique* from Germanistic editing and interpretation of genetic autographs is the fact that the French school is neither limited to the reader's concerns, nor confined to the text contents of the manuscripts. *Critique génétique*, directed towards the manuscripts themselves as the remains of the writing processes, in that sense focuses on *the author's genesis of the text*. The difference in interpretational aims between textual scholars and text geneticists can be more precisely defined with the help of Aristotle's terms "poiesis," i.e., purposeful production of a separable work, and "praxis," i.e., an action whose purpose cannot be detached from it. Textual scholars view the literary writing process as "poiesis," as a production of a work whose ultimate goal is by definition superior to the actions that led to its realization. The *géneticiens*, by contrast, see the genetic writing itself as "praxis," as an activity whose meaning does not exist outside of itself and, for that same reason, is superior to what derives from it. They tend to view texts more as relics of writing processes than as something intended. Whereas text genetics as practiced by German scholarly editors[29] *focuses on the author as speaker* and does not do adequate justice to the *writer*, *critique génétique* would seem on the

---

[28] For the sake of simplicity, I use throughout the term "book-reader." I have in mind the reader of texts set out in the typography of the printed book.

[29] The term "text genetics" has been adopted from Louis Hay, "Die dritte Dimension der Literatur: Notizen zu einer 'critique génétique,' " *Poetica* 16 (1984), 314, where it is mentioned only casually, and from Beda Allemann. Rolf Bücher quotes from Allemann's uncollected posthumous critical notes the following comments: "Jedenfalls ist nicht zu leugnen, dass die Literaturwissenschaft im allgemeinen von den Apparatbänden solcher Ausgaben [d.h. Ausgaben, die Textgenesen darstellen] bis heute nur selten den Gebrauch macht, der dem Aufwand bei ihrer Etablierung entsprechen würde. Was in dieser Lage Not täte, ist die Entwicklung einer eigenen Spezialdisziplin, der ich den Namen einer Textgenetik geben möchte." ("There is in any case no denying that critics seldom make use of the apparatus volumes of such editions [i.e., those that represent the textual genesis] commensurate with the efforts that have gone into establishing them. The need in this situation is for the development of a special discipline that I would call Text Genetics.") "Beda Allemann über Textgenese," in *Die Genese literarischer Texte, Modelle und Analysen*, ed. Axel Gellhaus with Winfried Ecke, Diethelm Kaiser, Andreas Lohr–Jasperneite, and Nikolaus Lohse (Würzburg, 1994), 328–38, esp. 330. The term itself means the exploration of creative processes by genetically oriented methods, whether in terms of a reconstruction of the genesis of texts from manuscripts as, for instance, in the preparation of an edition, or, in critical terms, on the foundation of genetic reconstructions of authorial drafts. The selective exploitation of genetic representation for the purpose of answering questions that the completed and communicated text poses in interpretation is an auxiliary strategy of text *interpretation* and does not methodologically belong to text genetics.

contrary so to emphasize the writer that the result is a modernistically one-sided notion of writing. ʼ

The task at hand, therefore, is to arrive at a more comprehensive understanding of literary production, based on the French and the German genetics of the text together, one that acknowledges both the author's *receptionally-productive double nature of authorship* and the *communicatively-creative double function of writing*. For scholarly editors, the consequence resulting from this more complex understanding is that, in principle, genetic presentation is not the goal but instead an aid in the study of manuscript traces. The path of cognition and interpretation should not unidirectionally lead away from the manuscripts to the edition. It should by apt means of representation also lead back to them (the editorial circle). The goal should be the unrestricted understanding of the manuscripts, and not merely of their textual substrate.

c. The Autograph-Enforced Editorial Approach to the Author as a Writer

Current scholarly editing has in its tasks and methods been decisively shaped by two factors: the discovery of *textual history*, i.e., those non-authorial textual changes that progressively occurred throughout the stages of its transmission (the history of its deterioration); and the discovery of the *genesis of the text*, that is, the author's work on a text as witnessed in the manuscripts. Consequently, literary works in transmission and reception have been doubly historicized according to their dual existence as between author and reader. Their receptional side has been configured as their *textual history;* their production side, hidden from the reader, has more recently become the history of the *genesis of the text*.[30] From time immemorial, textual history has served editorial scholarship's most important task, textual criticism, by uniquely supplying the basis in facts and knowledge for objective editorial decisions. But of what use can the reconstruction of textual genesis be? This question, properly considered, falls in the province of hermeneutics. But ever since its earliest Hellenistic examples, hermeneutics has been directed to texts already handed to readers, published and received texts that have been canonized and have become "classics"—a premise so seemingly self-evident as always to go unmentioned. On the basis of this premise, literary hermeneutics of texts can only respond negatively to the question. On its terms, the preliminary labor on a work might be of concern to the author, but to nobody else.

---

[30] See Klaus Hurlebusch, "Edition," in the revised *Fischer Lexikon Literatur*, ed. Ulfert Ricklefs (Frankfurt a.M., 1996).

Scholarly editors never could, nor can they now adopt this position. In preparing their critical editions, they cannot disregard the author's preliminary labor. Such disregard is precluded by the nature of the witnesses. They are, after all, not merely *texts* or *text materials*, but the author's manuscripts themselves.

d. The Ambiguity of Genetic Autographs

An author's genetic manuscripts pose a dilemma in evaluation for the scholarly editor. In strict consequence of his discipline's theory of understanding, no relevance could be ascribed to this text material because the autograph remains of the work on the text contain only dead letters drained of the spirit of the author. Metaphors from the visual arts (especially, sculpture) have popularly been invoked: these remains are the "cinders" and "shavings" from the workshop, which indicates an orientation towards a hermeneutics of "poiesis."

Nonetheless, despite their professional logocentrism, scholarly editors cannot overlook the fact that there is an individual gestural or expressive value attached to authors' manuscripts as such, comparable in effect to the semiotics of other non-linguistic expressions of a person, such as facial expressions or voice modulation. It is mainly such personal references that make autographs collectors' items.[31]

The expressive value of genetic autographs, recognised outside the realm of philology, has in the end had to be acknowledged by scholarly editors as well—without, however, their developing a concomitant sense or understanding of that value. It was a hesitating acknowledgement, though probably strengthened by the desire for total inclusiveness of the great nineteenth-century scholarly editions of the German classics. The ambivalent attitude of Franz Muncker, editor of the third edition of Lachmann's Lessing edition, towards manuscript material that the author had not intended for publication is symptomatic. His preface to the first volume in 1885 reads:

> At first I wanted to list as variants together with the readings of the older editions also those changes, as far as they still existed, which Lessing had performed before publication. They give a vivid impression of the way Lessing worked and allow a didactic insight into the creation especially

---

[31] See Günther Mecklenburg, *Vom Autographensammeln: Versuch einer Darstellung seines Wesens und seiner Geschichte im deutschen Sprachgebiet (On Collecting Autographs: An Essay Outlining its Nature and History in the German-speaking Countries;* Marburg, 1963). Mecklenburg quotes Joseph von Radowitz: "Von allem, was der Mensch hienieden zurücklässt, gehört ihm vielleicht nichts so ganz eigen an, als seine Handschrift [. . .] Keine andere Reliquie hängt so innig mit ihm selbst zusammen [. . .]"; ("Of all that man leaves behind in this world, nothing perhaps is so uniquely his as his handwriting. No other relic is so intimately related to him."), 44.

of several poems and of the dramatic fragments. However, as interesting as such knowledge might be for the specialist, I had to ask myself the question—whether these original readings of the manuscripts, ones that the author himself had quickly dismissed, should have a place in a critical edition. A critical edition should represent the completed work of art, to which (before the public eye) the author might perhaps have been putting the occasional finishing touch, or which he might even once more have recast into a new shape; but the edition should not preserve every half-hewn lump which the master himself had abandoned as unsuitable, nor all the cinders which he eagerly swept out of his covert workshop after casting the work. I began to shy away from including into Lessing's work those words or sentences in manuscripts that Lessing himself had heavily and repeatedly crossed out, so that they could only be deciphered with great trouble, which he therefore did not want to be read.[32]

However, starting with volume thirteen, Muncker began to include such changes into the edition, recording them as individual variants in the footnotes of the text in analogy with the classical presentation of variant readings.

Such wavering between inclusion and exclusion of the author's manuscript changes to the text can be explained by the fact that an appropriate understanding for the specific nature and author-related peculiarity of genetic autographs did not yet exist. One could not ignore them—they were, after all, authorial traces—but one could not quite recognize them as witness materials in their own right. Even today scholarly editing remains biased towards the perspective of the reader; that is, towards a hermeneutics of the text as a "completed work of art." It is the attitude of classical philology's editorial theory and technique that for a long time served as a model for Germanistic textual criticism.[33]

---

[32] *Gotthold Ephraim Lessings sämtliche Schriften*, ed. Karl Lachmann, 3rd ed., rev. Franz Muncker, vol.1 (Stuttgart, 1886), x–xi.

[33] How long this model remained relevant is demonstrated by Reinhold Backmann's 1923 article: "Die Gestaltung des Apparates in den kritischen Ausgaben neuerer deutscher Dichter" ("The Design of the Apparatus in Critical Editions of Modern German Writers"), *Euphorion* 25 (1924), 629–62. There he writes: "So sehr aber alle Herausgeber auseinandertreiben, von einem können sie sich doch nicht los machen: von dem noch immer verhängnisvoll vorherrschenden Vorbild der klassischen Philologie" ("However diverse the directions that editors everywhere take—they still cannot free themselves from the fatal dominance of classical philology."), 629. The longlasting influence of its editorial doctrine and technique is attributable not only to the age and the prestige of this discipline, but also to the fact that its editorial objects were mainly *received, authorative texts* and not drafts. Its exclusive focus therefore were texts, all the more as scribal manuscripts were and are of importance only as carriers of transmission.

ii. The Reader's Genesis of the Text

A way out of the ambiguity arising from the irrelevance of the draft manuscripts in terms of editing and hermeneutics on the one hand and their extra-editorially significative relevance on the other opens up if genetic autographs are regarded as *witness documents* distinguished only *materially* from other witness documents—such as printings of a work—and if they are accorded a mediate *hermeneutic significance* as "preliminary" or "developmental stages" of the achieved, valid text. The editorially posited linear connection between a finished text and its preceding stages is conceived in the spirit of a hermeneutics that is no longer a discipline of interpretation of individual passages but of the penetrative understanding of complex intellectual utterances based on the axiom of authorial intentionality. With its help, the inner unity, the meaningful coherence of externally different signs or successions of signs, is assumed.

a. Editorial Hermeneutics of the Genesis of the Text

The more comprehensive the claim to understanding, the more fundamental become the interpretative problems posed by semiotic differences in the given utterances that crave to be understood: "Every understanding of the particular depends on an understanding of the whole."[34] The solution to the problem here consists in the notion that, on the basis of a reader–author identification,[35] the idea of the whole as embodied at the end of the reception process is projected back on the author as his originally intended and germinal idea, incrementally developed. In this manner, synchronically existing semiotic differences are diachronically relativized as the *genetically different stages* of the realization of what the author intended.

It is therefore not surprising that, within Germanistic scholarly editing, confronted as it is with large textual disparities in the transmission of a work—especially the differences in kind between finished, communicated texts, on the one hand, that belong to the canonic

---

34 See Schleiermacher's drafts on hermeneutics in his aphorisms from 1805 and 1809 in *Fr. D.E. Schleiermacher, Hermeneutik*, ed. Heinz Kimmerle (Heidelberg, 1959), Abhandlungen der Heidelberger Akademie der Wissenschaften, Philosophisch–historische Klasse (1959), Sect. 2.

35 Schleiermacher writes in his aphorisms from 1805 and 1809: "Man muss suchen der unmittelbare Leser zu werden" ("One must seek to become the immediate reader"), and in a concise presentation of his hermeneutics from 1819: "Vor der Anwendung der Kunst muss hergehen dass man sich auf der objectiven und subjectiven Seite dem Urheber gleichstellt" ("To exercise art, one should begin by assuming a position of equality, both objectively and subjectively, with the originator"); Schleiermacher, 1959 (see preceding note), 32, 88.

realm of literary hermeneutics, and the "apocryphally" handwritten drafts, on the other hand, that do not so belong—a hermeneutics of the genetic coherence of meaning in heterogeneous documents has arisen. It became in fact possible to view the manuscript "remains of the unfinished work"[36] as the appropriate data for Schleiermacher's "positive formula" of the art of understanding, namely as the "historical, divinatory, objective and subjective reconstruction of a given utterance."[37] Where could the task of "perfectly reconstructing the author's whole internal compositional labor"[38] be better tested than in the original autograph traces of a text? Admittedly, Schleiermacher hardly had drafts in mind in designing his theory of understanding, for he conceived of such reconstruction as an essentially *intellectual* performance. The philological consideration of drafts would have interfered with the process of understanding he was striving for, the goal of which was to balance the receptivity and spontaneity of the interpreting scholar so as to assimilate it to the understanding of the creating writer. Despite his negative attitude to the medium of writing, Schleiermacher is a chief witness of the subjectivity-related school of thought that shifts the emphasis from the product to the process, from the work to the genesis of the work, from writing to speech, from the text to the author as realized in an idealized form by the recreation of speech from the text. For Schleiermacher the theologian, the agreement between the thoughts of the writer and those of the interpreting scholar stems from the relative identity of speech and thought, divinely vouchsafed, and from the unity of reason, similarly guaranteed. Thence ultimately arises the finalism with which he conceives of understanding as a process analogous to the process of production.

If it is appropriate to interpret literary production as an intentionally directed process, a creation existing "under the potency of a particular goal,"[39] as an action as it were analogous to speech, only reversed, then writing can essentially be regarded but as *a transposition*

---

36 See Muncker (note 32), xi.

37 See Schleiermacher (note 34), 87.

38 Schleiermacher, *Über den Begriff der Hermeneutik, mit Bezug auf F.A. Wolfs Andeutungen und Asts Lehrbuch* ("On the Concept of Hermeneutics, with Reference to F.A. Wolf's Suggestions and Ast's Primer"), (note 34), 135.

39 Schleiermacher, *Hermeneutik und Kritik mit besonderer Beziehung auf das Neue Testament: Aus Schleiermachers handschriftlichem Nachlasse und nachgeschriebenen Vorlesungen (Hermeneutics and Criticism, with Especial Reference to the New Testament: Edited from Unpublished Notes in Schleiermacher's Literary Remains and from Lecture Protocols)*, ed. Friedrich Lücke (Berlin, 1838). Schleiermacher, *Sämtliche Werke*, Sect.1: Zur Theologie, vol.2, p.150: "Ganz anders, wenn die Combination unter der Potenz eines bestimmten Zieles steht. Da ist zwischen den einzelnen Elementen

of something preconceived into something written. The possibility of a creative retroaction from the author's writing to his thinking is not taken into account here, at least not as an essential factor of the creative process. This is the price to be paid for including as objects of interpretation under the reception-oriented, *finalistic* or, more precisely, *"poietical" interpretation of genesis*—as well as those documents of the writer's work not meant for the eyes of the book-reading audience. However, *the finished text always remains the pivotal reference point of such interpretation.* To conceive of textual genetics in teleological terms is the ineluctable consequence of a reception-based orientation. "Finalism," therefore, is not only effective in those instances where it appears to be absolute, in metaphors of organic growth (as one encounters them, for example, with Friedrich Beissner); it is also potent where it is historicized and therefore expressed in a covert, pluralized manner. The typical argument then represents itself in the following manner: the author creates at different points in time a currently valid form of his work, "which reflects the author's will, skill and knowledge at that [. . .] moment [. . .]."[40]

The hermeneutic light that scholarly editing brings to the working manuscripts existing in the shadows of a private authorial ambience enhances merely their textual states. Their visually perceptible graphic features are conceded at best a marginal significance for their transcription, but no independent expressive value. Autographs are basically classed with apographs: as text carriers or text sources for text-critical and editorial exploitation.[41] It took considerable time

---

ein anderes Band des Fortschreitens, eine constante Grösse, ein bestimmtes Verhältniss jedes Punktes zu einem vorgesetzten Ziele in Vergleichung mit jedem vorhergehenden"; ("The matter is entirely different if the combinatory activity exists under the potency of a particular goal. There are then between the elements, as they advance, relational ties, a constant proportion, and from each point as against each other point of development a certain perspective towards the determined goal.").

[40] Siegfried Scheibe, "Zu einigen Grundprinzipien einer historisch–kritischen Ausgabe" ("On Some Basic Principles of Historical–Critical Editing"), in *Texte und Varianten: Probleme ihrer Edition und Interpretation*, ed. Gunter Martens and Hans Zeller (München, 1971), 4. Fredson Bowers tended more strongly towards a simple finalism in his textual criticism: "For example, suppose we took the easy attitude—very well, we have the author's earliest manuscript and the first printed edition that presumably contains all the revisions he made. What more do we want? I should say that we lose the opportunity to study the shaping development of idea as represented by stylistic and substantive revision, the manner in which one revision may have given rise to another or to a modification of the initial concept" (Bowers [note 12], 15).

[41] Here I quote one example among many others, Manfred Windfuhr: "Grundsätzlich wird daran festgehalten, dass die vorhandenen Handschriften in bezug auf Text und Chronologie vollständig *ausgewertet* werden [my emphasis]"; ("We uphold the demand that the surviving manuscripts be wholly *exploited* for the establishment of text and chronology"). Ute Radlik und Helga Weidmann, "Die Düsseldorfer Heine-Ausgabe," *Heine Jahrbuch* 9 (1970), 36.

to advance from the early editorial mode of selective inclusion of individual variants, referenced to the finished text, to the recent thorough penetration of all existing text materials—i.e., to the integral, genetic representation of every surviving manuscript. Our abbreviated account pursues a systematic, not a historical aim. It is an attempt to understand the genetic perspective in textual criticism and editing as an answer to a basic problem: namely, exactly what position to assume towards an author's working manuscripts and their contrary evaluation? The attitude taken in terms of a philologically oriented reading of books that decisively influenced the history of Germanistic scholarly editing of texts in manuscript constituted an innovation to the extent that the pre-communicative remains of the work process were viewed positively as the seminal and developmental stages of the finished work. However, this position was not in agreement with literary hermeneutics outside textual criticism. Its relation to editorial genetics has consequently been a distanced one, articulated at times somewhere between reserve and rejection.[42] On the other hand, the position taken by textual criticism has stayed well within the field of literary hermeneutics because the author's manuscripts have not been conceded *any expressive value in their own right*, but granted only a *mediate value as text-critical and editorial evidence*.

b. The Dialectics of Genetics in Scholarly Editing

Nonetheless: as spatio–temporal and graphic semiotic entities, authorial drafts pose a constant challenge to scholarly editors, who, if

---

[42] See Karl–Heinz Hahn and Helmut Holtzhauer, "Wissenschaft auf Abwegen? Zur Edition von Werken der neueren deutschen Literatur" ("Scholarship Off Course? On Editing Works of Modern German Literature"), *Forschen und Bilden, Mitteilungen aus den Nationalen Forschungs- und Gedenkstätten der klassischen deutschen Literatur in Weimar*, no.1 (1966), 2–22; Walter Müller–Seidel, "Edition und Leserschaft: Ein Diskussionsbeitrag" ("Scholarly Editions and Their Readers: A Contribution to an Ongoing Discussion"), *Frankfurter Allgemeine Zeitung*, 16.10, no.240 (1985), 111; Ulrich Ott, "Dichterwerkstatt oder Ehrengrab? Zum Problem der historisch–kritischen Ausgaben: Eine Diskussion" ("Workshop or Tomb of Honour? On the Problematics of the Historical–Critical Edition: A Discussion"), *Jahrbuch der deutschen Schiller-Gesellschaft* 34 (1990), 3–6. This short article contains references to other critical voices. The point on which the critics agree seems to be a reproach of the "perfectionistic"—and as such both time-consuming and expensive—over-specialized approach towards the author as writer, as one that increasingly leaves out the ordinary book-reader. It would seem, however, that (according to the German proverb) the critics beat the sack and mean the donkey. The auto-dynamics of specialization has long taken over literary studies as a whole, not only its Germanistic variety. How far this development has progressed, for instance, in editorial studies within the Anglo–American tradition has been demonstrated by D.C. Greetham's recent compendium, *Textual Scholarship: An Introduction* (New York; London, 1992).

required somehow to take them into account in their editions, must consider them more thoroughly and comprehensively than before. The more complex the manuscripts, the greater is their provocation to an editor's empiric conscience, to his or her professional duty to pedantry, to his or her allegiance to objectivity in terms of the highest possible faithfulness to transmission. However, in the measure that critical editions open themselves to the needs of integral and meticulous representation of complex manuscript states, they get entrapped in natural tensions with the *editorial hermeneutics* of text genetics. Genetic writing and habitual reading, as conditioned through the belletristic medium of print, are emphatically not analogous activities. The visual act of writing takes place spatially in two dimensions, the invisible act of reading proceeds in linear one-dimensionality. The spatial reading of a worked-over manuscript text cannot be harmonized with the linear process of book-text reading—although the attempt has been made over and over again. The history of the editorial treatment of genetic autographs, from the selective recording of individual changes to their integral transcription, lives off this tension between the *one-dimensional reading of the reader*, on the one hand, and *the two-dimensional reading of the writer*—that is, a reading of the manuscript through the eyes of the author, on the other, for it is the desire of the editorial reconstruction of the genesis of the text to approximate the writer's perspective. Yet in editorial practice, the perspectives of reader and writer have constantly oscillated.[43]

c. Reinhold Backmann: Theoretical Founder of Modern Editorial-Philological Genetics

With Reinhold Backmann the pendulum swung far for the first time towards the author–writer's side. Backmann's essay, "Die Gestaltung des Apparates in den kritischen Ausgaben neuerer deutscher Dichter" ("The Design of the Apparatus in Critical Editions of Modern German Writers "),[44] can be regarded as a founding document of modern editorial genetics. His model of a genetic apparatus, created for the Grillparzer Edition, took the two-dimensional spatiality of writing into account conceptually, descriptively, and representationally. It was essentially his conceptual distinctions that provided the analytical equipment for genetic editors in the second half of the twentieth century.

---

43 See Hans Zeller, "Zur gegenwärtigen Aufgabe der Editionstechnik: Ein Versuch, komplizierte Handschriften darzustellen" ("The Task at Hand in Editorial Technique: An Attempt to Represent Complicated Autographs"), *Euphorion* 52 (1958), 356–77. Zeller writes: "Die Geschichte der germanistischen Editionstechnik im 20. Jahrhundert lässt sich als eine Kette von Reaktionen verstehen" ("The history of Germanistic editorial techniques in the 20th century may be seen as a chain of reactions"), 356.

44 See Backmann, note 33, above.

He distinguished, for example, between "absolute chronology" (the sequence of changes to a given passage) and "relative chronology" (the chronological relation of changes to different passages). This definitional pair is of critical importance, since it is the main foundation for recognising and acknowledging the *syntagmatic aspect* of textual changes (to define "versions," "layers," "inscriptional strata") alongside their *paradigmatic aspect*. It is an essential distinction, because with it everything that precedes the superior finished form can be raised to a temporary textual state that mirrors the author–writer's reading activity. Backmann defines this raising as follows: "The emphasis on the finished form in the printed texts requires a balancing emphasis on the initial form in the apparatus." He continues: "It is the clarification of the development that gives the apparatus its independent value vis-à-vis the printed texts—indeed, when rightly done, it even gives it a significant predominance over the latter" (637, 638). In consequence, the emphasis on the given initial form has led to a chronologically differentiated identification of the changes in relation to the continuous inscription ("immediate," "early," "late" changes).

Like no other Germanistic textual scholar before him,[45] Backmann focused on the author as writer. Not only are changes as *acts* of change represented through descriptive information about the *kinds* of changes—something that Goedeke had already done in his historical–critical Schiller Edition—but also, by specifying the spatial positions of the changes, he recovered the author's own movements as he wrote, and for their own sake. The "restorability of the manuscripts"[46] through the use of the apparatus became an editorial goal. With that step, he had crossed the boundary line separating textuality and editorial scholarship.

d. The Manuscript: Point of Origin and Destination in the Exploration of the Genesis of the Text

To my knowledge, Backmann has had only one genuine follower: Hans Zeller, who early on adhered closely to Backmann's concept of a genetic manuscript representation, though without taking over his editorial model. In his epochal essay, published in 1958, "The Task at Hand in Editorial Technique: An Attempt to Represent Complicated Autographs" (see note 43), the reconstruction is still envisaged as an end in itself—if one observes closely the relevant wording:

---

45 Forerunners outside Germanistic studies were the editors of Luther's translation of the Bible in the Weimar Edition: IIIrd Division. *Die deutsche Bibel*, Vol.1., ed. P. Pietsch and E. Thiele (Weimar, 1906); vol.2, ed. K. Drescher, P. Pietsch, and E. Thiele (Weimar, 1909).

46 See Backmann (note 33), 653.

The editor [. . .] must unambiguously report [. . .] the manuscript record
[. . .], *not only for control*, but to enable the reader to visualize, by
means of it, the manuscript. I for my part, at least, feel the urge to
re-translate the printed account back into the manuscript. A poet's
manuscript lives; the transcription should retain as much as possible
of that quality. If it only reports the wording and the likely sequence
of the changes, then it is dead. It will speak only if it characterizes the
changes in the said manner. *Then one can visualize the manuscript or
reconstruct it on paper:* [. . .](my emphasis; 362, 359)

These are essentially no longer the words of a philologist or textual
scholar, but those of an collector of autographs sensible to their gestural expressivity and their closeness to the author.

It is no wonder that for this Zeller was criticized by his fellow guild
members.[47] He withdrew *intra muros*, back into the terrain of editorial scholarship, and relativized his principle of documentation. In the
first volume of the apparatus to Conrad Ferdinand Meyer's poems,
published in 1964, the third of the three self-imposed demands for
representation of the poetic manuscripts reads succinctly: "to give
an account of the graphic features of the manuscript *as far as is
required for the foundation and control of the interpretation.*"[48]
The manuscript is no longer a living thing, but instead has become
a semiotic basis for the editorial "constitution of the text": "By no
means does the representation of the manuscript in the Meyer Edition
pursue 'the account of the graphic record' or 'the reconstruction of
the manuscript' for its own sake; instead, it serves [. . .] primarily the
purpose of interpreting the manuscript [that is, of constituting the
text] and secondarily it renders possible a certain control by means of
descriptive information."[49] Zeller has, to my knowledge, never since
modified this instrumentalist position towards editorial documentation by means of description and representation of the manuscript.

As the example quoted from Franz Muncker (65–66, above) shows,
the oscillation between approximating the position of the author as

---

47 For example, Walther Killy, "Entwurf des Gedichts: Über den *Helian*-Komplex"
("Draft of a Poem: Reflections on the *Helian* Complex"). *Über Georg Trakl* (Göttingen,
1906; Kleine Vandenhoeck–Reihe 88/89), 81–82. Walther Killy and Hans Szklenar, eds.,
Introduction, Georg Trakl, *Dichtungen und Briefe*, Historical–Critical Edition, vol.2
(Salzburg, 1969), 9. See also Windfuhr (note 41), 35, 37.

48 Conrad Ferdinand Meyer, *Gedichte: Bericht des Herausgebers, Apparat zu den
Abteilungen I und II* (Bern, 1964); Sämtliche Werke, Historical–Critical Edition, ed.
Hans Zeller and Alfred Zäch, vol.2, p.110 (my emphasis).

49 Hans Zeller, "Befund und Deutung: Interpretation und Dokumentation als Ziel und
Methode der Edition," in *Texte und Varianten* (see note 40), 80. This essay is translated
in *Contemporary German Editorial Theory*, ed. Hans Walter Gabler, George Bornstein,
and Gillian Borland Pierce (Ann Arbor, Michgan, 1995), as "Record and Interpretation:
Analysis and Documentation as Goal and Method of Editing," 17–58.

author–writer, on the one hand, and of the author as author–speaker, or book-reader, on the other hand, characterizes not only scholarly genetics as a whole but affects the individual scholar as well. Even in cases where (in consequence of Zeller's Meyer Edition), the manuscript documentation has been further extended through facsimiles and diplomatic representation (as in the Frankfurt Hölderlin Edition), this extension is not intended to serve a better understanding of the originals themselves, but to offer a better edition, through enhanced control and potential reassessment of editorial decisions. The editorial model of the Frankfurt Hölderlin Edition is based on this axiom.[50] "An adequate scholarly edition should be modeled in such a way that the editing process could be repeated by the reader and its results revised" (D.E. Sattler). Only recently, in the outline announcement of a historical–critical facsimile edition of Georg Trakl's works and letters, the *editorial self-referentiality* that dominates the rationale for documentation seems to have dissipated a little, in favor of a more open view of the manuscripts themselves and their author–writers.[51]

Both within and outside Germanistic textual scholarship the opinion still prevails that Friedrich Beissner was the father of the modern, exhaustively genetic representation of draft manuscripts.[52] This assessment is, I believe, unwarranted historically (which is not to belittle Beissner's stature as the editor of Hölderlin). Yet it indicates to what extent editorial genetics are under the spell of the book-reader and his expectations, and to what extent the analytical records of the spatio–temporal manuscript structures have been subordinated

---

50 Dietrich E. Sattler, "Rekonstruktion des Gesangs," in *Edition und Interpretation / Edition et Interprétation des Manuscrits Littéraires*, ed. Louis Hay and Winfried Woesler (Bern, 1981), *Jahrbuch für Internationale Germanistik*, Series A, Vol.11, p.261. De facto, Sattler has weakened this instrumentalistic "axiom" with the excellent facsimile edition of the "Stuttgarter Foliobuch" and the "Homburger Folioheft." See Friedrich Hölderlin, *Sämtliche Werke*, Frankfurter Ausgabe, Supplement II: "Stuttgarter Foliobuch," ed. D.E. Sattler and Gerhard Steimer (Frankfurt a.M.; Basel, 1989); Supplement III: "Homburger Folioheft," ed. D.E. Sattler and Emery E. George (Frankfurt a.M.; Basel, 1986). See esp. Sattler's Introduction, Supplement III, 19.

51 Eberhard Sauermann and Hermann Zwerschina, "Historisch–Kritische Faksimile–Ausgabe der Werke und des Briefwechsels Georg Trakls," *editio* 6 (1992), 145–71. See also Georg Trakl, *Sämtliche Werke und Briefwechsel: Innsbrucker Ausgabe*, Historical–Critical Edition with facsimile and handwritten texts, ed. Eberhard Sauermann and Hermann Zwerschina (Basel; Frankfurt a.M., 1995–).

52 A recent example: Louis Hay, "Propositions théoriques: Passé et avenir de l'édition génétique. Quelques réflexions d'un usager," *Cahiers de textologie* 2, Problèmes de l'édition critique, ed. Michel Contat (1988), 7: "En introduisant la dimension temporelle de l'écriture dans sa présentation des variantes, F. Beissner inaugure d'un seul coup l'éditon génétique et l'édition moderne tout court" ("Introducing the temporal dimension of the writing into the presentation of the variants, F. Beissner inaugurates in a single action the genetic edition and that means, in short, the modern edition").

to the demand for readability. In reacting to Backmann's apparatus model, Beissner succeeded in forcing the two-dimensional complexity of genetic autographs (Wieland's and Hölderlin's) into a procrustean bed of a reader-friendly, interchangeable, graded linearity—virtually like a flight of stairs—neglecting once again the syntagmatic relationship of the variants so meticulously recorded. Book-readers gave him high marks for this; manuscript-readers, somewhat lower ones, as for instance Beda Allemann[53] and Hans Zeller.[54] Among scholarly editors who use the author's manuscripts as text sources but do not see them as writing *sui generis*, Backmann and temporarily Zeller were the odd men out. The editor of Grillparzer's works encountered next to no positive response, and the editor of C.F. Meyer found his way back to the discipline's merely instrumentalist use of autographs.

In France, by contrast, this species of transphilological boundary crossers is far more numerous. There the author's manuscripts have become, through *critique génétique* developed during the seventies, a research topic unto themselves, as printed texts have long been.

iii. The Author's Genesis of the Text

a. The Example of Critique Génétique

French genetic criticism owes its particular nature to the institutional and intellectual conditions of its origins: a group of literary scholars and linguists, the so-called "équipe Heine," that was formed for one reason—to research the Heine manuscripts at the Bibliothèque Nationale independently of any editorial tasks. French structuralism, the "nouvelle critique," provided the conceptual framework and methodology to lead the study of autographs from under the shadow of a discipline auxiliary to archival or philological concerns into the light of its own theoretical capability, and thus to allow its developing in its own right into a specialist sub-discipline of "critique littéraire." French text genetics therefore has emerged from the combination of manuscript research and a structuralist (i.e., linguistic, semiotic) orientation. From the beginning, the path followed by *critique génétique* differed from that of the German editorial genetics. Unlike the latter, the French approach did not have to ask itself the hermeneutical question: what

---

53 See Allemann's review of Beissner's Hölderlin Edition, vols. 1, 2 and 5, in *Zeitschrift für deutsches Altertum* 87 (1956/57), 75–82, esp. 79: "Es bleibt keine anderer Ausweg, als dass der ernsthafte Forscher wieder auf die Handschriftenphotographien zurückgreift, und das war offenbar gerade nicht die Absicht der Grossen Stuttgarter Ausgabe" ("There remains no way out for the serious scholar but to take recourse again to the photographs of the manuscripts, and that was clearly not the intention of the Greater Stuttgart Edition").

54 See note 43; 360–62, 368–69.

sense does it make to turn one's attention towards textual materials preserved in manuscripts that originally had been significant only to the author? The point of reference for the French was not, as it was for the Germanists, the book-reader, but rather the author–writer, the writer as reader of his own manuscripts. The structuralist "nouvelle critique" differed from traditional methodology in that it taught how one should see *through the eyes of the author* in order to understand the text as a product of a linguistic art of creation, as a spatial–temporal semiotic construct, not as a linear bodying forth of meaning.[55] And it taught how one should see the man of letters himself as a writer (*écrivant*), and not, in book-readerly terms, as an author (*écrivain*).[56] The statements of modern authors about the disappearance of the idols of reception—*the* work (Blanchot, Barthes)[57] and *the* author (Barthes, Foucault)[58] —and, furthermore, the programmatic statement of one of the founders of *critique génétique*, Louis Hay: "le texte n'existe pas,"[59] meaning the independent, closed text of the book-

---

55 See Barthes, "From Work to Text" (note 9): "Le Texte [. . .] pratique le recul infini du signifié, le Texte est dilatoire: son champ est celui du signifiant [. . .] Le pluriel du Texte tient [. . .] à ce que l'on pourrait appeler la *pluralité stéréographique* des signifiants qui le tissent [. . .] la métaphore du Texte est celle du *réseau*" (72, 73, 74); ("The Text [. . .] practises the infinite deferment of the signified, it is dilatory: its domain is the signifier [. . .]. The plural of the Text depends [. . .] on what might be called the *stereographic plurality* of its weave of signifiers [. . .] [and] the metaphor of the Text is that of the *network* [. . .]" [158, 159, 161].)

56 Barthes' distinction stresses the author's double nature—receptive and productive —and differentiates the two. The "écrivain" (the author) is integrated into institutions and traditions and is therefore primarily receptive to transsubjective formative powers governing authorship, whereas the "écrivant" (the writer), "situated at the borders of the institutions and transactions," understands himself above all as an acting individual subject. "The author performs a function, the writer an activity [. . .]. The author partici- pates in the priest's role, the writer in the clerk's; the author's language is an intransitive act (hence, in a sense, a gesture), the writer's an activity," "Authors and Writers," trans. Richard Howard, *Roland Barthes: Critical Essays* (Evanston, 1972), 144, 147.

57 See Blanchot (note 14) and Barthes (note 9).

58 Barthes, "The Death of the Author," in *Image Music Text* (note 9), "Linguistically, the author is never more than the instance writing [. . .] the modern scriptor is born simultaneously with the text [. . .] the modern scriptor can thus no longer believe, as according to the pathetic view of his predecessors, that his hand is too slow for his thought or passion and that consequently, making a law of necessity, he must emphasize this delay and indefinitely 'polish' his form. For him, on the contrary, the hand, cut off from any voice, borne by a pure gesture of inscription (and not of expression), traces a field without origin [. . .]." *Le bruissement de la langue* (note 9), 61–67, esp. 63–64; compare Michel Foucault, "What is an Author?", *The Foucault Reader*, ed. Paul Rabinow (New York, 1984), 101–20.

59 "Le texte n'existe pas: Réflexions sur la critique génétique," *Poétique* 62 (1985), 147–58, esp. 154. English translation: "It seems to me that it should be sufficient to agree

reader, are all complementary symptoms of the now predominant spirit of a producing subjectivity and artistic self-actuation that has seized authors as much as book-readers and among the latter especially the geneticists.

A reader who has put on the author's glasses, which structure writing and text two-dimensionally, is able to see the actual genetic manuscripts of an author as witness documents of the labor of writing, the *écriture*. The structuralist mode of perception, while proceeding in a text-immanent manner, was not tied from the outset—as was the case with literary hermeneutics—to the finished, communicated text.[60] For structuralist analysis, there was no barrier between communicativeness and private pre-communicativeness. The boundary line could easily extend to pre-communicative, handwritten "avant-textes,"[61] and even the borders of textuality were found permeable. Structuralism tends as such towards semiology.

b. The Semiotics of Manuscripts: "Rapport Nouveau entre la Main et la Page"[62]

The importance of semiology was that it opened a way of looking at writing as a physical movement of expression, executed in space and time. The graphic quality of genetic autographs could become the object of an "étude sémiotique." Even in France, it is as yet in its early stages. However, there it is at least possible: "Malgré des travaux remarqués, c'est loin d'être chose faite et l'étude sémiotique du manuscrit constitue, pour l'essentiel, un champ à explorer."[63] Louis Hay makes this statement in his introductory article to a book dedicated to the "sémiotique des manuscrits littéraires,"[64] in which several articles treat various aspects of manuscripts as graphic forms. One

---

that there is no absolute definition. And the above-mentioned criteria remain operative as long as we accept them as parameters in a variable field registering ever-differing realisations of the act of writing. Not *The Text*, but texts." "Does 'Text' Exist?" *Studies in Bibliography*, 41 (1988), 64–76, esp. 72–73.

[60] See Barthes (note 9), 157: "*[T]he Text is experienced only in an activity of production.* It follows that the Text cannot stop [. . .]. its constitutive movement is that of cutting across (in particular, it can cut across the work, several works)." "De l'oeuvre au texte," 71.

[61] See Jean Bellemin–Noël, *Le texte et l'avant-texte: Les brouillons d'un poème de Milosz (Text and Pre-text: Drafts of a poem of Milosz;* Paris, 1972).

[62] Louis Hay, "Critiques du manuscrit," in *La naissance du texte,* ed. Louis Hay (Paris, 1989), 9–20; here, 11.

[63] "Despite some noted studies, [the research] remains to be done and a semiotic approach to a manuscript is, essentially, a field still to be explored."

[64] "L'écrit et l'imprimé," in Louis Hay et al., *De la lettre au livre: Sémiotique des manucrits littéraires,* Textes et Manuscrits (Paris, 1989), 7–34, esp. 11.

reflects, for example, on the structures and the direction of writing on a page (Alain Rey, "Traces"). Another, on writing on the page's margins in printed material and manuscript pages (Jacques Neefs, "Marges"). A third, on Joyce's handling of paragraphs (Daniel Ferrer, Jean–Michel Rabate, "Paragraphes en expansion").[65]

To describe the format, the paper of manuscript pages, as well as the graphic spatialization of the writing inscribed thereon, means to visualize *what the author–writer himself had before his eyes during the writing process* and what influenced or could have influenced him or her while working on the text. Naturally, the effect of what has been written down on the imagination of the person writing will differ much in extent and intensity. Yet those authors who have gained a truly paradigmatic significance within French genetics, Flaubert and Valéry, represent, in quite an extreme fashion, the *constructive*, psycho-genetic *type of writer* among modern authors for whom the graphically visualized will exert from the beginning a comparatively large productive pull on the genesis of the text. Hence, a recent study of the genesis of the opening of Flaubert's story "Hérodias" contains passages about "La gestion de l'espace graphique": "Stratégie générale d'écriture" and "Écriture et mise en page."[66] But Stendhal, too, seems to have explored the writing process as a kind of open sesame for intellectual spontaneity: "La page que j'écris me donne l'idée de la suivante: ainsi fut faite la char[treuse]."[67]

However, approaching the author's perspective as a writer through description and reproduction of the autographs and transcription of their genesis not only makes sense in the case of a "man of letters" (homme-plume).[68] It is not a question of illustrating what is already known, but instead one of discovering the type of writer one is dealing with. The question whether the writing in a given instance tends more towards the constructive or towards the reproductive function should be posed and answered at the end and not at the beginning of a study. If, for instance, one dismisses from the start the visual "indications

---

[65] Hay et al. 1989 (note 64), 35–55; 57–88; 89–114.

[66] See Catherine Fuchs, Almuth Grésillon, and Jean–Louis Lebrave, "Flaubert: Ruminer 'Hérodias': Du cognitif-visuel au verbal-textuel," in *L'écriture et ses doubles: Genèse et variation textuelle*, ed. Daniel Ferrer et Jean–Louis Lebrave, Textes et Manuscrits (Paris, 1991), 27–109, esp. 38–58.

[67] "As I wrote one page led to the next: it was in such a manner that the Char[treuse] was created." Quoted from Jacques Neefs, *Objets intellectuels*, in *Les manuscrits des écrivains*, ed. Louis Hay (Paris, 1993), 111, "(note marginale de 'Lamiel'). Les manuscrits sont alors même de l'invention, écriture rapide, campagnes journalières" ("Thus the manuscripts are actual acts of invention, speed writing, [and] daily struggles").

[68] See Fuchs, Grésillon, Lebrave (note 66), 29.

de scription"[69] as pure formalities and fortuities of the writing hand—and this, within editorial genetics, is the heritage of classical textual scholarship and the result of a hermeneutics of ideas—then the answer can be anticipated. The author–writer is in principle seen according to the classical-philological scriptor model, that is, either as someone who reproduces a previously thought out "text" in the manner of a secretary dictating to himself, or as a copyist who transfers previously thought out material into writing, for whom the writing has an aesthetic (ornamental) function at most, not a genetic one.

c. The Absolution of Poetics from Hermeneutics within Critique Génétique

Because it awards the author's compositional manuscripts the same status that traditional literary studies have granted printed texts, *critique génétique* certainly represents a new fruit of the self-creating spirit of the modern age. Nowhere else, so far as I know, has critical scholarship approached the author–writer's perspective with comparable openness, decisiveness, and consistency of method. It has its intellectual roots in structuralism, not in scholarly editing or in the literary or stylistic study of variants. This is because the stylistic study of textual changes needs a normative frame of reference, be it an ideal of perfection, as in literature's "art period," or the final communicated version. Thus stylistic comparison of variants and versions belongs in the domain of reception, and, within literary studies, it is situated opposite to textual genetics oriented towards the author–writer. Even if it had been poets and writers who guided observation to changes in texts, they did so in their role as readers. Johann Christoph Wagenseil, for example, studied Petrarch's stylistic corrections in his "Canzonière,"[70] Lessing commented on the "changes and improvements" in Klopstock's Copenhagen edition of *Messias*,[71] and Goethe voiced appreciation of the "steps of correction" in Wieland, who had chosen to illustrate his own ever-honing hand by examples of textual variation in the edition of his complete

---

[69] Jean Bellemin–Noël, "Réproduire le manuscrit, présenter les brouillons, établir un avant-texte" ("Reproducing the manuscript, presenting the drafts, establishing a pre-text"), in *Littérature*, Genèse du texte (décembre 1977), 3–18, esp. 13.

[70] "Bericht von der Meister-Singer-Kunst" ("Account of the Art of the Master Singers"), in *De Sacri Rom. Imperii Libera Civitate Noribergensi Commentatio* [. . .] (Altdorf, 1697), 481.

[71] "Briefe, die neueste Litteratur betreffend" ("Letters Concerning the Latest Literature"; 19th Letter, 1759), in *Gotthold Ephraim Lessings sämtliche Schriften*, ed. Karl Lachmann, 3rd ed. rev. Franz Muncker, vol.8 (Stuttgart, 1892), 58.

works (Leipzig, 1794–1811)[72] —a self-demonstration of the receptional orientation towards models and patterns of the writer's "work
of bettering."[73] Uniting scholarly editors and these views taken by
writers on fellow writers is the common perspective of the receptive
reader.

French genetic criticism has relinquished this stance. It is a "discipline nouvelle" and not just a new form of editorial scholarship.[74] It
has turned production aesthetics the right way up, turning it from a
reflection on the condition and means of literary composition deduc-
tively dependent on literary aesthetics into an inductive exploration of
production, an aesthetics of creation itself. The notions that readers
love and value foremost in literature, *the* work, *the* author,[75] and
the text, have, one by one, become problematical and relative. The
process continues, and is now reaching out for the center-piece of
the heritage of editorial scholarship: the "variant."[76] The distinctive

---

[72] "Literarischer Sansculottismus" (first published in the "*Horen,*" 1795, vol.5), in
Goethes Werke, edition commissioned by the grand duchess Sophie of Saxony, Sect.1,
vol.40, 201.

[73] See Goethe, preceding note; see also Albrecht von Haller, who published his own
variants in his "Versuch Schweizerischer Gedichte" ("Attempt at Swiss Poems") from the
6th ed. (1751) onwards.

[74] Jean–Louis Lebrave, "La critique génétique: une discipline nouvelle où un avatar
moderne de la philologie?" in *Genesis: Manuscrits, Recherche, Invention: Revue internationale de critique génétique* 1 (1992), 33–72.

[75] The receptivity that contributes to defining the concept of "the author" is ignored in
favor of his or her producing subjectivity. The author is reduced to a factor of production,
an "instance écrivante" ("writerly event"; Hay, "Does 'Text' Exist?" [see note 59]; 154,
n. 56). Bernhard Beugnot does not even list the terms "auteur" and "écrivain" in his
brief terminological dictionary, listing only "scripteur." In explanation of this entry, he
quotes a paragraph from an essay by A. Grésillon and J.-L. Lebrave: "celui qui est à
origine des avant-textes et les produit [...] Plus neutre qu'écrivain ou auteur, il ne
préjuge pas de la qualité littéraire du document étudié et ne traîne après lui aucune
connotation idéologique" ("Scripteur" is "one who is at the origin of the pre-texts and
produces them [...] More neutral than [the term] writer or author, it does not prejudge
the literary quality of the document under study and does not carry any ideological
connotation"). "Petit lexique de l'édition critique et génétique," in Michel Contat, ed.,
Cahier de textologie 2, Problèmes de l'édition critique (1988), 77.

[76] See Daniel Ferrer and Jean–Louis Lebrave, "De la variante textuelle au geste d'écriture" ("From textual variation to the writing-act") in *L'écriture et ses doubles* (see note
66), 15–21. The applicability of the term "variant," as of the operation of "substitution," presupposes linear textualization, which is not always the case with the genetic
autographs of authors classifiable as psycho-genetic writers, for instance Flaubert and
Valéry: "Il faut ensuite que les données manuscrites obéissent à une linéarité au moins
potentielle. Chez Heine, les corrections ne font généralement que gonfler le texte
d'un 'feuilletage' qui matérialise l'axe paradigmatique sans remettre en cause l'unicité
de l'axe syntagmatique. Mais comment retrouver une linéarité dans ces brouillons

novelty of *critique génétique* shows in the titles of its studies: "Le manuscrit: langage de l'objet,"[77] *Leçons d'écritures: Ce que disent les manuscrits*,[78] "L'auteur et le manuscrit,"[79] "Critiques du manuscrit" (Hay, note 62), "Messages de l'écriture,"[80] or "Les manuscrits des écrivains" (Fuchs, Grésillon, Lebrave, note 66). One can hardly imagine the like within the Germanist discipline. The independence of such investigations is here way-laid and blocked off by a reception-oriented hermeneutics that appears tolerable at most as a preliminary to critical editing.

As for the French geneticists' own estimate of their enterprise, their self-declarations suggest that they believe themselves to be headed towards a "poetics of the writing process" ("poétique de l'écriture").[81] It is moot whether this is an achievable goal or only a regulative idea, and whether what may possibly be achieved—a phenomenology or

---

de Valéry où, même sans tenir compte de l'irruption du non-verbal (dessins, calculs mathématiques), la présence de paradigmes explicites (listes de mots ou de rimes) rend tout recours à la substitution problématique?

"En un mot, la substitution suppose que le manuscrit comporte un modèle énonciatif homogène et proche du modèle linéaire de l'énonciation définitive. Dans tous les autres cas, la notion est absolument inopérante, voire dangereuse" (18–19).

("Thereafter, the manuscript data must, at least, follow a potential linearity. In Heine's work, the revisions merely fill up the text with 'layers' that develop the paradigmatic axis without calling into question the work's uniqueness in Valery's drafts where, even if one does not consider the non-verbal irruptions [i.e., drawings, mathematical formulae], the presence of explicit paradigms (word lists or rhyme lists) makes any recourse to linearity and substitution problematic.

"In other words, substitution assumes that the manuscript is comprised of a homogeneous enunciative model, closely related to the definitive linear model of enunciation. In all other cases, this notion is totally inoperative, even dangerous.").

Editorial genetics has come to this conclusion as well, at least when dealing with prose manuscripts. In the edition of Klopstock's working diary, the notes on the genetic representation of the text were deliberately headed "authorial alterations," not "authorial variants." "Alteration," a wider term than "variant," was chosen because, in the case of immediate changes, it is not always obvious that a substitution was made, and if so, what was substituted; therefore, one cannot speak of a relationship of "substituens" and a "substituendum." *Klopstocks Arbeitstagebuch*, ed. Klaus Hurlebusch, in Friedrich Gottlieb Klopstock, *Werke und Briefe*, Historical–Critical Edition, ed. Horst Gronemeyer, Elisabeth Höpker–Herberg, Klaus Hurlebusch and Rose–Maria Hurlebusch, Addenda, vol.2 (Berlin; New York, 1977), 196–205, esp. 199–202.

77 Louis Hay, *Bulletin de la Bibliothèque nationale* (Paris, 1978), 77–84.

78 Almuth Grésillon and Michael Werner in hommage to Louis Hay (Paris, 1985).

79 Ed. Michel Contat, *Perspectives critiques* (Paris, 1991). See editor's Introduction: "La question de l'auteur au regard des manuscrits" (7–34).

80 Jacques Duvernoy and Daniel Charraut, in *La naissance du texte*, ed. Louis Hay (Paris, 1989), 33–40.

81 Louis Hay, "Reconnaître ses lois [i.e., de l'écriture], c'est constituer une poétique de l'écriture, en rapport (ou conflit) avec celle de l'écrit, mais à coup sûr différente" ("To

typology of writing processes?—should still be termed a "poetics" or better perhaps an "aesthetics," or whether it might turn into something like a genre and/or a theory. A poetics of the writing process appears irreconcilable with a poetics of the written ("poétique de l'écrit"), that is, a poetics of texts. There is no transition from the existing to the intended, not even to the historical formation of the intended. The discrepancy between the perspectives of production and reception cannot be bridged if the operational freedom of play in production as founded on the processual character of writing is taken seriously; the two-dimensional reading of genetic manuscripts cannot be transformed without distortion into linear book-text reading. The gradual severing of the *poetica in actu* from the *poetica in potentia*,[82] of an author poetics from a work poetics under the auspices of hermeneutics, first discernible in Klopstock and Herder, already advanced during the Weimar classical period, and theoretically fully effected in Valéry's self-reflexive poetics, has come to practical completion in *critique génétique*'s reconstruction of processes of literary composition as documented in actual manuscripts. That this has become a provocative alternative to established conventions of interpretation is evident in critiques of *critique génétique*. Interpreters, after all, are unlikely to take silently a questioning destabilizing at the core of their received ideas.

d. Sight-Lines on a Theory
of Process Structures of Literary Writing

The intellectual determinants that went into the first shaping of French genetic criticism appear equally to affect its objectives. Its concerns are again ultimately structures, namely, the process structures of compositional creation (one could say: the innate forces of writing), to which the author is a literary-productive auxiliary, almost merely a secretarial agent in the production of texts. Because, however, such

---

acknowledge its rules [i.e., the laws of writing], is to found a poetics of writing in relation to [or in conflict with] writing, but which will certainly be different"); see note 62, 15. See also Lebrave (note 74), 72: "Ils [i.e., les généticiens de l'écriture] ont ainsi dessiné les contours d'une nouvelle discipline et esquissé une poétique de l'écriture distincte de la poétique des textes. Dépasser le stade de l'esquisse, développer la critique génétique et bâtir autour d'elle une véritable théorie: tel est l'enjeu aujourd'hui" ("They [i.e., the geneticists of writing] have thus delineated the parameters of a new discipline and they have outlined a poetics of writing distinct from the poetics of texts. The challenge today is to push beyond the level of the outline, to develop a genetic critique and to build upon it an actual theory.").

82 August Buck, "Italienische Dichtungslehren: Vom Mittelalter bis zum Ausgang der Renaissance" ("Italian Normative Poetics: From the Middle Ages to the End of the Renaissance"), *Beiheft zur Zeitschrift für romanische Philologie*, no.94 (Tübingen, 1952), 7.

process structures are not simple givens but result from analysis and description, *critique génétique* has acquired a certain self-referential attitude towards authorial manuscripts, akin to that of the genetic transcription within critical editions, whose presentational objects also are the products of interpretation.[83] Hence, French geneticists have a substantial interest in their *own productivity:* in their developing a methodology potentially extensible into theory.

Yet where, in consequence, should the author's individuality, within which receptivity and productivity have interacted with each other, be thought to be positioned? It is only in reflections *about* genetics that an originator of writing processes fades into a hauntingly abstract notion. In French studies about individual works, a given author usually gains sufficient contour: the power of the autographs themselves is greater than that of the academic credo.

What understanding, then, is the "approche génétique,"[84] and perhaps it alone, capable of conveying?

iv. What Manuscripts Reveal: Or, What Writing Means to the Author

In Thomas Mann's *Magic Mountain*, Settembrini on one occasion remarks to Hans Castorp: "Two hundred years ago [. . .] you had a poet in your own country, a fine old confabulator, who set great store by beautiful handwriting, because he said it leads to a beautiful style. He should have taken that one step further and said that a beautiful style leads to beautiful actions."[85] This is fitting enough for a proponent of a literary, enlightened, and eloquent fellow humanity, whose very nature both issues and takes expression in beautiful handwriting, beautiful style and beautiful actions. Both speech and writing are governed by a *sensus communis*, by an orientation towards standards—stylistic models and calligraphic patterns—that exist outside the individual. Production is here guided a priori through reception, or rather recipient captivation: "The greatest genius is he, who takes in everything, knows how to assimilate everything to his self, without detriment to

---

[83] See Louis Hay, "Critiques de la critique génétique," in *Genesis: Revue internationale de critique génétique* 6 (1994), 11–23, esp. 13: "Derrière ces positions contradictoires on voit resurgir sur fond de génétique la vieille idée d'un conflit entre histoire et structure" ("The ancient debate between history and structure resurges in the background of the genetic frame behind [its] contradictory claims").

[84] See Hay, "Does 'Text' Exist?" (note 59).

[85] *Der Zauberberg*, at the end of the chapter "Aufsteigende Angst. / Von den beiden Grossvätern und der Kahnfahrt im Zwielicht." *The Magic Mountain*, trans. John E. Woods (New York: Knopf, 1995), 156.

his basic determination, what one may call his character, but on the contrary to the effect of its essential elevation and the enabling of its innate potential" (Goethe to Wilhelm von Humboldt, 17 March 1832).[86] Thus the process of literary creation has an objective goal from the beginning: the work, which not only has a significance for its author as a reader but for other readers as well, and which, in this sense, has an existence independent of him.

The author has already essentially severed himself from the work before its appearance in print—as when he submits his text, that is, its manner of articulation, to the examination of friendly and competent readers. This occurred frequently during the eighteenth century, when authors and their readers were still united in an artistic sensibility learned from the masterpieces. Klopstock, who enjoyed reading aloud from his manuscripts, found his advisers in Johann Jacob Bodmer, Johann Arnold Ebert, Johann Hartwig Ernst Bernstorff, Meta Klopstock, and others. Schiller found his in Körner, Wilhelm von Humboldt, and Goethe, as well as in Herder and Carl August Böttiger. Goethe sent the version in iambic pentameter of his *Iphigenie* to Herder, whom he also requested to pass it on to Charlotte von Stein and Wieland.[87] The friendly criticism of the author's literary art, essentially a matter of judgment, served not only the work's objective perfection but the author's *artistic* improvement as well. As a rule, the finished text was questioned by its first readers—the author included—only as to the choice of expression and the style, not as to substance of content, poetic scope, or unity of sense and meaning. Accordingly, the authorial post-publication changes were such that the resulting versions remained syntagmatically congruent. The changes were "improvements"[88] that did not affect the work's independence from its author.

---

[86] *Goethes Werke* (note 71), edition commissioned by the grand duchess Sophie of Saxony, sect.IV, vol.49, 281–82.

[87] Goethe to Herder, 13 January 1789, in *Goethes Werke* (see preceding note), sect.IV, vol.8 (Weimar, 1890), 133–34.

[88] Friedrich von Hagedorn to Johann Jacob Bodmer, 28.9.1745: "Ich habe sie [die Jugendode 'Der Wein'] also [...] mit gehöriger Strenge verändert, oder, wie die Autores sich erklären, gar sehr gebessert [...]" ("I have therefore altered it [the early ode 'Der Wein'] with due severity, or as the authors would say, bettered it"). See *Briefe*, ed. Horst Gronemeyer, (New York, 1997). About his work on *Messias* Klopstock writes on 5 May 1769 to Johann Arnold Ebert: "In meinem Exempl. wimmelts von Glättungen, u Wegglättungen, vornäml in Absicht auf das Sylbenmaass, u. dann auch des Ausdruks. Am Inhalte, dünkt mich, hab ich eben nichts zu verändern" ("My copy is crowded with smoothings-out, above all with regard to the syllabics of the meter, and to expression. As to contents, I feel there is little for me to change"), *Briefe 1767–1772*, vol.1, Text, ed. Klaus Hurlebusch (Berlin, 1989); Klopstock, *Werke und Briefe, Historical–Critical Edition*, ed. Horst Gronemeyer, Elisabeth Höpker–Herberg, Klaus Hurlebusch and Rose–Maria Hurlebusch. Sect. Briefe, vol.5.1, 146–47.

The author may be said to sever himself from his work, giving it autonomous status, when he hands it to a narrower or larger friendly audience and thus releases it into the public domain for reception. This severance is not, however, an external or arbitrary act, but founded in the work itself.[89] The author can sever himself from it only if he has expressed in it more than his own subjectivity, if it portrays a transsubjective meaning, a supra-individually valid central idea. Such works naturally assume within the author a receptivity—as a determinant of his character—for the historical above and beyond the individual (e.g., transmitted ideas, literary subjects or forms, etc.) as well as for the natural, or, in other words, a predisposition to distance himself from his self and thus, in consequence, from his own work. It is only on such terms that, for example, Goethe's poem "An Werther" in the *Triologie der Leidenschaft* may be understood. Eckermann reports on 17 February 1831 that Goethe had recognized a throwaway page as a piece of his own writing only on close scrutiny; he then cites Goethe as saying: "For since I always strive ahead, I forget what I have written and soon find myself in the situation of regarding my own things as something thoroughly alien." This author's constant supra-individual theme was his own creative self (or an idealized conception of that self) which enabled him to allow his creativity to culminate in independent works inwardly severable from him. But even this modern egocentric needed a conscious outward act of separation from *Faust*, the work that had been part of himself almost throughout his creative life. In the middle of August 1831, the eighty-two-year-old poet sealed the manuscript of the second part of *Faust*, "so that it be removed from my eyes and from all involvement in it."[90] Goethe's remarks about the conclusion of the "main business" of his later years show that an arbitrary act of separation was necessary so as not to have to think and feel further in terms of the problem-laden second part of *Faust*.[91] Yet, according to his diary (2–29 January 1832), Goethe took the manuscript in hand yet again before his death and worked on its, and his, text.

In what follows, I wish to differentiate between two types of literary composition: the mainly *reproductive, work-genetic* writing process ("poiesis") and the mainly *constructive, psycho-genetic* writing

---

[89] If the author's corrections did not meet a positive response, then their guiding principle could begin to waver; the author had to rely upon himself, and his corrections seemed to him in principle not completable. Compare the three oldest versions of Goethe's *Iphigenie*, ed. with a comparative critique by H. Düntzer (Stuttgart; Tübingen, 1854), 160.

[90] Letter to Reinhard 9 July 1831; see also the letter to Wilhelm von Humboldt 12 January 1831.

[91] See, for example, the letter to Boisserée, 9 August 1831, and conversations with Eckermann, 11, 13 and 17 February 1831.

process ("praxis"). Based on the author's double nature as receptor and producer, the distinction indicates the alternative dominance of receptivity and productivity, respectively. It is a distinction of ideal types made with heuristic intent. As an initial step towards a systematic understanding of individual compositional methods in authors, it may be taken to contribute to a hermeneutics of genetic writing. Its subject is the dialectic tension between the two types. To perceive their relational functionality can render comprehensible an individual compositional method as an author's expressive mode without hermeneutical recourse to finished, communicated texts on the one hand or a structuralist anticipation of general writing-process classifications on the other. The dialectics of genetic textual scholarship is thereby exploited to interpret its own subject matter.

a. The Mode of Work-Genetic Writing, Predominantly Reproductive

The basic feature dominant in work-genetic writing is the *purposeful reproduction* of an intellectual content, the translation of something previously thought into writing. The creative process is from the very beginning directed outwards from the writer's subjective precommunicative interior sphere into intersubjective communication, that is, into a *stable textual linearity*. Having attained this sort of structure, a text has already become independent of the author–writer; it possesses a permanent syntagma that remains intact during successive revisions. Subsequent changes only lead to paradigmatically differing variants or versions. The reader–writer responds to the textual syntagma in the manner of a reader. Its syntagmatic linearity conditions the reception of the written, constituting as it does the visual analogue to hearing a spoken utterance. The more homogeneous its linearity— in the form of fair copies and the final typography of print—the more readable, graphically rounded in itself, and autonomous the text in question becomes.

Linearity—or, in terms of content, directedness towards a goal— is the characteristic mode for this type of the literary work process. At the same time, however, linearity characterizes this creative mode only *by and large*, and by no means in every detail. Literary writing is fundamentally *complex* in nature, and is realized in the interplay of *reproduction* and *construction*. For an adequate understanding of an author's compositional method, it is essential to ascertain the typologically dominant mode: determinate reproduction or indeterminate construction? In case of the former, the two-dimensional spatiality of inscription is of only secondary importance. The horizontal and vertical dimensions belong to construction. No corresponding distinction can be made for spoken utterances. Here, alinear spatiality is subordinated to linearity: it serves to record the contents of memory not yet synthesized (keyword notations, outlines of content) in preparation of the text's inscription, or the sketching of alterations to individual passages. Textual linearity is established or re-established through *substitution:* in the case of notes and outlines in shape of the executed text; in the case of alterations, when a later variant replaces an earlier.

Two-dimensionality means for this type of the writing process something external, a means of fixation, of utilizing the available writing space. When measured against the progression and dominance of the previously thought, the author's perception of the written has a comparatively negligible genetic effect on the writing. The interaction between writing and thinking, between what is already inscribed and what yet remains to be written, affects only elocution and invention, that is, expression and subordinate ideas. In this manner Klopstock, for instance, would avoid isophones in the writing out of prose texts. Such literary writing is mainly *instrumental*: it serves the conception and the finalizing of the work; it is a means of giving "total ideas"[92] an artistically objectivized stability and supra-individual permanence. At the same time, all the more revealing are the constructive and generative elements in this type of genetic writing: the passages where its processes open up, where they must rely on the writer's spontaneous imagination, where they attain a mode of trying-out and groping ahead. Exemplarily, this *partial virtualization* of the inscription finds a material correlative in the *spatialization* of the written; as in the discontinuous writing out of portions of the text, or the columnarizing or marginalization of variants, especially variant alternatives. It is here that the other function of the writing process, that of stimulating the author–writer's imagination retroactively, becomes evident: through written (or pictorial) *visualization* of both the contents of thought and of ideas. By means of their material distancing, such variants

---

92 See Schiller to Goethe, 27 March 1801: "er [der Dichter] hat sich glücklich zu schätzen, wenn er durch das klarste Bewusstseyn seiner Operationen nur soweit kommt, um die erste dunkle Totalidee seines Werks in der vollendeten Arbeit wieder zu finden [. . .] Der Grad seiner [des Dichters] Vollkommenheit beruht auf dem Reichthum, dem Gehalt, den er in sich hat und folglich ausser sich darstellt, und auf dem Grad von Nothwendigkeit, die sein Werk ausübt. Je subjectiver sein Empfinden ist, desto zufälliger ist es; die objective Kraft beruht auf der ideellen"; ("The poet should consider himself happy, if by the clearest consciousness of his operations he may attain the point where he recognizes, in the finished labor, the first dark total idea of his work [. . .] The degree of his perfection depends on the richness and substance he has within himself and consequently represents outwardly, as well as on the strength of necessity that his work exerts. The more subjective his sensation, the more haphazard it is; the objective force depends on the ideal."). *Schillers Werke*, Nationalausgabe, vol.31, Correspondence. *Schillers Briefe 1.1.1801–31.12.1802*, ed. Stefan Orman (Weimar, 1985), 24–25.

may attain an innovating effect for their originator. He can perceive them as something that he encounters and experiences outwardly, as independent verbal entities, which at the same time, however, he can freely manipulate. At such junctures, therefore, writing acquires a potential of materially realizing and unfolding thought that becomes powerfully inductive of further writing. It is in this sense a medium of self-development and self-ascertainment, of the *subjectivation of the author.*

The extent of the constructive in a predominantly reproductive compositional mode is also of course genre-dependent. In the writing of brief lyrics, it will tend to play a lesser role than in composing large epics. Klopstock, for instance, composed some episodes of *Messias* disjointedly, discontinuously, not according to their sequence in the finished poem; as those of the Last Judgment (in Cantos 18 and 19), the Semida–Cidli episode (in Cantos 4, 15, and 20), or the "Triumphal Song at the Ascension" (in Canto 20). Only later did he write into them the contexts to situate them in the over-all thematic history of the salvation, which necessitated in turn compensatory changes in the already written text.[93] This compositional method, the genetic anticipation of episodes and their *subordinated text-syntagmatic construction* manifests a significant self-referential meaning of the writing for the author. It shows where the work's core segments lie hidden. Genetic priority signals dominance of thought. As a writer of prose, Klopstock, attracted to the ideal of conciseness, essentially only created "patch-work," not just because he lacked a conceptional talent for the *magnum opus,* but also because his self-referentiality barred him from opening up to readers so as to develop his ideas instead of merely expressing them. The reader was supposed to intuit their cohesion. The ideal reader for him was a person who realized "why I have left out this and that, and that again, and even more,"[94] almost a half-brother of the author in thought. In his prose (as latently also in his poetry), Klopstock was a fragmentalist—with great self-confidence, that is, with a psychagogical–imperatorical mindset, intent on self-intensification, yet in no need of introspection.

Insights into the dialectics between reproductive and constructive writing (which, particularly with the later Hölderlin, takes on almost

---

93 See the sections "Zum Werk, Konzeption und Arbeitsweise," "Textgenesen einzelner Gesänge und Episoden," ("Oeuvre, Conceptions and Working Habits"; "Textual Genesis of Individual Cantos and Episodes"), in Friedrich Gottlieb Klopstock, *Der Messias,* vol.3, ed. Elisabeth Höpker, and in Klopstock, *Werke und Briefe,* Historical–Critical Edition, ed. Horst Gronemeyer, Elisabeth Höpker–Herberg, Klaus Hurlebusch, and Rose–Maria Hurlebusch. Sect. Werke IV (Berlin, 1996), 177–254, 266–355.

94 *Die deutsche Gelehrtenrepublik,* vol.1, text ed. Rose–Maria Hurlebusch (New York, 1975); *Werke und Briefe,* Sect. Werke VII.1, 78 (Sections: "Guter Rath der Aldermänner"; "Besser ist besser").

dramatic features) may compensate for the undermining, caused by genetics, of the reception-oriented perspective on the text as a work unified in composition and spirit.

b. Psycho-Genetic Writing, Predominantly Constructive

The poet who embodies in an extreme manner the spirit of the modern times, the demiurgic maker over the respondent, is Paul Valéry, who should be counted among the ancestors of structuralism. The opposition against the reception-oriented response to literature and against its idols of *the* author and *the* work is far advanced with him. He reduces the idea of the author to the notion of an "Ego Scriptor,"[95] and the discrepancy between the poet's inward and outward perspectives seems to him impossible to bridge. The work—"le livre, l'écrit"— has become just "un accident"—"Limite factice d'un développement mental" (269).

"Les oeuvres, dans mon système, devenaient *un moyen de modifier par réaction l'être de leur auteur*, tandis qu'elles sont *une fin, dans l'opinion générale* [my emphasis]."[96] Texts are no longer the goals of the writing process; they are merely results left behind, transitional stages: the goal is intellectual self-ascertainment, the perfecting of the author: of the "créateur créé."[97] The creative process has therefore become, in principle, a never terminable activity, and thus a mode of existence that, removed from the determinant contingencies of everyday practical life, allows a free interplay of the senses and the imagination in which alone the author, now solitary, can realize his self, can gain a frail identity: "Travailler son ouvrage, c'est se familiariser avec lui, donc avec soi": "l'oeuvre modifie l'auteur."[98] Because he will not accept guidance from what exists transsubjectively above and beyond the individual and so distances himself from a communicative

---

95 *Cahiers*, vol.1, ed. Judith Robinson, Bibliothèque de la Pléiade (Paris, 1973), 233 ff.

96 Paul Valéry, "Fragments des mémoires d'un poème," in Valéry, *Oeuvres*, vol.1, ed. Jean Hytier, Bibliothèque de la Pléiade (Paris, 1957), 1465. ("According to my theory, a man's works were a means of modifying, by reaction, their author's inner being; whereas in the opinion of most people they are an end in themselves [. . .]"); "Memoirs of a Poem," *The Art of Poetry*, trans. Denise Folliot (New York, 1958, Bollingen Series 45, vol.7, *The Collected Works of Paul Valéry*), 101.

97 Paul Valéry, "Autres Rhumbs," *Oeuvres*, vol.2, ed. Jean Hytier, Bibliothèque de la Pléiade (Paris, 1960), 673. ("*The Creator created*"; "Rhumbs" is a nautical term: "The observations and opinions recorded in this volume might be described as swerves from the governing direction or 'set' of my mind; hence 'Rhumbs' "); in *Analects*, trans. Stuart Gilbert (Princeton, 1970, Bollingen Series 40, vol.14), 159, 230.

98 Ibid., 672, 673. ("To revise one's work means familiarizing oneself with it": "The work [itself] modifies its author"; ibid., 229, 230 [from "Rhumbs"].)

sense of belonging, the author is left with nothing but the literary work as the sole formative medium of his consciousness of the self: "On me reproche: V[aléry] ne s'intéresse qu'à V[aléry] [...] ce qui est vrai si V[aléry] signifie: ce qui est inconnu du V[aléry], en V[aléry]; et qui est, peut-être, connaissable? peut-être modifiable? Quelque autre objet peut-il,—doit-il, nous intéresser plus?"[99] An early modern protagonist, incidentally, of this open, author-poietic mode of writing was Montaigne, writing in his *Essais*: "Je n'ay pas plus faict mon livre que mon livre m'a faict, livre consubstantiel à son autheur, d'une occupation propre, membre de ma vie."[100]

It is to the process, not the product, that an autonomous value is attributed: "généralement très supérieure à celle que le vulgaire attache seulement au *produit*."[101] For the author, the question of his *internal* severance has here become pointless, because it never is "nécessairement *finie*, car celui qui l'a faite ne s'est jamais accompli, et la puissance et l'agilité qu'il en a tirées, lui confèrent précisément le don de l'améliorer, et ainsi de suite [...]. *Il en retire de quoi l'effacer et la refaire.*"[102] Since the creative subject is caught within itself, and so does not feel receptively bound to any supra-individual formative powers, there is no objective foundation for an objectivizable significance that could lend it inherent value and autonomy. Recalling Valéry's

---

99 ("I have been charged with: Valéry only cares about Valéry [...] which is quite true if by Valéry one means: what is unknown of Valéry, in Valéry; and who, perhaps, may be knowable? who may be modifiable? what other object could—should interest us more?"); see Valéry (note 95), 269.

100 Ed. Albert Thibaudet, *Bibliothèque de la Pléiade* (Paris, 1950), 748 (Book II, chapter 18); ("I have not made my book any more than it has made me—a book of one substance with its author, proper to me and a limb of my life." *The Essays of Michel de Montaigne*, trans. and ed. M.A. Screech [London, 1991], 755). Montaigne's *Essais* show characteristics typical of psycho-genetic writing: the open and improvisational, the associative, the discontinuous and aleatory, the methodically provisional, in principle interminable. See Hugo Friedrich, *Montaigne* (Berlin, 1949), 403–61, esp. 430: "Der Essay ist das Organ eines Schreibens, das nicht Resultat, sondern Prozess sein will, genau wie das Denken, das hier schreibend zur Selbstenfaltung kommt" ("The essay is the carrier of a mode of writing that does not tend towards the product but intends the processual, just like thought itself, that here unfolds in writing").

101 Paul Valéry, "Calepin d'un poète" ("Notebook of a poet"), in Valéry (note 96), 1450 ("generally much superior to that which the public attaches only to the *product*"); "A Poet's Notebook," *The Art of Poetry*, trans. Denise Folliot (New York, 1958, Bollingen Series 45, vol.7, *The Collected Works of Paul Valéry*), 177.

102 Ibid., 1450–51; "A work is never necessarily *finished*, for he who made it is never complete, and the power and agility he has drawn from it confer on him just the power to improve it, and so on [...] *He draws from it what is needed to efface and remake it*," trans. Folliot, 177.

famous dictum, "mes vers ont le sens qu'on leur prête,"[103] one could say that the text is understood as a projection screen for subjectively constituted meanings. The author's understanding has, admittedly, a more intimate character than that of the outside reader, because for him his understanding is linked back to experiences of a constructed spontaneity, of a voluntarily induced involuntariness.

If the author–writer's attitude towards the written is ruled by his "puissance de transformation toujours en acte,"[104] the work on a text will end only because of outward circumstances or for arbitrary reasons.[105] Publication will render a text only outwardly independent from its author. Inwardly, he cannot sever himself from it. The text is and remains a creature solely of its author's spirit: an entity that could have turned out totally differently. As an author, Valéry documented in an exemplary manner this special intellectual relationship between the originator and his poetic products. He printed a number of his poems in multiple versions, offering them as alternative solutions, so to speak.[106] Franz Kafka—resembling as he did one of his own fictive creatures, an author of books, who held "his theme [. . .] pressed against himself as the father held the child with whom he rode through the night"[107]—expressed this relationship to his writing by declaring

---

[103] ("My verses have the meaning attributed to them," trans. Folliot, 155.) "Commentaire de 'Charmes,' " in Valéry (note 96), 1509.

[104] ("[W]hich is a power of transformation always in action"; trans. Folliot, 140); "Au sujet du 'Cimetière marin,' " in Valéry (note 96), 1497.

[105] Ibid. See also Valéry (note 95), 254: "Une oeuvre est pour moi l'objet possible d'un travail indéfini. Sa publication est un incident extérieure à ce travail; elle est une coupe étrangère dans un développement qui n'est pas et ne peut être arrêté que par des circonstances externes"; ("A text for me is the potential object of work undefined. Its publication is an occurrence external to the work; it is a break which is foreign to an unstoppable process that is arrested only by external circumstances.").

[106] "Féerie" and "Féerie (Variante)"; "Narcisse parle, Première version" and "Narcisse parle, Deuxième version" (1926); in Valéry (note 96), 77–78; 82; 1543–44; 1551–61, esp. 1556. Compare Valéry's comment in "Fragments des mémoires d'un poème": "Il m'est arrivé de publier des textes différents de mêmes poèmes: *il en fut même de contradictoires* [my emphasis], et l'on n'a pas manqué de me critiquer à ce sujet. Mais personne ne m'a dit pourquoi j'aurais d m'abstenir de ces variations"; ("It has sometimes happened that I have published different versions of the same poem: *some of them have even been contradictory* [my emphasis], and there has been no lack of criticism on this score. But no one has told me why I should refrain from such variations"); trans. Folliot, 104; in Valéry (1957), 1467. See also Valéry (note 95), 254.

[107] The narrative fragment, beginning: "Ein junger Student wollte an einem Abend im Januar" ("A young student wanted one evening in January") is an example of the strong self-referentiality in Kafka's work. It seems to refer to the author's difficulties with the continuation of *The Trial*. Pasley describes the contents as follows: "Dieses Erzählfragment handelt von einem Buch, dessen Autor 'sein Thema [. . .] an sich ge-

to Max Brod as his last will that everything on which hands could be laid should share his own fate of annihilation.[108] Authors writing in the constructive, interminable mode will regard even published texts as if they had never left the creative inner space of their desks. Thus the significance their texts have for their authors is a private one; essentially, it cannot be generalized.[109] The texts are and remain for their authors a medium to realize an aesthetic–spiritual self-enhancement and are as such not severable from them.

For such authors, the process of writing serves visualization more than communication, that is, they serve an experiencing of the spiritual and sensory potential of the unfolding self: "Je prends la plume pour l'avenir de ma pensée—non pour son passé. / J'écris pour la voir, pour faire, pour préciser, pour prolonger—non pour doubler ce qui a été."[110] Through writing, thought comes under the power and dynamic of the eye and thereby under the power and dynamic of its own self; it becomes "hermaphroditic," fertilizes itself, and carries "itself to full term."[111] For the author–writer, writing acquires an heuristic value: it becomes a "lifting tool" for thought (memories,

---

drückt' hielt 'wie der Vater das Kind, mit dem er durch die Nacht reitet,' so wie von einem Studenten, dem dieses Werk merkwürdig nahegeht und von dem es heisst: 'Grosse seine Fassungskraft übersteigende Sorgen bedrückten ihn, das Gegenwärtige war zu erfassen, die vor ihm liegende Aufgabe aber erschien ihm undeutlich und ohne Ende ...'" ("This narrative fragment is about a book whose author holds 'his theme [...] pressed against himself as the father held the child with whom he rode through the night,' as well as about a student who is strangely taken with this work and about whom it is said: 'Deep anxiety oppressed him, beyond his strength of mind, the present to be grasped, the task before him seemed vague and endless'"), H 387. Franz Kafka, *Der Process*, Apparatus criticus, ed. Malcolm Pasley, in Kafka, *Schriften, Tagebücher, Briefe, Kritische Ausgabe*, ed. Jürgen Born et al. (Frankfurt a.M., 1990), 118.

[108] Franz Kafka, "*Der Process:* Die Handschrift redet" ("*The Trial*: The manuscript Speaks"), ed. Malcolm Pasley, with a contribution by Ulrich Ott, in *Marbacher Magazin* 52 (1990), 69–72.

[109] See T.S. Eliot's comment about *The Waste Land:* "Various critics have done me the honour to interpret the poem in terms of criticism of the contemporary world, have considered it, indeed, as an important bit of social criticism. To me it was only the relief of a personal and wholly insignificant grouse against life: it is just a piece of rhythmical grumbling"; "*The Waste Land": A Facsimile and the Transcript of the Original Drafts Including the Annotations of Ezra Pound*, ed. Valerie Eliot (New York; London, 1971, xxxiii). See also Paul Valéry, "Question de poésie," in Valéry (note 96), 1280–94, esp. 1287 ("c'est une affaire privée que la beauté"; "beauty is a private affair"), and 1292.

[110] "I write for my future thoughts—not for a thought's past. / I write to see that thought, to construct, to define, to expand—not to duplicate what has already been." See Valéry (note 95), 244.

[111] Paul Valéry, *Littérature*, in Valéry (note 96), 546: "La pensée a les deux sexes: se féconde et se porte soi-même" ("Thought is of both sexes: it impregnates itself and bears itself").

ideas, images, etc.). The effect of writing is twofold: on the one hand, as the practical pressures of decision cease, it opens up thought, it sets free the impulses of association, and thereby it gives free play to the expression of those secret wishes and stirrings of the soul that, outside of the writing situation, have been pushed into the realms of the subconscious and the semi-conscious; on the other hand, it brings such liberated thoughts under control, into relations through which the author's inner conflicts can be symbolically solved.

The writing process thus fulfills less a work-genetic than a psycho-genetic function, based as it is on the motorically stimulated interplay of the "higher" exterior senses—vision and hearing—with the imagination, even as body awareness is partly or wholly subdued. The situation of the author who in writing opens and guides his soul, voluntarily invokes the involuntary, bears a strong resemblance to that of the dreamer. Kafka, for instance, declared his main task to be the "representation of his dreamlike inner life."[112]   Or it resembles the psychoanalytic situation with patient and therapist both united in the person writing.[113]   What the psychoanalytic and the writing situation share is a sense of unburdening through utterance. And this is a double unburdening, since it can free behavior from the problems of the practical, real-life experience and can also relax internal tensions. That means that the inner voices become muted in their contradictoriness by being brought into privileged mutual relationships, as for instance in such a manner that the voice expressing the wish for harmony, for oneness with oneself and others, drowns out the voice of the reality principle. Authors do not write the world from out of their souls, but off their backs. They do so through fictive, illusory distortions based on a higher form-consciousness that has been raised to the level of a reference frame for perception.

The "alienation" of what is felt as a painful intrusion of the real world determines the poetic worlds of art. With Georg Trakl, it takes the shape of a melancholic disembodiment into spheres of sounds,

---

[112] *Tagebücher 1910–1923, Gesammelte Werke*, ed. Max Brod (Frankfurt a.M., 1954), 420 (entry from 6 August 1914).

[113] For a psychoanalytic interpretation of Kafka's work, see Hartmut Binder, "Kafkas Schaffensprozess mit besonderer Berücksichtigung des 'Urteils,'" ("Kafka's creative process with special reference to 'Das Urteil' ['The Judgment']"), an analysis of his statements about the writing process drawing on the manuscripts and on psychological theorems, in *Euphorion* 70 (1976), 129–74, and *Kafka: Der Schaffensprozess (Kafka: The Creative Process)*, Suhrkamp Taschenbuch Materialien (Frankfurt a.M., 1983). See also Jean Bellemin–Noël, "En guise de postface: L'essayage infini" ("By way of a postscript: the infinite variations") in *Littérature* (décembre 1983): "L'inconscient dans l'avant-texte" ("The unconscious in the pre-text"), 123–26.

rhythms, colours;[114] with Georg Heym it is expressed through the demonized unleashing of the bodily world in a rhythmic–tonal uniformity; with Kafka it becomes a contrasting of spiritual interior worlds with repulsive and enigmatic corporeal exterior worlds. All these are products of an inventive liberation, a redemption desired by these authors and not—as is often topically maintained—forced upon them by the social conditions of their lives and times. Writers who seek and find their self-realization only within their own artificial, solitary forms of existence also strive to legitimate for themselves this eccentric retreat through the contents of their writing, through repulsive, discouraging, humiliating, confusing, threatening, meaningless, labyrinthine, as well as through harmonizing, idyllizing representations of worlds. Their poetic worlds as written are "textual worlds,"[115] not the writers' experienced worlds, though, from the perspective of reception, the equation is often wrongly made. These authors are, as a rule, more self-willed and autocratic than their readers would like or concede.[116]

A main feature of psycho-genetic writing, characteristic of its process *by and large*, is the dialectic alternation between *release* and *control* of thought.[117] For this alternation, the spatialization of the writing becomes an important creative factor, whether it be in the shape of the page where, time and again, proto-textual jottings that are merely spatially correlated (keywords for the contents, metaphors, rhyme words, single sentences or sentence fragments, scenarios etc.) will occur, or whether it be in the shape of larger carriers of writing, where room is made, not for the sake of the space required for more

---

[114] See Georg Trakl, writing to Maria Geipel, at the end of October, 1908: "Ich bin immer traurig, wenn ich glücklich bin! Ist das nicht merkwürdig!" ("I am always sad when I am happy! Isn't that strange!"). *Dichtungen und Briefe*, Historical–Critical Edition, ed. Walther Killy and Hans Szklenar, vol.1 (Salzburg, 1969), 473.

[115] For an explanation of this term see Klaus Weimar, "Das Wandeln des Wortlosen in der Sprache des Gedichts" ("The Transmutation of the Word-Less in[to] the Language of the Poem"), in *Klopstock an der Grenze der Epochen*, ed. Kevin Hilliard and Katrin Klopstock with a biography of Klopstock by Helmut Riege (Berlin; New York, 1995), 33–45.

[116] See also Georg Trakl writing to Irene Amtmann in the early autumn of 1910 or 1911: "Nein die Losung ist für unsereinen: Vorwärts zu Dir Selber!" ("No, the watchword for the likes of us is: Forwards to your self!"). Trakl (note 114), 551. Walter Benjamin drew attention to examples of non-authorial, allegorizing interpretations with reference to the parts of Kafka's work he knew. See "Franz Kafka: Zur zehnten Wiederkehr seines Todestages" ("Franz Kafka: On the Tenth Anniversary of His Death"; note 23), vol.2, 196–228.

[117] About the polarity of these artistic forces see Friedrich Nietzsche's early "Artisten-Metaphysik" in *Die Geburt der Tragödie aus dem Geiste der Musik* (1871). This essay belongs among the key documents reflecting upon the wholly self-dependent self-creating artistic genius.

voluminous work, but for that of sessionally longer, externally uninterrupted durations of writing.

An exemplary implementation of a compositional method whose structure is mainly influenced by the page is, again, offered by Valéry, who used the page surface (and, in his *Cahiers*, the rectos and opposite versos together) in a very flexible manner and in every dimensional direction of the horizontal and the vertical.[118] Kafka, in turn, is an author whose writing seeks the extended inscription space; from 1909 onwards, he was in the habit "of writing his work immediately into notebooks."[119] Pasley has observed that the manuscript of *The Castle* provides "information about how an uncertainty of inscription—and with Kafka that means an uncertainty about the continuation of the story—arises apparently every time the paper of the notebook is almost used up"[120] and a disruption of the writing threatens.

As with Valéry, so with Kafka, the writing attains a gestural expressive value that never reaches beyond the trial and drafting mode. Even the written results, the texts, remain in a state of virtuality. A stable textual syntagma, expressive of an objective, unified sense of meaning, cannot here become manifest for the author–writer. Syntagmatic stability comes about only superficially; it may dissolve through a shuffling of parts or by a thorough reworking of the whole—as with Valéry, Heym, or Trakl—or it may be broken through discontinuation that leaves the contents unfinished—as with Kafka. A constructive release of the power of imagination takes place for these poets by means of the pretextual, spatial association of an expressive potential and by means of the transformative renewal of textual states. For Kafka, the author of narratives, it is effected through an alinear switching from a text syntagma no longer inspiring continuation to new ones, as for example from work on a longer fiction, e.g., the novel *Der Verschollene* (*The Vanished*) to the writing of a shorter narrative, e.g., *Die Verwandlung* (*The Metamorphosis*).[121] Kafka broke out of narrative singularity to productive plurality also during the writing-out of the

---

[118] See note 134, below; see also Valéry's description of the condition of his soul in view of a draft manuscript page of his lying before him on the table, "Autres Rhumbs" (note 97), 661–62.

[119] Malcolm Pasley, "Der Schreibakt und das Geschriebene: Zur Frage der Entstehung von Kafkas Texten" ("The Act of Writing and the Written: On the Question of the Origins of Kafka's Texts"), in *Franz Kafka: Themen und Probleme*, ed. Claude David (Göttingen, 1980), 11. See also Pasley (note 107), 17.

[120] See Pasley 1980 (preceding note), 12.

[121] Malcolm Pasley and Klaus Wagenbach: "Datierung sämtlicher Texte Franz Kafkas" ("Complete Dating of Kafka's Texts"), in Jürgen Born et al., eds., *Kafka-Symposion* (Berlin, 1966), 62–64.

chapters of *Der Prozess* (*The Trial*).[122] The changing back and forth between the different modes of representation, between diary and lyric poetry, and between different strands of narrative fiction, is of the very nature of this mode of writing.[123] As a result of its author-related finality, it is an intermittent and, as it were, an intertextual writing, whose variability signals that it should be capable of inciting anew the author's spontaneity over and over again.

It is also characteristic of the psycho-genetic and predominantly constructive mode of writing that its reproductive elements, organically reproducing something previously thought out, tend to be brief.[124] Larger texts result from a joining of text segments. This is due to the self-reflexivity of the writing process. The author's gaze on the written has a decisive genetic significance for the writing both in its continuation and in its rewriting. The generation of the text springs from the interaction of writing and thinking; texts emerge from acts of writing. Pasley has noted that interaction as fundamental for Kafka's compositional method: "One recognizes the especially close relationship between invention and notation [...] Through the act of writing itself, and through it alone, one may see emerging one by one those determinants for the continuation of the story that then prove irrevocable."[125] Another important circumstance is indicative of the crucial self-referentiality of Kafka's writing: "the changes in the autographs are almost always integral to the original inscription. They document the recognition and correction of false starts [...] This is true also for larger, structural changes [...] These too can almost without exception be called 'compositional corrections,' in the sense that they must have been performed before the story could have been continued" (ibid., 19).

---

[122] See Pasley 1990 (note 107), 17.

[123] Compare the text sequences in the octavo notebooks A, B, D and E, on which see Gerhard Neumann, "Der verschleppte Prozess: Literarisches Schaffen zwischen Schreibstrom und Werkidol" ("The Protracted Process: Creation between Writing Continuum and Idolized Work"), in *Poetica* 14 (1982), 92–112, esp. 100–101, 111–12.

[124] See Leopardi's notes for his "Zibaldone di pensieri": "Il poema epico è contro la natura della poesia [...] I lavori di poesia vogliono per natura esser corti. E tali furono e sono tutte le poesie primitive (cioè le più poetiche e vere) di qualunque genere" ("The epic poem is against the nature of poetry. [...] Poetic labors naturally strive to be short. And such were and are all primitive poems [that is, the ones most poetic and true] of whatever type"); Leopardi (note 24), 866–67. See also "Lyrik als Paradigma der Moderne" ("Lyric Poetry as a Paradigm of Modernism"), *Immanente Ästhetik. Ästhetische Reflexion. Lyrik als Paradigma der Moderne*, Kolloqium Köln 1964, Vorlagen und Verhandlungen, ed. Wolfgang Iser, Poetik und Hermeneutik (München, 1966).

[125] See Pasley 1980 (note 119), 13.

Georg Heym, too, who "actually almost always" was writing poetry,[126] let himself be led in poetic composition more by the written than by the imagined. This shows not only in his method of combinatorial amplification of keyword jottings,[127] but also in the circumstance that some semantically very divergent alterations were clearly provoked by the illegibility of his own handwriting; for example, the graphic similarity of "Häfen" and "Höfe," "Mond" and "Mord," "Baum" and "Raum."[128] Heym's compositional method generally, moreover, shows the typical signs of psycho-genetic writing: openness, interminableness, and dissolvability of the working results.[129] If one wants to call such insight a poetics, then maybe we should speak of a psycho-poetics of psycho-poiesis.

It is genetic autographs above all, as emerging from psycho-genetic writing processes, that are capable of "speaking"[130] about their authorial dynamics. Their graphic and spatio–temporal structures are incomparably more revealing than those in manuscripts of work-genetic production. It is not fortuitous that the chronological organization of the writing process has a more fundamental significance for the reconstruction of the genesis from these manuscripts than from those of the work-genetic type, while at the same time the frequent impossibility of deducing temporal circumstances from spatial circumstances carries a specific relevance for an understanding of the process of writing (though of course not of the genesis of the text).[131] In the realm of work-genetic manuscripts, terms such as "layer" (basic layer, or layers of reworking or revision) and "version" generally suffice for accurate

---

[126] Friedrich Schulze–Maizier, "Georg Heyms Nachlass" ("Georg Heym's Literary Remains"), in *Dresdner Neueste Nachrichten,* 21.10.1922, rptd. in Georg Heym, *Dokumente zu seinem Leben und Wirken,* ed. Karl Ludwig Schneider and Gerhard Burckhardt, Dichtungen und Schriften, vol.6 (München, 1968), 299.

[127] See Günter Dammann, "Theorie des Stichworts: Ein Versuch über die lyrischen Entwürfe Georg Heyms" ("Theory of the Keyword: An Essay on the Lyric Drafts of Georg Heym"), in Martens and Zeller (note 40), 203–18, and "Untersuchungen zur Arbeitsweise Georg Heyms an seinen Handschriften: Über die Entstehung der Gedichte 'Mortuae,' 'Totenwache,' 'Letzte Wache' " ("Investigations into Georg Heym's Working Process: On the Emergence of 'Mortuae,' 'Totenwache,' 'Letzte Wache' "), in *Orbis litterarum* 26 (1971), 42–67.

[128] See Gunter Martens, "Entwürfe zur Lyrik Georg Heyms: Möglichkeiten des Einblicks in die immanente Poetik seiner Dichtungen," ("Georg Heym's Lyric Drafts: Keys to an Immanent Poetics of His Poetry"), in *editio* 1 (1987), 250–65, esp. 260.

[129] See Dammann, "Untersuchungen" (note 127), 67.

[130] Pasley 1980 (note 119).

[131] Examples may be found in Almuth Grésillon, *Éléments de critique génétique: Lire les manuscrits modernes* (Paris, 1994), 121–40; see my review in *editio* 11 (1997), 233–36.

description, but autographs of the psycho-genetic type demand a distinct terminology to differentiate the written by external as well as internal evidence into states of textual development, "work phases,"[132] or "text stages." Abstraction is required from the appearance of the manuscript, such as from its inscriptional topography, its *ductus litterarium* and temporality. Such indicators serve critical insight only selectively and indirectly.

It would, however, mean overtaxing the manuscripts, both of the primarily work-genetic and of the primarily psycho-genetic type, to attempt to reconstruct from them the original course of the genesis of a text. To prize the documents as evidence for such reconstruction would lead to the genetic fallacy. And what truly, in the event, would be the literary critic's gain from the retracing of the original course of genetic development? Such knowledge would be of interest only to an empirical psychologist. Relevant to critical concerns, however, are the author's attitude to his writing as it manifests itself in his genetic autographs, as well as what part the writing itself plays in the formation of the text. Answers to such questions lie properly within the province of textual genetics.

v. The Editorial Circle

Textual genetics in editorial scholarship is oriented primarily towards linear book-reading. Even where the typographical transcription of genetic manuscripts has been largely adapted to the spatial–linear mode of manuscript reading—as, for instance, in Zeller's edition of Conrad Ferdinand Meyer's poems, Sattler's Frankfurt Hölderlin Edition, and Dammann's, Martens's, and Schneider's critical edition of Georg Heym's poems of 1910 through 1912[133] —book-oriented readability remains the guideline. What is still seen quite technically as the main editorial problem is how to reconcile descriptive accuracy in the representation of genetic manuscripts with readability, that is, how reading a manuscript can be made to conform with reading a book. At least in the case of complicated drafts—especially interesting documents from the genetic point of view—the task amounts to squaring the circle. Both *critique génétique* and some genetically oriented editions

---

[132] See Günter Dammann and Gunter Martens, "Einführung in die textgenetische Darstellung der Gedichte Georg Heyms" ("Introduction to the Textgenetic Representation of Georg Heym's Poems"), in *editio* 5 (1991), 178–98, esp. 181–87.

[133] Among such editions, finished or begun, may be included the recently inaugurated Brandenburg Kleist Edition, ed. Roland Reuss, Peter Staengle, and Ingeborg Harms, in so far as an assessment is possible from vol.I/5, *Penthesilea*, ed. Roland Reuss with Peter Staengele (Basel; Frankfurt a.M., 1992).

provide vivid examples.[134] However, the expressive value of genetic autographs, especially those resulting from the psycho-genetic mode of writing, justifies a reverse ranking of the two kinds of reading.

The end of genetic representation should be to render the genetic manuscripts themselves readable and interpretable, and their transcription should be the means to that end. The exploration of genetic autographs should no longer remain in the hands of textual editors alone; that is, its objective should not be editorial transcriptions and descriptions, but ultimately the originals themselves. It should not only lead out of the "underbrush of the drafts"[135] to the documentation of the genesis they imply, but it should lead back into that "underbrush" as well. Like a diplomatic transcription, a genetic transcription would become an instrument for reading and interpreting the manuscript itself. The manuscript or its reproduction would no longer simply serve as an illustration to the editorial representation. In fact, the first steps have already been taken on this upstream journey to cull not only the document contents from the "witnesses," but to recover from the documents' iconicity their paratextual nature. However, the mechanical reproduction of genetic manuscripts as found in the editions mentioned (especially the Frankfurt Hölderlin Edition)[136] needs yet to be endowed with a broader significance: it should be understood not only as a documentary medium for the justification and testing of editorial decisions, but, above all, as a portrayal of the originals themselves. This would establish the necessary—though naturally not the sufficient—precondition for increasing the mechanical reproduction of genetic manuscripts in number and quality.

The desirable extent and technical quality of facsimile reproduction must depend primarily on the author's individual compositional method; hence, no general rules can here be laid down. Only the individual editor can adjudicate the matter in each given case on the basis of his or her knowledge of the author's compositional method. The generalization may be hazarded, however, that in the case of

---

[134] See Giovani Bonaccorso et al., *Corpus Flaubertianum, I: Un coeur simple: En appendice édition diplomatique et génétique des manuscrits*, vol. 1 (Paris, 1983), and *Corpus Flaubertianum, II: Hérodias: Édition diplomatique et génétique des manuscrits*, Tome 1 (Paris, 1991). Compare, in both, especially the "Transcription diplomatique et génétique des manuscrits" and the facsimiles. See also Paul Valéry, *Cahiers 1894–1914*, ed. Nicole Celeyrette–Pietri and Judith Robinson–Valéry, vols.1–3 (Paris, 1987–1990).

[135] Afterword in Georg Trakl, *Gedichte*, ed. Hans Szklenar, Fischer Bücherei 581 (Frankfurt a.M., 1964), 134.

[136] With regard to the Meyer and Hölderlin editions, the facsimile portion is deplorably small. See Georg Heym, *Gedichte 1910–1912*, Historical–Critical Edition of all texts with genetic documentation, ed. Günter Dammann, Gunter Martens, Karl Ludwig Schneider, vols.1–2 (Tübingen, 1993).

work-genetic compositional methods, manuscript reproduction may be more easily limited to representative examples than in the case of psycho-genetic writing.

The proposition is of course liable to encounter opposition. Scholarly editors will object that we are, after all, *textual* scholars and that our interest in manuscripts should not extend beyond their serviceable function as sources or witness documents. True enough, but our interests should not end at the borders of the discipline. Manuscripts do not exist for the sake of textual scholarship, nor authors for the sake of editions. Our priorities must be reversed. If the nature of the object to be perceived and understood makes it necessary, the disciplinary borders must be crossed to broaden perspectives. Moreover: treating manuscripts in the psycho-genetic mode merely as witness documents is like responding to poems in the prosaic, narrow-minded fashion of only taking their lexical contents into consideration and ignoring their metrical and rhythmic, their tonal and also graphically line-structured, "co-expressiveness" (Klopstock).

Indecipherabilities and ambiguities, such as are typical for the genetic autographs of Trakl, Heym, Barlach, or Robert Walser's "Mikrogramme," cannot be laid to the account solely of critical deficits in perception; they must be recognized as expressive qualities, private signatures, as it were, of the ultimately self-reflexive authorial mode of writing. The phrase "ignorabimus" ("we shall not know"), if not rashly uttered, should here in many cases be felt to be as appropriate as vis-à-vis a hermetic poetry.

Authors have not only preceded scholarly editors in their communication of variants, they have also been pacemakers in reproducing autographs. In 1924 Valéry published a facsimile edition of one of his cahiers, the so-called "Cahier B. 1910."[137] From 1957 to 1961, a twenty-nine-volume facsimile edition of 261 cahiers (Paris: CNRS) was published posthumously. Francis Ponge documented in his edition several developmental stages of the poem "Le Pré" (*La Fabrique du Pré*).[138] And while Hans Magnus Enzensberger in his lecture "Über die Entstehung eines Gedichts" described but did not reproduce textual stages of the poem "an alle fernsprechteilnehmer" ("to all telephone subscribers"),[139] Peter Rühmkorf did exactly the same in providing an extensive facsimile edition of the working drafts of his long poem: "Mit den Jahren ... Selbst III/88"; "Selbst III/88. Aus der Fassung" (1989).[140] At the beginning of this study some authors and poets were quoted;

---

[137] In Valéry (note 97), 571–94, 1423.

[138] Geneva, 1971 (Les sentiers de la création).

[139] *Gedichte: Die Entstehung eines Gedichts.* Afterword by Werner Weber (Frankfurt a.M., 1965), 55–79.

[140] Haffmanns Verlag (Zürich) published 1,000 signed copies of the 736-page edition.

at its end, a poet again should have the final word. Rühmkorf reveals himself in the afterword to the facsimile edition mentioned above as an author in the psycho-genetic mode of writing:

> At the beginning of a poem is the idea and not the word [...] The poem as a genuine intellectual organ in the constitution of the ego, and the poet, who introduces himself as a token into it: we cannot give this away any cheaper. The certain narcissism/subjectivism that can be inferred therefrom has unfortunately to be accepted as part of the matter. As the recorder of his joys and sufferings and as an executor, constantly trying, the experimental lyrical poet is at every phase his own guinea-pig subject, one who has nobody else to send ahead, not even for sweeping out the workshop, and this is true before the world as it is on the paper [...] As a literary-medial self-experiment, 'Selbst III/88' is anything but a peaceful picture or freeze-frame produced before a domestic mirror. The subject that, believe it or not, only proceeds to discover itself in the course of the voyage and only begins to structure itself on the trip, works itself out—in this respect—only in and during the work, so that the wanderings of the ideas and detours of the words on paper must be read as the corresponding growing pains [...] What was to be demonstrated in the individual case were the stages of development of a subject in the lyrical longitudinal section.[141]

Rühmkorf did his part, so that the "groundwork of poetry" would no longer remain covered under the "airy strata of theory overlaying it," nor submerged under the yet higher-arching "sky of imagination" (ibid., 722). With this he attempted, at the same time, to become better understood himself.

---

[141] See Rühmkorf (preceding note), 715, 724, 727–28.

Scholarly Editing
in the Netherlands

H. T. M. van VLIET

i. Introduction

IN 1579, A UNION OF PROVINCES AND CITIES was created in the Netherlands that later evolved to become the Republic of the United Netherlands. For this Republic, the seventeenth century was to be a true "aurea aetas," a Golden Age. In the course of only two generations, the young Republic grew to become a global power: "the most formidable economic power stretched across the globe."[1] The unprecedented economic growth turned Amsterdam into one of the most important commercial and financial centres of Western Europe. Amsterdam already had its first stock exchange in 1611 where both goods and securities were traded. With its fleet of nearly 15,000 ships—four to five times the size of the English fleet—the Republic ruled the world's seas.

The prosperity in the Republic had a stimulating effect on both architecture and art. There was also a considerable amount of activity in the areas of literature and science. The Republic was "a world that was [...] surprisingly literate for its time."[2] At Leiden University, founded

---

[1] Simon Schama, *The Embarrassment of Riches: An Interpretation of Dutch Culture in the Golden Age* (New York, 1987), 8.

[2] *The Embarrassment of Riches*, 4.

in 1575, classical philology underwent enormous progress: "we are right to speak of a golden age of Latin studies."[3] Numerous editions compiled by the professors in Leiden were published by the famous publishing house Elzevier, which was located in Leiden. It launched a series of publications of the Latin and Greek classics in 1629 consisting of small, inexpensive books. This series in duodecimo grew rapidly, and was so popular both in the Republic and elsewhere that it was imitated on a grand scale.[4] The books became a status symbol: "no gentleman could afford to be without some of these volumes."[5]

At the beginning of the era of the blossoming of classical philology in Leiden, we see the Humanist editors from the fifteenth and sixteenth centuries, important representatives of which were Erasmus (± 1469–1536) and Lipsius (1547–1606), who was a professor in Leiden. Erasmus compiled more than forty editions of works by Greek and Latin authors; Lipsius' publications included Tacitus. The Leiden group also included the famous philologist Scaliger (1540–1609). They were all part of the Greek–Latin philology and developed the method of text reconstruction and textual criticism based on genealogical analysis of the available manuscripts that was characteristic of the Renaissance.

The classical philological method established in the Renaissance was continued in the following centuries. Textual scholarship in the Netherlands has always been dominated by the classical philology that was practised by classicists and later on by mediævalists. Starting in the second half of the nineteenth century, Dutch mediævalists produced an impressive series of scholarly editions. Based on their texts, numerous editions were made for schoolchildren and students. These editions reveal the great social importance of scholarly editing: it keeps the national literary inheritance accessible and therefore alive.

The nineteenth century saw the development of modern philology in Germany and France as well. The methods of classical philology were adapted, and totally new methods and techniques were later developed for vernacular literature. This trend was not followed in the Netherlands. Having missed this connection, all later academic discussions were lost to the Netherlands. The mediævalists continued their tradition into the twentieth century. The same was more or less true for the publication of sixteenth- and seventeenth-century literature, in which no consideration was taken of the specific bibliographical

---

3 J.H. Waszink, "Classical Philology," in *Leiden University in the Seventeenth Century: An Exchange of Learning*, ed. Th.H. Lunsingh Scheurleer and G.H.M. Posthumus Meyjes (Leiden, 1975), 167.

4 Cf. David W. Davies, *The World of the Elseviers 1580–1712* (The Hague, 1954), 146–51.

5 Charles Rosen, "The Scandal of the Classics," *The New York Review of Books*, 9 May 1996, 27.

problems of books printed in the hand press period. There was no academic interest for editions of modern literature. They were almost entirely left to publishers or compiled by editors who did not work according to a scholarly method, but who made their own decisions in ways that seemed best to them. Extensive bibliographic and text–critical research was not performed. The last edition was almost always taken as the starting point and was then "corrected" and modernised. All this resulted in unscholarly, unreliable editions of modern Dutch literature.

ii. The Constantijn Huygens Instituut

A change for the better did not occur until 1975, when an editing project was started at Utrecht University, following the German example of what is known as historical–critical editions. In September 1977 the board of the Royal Netherlands Academy of Arts and Sciences decided to take charge of the project. This made it possible for the first historical–critical edition in the Netherlands to be published in 1979. As a result of this publication and other plans, the former Dutch Ministry of Education and Sciences decided to provide the Academy with the financial resources needed to establish a centre for editing in the Netherlands. This resulted in the foundation of a Bureau for text editions on 1 June 1983. In addition to this bureau, the Academy also had several long-term classical philological editing projects, such as the publication of the *Opera Omnia Desiderii Erasmi*. In 1992 the board of the Academy finally decided to combine all the bureaux and institutes with editing projects into a single institute: the Constantijn Huygens Instituut. From the very beginning this institute combined both classical and modern scholarly editing. The institute was named after the great seventeenth-century "homo universalis," Constantijn Huygens (1596–1687).

The Constantijn Huygens Instituut produces editions of texts from every period of Dutch literature. All genres and types of editions are included: scholarly and more popular editions of poems, novels, letters, essays, etc. The scholarly editing at the Constantijn Huygens Instituut is performed within an international framework, but in service of the national heritage. Methods and techniques developed in the German-language area are followed with several adaptations. Theory and practice in America, France and England are also studied and followed where appropriate.

iii. Structure

The Institute consists of three work groups: Middle Ages, Renaissance and Modern Times. Each work group is responsible for a number of editing projects. The groups consist of a nucleus of permanent academic staff and a varying number of young temporary project staff. Because permanent staff is not appointed to all the available positions, there is a constant influx of young editors, who then leave after their projects have ended.

The Institute's research programme is divided into short- and long-term projects. The question of which editing project is to be included in the programme is decided after internal discussions and consultation with external experts. Prior to each new project, university colleagues are consulted. They can make their wishes known. These are then discussed internally and submitted to the Institute's academic committee. External experts are also involved in the implementation of the projects. In this way a broad consensus is achieved about the academic importance of the Institute's editing projects.

As a research institute of the Royal Netherlands Academy of Arts and Sciences, the Constantijn Huygens Instituut is thus a national centre for scholarly editing. The editing projects are funded by the Academy on the basis of total financing, not per project or cost item. The total amount is established on an annual basis by the board of the Academy. For 1999 the budget amounted to more than 1.3 million dollars.

Because of its national and central position, the Institute can develop its own short- and long-term policies. The Institute can also strive internally for methodical unity and uniformity. Thus in recent years several apparatuses for the presentation of variants have been developed that, in principle, can be used for all editions. This uniformity is not only important for editors. The user of the editions also benefits from it. In the long term the user becomes familiar with certain apparatuses, and this increases the accessibility of the editions.

iv. Contacts

There is also an inherent danger in the independent position of the Institute as a national centre. Editing is by definition solo work for which concentration and accuracy are essential. Due to the nature of the work, editors tend to prefer to withdraw into blissful isolation. In order therefore to prevent the Instituut from manoeuvring itself into an ivory tower, intensive contacts are maintained with universities and academic institutions at home and abroad. For example, the director of the Institute is also a guest professor at one of the Dutch universities, where he gives an annual seminar on scholarly editing. The links with universities make it possible for students interested in scholarly editing to establish contact with the Institute at an early stage. For this reason the Institute has introduced the possibility of a practical training programme. Together with five Dutch universities, training periods of three or six months are offered several times a year. The students are given the opportunity to actually work on an editing project for a longer period.

v. Projects

At the moment the Institute employs some twenty-five scholars working on various editing projects. Some of these projects involve editions for the general reader, but the result of most of the projects is a multivolume scholarly edition. These are published by the Institute itself in the series called Monumenta Literaria Neerlandica. In this series, a seven-volume edition was published in the 1980s of the poetry of Jan Hendrik Leopold (1865–1925).[6] Leopold is considered one of the most important representatives of Dutch symbolism, but his poems also show clear romantic characteristics, and because of his striking intertextuality he can also be considered a modernist. During his lifetime he published only one collection of poems and two small booklets in limited editions. After his death an immense poetic legacy was discovered, consisting of hundreds of documents of various types. These documents contain notes, sketches, quotations and a great many fragments of poems in varying degrees of incompleteness as well as a few dozen almost-completed poems. All the poems in Leopold's legacy are of a provisional nature. Even the almost complete poems copied out neatly cannot be said to be final. Further revisions were later added in these manuscripts, and in many places there is no punctuation.

Leopold's compositional method is characterised by continual revision and delay in making final decisions. He constantly wrote new versions of the poems and created new variants within these versions, but he did not delete the "early" versions and variants. As a result, it is difficult to decide which version should appear in a scholarly edition as the copy-text. In essence there is no final "definitive" version. All the versions and variants have "authority" that has not been overruled by another or a next "authority."

The first attempt to edit this complicated legacy was made by the family of the poet, one year after his death. In 1926 a small collection appeared without any explanation of or reference to the state of the

---

[6] J.H. Leopold, *Gedichten I. De tijdens het leven van de dichter gepubliceerde poëzie*, historical–critical edition, compiled by A.L. Sötemann and H.T.M. van Vliet (Amsterdam etc., 1983), 2 vols., Monumenta Literaria Neerlandica II,1–2. J.H. Leopold, *Gedichten uit de nalatenschap*, ed. G.J. Dorleijn (Amsterdam etc., 1984), 2 vols., Monumenta Literaria Neerlandica II, 3–4. J.H. Leopold, *Gedichten II. Nagelaten poëzie*, historical–critical edition, compiled by H.T.M. van Vliet in co-operation with A.L. Sötemann (Amsterdam etc., 1985), 3 vols., Monumenta Literaria Neerlandica II,5–6a/b.

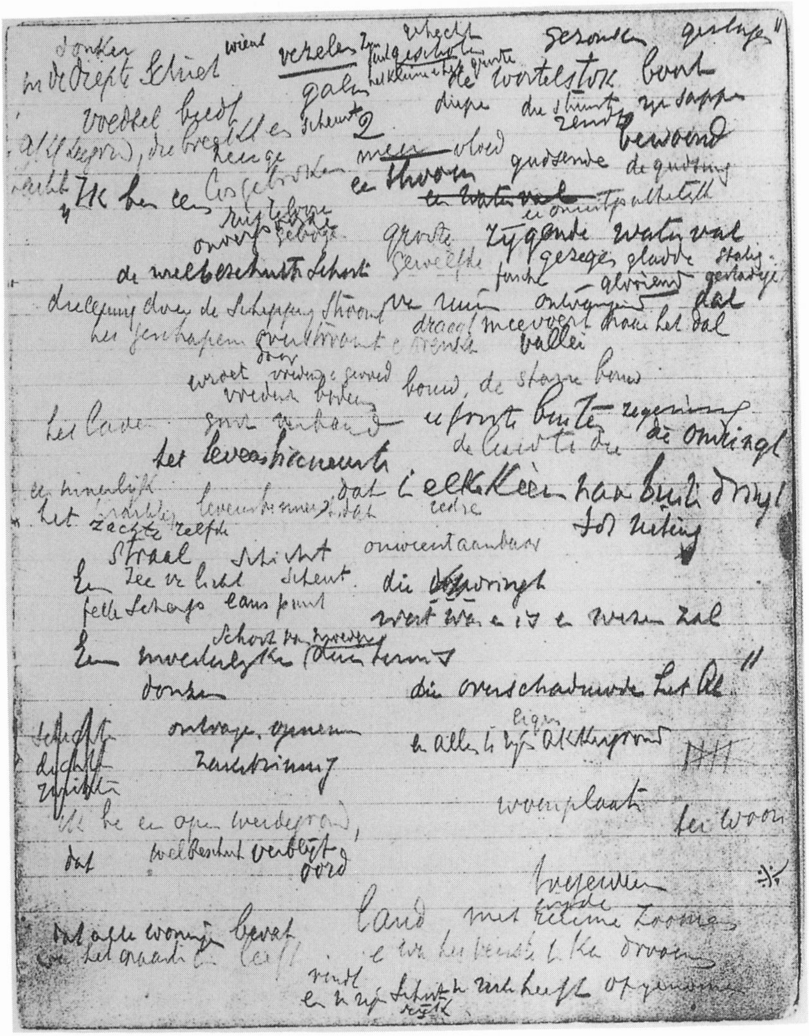

Illus. 1. Manuscript of J.H. Leopold (reproduced by permission of the Dutch Literary Archive, The Hague).

manuscripts.[7] This mystery resulted in a polemical exchange in the national newspapers. The family then felt it must entrust Leopold's entire legacy to the poet and critic P.N. van Eyck (1887–1954) early in 1928. He worked seven years on an edition of the complete poems, which was published in 1935.[8] According to Van Eyck, publishing Leopold's legacy was virtually impossible. His solution for the "unsolvable" problem was an extremely simplified, thus incorrect presentation of the state in which Leopold had left behind his unfinished poems, sketches and fragments. In an attempt to compile a readable text of the poems, Van Eyck based his choice of the variants on his own preference, even including readings that had been crossed out; he compiled virtually completed poems from what were really mere sketches, combined separate fragments of which the internal sequence had not yet been determined by Leopold into poems, and presented notes with no poetic structure as sketches or fragments of poems. These editorial decisions taken by Van Eyck actually resulted in *new* texts that can be attributed to the poet Leopold only to a limited extent. The reader cannot verify any of this, for his resources are limited to the extremely vague and often incomprehensible notes from Van Eyck; for example: "Sketch. Numerous words left out, others put more closely together." In another instance, Van Eyck presented the following, virtually finished poem:

Ik ben een rustelooze stroom,
      een groote, zijgende waterval
die het geschapene overstroomt
     en drenkt   meevoert naar het dal,

een zee van licht   die doordringt
     wat was en is en wezen zal,
een schoot van moederduisternis
     die overschaduwde het Al.

(I am a restless stream
     a great, sinking waterfall
that overflows the creation
     and drowns   carries to the valley

a sea of light   that penetrates
     that which has been and will be
a lap of motherly darkness
     that shadows the All)

---

7 J.H. Leopold, *Verzen*, Second Collection (Rotterdam, 1926).

8 J.H. Leopold, *Verzamelde verzen*, ed. with comments and notes, P.N. van Eyck (Rotterdam, 1935).

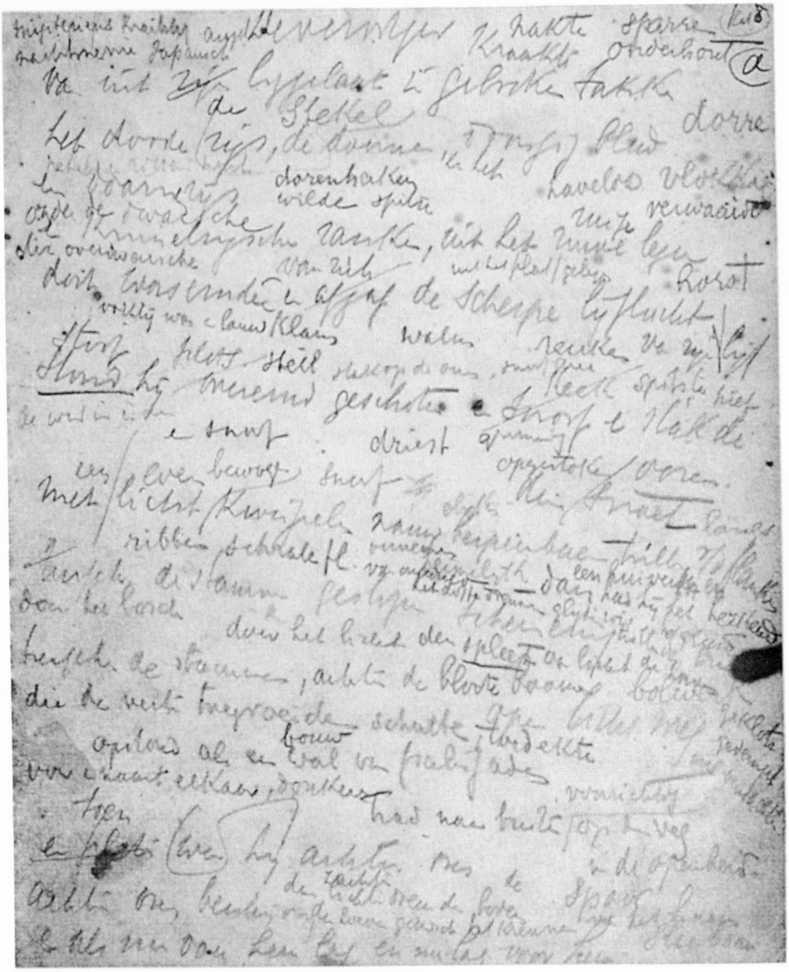

Illus. 2. Manuscript of J.H. Leopold (reproduced by permission of the Dutch Literary Archive, The Hague).

```
        c    [Van uit] de [ligplaats in ge]kraakte [takken]
        d    [Van uit de ligplaats in gek]nakte [takken]
        e                        ^sparren  ^onderhout
   (2)  a    het doode [rijs], de doornen, [drassig blad]
        b    [de] stekel[doornen] en het [drassig blad]        ^dorre
        c    en doorn<+en>rijs
        d    ^dorenhaken
        e    ^wilde spitse
        f    ^netels en rottend hout
   (3)  a                                    ^vlokkig
        b                                    ^haveloos
        c                                    ^verwaaid
   (4)  a    en kruiselingsche [ranken, uit het ruwe leger]
        b    onder de dwarsche [ranken, uit het ruwe leger]
        c    der overdwarsche [ranken, uit het ruwe leger]
             | en kruiselingsche |
        d    [{ onder de dwarsche } ranken, uit het] ruige [leger]
             | der overdwarsche  |
        e                                    ^uit het plat/gelegen
        f                                        ^horst
   (5)  a    [dat] wasemde͡ [en afgaf] de scherpe [lijflucht]
        b                        <>
        c    [dat wasemde en] van zich [gaf de scherpe lijflucht]
        d    [dat] vochtig was en lauw
        e    [dat vochtig was en] klam
        f                        reuken van zijn lijf
        g                        ^walm
   (6)  a    [stond hij] overeind geschoten en [snoof en stak de | ooren]
        b    [stond hij] plots [overeind en snoof en stak de | ooren]
        c    [stond hij] steil [overeind en snoof en stak de | ooren]
                       | plots |
        d    stoof [hij {       } overeind en snoof en stak de | ooren]
                       | steil |
                       | plots |
        e    stond [hij {       } overeind en snoof en stak de | ooren]
                       | steil |
             | stond |     | plots |
        f    [{       } hij {       } overeind en] keek [en stak
             | stoof |     | steil |
                                                    de | ooren]
        g                              <2 >
             | stond |     | plots |
        h    [{       } hij {       } overeind en] spitste [de | ooren]
             | stoof |     | steil |
             | stond |     | plots |
        i    [{       } hij {       } overeind en]   hief [de | ooren]
             | stoof |     | steil |
             | stond |     | plots |
        j    [{       } hij {       } overeind] stak op de ooren, snuffelde
             | stoof |     | steil |
        k    [stond hij] en snoof       ^driest  ^grimmig
   (7)  a                                    [den snoet]
        b                ^snoof          ^[den] opgestoken [snoet]
        c    ^de wind is in den
```

Illus. 3. Synoptic presentation (J.H. Leopold-edition, Constantijn Huygens Instituut, The Hague).

It is my belief that this poem does not exist. The relevant manuscript in Leopold's legacy contains a sketch with numerous added variants, from which no choice had been made (see illus. 1). First the poet wrote a framework for the poem with black pencil; then he used an aniline pencil to add many possibilities that could be used to fill in and complete the framework. For the first half of line 1 alone there are at least six alternative readings.

It is obvious that Van Eyck's edition of Leopold's legacy has nothing to do with scholarly editing. A scholarly edition of Leopold's posthumous poems should present the unfinished status of the poems and the multiple authority of the versions and variants. In some cases it is quite impossible to give one reading text or indeed make any reading text of the poem *in statu nascendi*. It would, however, be possible to reconstruct the genesis of the text of each poem in a historical–critical edition following the German tradition. Such an edition would include the complete documentation of one or all works of an author: all the extant versions of the work are presented in chronological order and in their historical form. An essential aspect of the historical–critical edition is the genetic approach. In our edition of Leopold's poetry, the genesis of the text is presented in the form of a synopsis. The synopsis is suitable for an edition of poetry because it simultaneously presents two essential aspects of the genesis in a manner that is almost ideal: the unity of each individual version—the synchronous or "horizontal" relationship—and the coherence of the changes per text fragment—the diachronous or "vertical" relationship. Extremely complicated manuscripts can, with considerable effort, be transformed into such a synopsis (see illus. 2, 3).

The scholarly importance of the historical–critical Leopold edition lies in the treasure of information it contains. This data can serve as the basis for a wide variety of scholarly research, including Leopold's compositional method, his idiom, his metaphors, his literary position, his development, and especially his intertextuality. In his poems, Leopold often entered into dialogue with various donor texts or other artistic expressions, including paintings. Numerous traces of this can be found in his legacy of manuscripts. One example is the genesis of the unfinished poem "Buiten de deuren en het balkon" ("Outside the doors and the balcony"), which starts with a French quote:

> Aussitôt que Katucha entrait dans la chambre, aussitôt que de loin il l'apercevait, c'est comme si tout lui aussitôt s'ensoleillait, tout lui paraisait intéressant, gai, important, la vie lui devenait une joie.
>
> (As soon as Katucha entered the room, as soon as he saw her from afar, it was as if everything was suddenly drenched in sunlight, everything seemed interesting, gay and important to him and life became a great joy.)

This quote concerning the effect of the entrance of a loved one is so general that, in principle, it could have been from any nineteenth- or early twentieth-century French novel. Only the Russian name Katucha and the knowledge that Leopold, like many of his Dutch contemporaries, read the great Russian authors in French translation, led us to the source: the French translation of Tolstoy's novel *Resurrection*.

During his visit to Italy in 1922, Leopold made numerous notes on small sheets that he kept in his pocket. In the Uffizi Gallery in Florence, for example, inspired by the famous painting *Primavera* by Botticelli, he noted the beginnings of a poem. Back in the Netherlands, he worked intensively on the poem in the years 1922–23, drafting eight stanzas with a large number of variants from which the poet had not yet made a selection (see illus. 4, 5). Leopold was clearly inspired by the painting for the setting of his poem: a field with many flowering plants. The violets and daisies were literally borrowed from the picture, and one of the drafts of the poem also uses Botticelli's irises and anemones. Botticelli's mythical garden turned into Leopold's spring-time scenery in which mythological figures are not seen, only two lovers. For both Botticelli and Leopold love is the main motif, but the poetic dialogue that Leopold entered into with his example brings a diametrically opposite result. Through the texts of the successive manuscripts of the poem, we see how Leopold moves further and further away from Botticelli: not Botticelli's blissful love in the closeness of a marriage for Leopold, but two lovers who remain separate and disillusioned. In Leopold's poem, the two lovers passionately attempt to come closer; they tell their innermost secrets, but this results only in confusion. The two lovers encounter a limit that they cannot pass. A barrier continues to separate them.

The synoptic reconstruction of the genesis of Leopold's poem not only reveals the dialogue with Botticelli's painting, but also renders important clues to the interpretation of the poem and insight into Leopold's view of life and his compositional method. The historical–critical edition makes relationships of this type visible, thus utilizable for continued scholarly research. However, this type of edition also has limitations, with reference to both practical–technical and intrinsic aspects. In a synopsis, for example, sketches and fragments without a clear poetic structure are difficult if not impossible to present. Refuge must be sought in a facsimile combined with transcription that is as accurate as possible. Moreover, there are various relationships between variants and versions that are not as evident when printed in a book as they can be when digitized on a computer. More importantly, the historical–critical edition has its intrinsic limitations. It cannot be stressed enough that a synopsis, and, for the record, any other apparatus of variants is *not* the genesis of the text, but is a

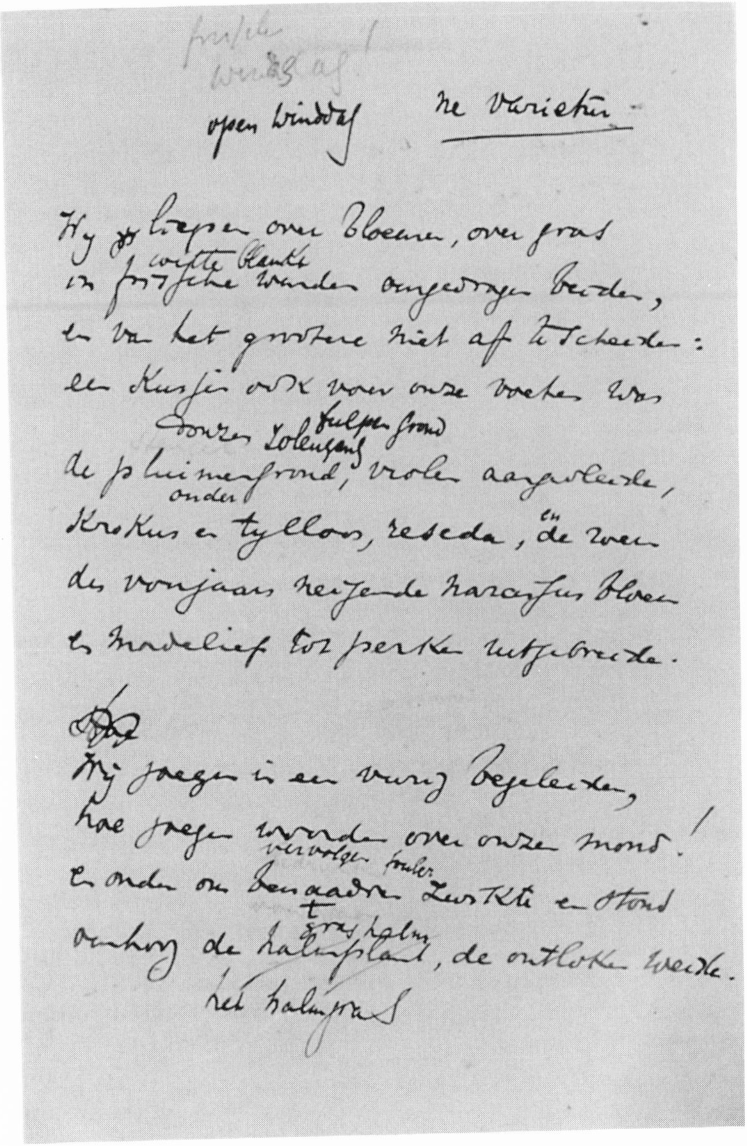

Illus. 4. Manuscript of J.H. Leopold (reproduced by permission of the Dutch Literary Archive, The Hague).

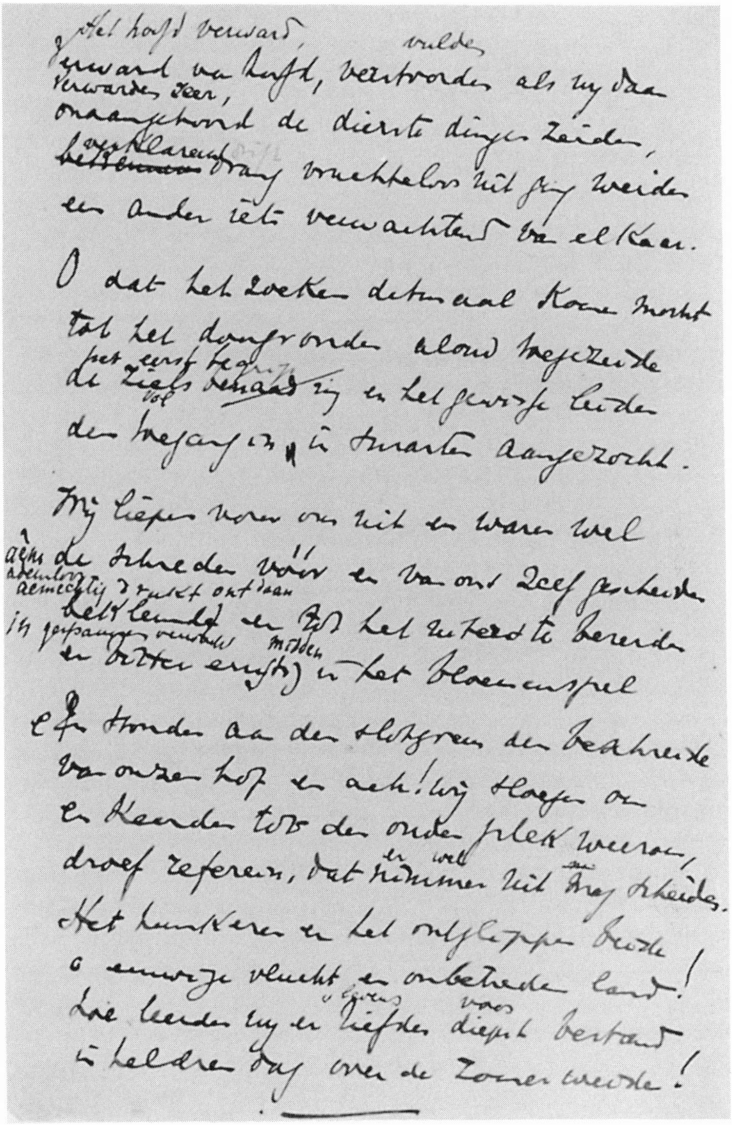

Illus. 5. Manuscript of J.H. Leopold (reproduced by permission of the Dutch Literary Archive, The Hague).

reconstruction of the genesis compiled by an editor, inescapably based on many subjective decisions. A different editor would probably arrive at a different interpretation of many places in the manuscripts, thus a different synopsis. Furthermore, the editor has access only to the extant manuscripts. What went on in the author's head that has not been written down is lost forever and cannot be reconstructed. Thus a genesis of a text can never be said to be *complete*.

vi. Van Gogh

Another large project of the Constantijn Huygens Instituut is a new scholarly edition of the letters of Vincent van Gogh (1853–1890). This is a collaborative venture with the Van Gogh Museum in Amsterdam.[9] More than 900 letters of Van Gogh are now known to exist.[10] The vast majority of these are addressed to his brother Theo. Only about 40 replies have been preserved. Other correspondents include Vincent's mother, his father and his sister Willemien, as well as artists including Anton van Rappard (1858–1892), Emile Bernard (1868–1941) and Paul Gauguin (1848–1903). The importance of Van Gogh's letters was recognised early on. In 1893 a series of articles was published in the *Mercure de France* containing extensive quotes from the letters to Emile Bernard. These were published in book form in 1911.[11] Three years later, Van Gogh's sister-in-law, Johanna van Gogh–Bonger, published the letters to Theo.[12] A more extensive edition was published in the 1950s.[13] For a long time, this edition formed the basis for the many translations of the letters and for Van Gogh research. The latest edition in four volumes dates from 1990.[14] However, all existing editions are incomplete, unreliable and modernised to a significant degree. Van Gogh–Bonger omitted entire passages, reduced to initials the names of persons who were still alive or whom she disliked, and adjusted words on her own initiative. The later editions also left out substantial parts of

---

9 The edition is being compiled by two experienced editors: Leo Jansen and Hans Luijten, supported by an editorial board and an advisory committee of experts.

10 The information given here on the Van Gogh project is based on two articles (see notes below) and an unpublished lecture by the two editors. Both have supplied me with additional information in informal discussions.

11 *Lettres de Vincent van Gogh à Emile Bernard*, ed. Ambroise Vollard (Paris, 1911).

12 Vincent van Gogh, *Brieven aan zijn broeder*, ed. J. van Gogh–Bonger (Amsterdam, 1914), 3 vols.

13 *Verzamelde brieven van Vincent van Gogh*, ed. J. van Gogh–Bonger and V.W. van Gogh (Amsterdam, 1952–54), 4 vols.

14 *De brieven van Vincent van Gogh*, ed. Han van Crimpen and Monique Berends–Albert (The Hague, 1990), 4 vols.

letters and included mangled sections of text. Furthermore, all existing editions contain—sometimes drastically—modernised versions of the texts and the French letters of Van Gogh only in translation. And none of the editions contain adequate commentaries or annotations to explain the letters. Thus a reliable scholarly edition of the correspondence of Van Gogh is urgently needed for Van Gogh research and for the compilation of reliable, complete translations.

The new scholarly edition will be based on letter-for-letter transcriptions of the original manuscripts. For the first time these transcriptions will include all variants. Every slip of the pen, deletion and addition will be registered. For example, in a letter of December 1883, Vincent confessed to his brother Theo: "In day time in daily life I sometimes look as insensitive as a wild boar perhaps and I can well understand that people find me crude. People are much like brushes: those with the finest looks are not the finest in practice." Van Gogh later deleted this analogy, but it is interesting to know that he did write it.[15]

The new transcriptions will provide a text of the letters that is as complete and as reliable as possible. Study of the manuscripts has already revealed many misreadings in the existing editions, varying from misspelled names to hilarious nonsense. In February 1885, Van Gogh wrote about a painting by Collin. Previous editions give the name Cottin. Elsewhere the name Hillen is given as Helleu. Mistakes of this type occurred easily because the letters were not annotated in previous editions and the editors were therefore never forced to deal with the problem of misspelled names that needed explanation. Every editor of letters knows that it is during the annotation phase that many mistakes are found in the texts. As a result of misreadings, the 1990 edition repeatedly puzzles the reader.

A scholarly edition of the letters of Van Gogh cannot ignore the fact that the manuscripts of the letters are aesthetic objects in themselves and that they, as material text carriers, also contain relevant information. Van Gogh was a spontaneous letter writer who visualised his emotions in his writing as he wrote. In several cases the handwriting is particularly expressive or emotional, with unusually large or sweeping script, multiple underlinings, etc. (see illus. 6).[16] This striking characteristic of Van Gogh's letters cannot be reflected in a traditional printed edition or in its annotations. During the transition from one medium—the original letter—to the other—the printed book—essential information is lost. This is even more true for the letters in which text and image are inextricably related. One of the

---

[15] Cf. Hans Luijten, "'As it came into my pen': A New Edition of the Correspondence of Vincent van Gogh," *Van Gogh Museum Journal 1996* (Amsterdam, 1997), 91–92.

[16] "'As it came into my pen,'" 98–99.

zeggen met de lippen — (vriendelyk of onvriendelyk) Zulke intentie meeningen
eigentlyk is dat minder dan niets
Gy moogt van my denken wat gy goedvindt Theo
maar ik zeg u dat het geen verbeelding van
my is ik zeg u Pa wil niet
Ik zie nu wat ik zag toen ik sprak toen
vierkant Tegen Pa ik spreek nu
in elk geval hoe het ook loope wederom tegen
Pa als willende niet als makende het
onmogelyk. Het is verdomd
handelden intelligent maar hier !!!!!!
En al wat gy er aan deed en doet het wordt 3/4 & rechteloos doorheen
Het is ... met een handdruk t.a.t. Vincent.
en dat is my te bar

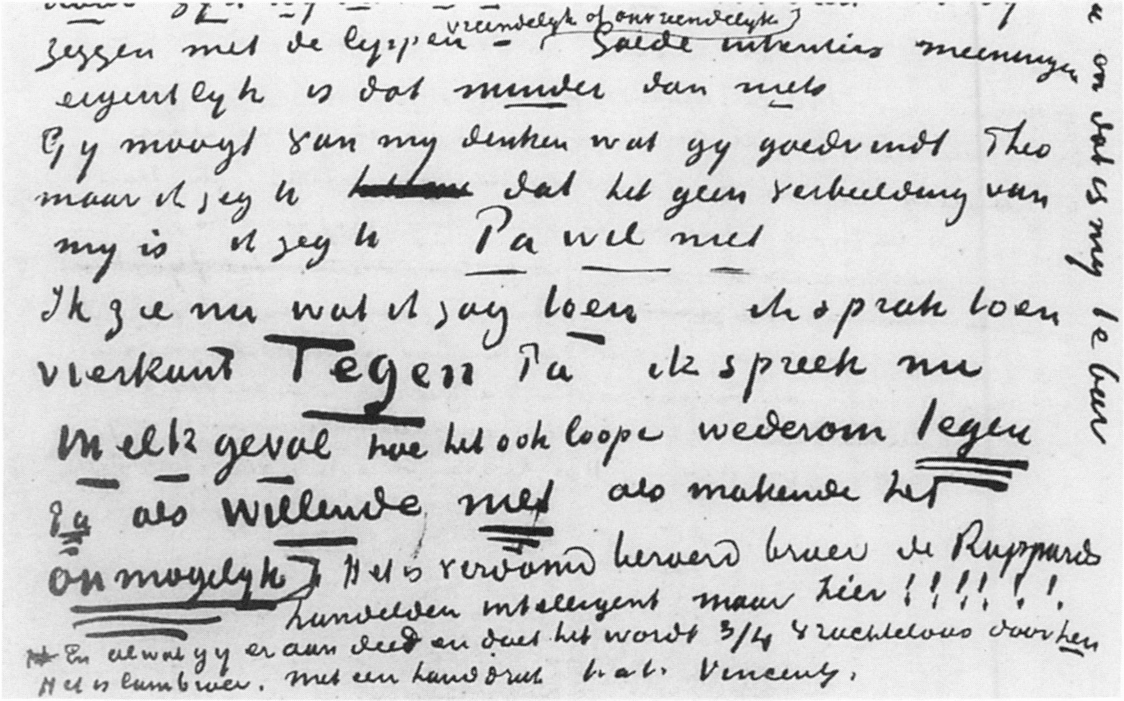

Illus. 6. Fragment of a letter of Vincent van Gogh (reproduced by permission of the Van Gogh Museum, Amsterdam).

best examples of this is a letter to Theo from September 1881. In this eight-page letter, Vincent informs his brother in word and image about changes in the manner in which he draws figures (see illus. 7–11). With the drawings that are part of the letter, one of the notes Van Gogh makes is: "This is a field or a stubble field, where people are ploughing and sowing, made a relatively large sketch of this with threatening storm." And: "The two other sketches are poses of diggers. I hope to make several more of these." Brief sketches of this type were sometimes part of the letter itself, and sometimes enclosed on separate sheets. Van Gogh's emotional handwriting and the fascinating combinations of word and image can only be seen in their fullest glory in the original manuscripts. The second-best solution is to add a CD-ROM to the scholarly edition containing facsimiles and transcriptions of all the letters.

The letters of Van Gogh will be included in the new edition with their original wording, spelling and punctuation. Parallel to the original text, an integral English translation will be given, and the comments and annotations will be in English only. The comments will contain extensive exposés of, for example, the art trade in which Theo and uncle Vincent were active, as well as correspondence conventions in the nineteenth century and within the Van Gogh family. The annotations to the letters include linguistic, biographical, literary and topographical notes as well as comments in the realm of art and cultural history. Every work of art referred to by Van Gogh, if at all possible, will be identified. The editors will also explore the likely source of the many quotations in the letters. Van Gogh read widely, and what he had read was assimilated in his letters. His quotes are often not literal; he modified quotations for his own purposes. In these cases one reads in the literature on Van Gogh that he must have made a mistake, or that he must have been quoting from memory, but in some cases these alleged errors are intentional or point to the edition which Van Gogh may have used. For the annotations, for the first time systematic use will be made of the remaining family correspondence. Father and mother Van Gogh, brother Theo and the sisters wrote several thousands letters to one another in which they also kept one another informed of and commented on Vincent's experiences and choices.

One of the most difficult problems confronting the editors is the dating of the letters. Extensive discussions in the Van Gogh literature address the problem of the dating. Many of the letters are undated, and in some other cases the date was added later by someone else. The combination of facts from different letters, the family correspondence and other external information may help to determine dates more precisely. This process has already led to several minor shifts and a few major ones. And, as a domino effect, new dates have consequences on the dating and order of other letters.

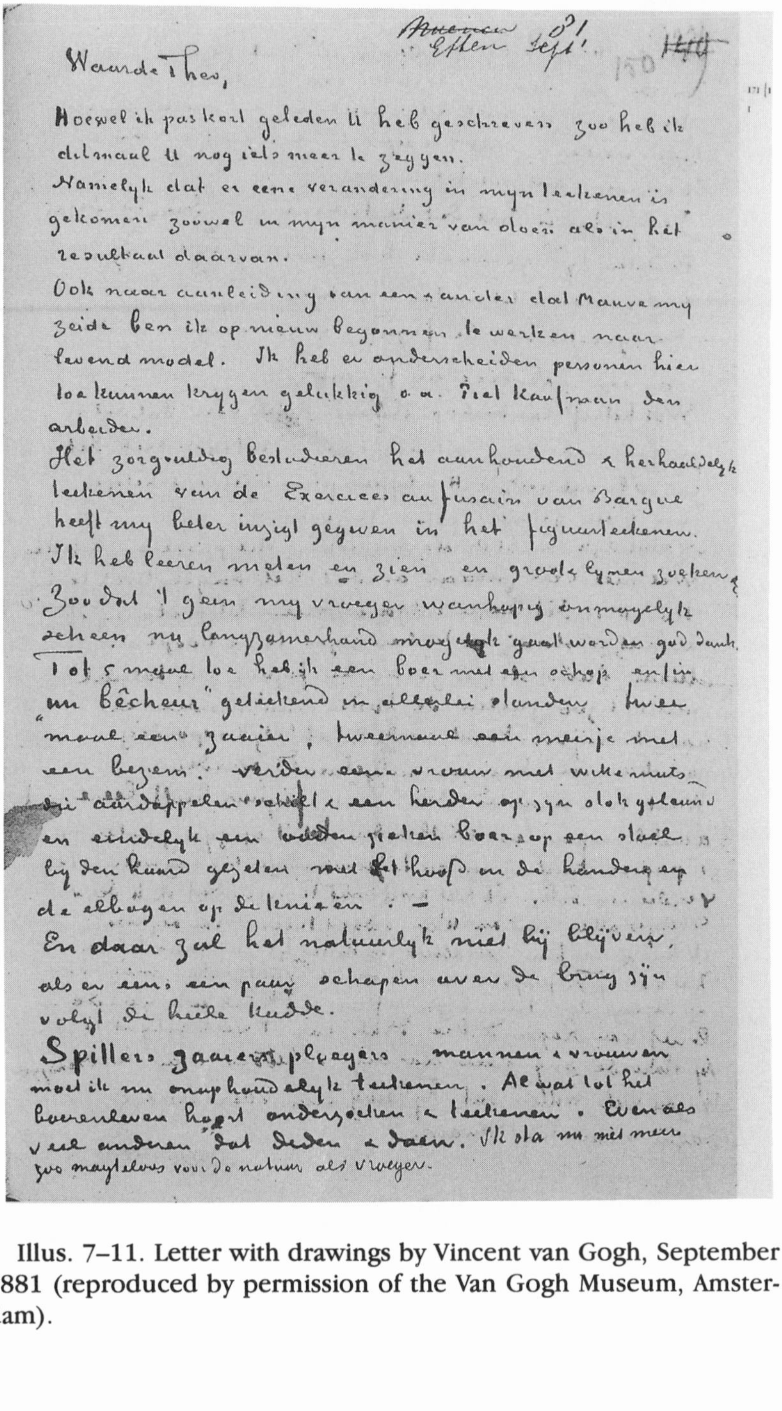

Etten Sept. 81

Waarde Theo,

Hoewel ik pas kort geleden U heb geschreven zoo heb ik dit maal U nog iets meer te zeggen.
Namelyk dat er eene verandering in myn teekenen is gekomen zoowel in myn manier van doen als in het resultaat daarvan.
Ook naar aanleiding van een & ander dat Mauve my zeide ben ik op nieuw begonnen te werken naar levend model. Ik heb er onderscheiden personen hier toe kunnen krygen gelukkig o.a. Piet Kaufman den arbeider.
Het zorgvuldig bestudeeren het aanhoudend & herhaaldelyk teekenen van de Exercices au fusain van Bargue heeft my beter inzigt gegeven in het figuurteekenen.
Ik heb leeren meten en zien en groote lynen zoeken & zoodat 't geen my vroeger wanhopig onmogelyk scheen nu langzamerhand mogelyk gaat worden God dank.
Tot 5 maal toe heb ik een boer met een schop enfin un "bêcheur" geteekend in allerlei standen, twee maal een zaaier, twee maal een meisje met een bezem. Verder eene vrouw met witte muts die aardappelen schilt & een herder op zyn stok geleund en eindelyk een ouden zieken boer op een stoel by den haard gezeten met het hoofd in de handen en de ellebogen op de knieën. —
En daar zal het natuurlyk niet by blyven, als er eens een paar schapen over de brug zyn volgt de heele kudde.
Spitters, zaaiers, ploegers, mannen & vrouwen moet ik nu onophoudelyk teekenen. Al wat tot het boerenleven hoort onderzoeken & teekenen. Even als veel anderen dat deden & doen. Ik sta nu niet meer zoo magteloos voor de natuur als vroeger.

Illus. 7–11. Letter with drawings by Vincent van Gogh, September 1881 (reproduced by permission of the Van Gogh Museum, Amsterdam).

Dit is een akker of aardappelveld waar men aan 't ploegen
& zaaien is. Ik heb daarvan een vrij groote schets
met opkomend onweer.

De twee andere schetsjes zijn poses van spitters.
Ik hoop er daarvan nog verscheiden te maken.

De andere zaaier heeft een korf.

Enorm graag zou ik eens een vrouw laten poseeren als met een zaaikorf om dat figuurtje te vinden dat ik in 't voorjaar U heb laten zien en dat ge op den voorgrond van 't eerste schetsje ziet

Enfin zooals Mauve zegt, "de fabriek is in volle werking".

Als ge niet en kunt denk dan aan het papier Ingres van de kleur van ongebleekt linnen zoo mogelijk het sterkere soort. Schrijf my eens spoedig als gij kunt in elk geval, en ontvang een handdruk in gedachten.

t. à t.
Vincent

A related problem is the fact that, in the course of time, the proper order of the manuscripts has been changed. Some pages have been exchanged or placed in other letters, or separate sheets have been grouped as a single letter. What is more, separate sketches have been removed from the letters in which they were originally enclosed. As a result, the editors have been forced to continually wonder which pages belong together, and which separate sketches were enclosed in which letters. The material study of the paper types, the ink used and any watermarks may give important clues in this respect. In a few instances, recent research has resulted in the discovery of an unknown fragment of a letter. For example, until recently a pen-and-ink drawing of a woman's head was classified as an independent sketch (see illus. 12), but the text on the back shows that it was originally an illustration within a letter (see illus. 13).[17]

Such a scholarly edition of the Van Gogh letters will have a considerable effect on the Van Gogh research. The authentic texts of the letters, the new dating, and the many annotations in which much information from the family correspondence is included will undermine many existing certainties, theories and assumptions. In the past, the letters served as the most important and final word in the many disputes concerning the life and work of Van Gogh, while the fragmentary legacy that the letters represent was not taken into consideration. Recently an exhibition of paintings from the Gachet collection was organised in the Grand Palais in Paris. Gachet was the doctor who attended Van Gogh in Auvers-sur-Oise during the last few months of his life. In addition to Van Gogh, Gachet knew other artists, acquiring a large art collection in the course of his lifetime. The problem, however, is that Gachet also liked to paint, and he sometimes copied paintings his friends had made. He urged his son Paul to do the same, as well as a girl that he was teaching to paint. In this game of copying and replicating, Van Gogh was sometimes a player, making the chaos complete. Doctor Gachet, for example, made an engraving based on a painting by Jacob Jordaens (1593–1678), Van Gogh made a painting based on the engraving by Gachet, and the girl made a copy of the painting by Van Gogh. The results are only logical: Van Gogh experts continue to debate the authenticity of paintings from Auvers-sur-Oise. One example is the famous portrait of Doctor Gachet in the Musée d'Orsay, which is said to be a poor copy of another portrait that was sold in 1990 for eighty-two and a half million dollars and now belongs

---

[17] Leo Jansen, "The Van Gogh Letters Project: New Findings and Old," *Van Gogh Museum Journal 1997–1998* (Amsterdam, 1999), 59–60.

Illus. 12. Drawing by Vincent van Gogh (reproduced by permission of the Van Gogh Museum, Amsterdam).

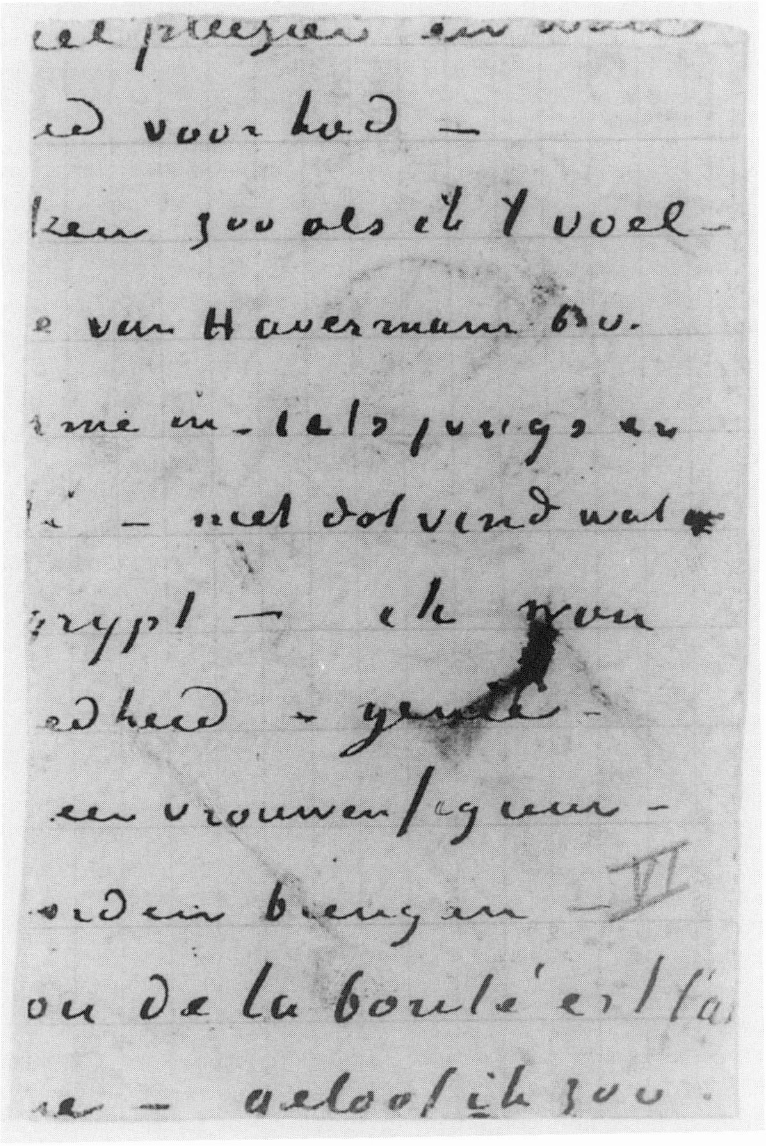

Illus. 13. Fragment of a letter of Vincent van Gogh (reproduced by permission of the Van Gogh Museum, Amsterdam).

to the Ryoei Saito collection in Japan. In the discussion concerning the Gachet portrait, the fact that it was never mentioned in letters from Vincent to Theo is considered an important argument against its authenticity. The other side claims that there probably was a letter but that it was lost. In the same way, the entire dispute involving the painting called the "Sunflowers," which the Japanese insurance company Yasuda purchased at Christie's in 1987 for more than forty million dollars, is based on a highly controversial interpretation of a passage in a letter that Vincent wrote to Theo. Discussions of this type, however, will bear little fruit as long as there is no scholarly edition of the letters that were not lost.

According to the editors of the new edition, the Van Gogh researchers must learn to live with uncertainty and doubt. We have much, but there is also much that we do not have. The remaining letters provide us with a report that is selective rather than complete of everything that Van Gogh read and saw. We therefore have nothing more than a fragmentary picture of Van Gogh's life and work. The editors estimate that half of Van Gogh's correspondence has been lost and that the losses started at a very early stage. In a newspaper dated 5 May 1934, Vincent's sister Lies answered a question concerning the letters as follows: "His letters? Yes, he wrote an incredible amount, sometimes about the same subject three times on one day. Mother would hide the others from Father." And the son of Hermanus Tersteeg, who was Vincent's former head of the art shop Goupil in The Hague, told an art historian that they had decided one day to raise the heating by a few degrees: "And we quite deliberately threw two or three hundred letters from Vincent van Gogh which were in our way into the fire; my father did not consider all that writing so important," under the motto "artists should not write, they should paint!"[18] These two examples clearly demonstrate that the remaining letters of Van Gogh will never be able to answer all questions or to solve every dispute involving his paintings.

The Van Gogh letters are not a separate entity, but are related to his drawings and paintings. It is for this reason that the new scholarly edition of the letters could have important consequences on the art market. Irrespective of the problem of the "real" or the "false" Van Goghs, there is the chronology of the paintings. Every shift in the order of the letters based on a new dating will, in many cases, change the chronological order of the paintings. And the value of the paintings is closely related to that chronology. An early Van Gogh is generally

---

18 " 'As it came into my pen,' " 100–101.

worth less than a later one. When you change the dating of a letter, the decision may involve millions of dollars. At last, we can say: we have made it. Scholarly editing has become big business, and editors have become a threat—or an asset—to art collectors and museums throughout the world. Is there anyone who would still dare to question the social importance of scholarly editing?

Dutch Scholarly Editing: The Historical–Critical Edition in Practice

ANNEMARIE KETS–VREE

WHEN MODERN SCHOLARLY EDITING started to develop into a specialized area of Dutch literary studies in the mid-1970s, it was only logical to look to research traditions in other countries. Dutch editors primarily turned to the Anglo–American and German-language traditions of scholarly editing. The establishment of a national institute for text editions—the Constantijn Huygens Instituut—made it possible for Dutch scholarly editing to take up relatively quickly a position in international discussions on editorial issues and, where it was useful, to develop its own working methods.

In keeping with German editorial studies, Dutch scholarly editing generally distinguishes three types of editions: historical–critical editions ('historisch–kritische Ausgabe'), study editions ('Studienausgabe') and reading editions, intended for the general public ('Leseausgabe'). All three types contain a sound scholarly text that has been purged of corruptions acquired through the years. The historical–critical edition distinguishes itself by documenting the genesis and development of the text, from the oldest known draft up to the final revised edition. The differences between the edited text and the other versions are presented in an apparatus of variants. In addition, all relevant secondary information is documented in summaries or incorporated in full: letters discussing the genesis, production and transmission of the work, contracts with publishers, reviews and so on. The historical–critical edition has been characterized as a 'semi-manufactured product',[1] because it supplies the basis for further literary research. The study edition is extensively annotated in order to elucidate the cultural and historical background of the text or to outline the current state of affairs in research concerning the text and its author. Finally, reading editions always contain a concise introduction concerning the textual history and an explanation of the criteria used in constituting the text. Sometimes these editions also include explanatory notes and a selection of variants.

These three categories and their relevant characteristics could suggest that there is a strict division between the edition types, but in practice the distinction is not all that clear. There are various reasons for this.[2] In a small language area like Dutch, texts are only rarely published in different types of editions. Editors therefore look for ways of achieving multiple objectives within a single edition, without compromising their scholarly principles. Developments in academic research and education also play a part. Initially, research in the Netherlands was largely text-oriented. Under the influence of the Anglo–American 'New Critics', efforts were concentrated on the analysis, interpretation, and evaluation of individual poems, narratives and novels. It was only through close reading that a literary work could be accessed, due to the fact that it was defined as an autonomous and sealed-off environment. Authorial variants were considered to be signals that could bring hidden meanings to light or point the way to the author's poetics.[3] The traditional historical–critical edition offers the very material that text-oriented research and research into poetics needed and still needs. In recent years, a shift can be seen towards a more context-oriented approach. Emphasis is increasingly placed on the conditions under which the texts were created, produced, and received. Editors now face the question of whether and to what extent it is possible to determine the effect of these conditions on the production of a certain text or version of a text, and to incorporate this in their editions.[4] Apart from these outside conditions, the edition is of course also determined by the nature of the text being published and by the primary and secondary documents available. In order to do

---

[1] G. J. Dorleijn, 'Stand van zaken moderne editietechniek.' In: *Nederlandse letterkunde* 3.IV (1998), 372–83; quotation on 374.

[2] H. T. M. van Vliet, 'Editionswissenschaft in den Niederlanden.' In: *editio: Internationales Jahrbuch für Editionswissenschaft* 8 (1994), 1–21. See also: Dick van Vliet, 'Das Constantijn Huygens Instituut—Ein Zentrum für Editionsphilologie in den Niederlanden.' In: *Philologie und Philosophie:* [. . .]. Ed. H. G. Senger (Tübingen, 1998), 122–34.

[3] *Varianten bij Achterberg*. Edited and annotated by R. L. K. Fokkema, 2 vols. (Amsterdam, 1973), 2: 11–25.

[4] Peter de Bruijn and Annemarie Kets–Vree, 'Produktion und Kontext: [. . .]' In: *editio: Internationales Jahrbuch für Editionswissenschaft* 12 (1998), 161–64.

justice to both internal and external conditions, the editor may choose to consolidate characteristics of different types of editions into a new configuration. This is the case, for instance, in the scholarly edition of the novel called *Max Havelaar or the Coffee Auctions of the Dutch Trading Company* (1860).[5]

Max Havelaar is an autobiographical novel, written by Multatuli (pseudonym of Eduard Douwes Dekker, 1820–87), and it is considered to be the unchallenged masterpiece of nineteenth-century Dutch literature. The work is strongly inspired by *Uncle Tom's Cabin* (1852): a critical message in an attractive wrapping. Multatuli's criticism focused on the colonial policy in the Dutch East Indies. He wrote from personal experience: the seed of his work was a conflict in 1856 between the author, who was a government official in the East Indies at the time, and his superiors, a conflict that ultimately led to his dismissal. The author's objective in writing the book was two-fold: to improve the position of the Javanese, which was an important issue in the conflict, and to rehabilitate himself.

Some interesting witness documents of *Max Havelaar* have come down to us, as well as numerous letters and other material containing information that sheds light on the genesis and development of the text, the author's compositional method, and the influence exerted by others on the transmission of the text.[6] In cases such as these, the historical–critical edition is a logical choice, because it is the only kind of edition that allows the presentation of a full range of material. The problem, however, is that an edition of this type does not do justice to another essential aspect of the text: *Max Havelaar* is also a text which is set in a historically remote world. The classes of nineteenth-century society, symbolized by the Coffee Auctions, no longer exist, and the former colony known as the Dutch East Indies is now an independent state. The gap between then and now could cause difficulties of understanding for the modern-day reader. Then there is also the question of genre. As already stated, *Max Havelaar* is autobiographical, and as such reflects reality. At the same time, it is an *apologia*; the main character, Multatuli himself, is made to appear in the best possible light, most of all when the facts were not entirely in his favor. This raises the question how fiction in this case relates to the facts. Therefore, in the case of *Max Havelaar*, it was decided to supply the text with a number of annotations, thereby combining two types of edition.

---

5 Multatuli, *Max Havelaar of De koffiveilingen der Nederlandsche Handelmaatschappy.* Historical–critical edition, compiled by A. Kets–Vree (Assen etc., 1992). Monumenta Literaria Neerlandica VI, 1–2.

6 Annemarie Kets–Vree, 'Wahrheit, Dichtung und Varianten in Multatulis *Max Havelaar*.' In: *editio: Internationales Jahrbuch für Editionswissenschaft* 12 (1998), 79–88.

*　　　*　　　*

Until now, the exchange of ideas between European and Anglo–American schools of scholarly editing has focused on theoretical aspects and issues. Central to this discussion is the volume called *Contemporary German Editorial Theory*, a selection in English translation of key essays on German textual scholarship.[7] Peter Shillingsburg, for instance, based his critical comments on German editing on this volume.[8] However crucial these discussions are—they concern the very heart of editorial theory—there is a risk that they will divert attention from the day-to-day reality of editing, where theory is applied in practical work and where compromises are sought. A balanced view on contemporary editing can only be achieved by taking into consideration both theory and practice. Language barriers between Anglo–American and European scholars, however, form an obstacle to each side's becoming acquainted with the other's practical results. In this essay, therefore, I will focus attention on the manner in which Dutch scholarly editing has put the theoretical concept of the historical–critical edition, as defined by German scholars, into practice, by drawing on the experience of two recent editions. I will be concentrating on two issues: first of all, the diversity and complexity of the material available, and secondly, the implications for the choice of the base text and the presentation of the variants, which are two major aspects of the historical–critical edition.

*　　　*　　　*

Let us return to *Max Havelaar*. The textual history of this novel and the authorisation of its different versions are highly complex.[9] This is largely due to the influence exerted by outsiders, such as publishers, compositors and printers, on the transmission of the text. The sizable volume of letters written between the author and his publishers provides a fair insight into the course of that transmission, but leaves a number of questions unanswered. This prompted the editor to turn to the Anglo–American tradition. It was through analytical-bibliographical research—which is a new element brought into the historical–critical edition—that an edition came to light which was

---

7 Edited by Hans Walter Gabler, George Bornstein and Gillian Borland Pierce (Ann Arbor, Michigan, 1995).

8 'A Resistance to Contemporary German Editorial Theory and Practice.' In: *editio: Internationales Jahrbuch für Editionswissenschaft* 12 (1998), 138–50.

9 Siegfried Scheibe, 'Theoretical Problems of the Authorization and Constitution of Texts.' In: *Contemporary German Editorial Theory*, 171–91.

hitherto unknown and which forms a vital link in the textual history.[10]

M   (1859)
↓
D1   (1860)
↓
D2   (1860)
↓
D2d   (?)
↓
D3   (1871)
↓
D4   (1875)
↓
D5a ⎫
D5b ⎬ (1881)
D5c ⎪
D5d ⎭

1. Stemma of *Max Havelaar*.

This stemma (Figure 1) summarizes all witness documents relevant to *Max Havelaar* and provides an insight into how they relate to one another. The draft manuscript is not extant, but the fair copy is (M, 1859). It consists of 123 densely filled double sheets of paper in the author's handwriting. Various circumstances prevented Multatuli from preparing the text for publication. He left this to Jacob van Lennep, an influential man of letters at the time. Van Lennep did not limit himself to the usual editorial activities of correcting writing and spelling mistakes, but he was very liberal in altering Multatuli's text. For example, he divided it into chapters, omitted controversial passages and added comments of his own. He did not discuss these measures with the author, even though they frequently wrote to one another. He did, however, discuss the delicate balance between the actual background and how it was reflected in the novel. Multatuli had already applied a level of fictionalisation by renaming the main characters in the conflict—often high-ranking dignitaries in official political circles. But because actual places and dates were used, it was not difficult to discover their true identity. Van Lennep wanted to leave out the dates because he feared charges of slander. After lengthy discussions Multatuli finally agreed, but the place names were to remain

---

[10] Annemarie Kets–Vree, 'Een onbekende druk van "Max Havelaar" uit de negentiende eeuw.' In: *De nieuwe taalgids* 78.IV (1985), 330–40.

as they were, because his criticism was exclusively aimed at the region where he had been employed. Van Lennep went his own way, however, and substituted also the names of places with dots (Figure 2), and this is how the book was published (D1, 1860; Figure 3).

Although one would expect Multatuli to respond to this interference with his text, he did not. On the contrary, he thanked Van Lennep for his meticulous efforts and remarked, mostly in a positive manner, on a few of the changes that he had noticed. He did not voice any criticism until many months later, when the book did not have the desired effects, despite the commotion it had caused. According to Multatuli, this was because of the changes made by Van Lennep, which he now referred to as 'mutilations' and which he wanted corrected in subsequent editions. Three more unauthorised editions followed; one of which was an illicit so-called duplicate edition, based on the second edition, which was released entirely without the author's knowledge (D2, 1860; D2d, ?; D3, 1871).

In 1874 Multatuli had the opportunity to revise his work. Two factors had an important effect on that revision. First, he was by then an experienced author, and second, his original idealism had been replaced by feelings of bitterness and disillusionment. The first resulted in numerous stylistic changes; the second in extensive additions to the text. In almost two hundred 'Notes and Clarifications', Multatuli gave the actual background of the events, responded to all of the criticism he had received in the intervening period, and gave his views on current colonial matters. He was also closely involved in the production process. He meticulously corrected the proofs, repeatedly asked for revisions, and even occupied himself with typographical details. In 1875, the 'First edition revised by the author' was published (D4). The 'Second edition revised by the author' was published six years later, in 1881. The process that had been initiated in 1875 was continued and perfected, and the number of notes and clarifications was increased. Multatuli died in 1887, which made the 1881 impression the final revised edition. Variants within this one impression arose from corrections made during its printing (D5a, D5b, D5c and D5d, 1881). Comparing these variants has established that D5d corresponds most closely to the final intentions of the author. The other copies contained rejected readings, but were not destroyed by the publisher for reasons of economy.[II]

The 'family tree' of *Max Havelaar* contains a number of reprints that Multatuli never assisted in nor gave his consent to. However, these unauthorised versions cannot be left out of the textual research,

---

[II] Annemarie Kets–Vree, ' "Tweede door den auteur herziene uitgaaf": Een stukje tekstgeschiedenis van *Max Havelaar*.' In: *Over Multatuli* 25 (1990), 46–55.

2. Manuscript of *Max Havelaar*, with censoring interferences by Van Lennep.

VIJFDE HOOFDSTUK.

(Door Stern opgesteld.)

Er was 's morgens te tien ure eene ongewone bewe-
ging op den grooten weg, die de afdeeling *P....ng*
verbindt met *Leb....* //Groote weg", is misschien wat veel
gezegd voor het breed voetpad, dat men, uit beleefd-
heid, en bij gebrek aan beter, de //weg" noemde; maar
als men met een vierspannig rijtuig vertrok van (*S....ng*)
de hoofdplaats van *B....* met het voornemen zich te
begeven naar *R.... B....ng* de nieuwe hoofdplaats van
het *Leb.... sche*, kon men nagenoeg zeker zijn, te eeni-
ger tijd daar aan te komen. 't Was dus een weg. Wèl
bleef men gedurig steken in den modder, die in de
B....sche laaglanden zwaar, kleijerig en klevend is, wel
was men telkens genoodzaakt de hulp in te roepen
van de bewoners der naastbij gelegene dorpen — ook
al waren ze niet zeer nabij, want de dorpen zijn niet
menigvuldig in die streken —; maar als men dan ein-
delijk geslaagd was een twintigtal landbouwers uit den
omtrek bijeen te krijgen, duurde het gewoonlijk niet
zeer lang, voor men paarden en wagen weder op vas-
ten grond had gebragt. De koetsier klapte met de zweep,

3. First edition of *Max Havelaar*,
with censoring interferences by Van Lennep.

because printer's errors and other interventions in one of these versions may well have inadvertently been incorporated in the authorised
fourth and fifth editions. Of course this does not mean that all versions
in the stemma are qualified to be the base text for the edition.

The choice of the base text is one of the most important decisions
pertaining to the edition. The base text is the version which is usually
the only one to be included in full in the edition. The editor subjects
the base text to a critical study, corrects spelling, printing and typesetting errors and thus constitutes the so-called edited text. The other
versions, in so far as they deviate from the base text, are included in
the apparatus of variants.

Following the German school, Dutch editors in their choice of base text take as their guiding principle that there is no guiding principle. The premise is that all versions are equal, providing they are authorised.[12] Thus there are no fixed rules, and there is even no preference for, for example, either the *editio princeps* or the *ultima manus*-edition. In the series of scholarly text editions published by the Constantijn Huygens Instituut (the Monumenta Literaria Neerlandica), both extremes are represented. The historical–critical edition of the Poems of J. C. Bloem (1887–1966), for example, is based on the first completed version of each poem. That could be a completed draft version, a manuscript or typescript, or a version published in a periodical or a volume.[13] For the edition of the Poems of J. H. Leopold (1865–1925), on the other hand, the last version authorised by the poet and published during his lifetime was used.[14] The editors of the Bloem edition opted for the early versions in order to establish a well-organized, progressive presentation of the further textual development in the apparatus of variants. In the Leopold edition, the reliability of the versions played an important part. Although the early versions were authorised, the author himself had not corrected them, which is why the *ultima manus*-edition was used.

The criterion of authorisation limits the number of possible base texts for *Max Havelaar* to the two extremes that history has handed down to us: the manuscript and the first edition at the one end and the revised editions of 1875 and 1881 at the other. In order to choose between these, various elements must be taken into consideration. In the case of the Bloem and Leopold editions, three arguments played a part: the type of edition, the structure of the apparatus of variants, and the status of the various versions. These are of course also important arguments with reference to *Max Havelaar*. In addition, there are a number of other factors: the compositional method of the author and biographical and literary-historical circumstances must be considered, as must matters that pertain to the reception and influence of the various versions.

---

[12] Siegfried Scheibe, 'Zu einigen Grundprinzipien einer historisch–kritischen Ausgabe.' In: *Texte und Varianten: Probleme ihrer Edition und Interpretation*. Ed. Gunter Martens and Hans Zeller (München, 1971), 1–44. See also: Waltraud Hagen, 'Frühe Hand—späte Hand? Methodische und praktische Überlegungen zur Wahl der Textgrundlage in Werkeditionen.' In: *Zu Werk und Text: Beiträge zur Textologie*. Ed. Siegfried Scheibe and Christel Laufer (Berlin, 1991), 111–24.

[13] J. C. Bloem, *Gedichten*. Historical–critical edition, compiled by A. L. Sötemann and H. T. M. van Vliet (Amsterdam etc., 1979). Monumenta Literaria Neerlandica I, 1–2.

[14] J. H. Leopold, *Gedichten*. Historical–critical edition, compiled by A. L. Sötemann and H. T. M. van Vliet (Amsterdam etc., 1983). Monumenta Literaria Neerlandica II, 1–2.

Multatuli is one of those authors who continually revise their work. This working method, which the author believes results in an improved text, justifies using the last authorised edition as the base text. The problem, however, is that the 'late' *Max Havelaar* is the work of a man who had undergone extensive development in terms of both his views and his profession. The manuscript and the first edition are much closer to the events of 1856 and the literary processing thereof in 1860. The objection to the manuscript as Multatuli gave it to Van Lennep is that it still contained gaps and other shortcomings. Although the last 'layer' of the manuscript no longer contained these flaws, it was, like the first printed edition, also altered to a significant degree by Van Lennep's actions. The authorisation of these versions is further complicated by Multatuli's continually changing views in this respect. From the perspective of reception, the first printed version is to be preferred: it was the censured version that had an enormous effect in both literary and social and political terms. That effect was witnessed by a large number of reviews and essays, some of which in turn demonstrably resulted in certain changes in the last two printed editions.

The only conclusion which can be drawn is that there is no single logical base text for *Max Havelaar*. Each choice could well be defended with varying degrees of success. Each version has its advantages and disadvantages. Because they differ so much, these do not cancel each other out. For this reason practical arguments tipped the balance. In the historical–critical edition the primary function of the base text is to support the apparatus of variants. If the various versions differ significantly in terms of the size of the texts, the arrangement of the apparatus is best served by using the most extensive version as the base text. In the case of *Max Havelaar*, this is the final revised edition of 1881 (D5d). The variants in the other sources were included in a lemmatized apparatus that is partly regressive and partly progressive: regressive in that the *ultima manus*-edition is its starting point, progressive because the variants were presented in the order in which they came into being (see Figure 4).

Although, as already indicated, all versions are equal in principle, some versions are more equal than others. The base text is given undue preference, a fact which is hard to avoid. It is, after all, the only version of the text that is transformed into an edited text and included in full, and it is also, in the case of *Max Havelaar*, the basis for the annotations. It will also usually be the version that will be quoted in later studies. Nevertheless, the historical–critical edition is not intended to present a sort of 'standard text'. This is done by the

ACHTSTE HOOFDSTUK < [streep]	M^a
Achtste Hoofdstuk [streep]	M^b
ACHTSTE HOOFDSTUK.	D^1-D^4

1

Havelaar < *Havelaar*	M^a
Vervolg van het opstel van Stern Havelaar	M^{b*}
(Vervolg van het opstel van Stern.) Havelaar	D^1, D^3
(Vervolg van het Opstel van Stern.) Havelaar	D^2, D^{2d}

1-2

te *Rangkas-Betoeng* aanwezig waren < aanwezig waren te *Rangkas-Betoeng*	M^a
aanwezig waren te R( )-Bet( )	M^b
aanwezig waren te R... B...ng	D^1-D^1

2-3

tot den volgenden dag te vertoeven <	
te vertoeven tot den volgenden dag	M-D^3

3

Sebab[11] < 'Sebab' (raadsvergadering)	M
Sebab (raadsvergadering)	D^1-D^3
Sebab[47]	D^4
Sebab[1a]	D^{4a}

4

eens in de maand plaats < plaats eens in de maand	M-D^3

4-5

aan sommige < sommigen	M-D^3

4. The apparatus of variants of *Max Havelaar*.

reading edition, in which the base text is autonomous. Sometimes, as with *Max Havelaar*, the same base text is chosen for both editions.[15] But in other cases a work can be published in two different versions. As mentioned above, the scholarly Bloem edition is based on early versions of the poems, while the reading edition of the same texts is based on the *ultima manus*-edition because the editors wanted to honor the final self-presentation by the author.[16] The material required for this was taken from the historical–critical edition, which can therefore also in this respect be considered a 'semi-manufactured product'. The Constantijn Huygens Instituut consciously strives towards marketing editions for the general reading public through commercial publishers as a spinoff of the specialized scholarly editions. The two different Multatuli and Bloem editions serve as examples of this policy.

*   *   *

Sometimes it is impossible to select a single base text and then include the other versions in a variant apparatus because the versions differ too much. That was the case with the narrative called *De uitvreter* (*The Sponger*) by Nescio (J. F. H. Grönloh, 1882–1961).[17] *The Sponger* is a story about a group of friends who are impractical idealists and artistic bohemians. The main character is Japie, who continually lives off of others and is therefore called 'the sponger'. He prefers to spend his days staring at the water. On a nice summer day he puts an end to his life: he steps off a bridge and drowns. *The Sponger* is an apparently simple story that actually resulted from a lengthy and difficult process of genesis. Because Nescio saved nearly all of his papers, including scribbled notes and the beginnings of a few lines, that process can be followed virtually step by step. It started in 1903, when he wrote a short sketch entitled 'Heimwee' ('Homesick'). The main character is a poor painter. In certain ways, this painter is a preview of the later 'sponger' character: he is a bon-vivant, but does not sponge on others. In the six years that followed, Nescio wrote another eleven, usually incomplete sketches and stories, all of which can be related to the story *The Sponger* and/or its main character. Collectively, they represent the first phase of the genesis of *The Sponger*.

Nescio's compositional method during this first phase cannot be placed in one of the two usual categories, which can be characterized

---

[15] Multatuli, *Max Havelaar of De koffiveilingen der Nederlandsche Handelmaatschappy*. Edited and annotated by Annemarie Kets–Vree (Amsterdam, 1998).

[16] J. C. Bloem, *Verzamelde gedichten* (Amsterdam, 1981).

[17] Historical–critical edition with comments on the genesis of the story and the story characters, compiled by Lieneke Frerichs (Assen etc., 1990). Monumenta Literaria Neerlandica IV, 1–2. See also: A. Kets–Vree, review of 'Nescio, *De uitvreter*. Historical–critical edition [. . .].' In: *De nieuwe taalgids* 86.I (1993), 75–79.

as the Mozart versus the Beethoven procedure. Manuscripts of the Mozart type contain few or no variants because the genesis did not take place on paper, but in the author's mind. The author who works according to the Beethoven method, by contrast, starts with a rough version and then proceeds to delete and refine. Nescio's approach was different: the genesis of his work runs in circles around a core of anecdotes, motifs, formulations and ideas which continually resurface. Certain elements—the suicide motif, for instance—are linked first to one and then to another character. Nescio was concerned, at least during this phase, not with improving details, for instance choice of words or sentence structure, but with structural changes. His problem was finding an intrigue, a plot. This is why the same individual elements repeatedly resurface in continually changing combinations. This kind of method can be referred to as 'text transplantation' or 'assembly technique'. The fact that this cannot be taken literally enough is evident on a reconstructed manuscript page, written by Nescio and his wife. The page was cut and pasted into a later version: the top half was left out while the bottom half was fitted into page 29 of the new version (see Figure 5).

After years of toiling, the pieces of the puzzle fell into place on a Sunday in September of 1909. Characters, locations and anecdotes finally found their way to a harmonious entity. This resulted in the first fair copy in a series of four. These were written during 1909 and 1910. In 1911 the story was published for the first time in a periodical. Four other reprints were made during the author's lifetime, this time in a collection together with a number of other narratives.

Different types of genesis and compositional methods must be represented in different ways. In order to do justice to the complex genesis of *The Sponger*, the historical–critical edition contains a combination of various apparatuses. The first phase of the genesis could not be presented in one of the traditional apparatus models, such as the lemma apparatus or the synopsis, but demanded a fresh approach. Thus the usual base text and apparatus of variants are not included. Instead, the last layer of each of the twelve hand-written sketches and stories is given. The editor paid no attention to the differences *within* the individual texts, but concentrated on shifts *between* these texts. This resulted in an essay in which the genesis of the story and the main character, meaning Nescio's search for a meaningful entity, are described in detail. The essay is supported by diagrams, which show how certain characters and their characteristics ended up in the final story (see Figure 6).

The four fair copies (V1, V2, V3 and V4) show a much more usual method of composition, making a parallel presentation of the variants

5. Example of Nescio's 'assembly technique':
reconstructed page of the manuscript of
De uitvreter (*The Sponger*).

Schema 7. Japi, Jagers, Laan in 'De uitvreter' [redactie B]

Heimwee	Lenteavond / Het begon eerder	Venloër Grensbode	Japi stond op 't zuiderhoofd	De uitvreter
Heldring-de-bon-vivant →	Japi-de-bon-vivant		Jagers-de-bon-vivant	Japi-de-bon-vivant →
		X: doodsangst		Japi-de-gekwelde →
	ik-de-harde-werker		Laan-de-harde-werker	Japi-de-harde-werker →
		X: gemoedsrust →	Japi-de-berustende	Japi-de-berustende →
		X: zelfmoord	Japi: potentiële ... zelfmoord	Japi-de-zelfmoordenaar
			Laan: zelfmoord	
1903	1906	24-1-1907	juli 1908	sept. en dec. 1909

6. Diagram from the historical-critical edition of *De uitvreter* (*The Sponger*).

possible. They are, again based on the last layer, presented in a row, with the oldest version at the bottom of the page and the youngest at the top. Fragments that are identical are combined. If a certain scene is not found in one or more of the manuscripts, this is indicated by a blank (see Figure 7). The edition concludes with two lemmatized apparatuses: one with the variants from the hand-written sources (Figure 8) and one with the printed variants (Figure 9).

No matter how different they appear to be, all the apparatuses of *The Sponger* serve the same purpose: to document the genesis and to demonstrate the highly personal composition by the author. The documentary aspect is subordinate, the subjective and interpretive comments are dominant, especially in the essay on the first phase of the genesis. This is unusual in the Monumenta series and may seem to conflict with the historical–critical method. In fact, however, the re-construction of a genesis, which means determining the chronological order of and interrelationships between the genetic variants as they came into being, is *always* the result of interpretive work, certainly when complicated drafts are involved.[18] Presenting that reconstruc-tion in a synopsis, for example, means that the editor's assumptions must remain implicit, as a result of which the impression can be given that the apparatus reflects the only true course of events rather than the editor's view of those events. The Nescio edition is therefore not exceptional in the interpretive element, but in the fact that the editor had to make her uncertainties, assumptions and decisions explicit.

*　　　*　　　*

Research at the Constantijn Huygens Instituut is aimed at preserving the Dutch national heritage, but always from an international perspec-tive. The sources are national, the methodology international. For the Dutch historical–critical edition, German editorial theory served as a point of departure into which elements from the Anglo–American tra-dition have been incorporated. This approach, which is characterised by methodological eclecticism, is typical of Dutch scholarly editing and it results in a solid theoretical foundation. What is further typical is the realistic and pragmatic approach, as demonstrated by the cases discussed in this essay: they are based on the same premises and they share their research methods and terminology, but the results vary significantly, because the primary and secondary witness documents of the texts and the objectives for further use differ case by case.

---

18 See H. T. M. van Vliet, 'Scholarly Editing in the Netherlands', 132 n2, above.

volgenden middag was i op straat Loef tegengekomen dien i ook al
kende. Loef die later met zwemmen verdronken is juist toen i er zoo'n
beetje begon te komen en die had hem weer meegenomen naar Bavink
en gezegd: 'Bavink ik breng je kaduukstoker mee.' En Bavink had om
5   't geval gelachen. En Japi was dadelijk naar 't plankje geloopen en had
op 't bekende plaatsje 'naast Dante' een nieuw kruikje Bols gevonden.
En met z'n drieën hadden ze 't een heel eind soldaat gemaakt, en toen
had Japi dikke boterhammen gesneden van Bavink z'n brood en toen
waren ze met hun drieën naar 't Amstelveld gegaan en hadden voor 70
10 cent een nieuw kacheltje gekocht ('t was Maandag) een kachel van een
voorwereldlijk model en met z'n drieën hadden ze die op een handkar
naar huis gekruid.

V^2

»

bij Loef die naderhand met zwemmen verdronken is juist toen hij er
zoo'n beetje begon te komen (p. 98, V^2).

op dien avond dat hij hem bij Bavink bezig vond dikke boterhammen
te snijden en Japi hem een degelijk borreltje schonk uit de flesch die Bavink altijd op 't bekende plaatsje had staan, 'op 't plankje naast Dante'
(p. 98, V^2).

V^1 [,2]

»

die doodouwerwetsche buikkachel die Bavink en ik voor zeventig cent
op 't Amstelveld hadden gekocht, en zelf op een handkar naar zijn hok
hadden gekruid (p. 105, $V^{1,2}$).

7. Apparatus of variants: the four fair
copies of *De uitvreter* (*The Sponger*).

Overlevering M^{15}

Tekstverantwoording   *Voor de status van dit fragment zie hoofdstuk 8, p. 177 en 180.*

123,1	Wbd] Wijk bij Duurstede
123,3	van *[het zinloze van is waarschijnlijk een verschrijving voor wat, zoals uit 123,19 zou kunnen worden afgeleid: dien middag had i nog al wat gedaan. Dit moet echter een gissing blijven; reden waarom deze plaats niet is gecorrigeerd. Zie Verantwoording, p. 46-47.]*
123,4	ezeltje ⟨-s⟩
123,6/7	⟨geschilderd,⟩»geteekend en⟩ [*p.1ᵛ*] een beetje geschilderd
123,7	gelanterfand] gelanterfant
123,7	all⟨e⟩»erlei⟩
123,10	middernacht//schemering] middernachtschemering
123,14	⟨ve⟩»bijzonder⟩ veel
123,17	kastanje//boomen] kastanjeboomen
123,20	zuid westen] zuidwesten

DE WALCHERSCHE REIS

Overlevering $M^{17}, p.\ 1^r - 3^r$

Tekstverantwoording   *Tekst deels in inkt, deels in potlood. Het is onzeker of de potloodtekst al dan niet deel uitmaakt van de inkttekst. Zie hoofdstuk 8, p. 177.*

125,4	De Walchersche Reis *[deze subtitel staat midden op p.2ʳ]*
125,5	I // ⟨-Een zonnetje⟩ // *[witregel]* // ⟨-Die man die dit schrijft // is een verloren man.⟩ *[Deze, evenals het voorafgaande, met inkt geschreven regels zijn met potlood doorgehaald, waarbij het hoofdstuknummer I (mogelijk abusievelijk) is blijven staan. Daarna volgt, in potlood, de tekst vanaf 125, 6.]*
125,6	da⟨t⟩»n⟩ dat
125,7/8	koeke//loeren] koekeloeren
125,8	de⟨-n⟩ Groenburgwal
125,10	zon, De zon] zon. De zon
125,11	zuidertoren] Zuidertoren

8. Apparatus of variants: manuscript variants
in *De uitvreter* (*The Sponger*).

p. 59	59,1	DE UITVRETER. $D^{a,b}$: DE UITVRETER [*geen punt*] D^{c-e}
	59,2	I. $D^{a,b}$: I [*geen punt*] D^{c-e}
	59,3	den man, D^{a-e}
	59,5	Den uitvreter, D^{a-e}
	59,5	vondt D^{a-c} : vond $D^{d,e}$
	59,8	op-droeg D^{a-d} : opdroeg D^{e} [*als gevolg van* D^{d} op-//droeg]
	59,10	een ander; D^{a-e}
	59,11	de lui; D^{a-e}
	59,12	terugbracht; D^{a-e}
	59,12	tweede hands D^{a-c} : tweedehandsch $D^{d,e}$
	59,13	Bavink; D^{a-e}
	59,14	Appi, D^{a-e}
	59,15	afgezet, D^{a-e}
	59,15	droeg, D^{a-e}
p. 60	60,1	had-i D^{a-e}
	60,3	gedacht: wat is dat toch voor een kerel? D^{a-e}
	60,3	wist 't, altijd D^{a-e}
	60,4/5	onbewegelijk. D^{a-d} : onbeweeglijk D^{e}
	60,5	ging i D^{a-d} : ging-i D^{e}
	60,6	eten; D^{a-e}
	60,6	zat i D^{a-d} : zat-i D^{e}
	60,7	drie; D^{a-e}
	60,12	zat i D^{a-d} : zat-i D^{e}
	60,12	ochtend; D^{a-e}
	60,15	dicht; D^{a-e}
	60,17	diezelfde kerel D^{a-e}
	60,22	plons water D^{a-e}
	60,22/23	[*alinea*] 'Nogal', zei Japi. D^{a-e}
	60,24	den glazen salon D^{a-e}
p. 61	61,1	golven, Bavink D^{a} : golven. Bavink D^{b-e}
	61,3	Japi: 'kijk D^{a-c} : Japi: 'Kijk D^{d-e}
	61,7	verdomd leuk D^{a-e}
	61,8	[*alinea*] 'Moet u D^{a-e}
	61,9	[*alinea*] 'Dat wil zeggen D^{a-e}
	61,9	vanavond D^{a-e}
	61,10	is u D^{a-e}
	61,10	[*alinea*] 'Ja D^{a-e}
	61,11	is u D^{a-e}
	61,12	zit?' moest Japi D^{b} [*corr. in* D^{bm} *en* D^{bp}: *zetfout*]

9. Apparatus of variants: printed variants
in *De uitvreter* (*The Sponger*).

Selling Sidney:
William Ponsonby, Thomas Nashe,
and the Boundaries of Elizabethan
Print and Manuscript Cultures

STEVEN MENTZ

Gentle Sir Phillip Sidney, thou knewst what belongd to a Scholler, thou knewst what paines, what toyle, what trauel, conduct to perfection: wel couldst thou giue euery Virtue his encouragement, euery Art his due, euery writer his desert.

Thomas Nashe[1]

IN THE YEARS FOLLOWING Sir Philip Sidney's death, Elizabethan publishers clamored to print his unpublished literary works. He was the biggest game in town: a national hero, Protestant martyr, and superlative poet. During the period between his death and first publication (1586–90), Sidney's manuscripts were held by his aristocratic family circle, especially his sister, the Countess of Pembroke, his longtime friend, Fulke Greville (later Sir Fulke and first Baron Brooke),[2] and his father-in-law Sir Francis Walsingham.[3] Once published, however, Sidney's works found broad popularity beyond coterie circles.

---

[1] *Pierce Pennilesse,* in *Works,* I: 159.

[2] Greville was knighted by Elizabeth in 1597, and made first Baron Brooke in 1621 by James I.

[3] See Woodhuysen for thorough consideration of the manuscript circulation of Sidney's texts.

The Countess of Pembroke's Arcadia in particular reigned from the sixteenth- to nineteenth-centuries as one of the most reprinted and best loved prose works in English.[4] From the Elizabethan period forward, Sidney loomed large in the imaginations of both aristocrats and more humble readers.[5] The process of transferring him from coterie circles to printed publication maps the changing boundaries and common spaces of Elizabethan print and manuscript cultures.

Sidney's print publication brought two prominent players from the Elizabethan book market, William Ponsonby and Thomas Nashe, in contact with Greville, Walsingham, and the Countess of Pembroke. Two seldom-read texts document their interaction: a letter from Greville to Walsingham describing his encounter with Ponsonby in 1586, and Nashe's preface, addressed in part to the Countess of Pembroke, to the unauthorized 1591 Quarto of *Astrophel and Stella*. These texts reveal an overlap between Elizabethan print and manuscript cultures once obscured by an absolutist belief in the "stigma of print."[6] The evidence that many aristocrats avoided print during their lifetimes is incontrovertible, but not unmixed.[7] The anti-print attitudes of many literary aristocrats (including Sidney) did not, however, preclude significant interaction between manuscript and print circles, especially regarding the posthumous publication of aristocratic works.

It may seem incongruous to compare two texts involving actors as disparate as a publisher (Ponsonby), a mercantile writer (Nashe), and a courtier poet (Greville), but each of them appears surprisingly similar in his approach to the Sidney circle. Each contributed to Sidney's early publication: Ponsonby in the literal sense as his authorized publisher, Greville because he provided the manuscript copy of the 1590 *Arcadia*, and Nashe because he introduced the (unauthorized) first edition of *Astrophel and Stella* to the reading public. The Sidney that finally appeared in print was a composite product.

It is of course an oversimplification to treat "Elizabethan print culture" as a monolithic entity to which Ponsonby and Nashe owed

---

4 See Lindbaum, 80 and n. He cites Ringler, among others, on Sidney's continued popularity, and also describes Samuel Richardson's use of the *Arcadia*, which he would republish in 1725. For the Countess's "ownership" of a text so prominently addressed to her, see Lamb, 72 ff.

5 See, e.g., Ringler, "Sir Philip Sidney: The Myth and the Man."

6 For the classic formulation of the "stigma of print," see Saunders. For consideration of work influenced by Saunders, especially studies of manuscript circulation, see Traister and Woodhuysen.

7 For a persuasive rejoinder to Saunders' formulation of the "stigma," see May, who focuses on counter-examples of aristocrats, including King James VI/I, who sought printed publication during their lifetimes. His data, however, do not fully justify his conclusion that "no 'stigma of print' is discernible during the Tudor age" (17). Rather, print appears to carry both stigma and practical value for aristocrats in this period.

allegiance and which Greville manipulated to serve his ends. The imagined unity among publishers, writers, and printers—the complex we call "print culture"[8] —can blind critics to the substantial diversity of interest within the growing publication communities.[9] The social phenomenon of "Elizabethan print culture" took shape through the competitive efforts of men as unlike each other as Ponsonby, Greville, and Nashe. Attention to their interaction in this case yields several important insights. First, Greville's involvement in publishing the 1590 *Arcadia* suggests that the "stigma" which kept living aristocrats away from print publishers was more malleable than previously supposed. Greville's refusal to publish his own works during his lifetime did not prevent him from taking an active part in publishing Sidney after the latter's death. Second, both Greville's letter and Nashe's preface employ the deferential rhetoric of class in order to conceal practical self-interest. These texts show that the intellectual property of print emerged through accommodation with, more than rebellion against, class hierarchy. The discourse of class facilitated two-way communication between aristocrats like Greville and businessmen like Ponsonby and Nashe. Third, Nashe's preface recalls the erosive force of market realities on aristocratic pretensions. Nashe manipulated his own and the public's fascination with Sidney in an attempt to promote himself as a brand name author. Nashe's preface makes a potent rejoinder to Greville's letter, emphasizing the rift in literary culture as well as Nashe's belief that he, at least, could cross it.

Recent critical work on the early modern book market has explored the various ways texts interact with their intended (or unintended) audiences.[10] As Alexandra Halasz has described the effect of print on Elizabethan England, "Print permanently altered the discursive field ... by enabling the market place to develop as a means of producing, disseminating, and mediating discourse independent of the sites and practices associated with and sanctioned by university, Crown, and Church."[11] In the "marketplace of print" texts that are commodities in Marx's sense are produced and manipulated by publishers like Ponsonby and writers like Nashe to create a new form of literary

---

[8] For an influential formulation of "print culture," see Eisenstein. For a critique of Eisenstein's methodology, see Johns, 10–20.

[9] See Johns, 58–186, for detailed analysis of print culture and its many components in early modern London.

[10] For influential studies that expose the complexity of early modern books and print culture, see Blayney, Chartier, Davis, and Marcus.

[11] See Halasz, 4. For two recent essay collections concerned with print culture, see Masten et al., and Brown and Marotti.

culture.[12] As both the texts I treat show, however, the independence of the marketplace as a site of cultural meaning should not be overstated. Literary aristocrats like Greville did not stand idly by, prohibited from entering the fray by an exaggerated distaste for mercantile publication. They too had a stake in the marketplace, and they too manipulated their social superiors by genuflecting to the still-potent old order. That Nashe authored texts as well as sold them, and that Greville refused to publish his own works while he was alive, did not lessen either man's desire to advance personal agendas by selling Sidney.

The postulated separation between the "coterie aristocracy" and the "print industry" raises perhaps the largest conundrum in early modern publication studies, the dilemma of readership. It is seldom possible to reconstruct who, exactly, bought and read early modern texts. The efforts of cultural historians from Louis Wright to Natalie Davis to Roger Chartier have expanded our insight into early modern reading, but knowledge of reading habits and tastes remains elusive. The older notion that readers separated themselves by social class, implicit in Wright's title, *Middle-Class Culture in Elizabethan England*, has come under attack from later critics and historians.[13] The division of literary production between manuscript and print appears to divide Elizabethan producers (if not necessarily readers) of literature by social class.[14] Market operators like Ponsonby and Nashe, however, straddled the divide by appealing simultaneously to aristocratic patrons and anonymous book buyers. Greville also operated on both sides of the print-manuscript split. The practice of aiming at two audiences at once explains the disorienting frequency with which formulaic pleas for patronage shared front matter space in Elizabethan books with overt grabs at market share.[15]

---

[12] See Halasz, 28–29, for discussion of Marxist commodities and the early modern book market. The classic formulation of "commodity fetishism" appears in Marx, 302–29.

[13] For an influential reading of Elizabethan England as a "one-class society," see Laslett, 23–54.

[14] Theorists of cultural transformation such as McLuhan, Ong, and Eisenstein connect the innovation of print to the emergence of a body of self-consciously non-elite readers. In Elizabethan England, however, this process is caught in transition; it is not clear that the "middle-class" is a viable social category yet. Wall, who relies on the category of class in her reading of early modern publishing, defends its use in an "expansive" rather than "narrow" sense (11n).

[15] Among numerous examples, Nashe's *The Unfortunate Traveler* (1594) combines a plea to the Earl of Southampton for "gracious favor" with a spirited address to "The Dapper Monsieur Pages of the Court," presumably Nashe's intended readers. Numerous critics, including Ferguson and Suzuki, have noted that Nashe's address to the readers sits uneasily next to his appeal for patronage.

Historians since R.B. McKerrow have pointed to Ponsonby as a key figure in the Stationers' Company's growth in the latter Elizabethan years.[16] McKerrow's pronouncement that Ponsonby was "the most important publisher of the Elizabethan age" has been widely accepted.[17] Ponsonby's prominence foregrounds the perplexing nature of Elizabethan print publishing: what exactly did he contribute to the books he published? Justly famous for his editions of Sidney and Spenser, Ponsonby nonetheless did not edit them in the modern sense, nor did he (so far as we know) solicit or shape additional works from his authors. Ponsonby did not print texts himself but relied on various London printers.[18] As publisher Ponsonby gave his enterprise two things: the capital needed to begin a print run, and a shop in which to sell the books.[19] Additionally, and in this case more importantly, he received copy from Sidney's family.[20] Playing the role of economic midwife, Ponsonby converted the manuscripts of the Sidney circle into his own intellectual property. He manipulated the Sidney circle's elitism, attachment to fictions of generosity and allegiance, and their refusal (or inability) to consider the profit motive. He was not, however, the only one who gained by the 1590 *Arcadia*.

Greville's stake in selling Sidney involved content and presentation rather than economic profit. Greville was determined that only a particular image of Sidney—religious, ethical, and politically serious—

---

[16] While print had been part of English cultural life since Caxton, the increased volume of publishing in the latter half of the sixteenth century marks the industry's arrival as a challenge to the established patronage system, according to critics from Sheavyn (10–11) to Wall (x).

[17] See McKerrow, 217. For an account of Ponsonby's career, see Brennan. For a recent critique of Brennan, which emphasizes Ponsonby's lack of economic independence, see Bland (109n).

[18] See Brennan, 104–5, for a table of Ponsonby's publications, with printer's names where known.

[19] For an overview of Elizabethan publishing of play quartos, see Blayney, "Publication." Elizabethan publishers are often called "booksellers" (as in the title of McKerrow's *Dictionary*) since the two tasks were generally done by the same person. Bland notes that Greville and John Ramsey call Ponsonby a "booke bynder" (109n). Ponsonby had owned his own bookshop since 1576; he entered his first book in the Stationers' Register in 1577 and took his first apprentice (Edward Blount) in 1578 (Brennan, 91). By 1586 he had begun a promising career, having published 17 volumes, including two prose romances by Robert Greene (*Mamilia*, Part II, 1583; *Gwyndonis*, 1584) and a translation of Cicero's *Consolatio* (1583). The bulk of his publications at this time were Protestant sermons and tracts. See Brennan, 104–6.

[20] Brennan notes that Ponsonby's career disproves the "popular bibliographical theory that for every 'high-class' publication . . . the Elizabethan stationer needed a regular supply of popular material . . . to keep his cash flow healthy" (91). Ponsonby's cultivated relationship with the aristocracy illuminates the tactics behind his ability to break this mold.

appear to the public.[21] To protect this image, Greville substituted the unfinished *New Arcadia* for the completed *Old* version, replacing a text Sidney had called an "idle toy"[22] with the revision that Greville, based on his relationship with Sidney, considered superior.[23] To publish the version he preferred Greville needed a publisher acceptable to the Sidney circle. As Nashe would later attempt to do for *Astrophel and Stella*, Greville acted as intermediary between the Sidneys and a publisher's market.

Neither a member of the Stationers' Company nor a friend of Sidney's, Nashe was an ambitious writer who maintained close ties to various figures in the publishing business, including the printer John Danter.[24] He acted as a front for various publishing ventures, bouncing between the ill-defined roles of writer, critic, publicist, and possibly even editor.[25] Lacking the capital (and probably the inclination) to set up his own book shop,[26] Nashe sought multiple venues for literary success. To foster his twin careers as writer and publisher's aide he attached himself to the famous dead poet.[27] His preface attempts to make him both a popular and a courtly writer, to befriend market readers as well as coterie poets. The preface's polite veneer hardly conceals, however, that the book it introduces was published without the Sidneys' consent. Nashe wanted to bridge the print-manuscript divide on his own terms. When his preface asks the Countess of

---

[21] See Woodhuysen, 416–20.

[22] See Sidney's letter to the Countess of Pembroke, which properly precedes the *Old Arcadia*, although it has generally been printed with both versions. See Sidney, *Old Arcadia*, 3.

[23] For a recent biography of Greville that takes note of his lifelong attachment to Sidney, see Larson, esp. 94–108.

[24] He later lived with and worked for Danter from 1593–95. See Hibbard, 233, and Nicholl, 24–31.

[25] Nashe was involved with the publication of Robert Greene's *Menaphon* (1589), to which he contributed a preface, two years before he wrote the preface to *Astrophel and Stella*. Especially in these early years, before the commercial success of *Pierce Pennilesse* (1592), Nashe seems to have pursued careers as what we might now call a publicist, publisher's aide, or possibly an editor. (Nashe's practices are murky and undocumented, but it seems that he had a hand in the 1591 Sidney Quarto, Greene's *Menaphon*, and possibly other texts later when he lived with Danter.) See Nicholl, 2–3, on Nashe's multifaceted roles in Elizabethan print culture. Nicholl is one of several critics who suggest that Nashe may have been a journalist whose misfortune was to write before popular journalism existed (2–6).

[26] See Nicholl, 39–47, for discussion of Nashe's finances when he arrived in London around 1589.

[27] Halasz notes that Nashe "embraces ... the degradation of the marketplace ... but with an awareness of its cost" (96). I suggest that nowhere can Nashe's ambivalence about his need for the market be seen more clearly than in his attitude toward Sidney.

Pembroke to approve the book that he and Newman had (perhaps surreptitiously) acquired from her family, it exposes the self-interest of Nashe's traffic in Sidney's literary relics.[28]

These texts reveal a three-part chain of communication in each interaction between the market and the Sidneys: a publisher (Ponsonby or Newman) acts through a writer (Greville or Nashe) to reach an aristocrat (Walsingham or the Countess) who holds—or thinks she holds—the keys to Sidney's literary estate.[29] These interactions describe the nexus between the emerging "public sphere" of marketplace literary discourse and established aristocratic coterie culture, revealing an interrelationship that broad generalities about "print" and "coterie" cultures often overlook.[30] The resulting picture of Elizabethan print and manuscript cultures is more varied than either the democratizing panacea that print historians celebrate or the "closing" of a previously "open" manuscript culture that manuscript historians decry.[31]

i. Publishing a Hero: Ponsonby and Greville

In November 1586, at St. Paul's Churchyard in London, Ponsonby initiated his trade in Sir Philip Sidney by approaching Fulke Greville. Sidney had died one month before,[32] and he was already a national hero. The state funeral being planned would keep his name in the public spotlight.[33] Greville, Sidney's childhood friend, was likely still in mourning when Ponsonby approached him. The Sidney circle's

---

[28] For discussions of the still uncertain provenance of the copytext, see Warkentin, 461–62; and Woodhuysen, 367–69. For an overview of the "book pirates" who stole copy and printed it for their own profit, see Judges.

[29] As I discuss below, this chain is complicated because the figures on top—Walsingham and the Countess—did not have the total access to Sidney's text that they were presumed to have. For the *Arcadia*, Greville had possession of the copytext, and for *Astrophel and Stella* Nashe's address to the Countess postdates the acquisition of the copy for the Quarto. What the writers and publishers wanted from the high-level aristocrats was permission and immunity from legal action.

[30] I adopt the term "public sphere" from Jürgen Habermas. For its value in considering the overall project of early modern publishing, see Halasz, 42–45.

[31] For a reading of print as part of a progressive narrative, see Eisenstein. For the terms "open" and "closed" referring to manuscript and print culture, see Wall, 8–9 and n. For a witty distinction between print as a negative force destroying a prior social innocence (the "Jack Cade" reading) and print as a positive diffusion of information (the "John Wolfe" reading), see Wall, 341–45.

[32] Sidney was wounded on September 22, 1586, and he died of those wounds on October 17.

[33] The funeral was held at St. Paul's three months later, on February 16, 1587, eight days after the execution of Mary Queen of Scots.

evident distaste for print forced Ponsonby to tread lightly, even if he knew—or guessed—that Greville might no longer be bound by it now that Sidney was dead.

Significantly, Ponsonby approached Greville, Sidney's friend and fellow poet, rather than Walsingham, Sidney's father-in-law and executor. He approached Greville not as a prospective publisher but ostensibly as a helper in preventing unlicensed publication. As Greville described the meeting in a letter to Walsingham, Ponsonby warned about less scrupulous publishers:

> Sir this day one ponsonby a booke bynder in poles church yard, came to me, and told me that ther was one in hand to print, Sir philip sydneys old arcadia asking me yf it were done, with your honors co[n]s[ent]...
> I told him to m[y] knowledge no, then he advised me to give w[ar]ning of it, ether to the archebishope or doctor Cosen, who haue as he says a copy of it to pervse to that end / Sir I am lothe to reneu his memori vnto you, but yeat in this I might presume, for I haue sent ... a correction of that old one ... which he left in trust with me wherof ther is no more copies, & fitter to be printed then that first which is so common, ...[34]

The "correction" Greville mentions, the *New Arcadia*, would be published by Ponsonby in 1590. That publication appears to have been the direct product of the meeting described in Greville's letter.

William Brennan describes Ponsonby's meeting with Greville as "the most important business contact of [Ponsonby's] career" (92). As the most important moment in the most important career of Elizabethan publishing, the meeting bears renewed scrutiny. There are at least three ways to interpret the encounter, relying on three different centers of agency and control. Each of the three figures in the transaction (Ponsonby who approached Greville, Greville who wrote to Walsingham, and Walsingham who received the letter) had some claim to power over the other two. Ponsonby knew the book market and (presumably) the prospective publisher; Greville was Sidney's confidant and possessed the manuscript of the *New Arcadia*;[35] and Walsingham was Sidney's executor and the highest-ranking man involved.

The simplest explanation is that the letter means what it says, and that the chain of command leading upward to Walsingham dominates. Walsingham was Sidney's father-in-law and a powerful nobleman, and if he had become directly involved in the publication he probably

[34] As quoted in Robertson, xl, citing Ringler, 530. See also Brennan, 93. For a recent transcription with commentary, see Woodhuysen, 416–21. For a facsimile reproduction of the letter, see Skretkowicz, 114–15.

[35] According to Woodhuysen, a second copy of the revised manuscript did exist, but Greville appears (or claims) not to have known of it (311).

would have wielded ultimate control over Sidney's legacy. (It was Walsingham, for example, who remarried his daughter, Sidney's widow,
to the Earl of Essex.)[36] Walsingham served as the absent authority
in the interaction between the market and the Sidney circle. Both
Greville, and Ponsonby through Greville, endeavored to win him over.
It is unclear, however, that Walsingham ever took any great interest in
publishing Sidney's literary works.[37]

An alternative reading makes Greville the primary agent. Greville
describes himself as wanting to substitute his copy of the revised *New
Arcadia* for the "common" *Old Arcadia* to which Ponsonby alerted
him. Greville implies that his bond of friendship with Sidney gave
him a right to the revised text "which [Sidney] left in trust with me."
Greville's word "trust" indicates a legal status of ownership exercised
on another's behalf, and it implies that Greville was essential to any
publishing effort.[38] Apparently released from anti-print inhibitions
because Sidney was dead,[39] or perhaps because he was convinced by
Ponsonby that a bad text was "in hand to print," Greville wanted to
print his copy of the *Arcadia* forthwith, without the "common errors of
mercenary printing."[40] These errors included not simply the mistakes
in typesetting and proofreading common in Elizabethan print shops,
but the fundamental error of using the wrong text.[41] The *New Arcadia*, once printed, would help create a serious, moral, and religious
Sidney, whose fiction Greville would supplement with translations of
the Psalms which Sidney had begun in his final years.[42] While he

---

[36] See Read, III: 423–25, for details of the marriages of Frances Walsingham Sidney.
Read notes that her marriages to both Sidney and Essex appear to have been part
of Walsingham's political alliances, and that the wedding to Essex may have occurred
anytime after 1587, most likely before Sir Francis's death in 1590.

[37] Read suggests that Walsingham had little interest in Sidney's literary career (III:
436), although he was a well-known patron of both universities (III: 437–42).

[38] This meaning of "trust" was current since at least the fifteenth century (OED 6).

[39] Greville's works in poetry and prose, including his *Life of the Renowned Sir Philip
Sidney*, would be printed only after his own death in 1628. See Larson.

[40] See Ringler, 530. Greville apparently recognized that there would be profit from the
publication, but he was careful to downplay any mercenary motives: "Gayn ther wilbe
no doubt to be disposed by you, let it help the poorest of his seruants" (Woodhuysen,
416).

[41] For an account of the systematic errors associated with early modern printing, see
Johns, 58–186.

[42] Woodhuysen notes that Greville's letter is also concerned to suppress Sidney's
partial translation (completed by Golding) of Mornay's *De la vérité de la religion
chrétienne* (420). This text was not suppressed successfully, and in fact the volume,
almost entirely Golding's translation, bears Sidney's name prominently on its title-page:
exactly what Greville wished to avoid. See Woodhuysen, 420–21.

may have had publication "forced on him by the possibility . . . [of] a corrupt text" (Saunders, 154), Greville also wanted to issue his version of Sidney. The 1590 *Arcadia* was Greville's text, containing only the incomplete two and one-half books of his revised manuscript, along with chapter divisions and elaborate descriptive headings written by Greville himself.[43]

A third reading, that Ponsonby manipulated the encounter to get what he wanted out of Greville and the Sidneys, is also plausible. In this interpretation, the image the letter creates of Ponsonby— deferential, unthreatening, loyal—served as bait to secure the Sidneys' trust. Greville accents Ponsonby's humility by calling Ponsonby a "booke bynder," a term that minimizes his motivation as a businessman and his potential threat to the Sidney circle. (It may be that Greville was simply ignorant of Ponsonby's profession, but that ignorance would have worked to Ponsonby's advantage.) Securing the literary rights to Sidney's estate was a great coup, and evidence that Ponsonby was the primary beneficiary of the encounter seems strong.[44] The publisher appears to have initiated the contact: Greville's letter reports that Ponsonby "came to [Greville]" to report the unauthorized *Arcadia*'s existence, and that subsequently Ponsonby "advised [Greville]" to start action against the unlicensed publication. According to the letter, Ponsonby paid lip service to "your honours consent," but he seems much more an active agent in the transaction than Greville conveys. The crucial phrase, "He [Ponsonby] advised me [Greville]," provides a possible grammatical microcosm of the encounter, with Ponsonby as subject imposing his advice on Greville the direct object. The meeting helped quash whatever *Arcadia* was "in hand to print," clearing the way for Ponsonby's authorized edition.

---

43 As Skretkowicz notes, these headings were attacked by the Countess of Pembroke and Hugh Sanford and kept out of subsequent editions (111–16).

44 The first edition of the *Arcadia* was registered August 23, 1588, and published in 1590. In 1588 Ponsonby also registered Sidney's translation of Salust du Bartas. He would continue as the authorized publisher of Sidney's works for the rest of his career. See Brennan, 93, and Arber, II: 486. Brennan suggests that the time between the meeting in 1586 and the agreement of 1588 was spent in "editorial matters" (107n). Bland suggests that work on printing of the 1590 *Arcadia* began just after it was entered in August 1588 (108). Ponsonby would go on to publish all authorized editions of Sidney in the sixteenth century, including three versions of the *Arcadia*: the revised Books I–III, ending with the sentence fragment that marks the end of the revision (1590); the cobbled-together version that splices the last three books of the *Old Arcadia* onto the *New* (1593); and a second version of the composite *Arcadia* as part of Sidney's collected works (1598). Ponsonby also published the first authorized edition of the *Defence* (1595), Sidney's translations of du Bartas, the Countess of Pembroke's translations of Mornay, and both the 1590 and 1596 versions of *The Faerie Queene* along with minor works by Spenser.

Most readers of the letter have assumed its basic truthfulness, especially since the Sidneys did later give Ponsonby the rights to Sidney's
works. It is worth noting, however, that there is no independent
confirmation of the rival publisher. The *Stationers' Register* mentions
no names, nor do any other records survive.[45] The particular "copy"
of the "old" *Arcadia* Ponsonby mentioned to Greville has never been
identified, although several manuscripts have been discovered in the
twentieth century.[46] That a potential publisher might have been scared
off by the Sidneys seems possible, since emerging publishing laws
were starting to develop teeth in this period.[47] As it was publishers,
not authors or authors' estates, who owned "copy" in early modern
England, it was generally publishers who successfully attacked pirated
editions.[48] Sidney's executors were well positioned to press their
claim,[49] and the letter describes Ponsonby reminding Greville to apply
to the proper authorities to block publication ("ether to the archebish-
ope or doctor Cosen").[50]

The letter of the law, moreover, was not always observed in St.
Paul's Churchyard. Even after the mysterious first publisher withdrew
from the scene, unauthorized editions of *Astrophel and Stella* and
the *Arcadia* were printed, attacked, and eventually recalled.[51] In this
climate, if a copy of the *Old Arcadia* were really "in hand to print,"

---

[45] Jean Robertson, editor of the Oxford *Old Arcadia*, obviously accepts Ponsonby's
version of events when she observes, "That a copy had already been submitted for
licensing indicates how narrowly the *Old Arcadia* escaped printing" (xln). She does
not, however, offer independent evidence that such a submission actually took place.

[46] Woodhuysen, 299–303.

[47] The quick recall of the 1591 Quarto of *Astrophel and Stella* is a case in point. For
documentation of some of the Company's most celebrated legal battles over copy, see
Judges. In the 1580s Ponsonby had been involved in an elaborate legal struggle over the
A.B.C. once licensed to John Day (Judges, 61–89).

[48] For the developing notion of "copy" in early modern England, see Johns, 187–
89. When unauthorized editions of Sidney's works were published in the 1590s, it was
generally Ponsonby himself, then the authorized publisher, who successfully attacked
them.

[49] Warkentin believes that in the case of the *Astrophel and Stella* Quarto, Sidney's
family brought the action against the publishers (467–68). Her assertion, however, does
not seem definitive, as Woodhuysen notes (368–69).

[50] These two, Archbishop Whitgift and his protégé and former student Richard Cosin,
controlled the licensing of books at this time. See *DNB*, 21: 128–37 (Whitgift); 4: 1196
(Cosin).

[51] In 1591, Thomas Newman published the unauthorized *Astrophel and Stella* that I
discuss below. In 1599, a consortium of London publishers, including John Harrison
the younger, Paul Lynley, Richard Banckworth, and John Flaskett printed the *Arcadia* at
the Edinburgh print-shop of Robert Waldegrave, and then attempted to sell it in London
for 3 shillings less than Ponsonby's 1598 folio. Lynley had been Ponsonby's apprentice

there seems a decent chance it would have been printed by someone despite any action by the Sidneys. Lacking Ponsonby's connections, Newman published the 1591 *Astrophel and Stella* without permission or registration. Furthermore, if the "old" text were to go forth unlicensed, there would have been no reason to submit it to the authorities; works that were printed illegally—like Newman's *Astrophel and Stella*—were not registered beforehand. The circumstances of the "old" text remain obscure; perhaps some other publisher was hoping to obtain the family's permission. If another publication, legal or not, was in the offing, however, Ponsonby's approach to Greville forestalled it.

In the absence of further data, Ponsonby's veracity has usually been assumed, especially since being caught in a lie would have damaged his credibility with the Sidneys. Skepticism about his approach, however, remains valuable. He had practical reasons for presenting himself to Greville, and through Greville to Walsingham, as a defender of the Sidney circle's monopoly of Sidney's literary works. His intervention reminded the Sidneys that time was running out on that monopoly. St. Paul's was not as distant as they might have wished. Ponsonby's intervention let Greville and the Sidneys infer that after avoiding an unwanted publisher they would be well advised to acquire one of their choosing. It is unclear how close the *Old Arcadia* was to licensing or print, but in any case Ponsonby's goal was to secure the rights to Sidney's works for himself. It should be stressed that in November 1586 Ponsonby was not yet a friend of the Sidneys, or even known to them at all. He was simply a young publisher seeking marketable material.[52]

---

and may have stolen the copy from his shop (Judges, 101n). Each of the editions were recalled, and the Edinburgh consortium repaid Ponsonby for his loss. See McKerrow, 218.

52 Ponsonby's encounter with Greville was perfectly timed for his own career. His early publications had centered around Protestant theology, another reason he might have sought and been accepted by the Sidneys (Brennan, 91–92). He would subsequently use his connections with the Sidneys to advance himself in the clannish world of the Stationers' Company. He had been free of his apprenticeship since 1571, and was successful enough during the 1570s to take two apprentices, one of them Edward Blount, future co-publisher of Shakespeare's First Folio. Around this time he also made a fine match for himself in the narrow world of Elizabethan publishing by marrying Joan Coldocke (Brennan, 91). Her father Francis Coldocke's rise in the Company began soon thereafter, from Junior Warden in 1580–82, to Senior Warden in 1587–89, to twice Master of the Company, in 1591–92 and again in 1595–96 (Brennan, 91; McKerrow, 72). Coldocke had launched his career with a popular prose romance, the English translation of Heliodorus' *Aethiopian History*, which he published three times, in 1569, 1577, and 1587. Ponsonby's acquisition of the *Arcadia* thus parallels the career narrative of his successful father-in-law. In the *Arcadia*, Ponsonby chose a text singularly aligned with Coldocke's Heliodorus, which was one of the major sources for Sidney's text. (See

While Ponsonby may have exaggerated, manipulated, or even invented the rival publisher for the purpose of obtaining an introduction to the Sidney circle, I do not suggest that he was merely an unscrupulous publisher manipulating the recently bereaved. Rather, the mutual benefits of the arrangement he came to with Greville and the Sidneys, in which he protected them from unauthorized publication, served the interests of all the agents in the interaction. Ponsonby wanted to sell books, Greville to suppress the *Old Arcadia* in favor of the *New*, and Walsingham to preserve Sidney's reputation. The threat of illegal publication aligned these separate goals.

The irony is that this coterie–print alliance was viable only after the death of the author. Sidney's absence helped make his name a commodity recognized as such by London audiences both mercantile (Ponsonby, and later Nashe) and aristocratic (Greville and the Sidney circle). All these actors sought success through Sidney, and they were not alone in trying to sell him at this time.[53] Ponsonby and Greville succeeded by acting in concert, combining Ponsonby's professional knowledge with Walsingham's approval and Greville's text.

ii. Making a Name: Nashe and the Countess of Pembroke

Ponsonby's coup left other publishers out in the cold. Not only did Ponsonby have the rights to all of Sidney's works sewn up by 1588, but the published *Arcadia* also helped foster a growing taste for prose romance. Competing publishers had two choices: publish Sidney illegally, or market pseudo-Sidneian authors.[54] Thomas Nashe became involved in the first of these, the earliest pirated edition of Sidney. The publisher Thomas Newman issued an unlicensed Quarto of *Astrophel*

Hamilton, *passim*.) Acquiring the rights to the *Arcadia* may also have helped bring about Ponsonby's first major promotion; he was received into the livery of the Company in July 1588, one month before registering the *Arcadia*.

[53] As Brennan notes, many publishers had tried to publish Sidney immediately after his death. In addition to Thomas Newman, whose *Astrophel and Stella* I discuss below, Thomas Dawson published a letter of Henry Sidney's in 1591, Henry Olney published a pirated edition of the *Defence* under the title *An Apologie for Poetrie* in 1595, and Thomas Cadman published two books that mention Sidney in their titles in 1587. See Brennan, 100. The Puritan publisher Robert Waldegrave, the main printer of the Marprelate tracts, also published Angel Day's *Life and Death of Sir Philip Sidney* around 1586 or later and was involved in the Scottish pirated *Arcadia* in 1599. See McKerrow, 277–79.

[54] The more common, and successful, approach was the second of these, which I do not have space to consider here. Pseudo-Sidneian works in the 1590s include the romances of Robert Greene, Thomas Lodge, John Dickenson, Anthony Munday, Barnabe Riche, and to some extent Nashe himself (whose *The Unfortunate Traveler* contains a series of episodes based loosely on the *Arcadia*). For a bibliography of Elizabethan fiction, see Salzman, 351–55.

and Stella in 1591, with a prefatory epistle by Nashe.[55] This direct approach provoked legal action and resulted in the prompt confiscation of the book.[56]

The source of the printer's copy for the 1591 Quarto remains obscure. Neither Newman nor Nashe seems to have approached any member of the Sidney circle to secure permission, and if they had they would likely have been refused in favor of Ponsonby. Critics have noted "general agreement" that the copy was obtained "surreptitiously,"[57] but that judgment seems based on the reaction against the publication more than any firm proof. Nashe's preface speaks provocatively about "some private penne (in steed of a picklock) [being used] to procure [the text's] violent enlargement."[58] This striking phrase cannot serve as proof that Nashe stole the copy, but it does highlight the aggressive stance of Nashe and Newman versus the coterie text-holders. This market–coterie interaction commenced with an aggressive theft, rather than the gentle warning Ponsonby gave to Walsingham through Greville.

Nashe's preface attempts to forge a direct link between the Sidney circle and the marketplace. Like Greville's letter, the preface occupies the center of a three-person exchange. Speaking publicly in print, Nashe approached the Countess of Pembroke on behalf of Newman's book in an odd inversion of Ponsonby's approach to Greville and Walsingham. Unlike Ponsonby, Nashe neither simulated disinterest nor respected the family's privacy. As a market-to-coterie communication, the preface attempts to duplicate the success of Greville's letter in mediating between publisher and aristocrat. Nashe, however, lacked Greville's close relationship with Sidney to authorize his possession of the manuscript, and he also eschewed Greville's respectful tone. While

---

55 Newman was a shadowy character, only in business from 1587–98. For a reading of his epistle to the 1591 Quarto, see Warkentin, 470–82. For a brief summary of his career, see McKerrow, 200. Nicholl notes that Newman himself suffered little from the calling-in of the 1591 Quarto (84).

56 See McKerrow, 200; Arber, II: 475; Warkentin, *passim*; and *STC* 22536–38. It remains unclear who initiated the calling-in and why; Warkentin blames it on Newman's prefatory letter to Francis Flower (470–80); Woodhuysen, more tentatively, on the unreliable text of Samuel Daniel's sonnets which were included (371–81). Neither critic gives much consideration to the Countess of Pembroke's reaction to Nashe's preface, but Nicholl notes that Nashe suffered most from the calling-in of the text, since his preface was definitively suppressed (82–84).

57 See Warkentin, 461–62. She cites Ringler, *Poems*, 543.

58 Thomas Nashe, "Somewhat to reade for them *that list*," III: 330. Further citations in the text.

Greville's letter does not assert himself overtly, Nashe's desperate persona overflows his text.[59]

Nashe's preface attempts to do three separate things at once: sell the Quarto, attract the patronage of the Countess (belatedly to this volume and perhaps also to Nashe's future work), and create the literary brand-name "Thomas Nashe." In the first two goals he mirrors, respectively, Ponsonby and Greville: like Ponsonby he wants to sell the book at hand, and like Greville he invokes his (in this case wholly invented) closeness to Sidney. These efforts would fail dramatically when the Quarto was called in and suppressed. It is Nashe's third goal, however, authorial self-creation, that his preface advances most determinedly. The "Thomas Nashe" it creates derives seductive appeal from the proximity to Sidney that the preface asserts.

The preface's title, "Somewhat to read for them *that list*," captures Nashe's ambivalent egotism. He courts and dismisses his reader; someone can read his dashed-off "somewhat" if he or she "*list*," but Nashe woos the audience backhandedly. The text opens with a series of attacks on other men's writing, which he characterizes as a "thousand lines of folly" and "the ecco of Fames brasen towres" (III: 329). Nashe attacks to clear the field; he seems intent that only he and Sidney be left standing.[60] He wants to narrow the category of desirable authors to Sidney and himself. He half-heartedly diffuses this hubris by saying, "peraduenture my witles youth may be taxt with a margent note of presumption" (III: 329). This caveat, however, does not impede his attacks on all and sundry.

Nashe grants Sidney fulsome praise. In an oft-cited passage he writes, "here you shal find a paper stage streud with pearle, an artificial heau'en to ouershadow the faire frame, & christal wals to encounter your curious eyes, whiles the tragicommody of loue is performed by starlight" (III: 329). The terms of the praise—pearls, crystal, love, starlight—recall the intimacy and wealth of the coterie environment to which Nashe craved admittance. He also shows off his apparent familiarity with Sidney's still unpublished *Defence of Poesy*, where the poet's "golden" artifice overshadows the "brazen" world.[61] At

---

[59] This image may be a pose that Nashe was cultivating at that stage of his career. It does, however, resonate with the desperate economic conditions of his life, so far as they are known, as well as with the authorial personae of his later works. See Nicholl, *passim*.

[60] This scorched-earth policy of literary attack had already distinguished Nashe's preface to Greene's *Menaphon* (1589), his *Anatomie of Absurdities* (1590), and his writings as official attacker of Martin Marprelate around 1590. He would go on to assault Gabriel Harvey in print between 1592 and 1596, and this debate ultimately led to the calling-in of all his works.

[61] See Sidney, *Defence*, 216.

this point, Nashe's Sidney seems not unlike Greville's: aristocratic, peerless, and idealized.

Notably absent in the early pages of the preface is praise of the Countess, whose approval, had Nashe attained it, might have enabled him to replicate the marketplace–coterie alliance of Ponsonby and Greville's 1590 *Arcadia*. Only halfway through his text does Nashe turn to the flattery customary in dedicatory prefaces.[62] At this point he calls the Countess the "fayre sister of *Phoebus*" in whom "Learning, wisedome, beautie, and all other ornaments of Nobilitie whatsoeuer, seeke to approue themselues" (III: 331). While making this plea, however, he emphasizes his ambivalence by saying, "I feare I shall be counted a mercenary flatterer" (III: 331). If the Countess was not immediately put off by the unauthorized edition, or by being buried in the back half of the preface, she must have distrusted Nashe's double-talking appeal.[63]

Nashe's Sidneolatry does not bear close scrutiny. He writes, "the least sillable of [Sidney's] name, sounded in the eares of iudgement, is able to giue the meanest line he writes a dowry of immortality" (III: 329). Here Nashe's hyperbole becomes ironic: Sidney's aristocratic name alone suffices to make the text memorable. The Sidney name as fetishized commodity awakens desire in book buyers and provokes envy in Nashe. Nashe wants the Countess as a patron, but he wants even more to make his own name by connecting himself to Sidney.[64] Like Ponsonby, but with different results, Nashe saw Sidney as his ticket to commercial success.

Nashe's preface also ties Sidney to a base stratum of the literary marketplace, the "stage" of public drama. This popular form, mocked by Sidney,[65] occupied the opposite cultural register from courtly poetry. That the Quarto itself should be a "paper stage" and the sonnet cycle a "tragicommody" links the aristocratic poet to a social sphere

---

[62] It was customary to use a patron's name as the title of a dedicatory letter, as Warkentin notes (470–71).

[63] Woodhuysen emphasizes Nashe's praise of the Countess in the preface (373), and Nicholl notes that the material "seems innocuous enough" (83), but as keen a reader as the Countess surely would have recognized the presumption that accompanied Nashe's praise. Nicholl notes that later, in *Lenten Stuffe* (1599), Nashe would poke fun at the Countess (84).

[64] Nashe's attitude toward Sidney over the course of his career remains complex. Critics of Nashe's works who discuss his references to Sidney seem about equally divided between those who think Nashe mocks Sidney, those who think he celebrates his example, and those who suggest a little of both. See, e.g., Duncan–Jones; Suzuki, 365–66; Barbour, 72.

[65] For Sidney's anti-theatricality, see *Defence*, 243–45. For Nashe's, see *The Anatomie of Absurditie* (1589) and the preface to *Menaphon* (1588).

neither he nor his family cared to enter. Mixing the "paper stage" with the "christal wals" of an upper-class house reveals the aggressive undertones of Nashe's preface. Nashe himself scorned the stage,[66] but the connection he makes between coterie poems and public drama suggests that he was aware that the medium of print was lessening the distance between opposite ends of the literary spectrum. When book stalls carried copies of Sidney's *Arcadia* alongside Greene's romances, and popular plays and broadsides could be had next door, the social distinctions of aristocratic culture were threatened. Nashe's preface captures that threat. If Greville's desire to publish the *New Arcadia* undercuts the force of the "stigma of print," Nashe's metaphoric connection of a volume of Sidney's poems to the stage recalls the social differences among literary modes.[67]

Nashe's precise intentions in first celebrating and then mocking Sidney are difficult to recover. One possible explanation arises from his juxtaposition of attacks on Sidney with increasingly direct references to the urban book market. This combination brings Sidney down to Nashe's level. Nashe trivializes the social fate of Sidney's volume when he writes that *Astrophel and Stella* will be, "oftentimes imprisoned in Ladyes casks" (III: 330). He echoes here a notorious phrase from John Lyly's preface to *Euphues and his England* (1580), "Euphues had rather be shut up in a Lady's casket than open in a scholar's study."[68] Linking Sidney to one of the most widely popular prose writers of the 1580s cannot have been welcome to the Countess, although it may have made Sidney's poems enticing to readers of *Euphues*.[69]

In the concluding pages of the preface Nashe consigns Sidney to a pastoral never-never land and concentrates on himself. Nashe notes that he—unlike Sidney—cannot write pastoral lyrics in the style of "oh my loue, all my loues gone, as other Sheepheards" (332).[70] Nashe himself prefers urban grit to pastoral grass: "Onely I can keepe pace with Grauesend barge, and care not if I haue water enough to lande my

---

[66] He did write one play, *Summer's Last Will and Testament*, probably in 1592 while living on the Isle of Wight after fleeing London because of plague. That this play was a plea for patronage never performed on the public stage accents Nashe's contempt for popular drama.

[67] Himself openly a "man in print," Nashe appears to have found in the stage a site for the contempt that coterie writers heaped on printed publication.

[68] Dedicated to Sidney's rival the Earl of Oxford, Lyly's text connects *Astrophel and Stella* to decadent, Italianate, and possibly Catholic circles. See Lyly, 200.

[69] Lyly was a minor aristocrat and a courtier, but his notoriety in the marketplace would likely have placed his texts beyond the pale in aristocratic eyes. On the popularity of *Euphues*, see Croll, intro.

[70] This mock-pastoral jabs at Sidney's eclogues and Spenser's *Shepheardes Calendar*, dedicated to Sidney in 1579.

ship of fooles with the Tearme (the tyde I should say)" (III: 332). Here he rejects the "faire frame" of *Astrophel and Stella* for his preferred place, London, and abandons the Countess of Pembroke to address his readers as "Gentlemen" (III: 333).[71] Having relegated Sidney to an "artificial heau'en," Nashe claims urban reality as his own.

As Nashe's self-assertion nears hysterical proportions, he loses control of his hyperbolic metaphors. He concludes with a flourish of mismatched imagery:

> if learning had lost it selfe in a groue of Genealogies, wee neede doe no more but sette an olde goose ouer halfe a dozen pottle pots, (which are as it were the egges of inuention,) and wee shall haue such a breede of bookes within a little while after, as will fill all the world with the wilde fowle of good wits. (III: 333)

In Nashe's urban playground, books are not written in pastoral retreat but coaxed into being amid the chaos of the city. Aristocratic poetry gives way to books that cannot be distinguished from goslings hatched from an old bird's eggs.[72] Nashe confusingly imagines the "pottle pots" themselves to be the "egges of inuention," although he may be referring to the ale that filled pottle pots in London taverns.[73] How the pots and geese create literature remains unclear, but the process rejects the "artificial heauen" of Nashe's earlier description of Sidney. City street replaces country house as the site of creative gestation.

The old yet fecund goose amid pottle pots urbanizes Aesop's goose that laid golden eggs.[74] As the ultimate producer of literary value, the goose recalls Sidney himself, who, dead for five years, had to some extent become "old" by 1591. By producing a variety of texts to circulate in the urban marketplace, however, the goose also appears analogous to Nashe, or at least to the thriving, successful "Thomas Nashe" that he was hoping to become. The image blurs the two writers together to ensure that even after Sidney's death more golden eggs can

---

[71] As Nicholl puts it, "Nashe's genius was urban, lurid, grotesque, and low" (3).

[72] Eggs also make a suggestive image of mass production, as one of few products of a pre-industrial society that look substantially the same in large numbers. Shakespeare's Leontes plays on the notion of eggs as identical products when he describes himself and his son as "almost as like as eggs" (*Winter's Tale*, 1.2.130). Copies of books were only starting to become this identical in early modern England (see Johns, *passim*).

[73] The word "pottle" is not recorded as a synonym for the ale inside these pots until 1698 (OED 1c), but pots of this description had been used to carry ale since at least 1300 (OED 1a).

[74] Aesop's fable had been published in English by Caxton in 1484. Lyly had recently referred to the fable in his anti-Marprelate tract in 1589 (see OED, "goose," 1d).

be produced; the mantle merely passes from Sidney to Nashe.[75] Nashe relies on the dead poet's star power for a boost, and his imagined closeness with Sidney helps make him the new dominant author. The image of the goose suggests that the two together, or Nashe having assumed Sidney's place, can create a "breede of books" to fill "all the world."

Conscious of using the preface to Sidney's book as his platform, Nashe finally apologizes for "talking all this while in an other mans doore" (333), backing down from his startling assertion of connection with Sidney. The final image leaves Nashe just inside the doorway of Sidney's house, almost but not quite within his world. Nashe has also, however, loosed the "wilde fowle of good wits" into the streets. In this urban literary commonwealth, Nashe was well suited, he believed, to take over Sidney's status. Nashe's cityscape describes a fantasy of literary community, in which an urban writer can replace an aristocratic poet as producer of literary value.

Nashe's stylized aggression eventually developed into a widely known authorial persona. Despite the popularity of his fictionalized autobiography *Pierce Pennilesse* (1592), however, he never secured the market currency that Sidney embodied for Nashe's generation.[76] His preface suggests that he coveted success in a variety of arenas—seller of books, beneficiary of a prominent patron, and literary celebrity—but was never able to reconcile these ambitions. His struggle toward self-definition exposes the underbelly of the process that went so smoothly for Ponsonby, Greville, and their edition of Sidney's *Arcadia*.

iii. Selling (off) Sidney

The efforts of Ponsonby and Nashe in selling Sidney expose the shifting boundaries of aristocratic manuscript culture and the marketplace of print. Ponsonby's methods for crossing the boundary were designed to work in concert with class hierarchy, so that manipulation of aristocratic codes—attention to "your honours consent"—gained him access to valuable texts. Ponsonby's position was not, however, secure: *Astrophel and Stella* was printed illegally by Newman, recalled, printed a second time by Newman in 1591, and then finally licensed

---

75 Nashe notes that receiving Sidney's mantle does not make literary creation easy: "I can tell you this is a harder thing than making golde of quicksiluer" (III: 333).

76 Authors like Robert Greene and Thomas Lodge, who borrowed from Sidney and the genre of romance with less hostility, achieved greater market success than Nashe, based on the number of reprinted editions in the sixteenth-century. Publishers like Nicholas Ling and John Busby, among others, advanced themselves by publishing Greene and Lodge, but neither rivaled Ponsonby in terms of professional success.

and published legally by Ponsonby in 1597. Elizabethan publishing's notion of intellectual property was not a simple or inevitable system; the control Ponsonby secured over Sidney's texts was repeatedly threatened. Nashe's attempt to bridge print and manuscript cultures further underscores the instability of the boundary. Nashe's preface proclaimed the social barrier to be powerless over him. By asserting a link between himself and Sidney in the preface to an illegal edition, however, Nashe sabotaged his dual goals of admission to the Sidney circle and advancement for both the Sidney and Nashe names in print. While the boundary was permeable, Nashe failed to cross it simply by pretending it did not apply to him.

In the interactions around Sidney's early publication, print and manuscript cultures seem less separate than formerly believed. The privileged view that Sidney's case provides suggests we revise the standard history of these cultural spheres in Elizabethan England. In a revised view, the two modes seem less stark alternatives than complementary, intertwined social forces. The boundary between print and manuscript was negotiable. This reminder of the mutual implication of these modes of dissemination returns much-needed flexibility to the history of technological and social transformation in early modern England.[77]

Seventeenth-century England would not prove hospitable to print-manuscript interaction. The social dislocations of mid-century brought to a climax an era of conflict between aristocrats and commoners, between country estates and the city. Sidney's *Arcadia* would be appropriated by royalist circles during the Civil War.[78] This cultural split, however, should not obscure the difficult but productive interaction between print and manuscript in the late Elizabethan era. The maneuvering of Ponsonby, Greville, and Nashe around Sidney's works provides a counter-example to influential studies of separation by class in Tudor–Stuart literary culture, such as Alfred Harbage's "rival traditions" of "popular" and "coterie" drama (see esp. 3–57).

Ponsonby and Nashe's subsequent careers anticipate the increasing rift in literary culture in the seventeenth century. Ponsonby joined the market elite, and Nashe was treated as an inferior hack. Ponsonby's stable of writers became increasingly courtly and aristocratic: Sidney, Spenser, Raleigh, Guicciardini, Plutarch. (His apprentice Blount would also publish Montaigne and Cervantes, and have a hand in Shakespeare's First Folio.) Nashe became part of a popular group of

---

77 This flexibility may also serve as a caveat in our own age to dire prophecies about the "death of the book" in an era of rapidly changing, antagonistic communications technologies.

78 See Patterson, 32–51.

writers who self-consciously wrote for sale to an anonymous audience, including Greene, Lodge, Deloney, and Dekker. The possibility of cultural exchange that Ponsonby maneuvered into being, and that Nashe trumpeted in his preface, provides a glimpse of the common ground of print and manuscript cultures, just as their later careers describe the subsequent contraction of that shared space.[79]

79 I would like to thank Douglas Brooks and the other participants in his 1998 MLA panel for providing a forum for an early version of this paper. I also would like to thank W. Speed Hill and the two readers for *TEXT* for their valuable comments and suggestions.

Works Cited

ARBER, EDWARD. *Transcript of Register of the Stationers' Company.* Volume II. London: privately printed, 1875.

BLAND, MARK. "The Appearance of the Text in Early Modern England." *TEXT* 11 (1998): 91–154.

BLAYNEY, PETER W. M. *The Texts of King Lear and Their Origins.* Cambridge: Cambridge UP, 1979.

———. "The Publication of Playbooks." *A New History of Early English Drama,* ed. J. C. Cox and D. S. Kastan (New York: Columbia UP, 1997), 385–422.

BRENNAN, WILLIAM. "William Ponsonby: Elizabethan Stationer." *Analytical & Enumerative Bibliography* 7 (1983): 91–110.

BROWN, CEDRIC C., and ARTHUR F. MAROTTI, eds. *Texts and Cultural Exchange in Early Modern England.* New York: St. Martin's, 1997.

CHARTIER, ROGER. *The Cultural Uses of Print in Early Modern France,* trans. Lydia G. Cochrane. Princeton: Princeton UP, 1987.

DAVIS, NATALIE ZEMON. *Society and Culture in Early Modern France.* Stanford: Stanford UP, 1975.

DUNCAN–JONES, KATHERINE. "Nashe and Sidney: The Tournament Scene of *The Unfortunate Traveler." Modern Language Review* 63 (1968): 3–6.

EISENSTEIN, ELIZABETH. *The Printing Press as an Agent of Change: Communications and Cultural Transformations in Early-Modern Europe.* 2 vols. Cambridge: Cambridge UP, 1979.

FERGUSON, MARGARET. "Nashe's *Unfortunate Traveler*: The 'Newes of the Maker' Game." *English Literary History* 11 (1981): 165–82.

HALASZ, ALEXANDRA. *The Marketplace of Print: Pamphlets and the Public Sphere in Early Modern England.* Cambridge: Cambridge UP, 1997.

HAMILTON, A. C. "Sidney's *Arcadia* as Prose Fiction: Its Relation to Its Sources." *English Literary Renaissance* 2 (1972): 29–60.

HARBAGE, ALFRED. *Shakespeare and the Rival Traditions.* New York: Macmillan 1952.

HIBBARD, G. R. *Thomas Nashe: A Critical Introduction.* Cambridge: Harvard UP, 1962.

HUTSON, LORNA. *Thomas Nashe in Context.* Oxford: Clarendon, 1989.

JOHNS, ADRIAN. *The Nature of the Book: Print and Knowledge in the Making.* Chicago: U of Chicago P, 1998.

JUDGES, CYRIL BATHURST. *Elizabethan Book-Pirates.* Cambridge: Harvard UP, 1934.

LAMB, MARY ELLEN. *Gender and Authorship in the Sidney Circle.* Madison: U of Wisconsin P, 1990.

LARSON, CHARLES. *Fulke Greville.* Boston: Twyane Publishers, 1980.

LASLETT, PETER. *The World We Have Lost: England Before the Industrial Age*. 2nd Edition. New York: Charles Scribner's Sons, 1965.

LINDENBAUM, PETER. "Sidney's *Arcadia* as Cultural Monument and Proto-Novel." *Texts and Cultural Exchange in Early Modern England*, ed. Cedric C. Brown, and Arthur F. Marotti. New York: St. Martin's Press, 1997.

LYLY, JOHN. *Euphues*, ed. Morris William Croll and Harry Clemons. London: Routledge & Sons, 1916.

MARCUS, LEAH. *Unediting the Renaissance: Shakespeare, Marlowe, Milton*. London: Routledge, 1996.

MARX, KARL. *The Marx–Engels Reader*, 2nd edition. ed. Robert C. Tucker. New York: W. W. Norton, 1978.

MASTON, JEFFREY, PETER STALLYBRASS, and NANCY VICKERS, eds. *Language Machines: Technologies of Literary and Cultural Production*. New York: Routledge, 1997.

MAY, STEPHEN W. "Tudor Aristocrats and the Mythical 'Stigma of Print.'" *Renaissance Papers* 10 (1980): 11–18.

MCKERROW, R. B., ed. *A Dictionary of Printers and Booksellers in England, Scotland, and Ireland, and of Foreign Printers of English Books, 1557–1640*. London: Bibliographical Society, 1910.

MCLUHAN, MARSHALL. *The Gutenberg Galaxy: The Making of Typographic Man*. New York: New American Library, 1969.

NASHE, THOMAS. *The Works of Thomas Nashe*, ed. R. B. McKerrow, rev. F. P. Wilson, 5 vols. Oxford: Blackwell, 1958.

NICHOLL, CHARLES. *A Cup of News: The Life of Thomas Nashe*. London: Routledge & Kegan Paul, 1984.

ONG, WALTER. *Orality and Literacy: The Technologizing of the Word*. New York: Methuen, 1982.

PATTERSON, ANNABEL. *Censorship and Interpretation: The Conditions of Writing and Reading in Early Modern England*. Madison: U of Wisconsin P, 1984.

READ, CONYERS. *Mr Secretary Walsingham and the Policy of Queen Elizabeth*. 3 volumes. 1925; New York: Archon, 1967.

RINGLER, W. A., Jr. "Sir Philip Sidney: The Myth and the Man." *Sir Philip Sidney: 1586 and the Creation of a Legend*, ed. Jan van Dorston, Dominic Baker–Smith, and Arthur F. Kinney. Leiden: Leiden UP, 1986.

SALZMAN, PAUL. *English Prose Fiction 1558–1700: A Critical History*. Oxford: Clarendon P, 1985.

SAUNDERS, J. W. "The Stigma of Print: A Note on the Social Bases of Tudor Poetry." *Essays in Criticism* 1 (1951): 139–59.

SHAKESPEARE, WILLIAM. *The Winter's Tale*, ed J. H. P. Pafford. London: Routledge, 1963.

SHEAVYN, PHOEBE. *The Literary Profession in the Elizabethan Age*. 1909; New York: Haskell House, 1964.

SIDNEY, SIR PHILIP. *The Countess of Pembroke's Arcadia (The Old Arcadia)*, ed. Jean Robertson. Oxford: Oxford UP, 1973.

——. *The Poems*, ed. W. A. Ringler, Jr. Oxford: Oxford UP, 1962.

——. *The Defence of Poetry. Sir Philip Sidney*, ed. Katherine Duncan–Jones. Oxford: Oxford UP, 1989.

SKRETKOWICZ, VICTOR. "Building Sidney's Reputation: Texts and Editors of the *Arcadia*." *Sir Philip Sidney: 1586 and the Creation of a Legend*, ed. Jan van Dorston, Dominic Baker–Smith, and Arthur F. Kinney. Leiden: Leiden UP, 1986.

SUZUKI, MIHOKO, " 'Signiorie ouer the Pages': The Crisis of Authority in Nashe's *The Unfortunate Traveler*." *Studies in English Literature* 28 (1988): 18–38.

TRAISTER, DANIEL. "Reluctant Virgins: The Stigma of Print Revisited." *Colby Quarterly* 26 (1980): 75–86.

WALL, WENDY. *The Imprint of Gender: Authorship and Publication in the English Renaissance*. Ithaca: Cornell UP, 1993.

WARKENTIN, GERMAINE. "Patrons and Profiteers: Thomas Newman and the 'Violent Enlargement' of '*Astrophil and Stella*.' " *Book Collector* 34 (1985): 461–87.

WOODHUYSEN, H. R. *Sir Philip Sidney and the Circulation of Manuscripts, 1558–1640*. Oxford: Clarendon P, 1996.

WRIGHT, LOUIS B. *Middle-Class Culture in Elizabethan England*. Chapel Hill: U of North Carolina P, 1935.

Evidence for an Authorial Sequence in Donne's Elegies

GARY A. STRINGER

B EGINNING SOMETIME IN THE LATE 1580s or early 1590s and continuing into the next century, John Donne composed a body of seventeen love elegies that proved extremely popular among his contemporaries. According to the surviving evidence, some 136 different scribes participated in the transcription of these poems into assorted diaries, commonplace books, and poetical collections during and soon after Donne's lifetime, leaving 705 complete or partial copies in the manuscript record. The average number of copies per poem is 41.76, and some appear much more widely: the three most popular are "The Anagram" at 69 manuscript copies, "Going to Bed" at 67, and the 114-line "The Bracelet" at 63. As might be expected, such uncontrolled proliferation not only produced an enormous amount of verbal variation in the texts of individual poems, but also left the poems ordered in virtually every conceivable way within the body of surviving artifacts; indeed—to take a representative detail—of the twelve elegies that I want to focus on in this paper, all but one ("By our first strange and fatal interview" [*ElFatal*]) appear as the first elegy in at least one of the major manuscript collections of these poems (see Figure 1). Merely as a practical matter, of course, an editor is obliged to deal with the question of sequence—poems must be fixed in some order or other (at least this is true if the medium is print)—but the issue also has thematic and historical dimensions. We know that Renaissance / Early Modern writers employed the sequence as an important device for the creation of meaning as they organized shorter poems of various kinds into larger narrative structures (the sonnet cycle being perhaps the most familiar example); we know that such classical elegists as Ovid organized their poems generically into "books"; and we know that this generic organization was part of the art of the elegy that Donne and his contemporaries learned from their classical predecessors—Thomas Campion's *Poemata* (1595), for example, a copy of which Donne had in his library, included as a separate section a "Liber Elegiarum."[1] Thus the extent to which Donne thought of his elegies as a discrete, coherent collection and, more specifically, the question of whether they are intended as an ordered, step-by-step sequence are issues worthy of our attention.

From their first entry into print in 1633 (and even before that, as I will demonstrate below), the ordering of Donne's elegies was affected by extra-literary factors. According to Edward Arber's transcript, John Marriot brought a book of verses and poems by John Donne for entry in the Stationers' Register on 13 September 1632. The five satires and "the first, second, Tenth, Eleyenth, and Thirteenth *Elegies*," however, were "excepted" until such time as Marriot could produce "lawful authority."[2] A subsequent entry on 31 October indicates that Marriot, presumably having obtained the requisite permission, resubmitted the five satires (Arbor 261). But the excluded elegies are not mentioned, and they remain absent from the first printing of Donne's collected *Poems* the following year.[3] As Figure 2 indicates, the principal manuscript of the elegies that Marriot produced was a member of the traditional Group I, as first defined by Herbert Grierson in 1912.[4] Marked with a capital "E" in Group I and shown as omitted (*om*) in 1633 on Figure 2, the prohibited elegies are "The Bracelet" (*ElBrac*), "Going to Bed" (*ElBed*), "Love's War" (*ElWar*), "By our first strange and fatal interview" (*ElFatal*), and "Love's Progress" (*ElProg*). "Love's Progress" and "Going to Bed" were not printed among Donne's *Poems* until the Restoration edition of 1669 (G), and "Love's War" did not see print until 1802;[5] but "The Bracelet" and *ElFatal* appeared in the expanded

---

[1] See Geoffrey Keynes, *A Bibliography of Dr. John Donne, Dean of Saint Paul's*, 4th ed. (Oxford: Clarendon P, 1973), 266.

[2] Edward Arber, ed., *A Transcript of the Register of the Company of Stationers of London; 1554–1640 A.D.*, vol.4 (London: Privately Pr., 1877), 249.

[3] *Poems, by J. D. With Elegies on the Authors Death* (London: John Marriot, 1633).

[4] In *The Poems of John Donne*, vol.2 (Oxford: Oxford UP, 1912), lvi–cxxiv. Subsequent editors have expanded and refined Grierson's classified listing, but his taxonomy has endured.

[5] Lines 29–46 of "Love's War" were excerpted in Robert Chamberlain's *Harmony of the Muses* (London, 1654; Wing C105), and lines 29–32, 35–36, 39–40, and 43–46 appeared

and reorganized edition of 1635 (B), though Marriot still had no permission to include them. One part of his method of circumvention was to slip them in from manuscripts other than the one in which they had been explicitly proscribed by number and in which their texts differed from those in Group I;[6] the second part of his method consisted in repositioning them in the sequence, so that "The Bracelet," which should have been "Elegy I" in 1633, became in 1635 "Elegie XII"; and *ElFatal* was not included among the Elegies section at all, instead appearing among funeral poems more than 150 pages away. Having further muddied the waters by importing a number of new poems into the newly established Elegies section, Marriot then numbered the whole sequence from I to XVII, and this order and numbering carried over intact until 1669, when it was finally deemed possible to include "Love's Progress" and "Going to Bed." With some slight adjustments and additions, the 1669 arrangement of elegies has appeared in every subsequent edition except for those of Helen Gardner (*John Donne: The Elegies and the Songs and Sonnets*, 1965), John T. Shawcross (*The Complete Poetry of John Donne*, 1967), and John Carey (*John Donne* [Oxford Authors], 1990; *John Donne: Selected Poetry* [World's Classics], 1996).[7]

Carey's arrangement is that of the Group I manuscripts—what would apparently have appeared in 1633 had the licenser not intervened (see the leftmost column of Figure 2)—and I cannot believe it has any real authority.[8] Gardner, however, though she uses 1633 as copy-text for the elegies it contains, praises the extrinsic authority of

---

in John Cotgrave's *Wits Interpreter* (London, 1655; Wing C6370), but it remained for F. G. Waldron to publish the full text, which he did twice in London in 1802—in both *A Collection of Miscellaneous Poetry* and *The Shakespearean Miscellany*.

[6] Marriot drew his text of "The Bracelet" from a (now unidentified) manuscript whose text was only a distant cousin of that in the Group I and his text of *ElFatal* from the well-known O'Flahertie manuscript (H6), where it was numbered "Elegie 9."

[7] Pre-twentieth-century editions of Donne that include full sequences of the elegies are those of Jacob Tonson (*Poems on Several Occasions*, 1719), John Bell (*The Poetical Works of Dr. John Donne*, 1779), Robert Anderson (*The Poetical Works of Dr. John Donne*, 1793), Alexander Chalmers (*The Poems of John Donne*, 1810), James Russell Lowell (*The Poetical Works of Dr. John Donne*, 1855), Alexander B. Grosart (*The Complete Poems of John Donne*, 1872–73), James Russell Lowell (*The Poems of John Donne*, 1895), and E. K. Chambers (*The Poems of John Donne*, 1896). Twentieth-century editions that follow the 1669 arrangement are Grierson (1912), John Hayward (*John Donne, Dean of St. Paul's: Complete Poetry and Selected Prose*, 1929), Roger D. Bennett (*The Complete Poems of John Donne*, 1942), A. J. Smith (*John Donne: The Complete English Poems*, 1971), and C. A. Patrides (*The Complete English Poems of John Donne*, 1985).

[8] Carey presents the elegies in the same order in both his editions. In the World's Classics volume, they are all printed together as a generic group; in the Oxford Authors volume, however, they are scattered among other poems and prose pieces in a

the Westmoreland manuscript (NY3), written in the hand of Donne's friend Rowland Woodward, and follows its ordering of the elegies—except that she inserts "Love's Progress" (which does not appear in NY3) after "Going to Bed," which she deems "an appropriate place" (111). And Shawcross—without addressing the issue at all—follows Westmoreland's order exactly, adding "Love's Progress" after "His Picture"; he, too, prefers the earliest printing as copy-text. The fact that Shawcross does not discuss the matter and that Gardner does not respect the matter indicates that both have failed to treat the sequencing of the elegies in NY3 with the importance that, in my judgment, it deserves.

We may begin our investigation of this issue by attending to the information encoded in the letters and numbers on Figure 3. In the leftmost column of the Figure are shown the Donne Variorum short forms for the elegies, from "The Bracelet" (*ElBrac*) at the top to "Variety" (*ElVar*) at the bottom. At the top of the other columns are the sigla for various textual sources—beginning with the manuscript C9 in column two and moving rightward through H6, NY3, B13, the NY1–VA2 pair, the Group I family (B32 to SP1), and on to the Group II manuscripts (which include B7–CT1 and DT1–H4) at the far right-hand side. The left-to-right arrangement of these sigla reflects at least generally the chronological sequence of the texts of the elegies they contain. Indicated with an arabic numeral in the leftmost position in the column under each siglum is the ordinal position that each poem occupies among the elegies in the artifact in question, and to the immediate right of that numeral is printed the heading given the poem in that artifact (e.g., in C9 *ElBrac* is the fifteenth elegy and is headed "Elegye"). In parentheses under some headings are given line numbers and variant readings, which I will refer to below. Alterations between regular and boldface type as we move through the sequences of arabic numerals in each column indicate interruptions in the physical sequencing of the poems (e.g., in C9 other poems intervene between *ElPart* [numbered "13"] and *ElExpost* [numbered "14"]).

The single most authoritative artifact cited on the chart is NY3—not only because its scribe was a long-time friend of Donne's, but also because the general verbal quality of its texts is exceedingly high. And though it does not contain every poem Donne wrote, it contains several that are found nowhere else, and it records some

---

scheme intended to show chronologically "Donne's development, as writer and thinker" (xxxviii). In assuming that the Group I arrangement reflects the order of composition, Carey presumably follows I. A. Shapiro, "The Date of a Donne Elegy, and Its Implications," in *English Renaissance Studies Presented to Dame Helen Gardner in Honour of Her Seventieth Birthday*, ed. John Carey (Oxford: Clarendon P, 1980), 141–50, who advances this view.

individual readings that are uniquely correct.[9] If this manuscript was not copied directly from Donne's papers, it undoubtedly stands very close to them, and its sequencing of poems may be as authoritative as the verbal constitution of its texts. Thus, even if NY3's ordering of the poems were unique, the pedigree and intrinsic virtues of this manuscript would still compel us to consider whether that ordering reflected the author's intentions. Significantly, however, as is shown on Figure 3, NY3's numbered sequence of twelve elegies reaching from "The Bracelet" (*ElBrac*) at the top of the column to "His Picture" (*ElPict*) at the bottom is recapitulated in several other artifacts. Even more significantly, as I will demonstrate below, these artifacts do not derive from NY3 or even subsist in its general line of transmission. The likelihood that NY3 reflects the author's intended order for the elegies is thus considerably strengthened by the recurrence of that order in other artifacts that can be traced back to Donne's holograph in independent lines of transmission.

Traditionally designated Group III manuscripts, C9 and H6 (the Luttrell and O'Flahertie manuscripts)—listed to the left of NY3 in Figure 3—are siblings. The compiler of H6 (whom I suspect was also the keeper of the parent manuscript) was someone who knew how to get his hands on Donne poems, and this artifact not only stands as the largest single manuscript collection of Donne's verse (174 poems), but also preserves some exceedingly rare items—it contains the sole manuscript copy of Donne's "Upon the Translation of the Psalms by Sir Philip Sidney" and one of only two surviving copies of "To the Countess of Bedford: Begun in France" and of the epigrams "Cales and Guiana" and "Sir John Wingfield." Though this scribe accepted into his manuscript a number of poems that are not Donne's, his zeal as a collector and his success at acquiring scarce items lend his manuscript a great deal of importance.

As is shown on Figure 3, the collection of elegies in the C9–H6 prototype begins with "The Comparison" (*ElComp*)—the C9 scribe for some reason failed to enter the poem, though he did leave space for it—and proceeds in a numbered sequence that matches that in NY3 except for the positioning of "The Anagram" (*ElAnag*), which immediately precedes *ElFatal* and "His Picture" in NY3, but follows them in C9–H6. As for "The Bracelet," at the top of the column, the H6 scribe appears to have obtained a copy only at the last minute. Following a number of noncanonical and dubious items as the last of 27 entries in the "ELEGIES" section, "The Bracelet" is entered under the generic heading "Elegy" and is not given a number at all. H6

---

9 NY3 is our sole source for the Holy Sonnets "Since She whome I lovd," "Show me deare Christ," and "Oh, to vex me." Among its unique correct readings is "dearth" in line 6 of "At the round Earths imagind corners," where all other sources record "death."

thus records the twelve elegies of NY3, but evinces two differences of order—one involving "The Bracelet," the other "The Anagram."

Let us now hold these considerations in abeyance for a moment while we bring a different kind of evidence to bear on the problem. As my colleague Ted–Larry Pebworth suggests in the following essay, Donne seems to have revisited a number of the elegies to effect slight adjustments of one kind or another, and two such instances—one each in "The Perfume" and in "Jealousy"—are particularly relevant to the discussion here because they occur in the sequence of poems shared by C9–H6 and NY3.[10] As noted in Figure 4, C9–H6 record the early "dandled" version of line 29 of "The Perfume" (as opposed to the revised "ingled" version that appears in NY3); and these artifacts also give the early "high fare" reading of line 21 of "Jealousy" (as opposed to the revised "great fare" found in NY3). It is also true that while C9–H6 preserve such demonstrably erroneous readings as "Coronets" (for NY3's correct "carcanetts") in line 6 of "The Comparison" and "Peeres" (for NY3's correct "pres") in line 6 of "Love's War," C9–H6 also preserve the correct "wordes" in line 18 of "The Anagram," where NY3 evinces the eyeskip error "Letters." That the C9–H6 pair and NY3 are each right in places where the other is wrong shows that both descend from the holograph in independent lines of transmission. That the poems are transmitted in the same order even as specific readings change in response to Donne's tinkering suggests that maintaining them in a particular arrangement was a matter of ongoing authorial concern.

What the evidence with respect to C9–H6 suggests to me is that, at a fairly early stage in the development of his collection of elegies, Donne circulated a group of eleven poems—beginning with "The Comparison" and extending to "His Picture"—that did not include "The Bracelet." These are elegies 1–11 of H6 and elegies 2–12 of NY3. Whether "The Anagram" originally came at the end or whether it was mishandled in the C9–H6 parent manuscript is impossible to determine, although that it precedes *ElFatal* in NY3 (as well as in NY1–VA2 and B13) argues the latter—and "His Picture," in which a lover contemplates going off to war and leaving his mistress alone, seems more like a concluding poem than does "The Anagram." The reason for the absence of "The Bracelet" from the C9–H6 collection is also

---

[10] The changes in question occur in *ElPerf* 29 and *ElJeal* 21. In *ElPerf* the original "And kist and **dandled** on thy fathers knee" has been altered to "And kist and **ingled** on thy fathers knee"; in *ElJeal* the original "pamperd with **high** fare" has been revised to "pamperd with **great** fare." Briefly stated, the reasons to regard these changes as authorial are three: (1) the contexts in which they occur do not otherwise reflect strong interventionist tendencies on the part of the manuscript copyists—each of these is an isolated, specifically targeted alteration; (2) in neither instance does the change seem necessary, but in each it seems for the better; (3) neither change seems likely to have resulted from scribal misreading or mistaking one word for the other.

not susceptible of absolute proof, but the most likely explanation—given the diligence of this collector and the fact that he has the earliest versions of at least two of the poems—is that it had not yet been written: the poem also appears not to have been initially available to the scribes of B46 and H5, the other two Group III manuscripts, for it appears late in their sequences of elegies and stands apart from the other members of the genre (see Figure 1). If we accept, at least provisionally, that "The Bracelet" did not exist at the time Donne circulated his initial collection of elegies, this additional evidence on the order of composition may lead to a more precise dating of the entire sequence, since "The Bracelet" contains specific topical allusions that link it to contemporary events.[11] Whether or not this is the right explanation for the original absence of "The Bracelet" from C9–H6, the poem's appearance at the head of the sequence in NY3 is matched by its similar placement in B13 and in the NY1–VA2 pair and—even though they do not otherwise preserve NY3's sequence—in the later Group I and Group II manuscripts. That Donne at a fairly early point intended "The Bracelet" for position number 1 does not seem to me open to doubt.

As Figure 3 shows, the twelve-elegy sequence of NY3 also appears in B13 and in the parent-child pair NY1–VA2. These artifacts entitle each poem simply "elegy" and number them sequentially from 1 onward, and—except for one deviation in B13—the sequence in each is entered continuously and in a single scribal hand. I would cite these sequences in support of the authenticity of the NY3 sequence and argue the case in much the same way as I did for C9–H6: both B13 and NY1 evince correct readings in places where NY3 errs—the "words/letters" crux in line 18 of "The Anagram" being an obvious example—and both err (in many places) where NY3 reads correctly. Thus neither they nor NY3 can have been copied one from the other—not even through a series of intermediaries—and must descend from Donne's holograph in separate lines of transmission. And the same reasoning shows that B13 and NY1 do not belong on the same family tree with each other, leading us to see that these artifacts provide two parallel corroborating instances—rather than one—of the authenticity of the NY3 sequence.

Among the verbal variants listed parenthetically in Figure 3 are one instance apiece in which the B13 and NY1 sequences diverge from the NY3 reading—B13 with "fault" in line 11 of "The Bracelet" and NY1 with "due to" in line 46 of "Going to Bed." B13's "fault" reading, as Ted Pebworth explains below (195), is a Donnean revision appearing otherwise only in the later texts represented on this chart by Groups

---

[11] In an analysis generally accepted by Donne scholars, Gardner surveys various kinds of topical material in the poems and dates the poem c. 1593–94, "at the time when Donne was writing his first *Satires*" (113).

I and II. Primarily because of this reading, B13 appears far down the stemma for "The Bracelet." Above B13 on that stemma are artifacts whose order for the elegies is quite different from that in B13. Fortunately, this incongruity—which might otherwise seem irreconcilable with the notion that these elegies circulated as an ordered group—is explained by the recognition that in B13 only the second through the twelfth elegies, scribally numbered "2" through "12," are written in the primary hand. *ElBrac*, numbered "i" in the manuscript, has been entered by a different copyist. The first scribe seems to have received the eleven elegies from *ElComp* through *ElPict* as a set, but somehow knew that *ElBrac*—or something—was missing from the beginning and so left space for its later entry (much as the scribe of C9 did with *ElComp*); he then proceeded to enter the poems he had in hand, beginning each immediately where the previous one left off on the page and numbering them as he went. Though it is also possible that the later scribe appended an extra quire of pages containing *ElBrac* to the beginning of the manuscript, the presence of an extra leaf between the conclusion of *ElBrac* and the beginning of *ElComp* makes the former explanation more likely (the volume is bound too tightly for definitive physical analysis); either explanation can accommodate the anomaly of a later-version text of "The Bracelet" in the otherwise early-version sequence of B13 and leave B13 as a valid witness to the authenticity of the NY3 sequence.

NY1's "due to" (for the normative "much less") in *ElBed* 46 ("There is no penance, **much less/due to** innocence") cannot be so simply explained, for "due to" is a scribal expurgation and constitutes the watershed variant that separates the sixty-seven manuscript witnesses into two major lines of transmission. In other instances in which the artifacts divide into distinct lineages, NY1 aligns itself with NY3, and discrepancies between their texts of particular poems result from individual scribal initiative, not from NY1's having imported a text across lineal boundaries. The latter seems to have happened here, however, for the separate identity of the text preserved in NY1 (and a score of other manuscripts) consists not only in the line 46 crux, but also in several other variants scattered throughout the poem. We cannot, of course, know the exact procedures followed by John Cave (the scribe of NY1) in acquiring his collection of Donne's poems—in some instances he may simply have accepted whatever poems happened his way; in others he may have deliberately set out to track down copies of specific poems whose titles he carried about on a "poems-to-get" list. The artifact he finally compiled, however, is the product of an assiduous and discriminating collector; and no other manuscript of Donne's poems shows a greater concern with generic organization. After an opening section of "FIVE SATYRES: THE LETANIE: THE STORM, AND CALME BY Mᴿ IOHN DONNE," Cave inscribes a new title page—"ELEGIES: AND EPIGRAMMES: BY MR IOHN DONNE:"—and proceeds to replicate the NY3 sequence of elegies exactly (including the funeral elegy *Sorrow* at the end), following it immediately with another title page introducing a selection of "Miscellanea Poems Elegies Sonnetts by the same Author." Though Cave failed to obtain Donne's epigrams, his section heading shows that he was aware of their existence and marks him as a deliberate and knowledgeable collector who, if he did not receive his mixed-lineage sequence of elegies as a pre-existing set, was capable of constructing it on his own.

The final manuscript sequences of elegies listed on Figure 3 are those preserved in Groups I (B32–SP1) and II (B7–H4), which Donne's editors have historically regarded as centrally important. Generally speaking, these artifacts preserve later texts than those in the Group IIIs and in NY3, and previous editors and commentators have speculated, primarily on biographical grounds, that the ur-texts from which these groups descend were authoritative collections that Donne himself put together in 1614 and 1619, respectively. If this were true, we should of course wish to pay attention to any sequencing of poems they contain as well as to individual texts (reciprocally, how they handle sequence and text might affect our judgments on their overall reliability).[12] It is therefore worth examining such biographical

---

[12] Grierson first suggested in 1912 that the "nucleus" of the Group I collection "may have been a commonplace-book which belonged to Sir Henry Goodyere" (2: xc) and briefly quotes from the 20 December 1614 letter of Donne to Goodyer that I quote at length below (unless otherwise noted, I cite Donne's prose letters from the 1651 *Letters to Severall Persons of Honour*, ed. M. Thomas Hester [New York: Scholar's Facsimiles, 1977]). Though Grierson enumerated both the Group I and the NY3 orderings of the elegies (2: 60–61), he seems never to have addressed the possibility that either order might be authorial or significant. In her Oxford edition of the *Divine Poems* in 1952, however, Gardner took Grierson's suggestion further, arguing that the prototype of the Group I collection (X) "was a copy of Donne's own collection, which he speaks of in … [the] letter to Goodyer" (lxiv) and proposing that "the Group I manuscripts … preserv[e] the 'text of the "edition" of 1614' " (lxvi). Gardner additionally thought the "order of the collection" reflected in *H 49* (B32) and *C 57* (C2) "suggest[ed] that when [X] was copied the collection had not been finally arranged" (lxviii). Citing its inclusion of "the Hamilton Elegy" (dated 1625), Gardner believed that the progenitor of the Group II manuscripts must have been copied "from Donne's own papers … some time after 1625" (xlvii). In her subsequent edition of *The Elegies and the Songs and Sonnets* (1965), Gardner called the Group II order "rather chaotic" (lxxi). Though, as explained above, she violated it, Gardner claimed to "prefer the order of the set" of elegies in NY3 because of the artifact's "high extrinsic authority" and because "it brings together at the close the three most serious poems" (111). The proposal that the Group II collection "came from the poet himself" in 1619 was advanced by Alan MacColl ("The New Edition of Donne's Love Poems," *Essays in Criticism*, 17 [1967], 258–63), who speculated that the "Poems, of which you took a promise" alluded to in the letter Donne wrote to accompany a copy of *Biathanatos* that he sent to Sir Robert Ker (*Letters* 21) were "those that make up the Group II collection." In MacColl's view,

evidence as we have for what it can tell us. Before doing so, however, we might note that information contained in Figures 3 and 5 allows us to dismiss the Group II order out of hand and thus to simplify our task considerably, for in both the B7–CT1 and DT1–H4 branches of Group II (for ease of examination the DT1 arrangement is isolated in Figure 5), the poems are scattered about in small clusters that form no sequence at all. The Group I order, therefore, is the only one with which we must deal here.

Both the 20 December 1614 letter to Goodyer cited above (note 12) and another to Henry Wotton "probably written in the latter part of 1600"[13] cast light on the possible origins and authority of the Group I manuscripts. In the epistle of 1614, having already determined to enter the Church, Donne reminds Goodyer that he has not complied with Donne's previous request to "borrow" an "old [manuscript] book" of poems:

> ... I am brought to a necessity of printing my Poems, and addressing them to my L[ord] Chamberlain [Robert Ker, Earl of Somerset]. This I mean to do forthwith; not for much publique view, but at mine own cost, a few Copies. I apprehend some incongruities in the resolution; and I know what I shall suffer from many interpretations: but I am at an end, of much considering that; and, if I were as startling in that kinde, as ever I was, yet in this particular, I am under an unescapable necessity .... By this occasion I am made a Rhapsoder of mine own rags, and that cost me more diligence, to seek them, then it did to make them. This made me aske to borrow that old book of you, which it will be too late to see, for that use, when I see you: for I must do this, as a valediction to the world, before I take Orders. But this is it, I am to aske you; whether you ever made any such use of the letter in verse, *A nostre Countesse* [of Huntington] *chez vous*, as that I may not put it in, amongst the rest to persons of that rank; for I desire very very much, that something should bear her name in the book .... (*Letters* 196–97)

What this letter tells us for certain is that Donne was attempting to gather his poems for publication late in 1614 and did not have copies of at least some of them. It does not, of course, tell us whether Goodyer ever forwarded the book, what its contents might have been, what other efforts to collect his "own rags" Donne may have been

---

"Everything about the Group II collection is consistent, as no other manuscript is, with its having come from the poet himself at this time" (259). More recently, Peter Beal (*Index of English Literary manuscripts*, vol.1, pt. 1 [London: Mansell, 1980], 249), has tentatively endorsed these notions of the origins of Groups I and II.

[13] Claude Summers and Ted–Larry Pebworth, "Donne's Correspondence with Wotton," *John Donne Journal* 10 (1991), 25. Derived from ff. 308v–309 of the Burleigh manuscript, this is the letter designated number 11 and quoted by Evelyn M. Simpson, *A Study of the Prose Works of John Donne* (Oxford: Clarendon P, 1948), 316–17; I here follow the new transcription of the letter provided by Summers and Pebworth.

pursuing simultaneously, nor indeed even whether Donne actually completed the task of assembling a large collection of his poems at this time.

The letter also drips Donne's distaste for the "necessity" forced upon him. It is possible that his worry over the "interpretations" he dreads having to "suffer" refers to a general disapprobation of the act of publication itself—what he elsewhere labels the "fault" of having "descended to print" (*Letters* 238)—but the exculpatory claim that he is not now "as startling [i.e., liable to offend] in that kinde, as ever ... [he] was" makes it more likely that he is here thinking of the specific imputations of moral and/or political impropriety that he knows some of the poems will draw upon him. That is certainly the worry he had privately expressed to Wotton a decade before in a letter accompanying a collection of his prose paradoxes. Demanding Wotton's assurance "upon the religion of your frendship that no coppy shalbee taken for any respect of these or any other my compositions sent to you," Donne promises "to acquaint you with all myne" and concedes: "to my satyrs there belongs some feare and to some elegies and these [the enclosed paradoxes] perhaps shame"—attributes that make him "desirous to hyde" the poems" in order to avert "any over reconing of them or there maker" (Summers and Pebworth 27).

No published volume of Donne's poems dating from 1614 or 1615 has ever been found. If Donne did succeed in collecting his poems at that time, however, the concerns expressed in these widely separated letters to Wotton and Goodyer are difficult to reconcile with the notion that the Group I manuscripts represent what he finalized for submission to the press. Despite his declaration to Goodyer that he had steeled himself against whatever adverse "interpretations" publication might entail, it seems unlikely that he would have felt obliged to throw discretion to the winds and include every last poem he had ever written; and one can hardly imagine that he would have organized a volume that—as the Group I manuscripts do[14] —opened with the "fear[ful]" satires and followed them immediately with the "shame[ful]" elegies. Indeed, as noted above, these are the very poems refused a license seventeen years later when Marriot was preparing the 1633 *Poems*, an official response confirming the prophetic accuracy

---

[14] Of the five principal Group I manuscripts (B32 [*H 49*], C2 [*C 57*], C8 [*Lec*], O20 [*D*], SP1 [*SP*]), four open with satires and follow them immediately with elegies, which suggests that this was the order of the group's progenitor. Perhaps anticipating the objections to this arrangement that I advance above, however, the compiler of C2 places "Metempsychosis" (*Metem*), "La Corona" (*Cor*), and twelve Holy Sonnets before the satires and elegies. No other Group I manuscript contains *Metem*, and C2's cognate C8 lacks both *Cor* and the Holy Sonnets. B32, and the cognates O20 and SP1, contain *Cor* and the Holy Sonnets, but place them later in their respective collections.

of Donne's earlier pronouncement on these works. In light of the expressed necessity of dedicating the poems to Somerset and his concern not to overlook the Countess of Huntington in the section of poems "to persons of that rank," it is more probable that the volume would have opened with verse letters to persons of honor or holy sonnets or even love lyrics and that the satires and elegies would have been relegated to a far less conspicuous place in the volume.

A further, more strictly bibliographical reason to question the authority of the Group I ordering of the elegies lies in the quality of the text preserved in these artifacts. Group I corruptions in the thirteen love elegies listed in Figure 5 (taking the poems in Figure 5 order and omitting the funeral elegy *Sorrow*) include omission of "me" from the normative "love me less" in *ElBrac* 54, "softly tread" (for the normative "safely tread") in *ElBed* 17, "pure" [for the normative "poor"] kindred in *ElJeal* 9, "leane dearth of Letters" (for the correct "leane dearth of words") in *ElAnag* 18, "these [for the normative "those"] meanes" in *ElChange* 8, omission of an entire couplet (ll. 7–8) in *ElPerf*, "cares rash sudden stormes" (for the normative "cares rash sudden horines") in *ElPict* 8, "nor to write my name" (for the normative "nor so write my name") in *ElServe* 4, the rhyme-destroying and ungrammatical "giues" (for the correct "giue") at the end of *ElWar* 17, "Will quickly know Thee, and alas" (for the authorial "Will quickly know Thee, and know thee, and alas") in *ElFatal* 37, "graces and good works" (for the correct "graces and good words") in *ElNat* 25, and "bringes/breeds blood" (for the normative "enrageth blood") in *ElAut* 26. Indeed, of all the Group I elegies, only *ElProg* (last in the unbroken sequence of thirteen) is without flagrant verbal error, perhaps because the family progenitor derived its text of the poem immediately from a revised holograph copy of the poem.[15] If Donne had any hand in preparing the Group I prototype, this evidence suggests that it did not involve detailed attention to the texts of the elegies.

If both the placement of the generic group within the overall collection and the texts of individual elegies raise questions about the author's alleged involvement with Group I, the sequencing of the poems is equally suspect. Subjective impressions are perhaps more open to dispute than are bibliographical details, but I would point especially to the placement of "Going to Bed," the funeral elegy "Sorrow, who to this house," and "Love's Progress" in Group I as locations that seem highly unlikely for Donne to have chosen in any gathering of

---

[15] As will be demonstrated in the forthcoming Elegies volume of the Donne Variorum, *ElProg* circulated widely in an early version containing the authorial misstatement "Then hee that tooke her mayd" in line 27, and this is the version contained in C9 and H6. A revised version bearing the correction "Then if hee took her maide" appears in the Groups I and II artifacts.

his poems for public exhibition on the eve of ordination. Since both "Going to Bed" and "Love's Progress" were regarded as unprintable among the collected *Poems* until 1669, one wonders whether a Donne reluctant to publish his poems at all would have deliberately chosen to place these provocative elegies in positions number 2 and 13—last and very nearly first. And what of the funeral elegy? It might provide a sense of closure at the end of the Ovidian sequence in NY3, marking a turn from carnal to spiritual concerns rather like the sonnets on divine love at the end of the *Amoretti* or *Astrophil and Stella*, but as the eighth poem—between "His Picture" and *ElServe*—it makes no sense. In sum, this Group I order to me seems no order at all, but a random shuffling together of poems that, in the earlier arrangements that I have described, seem to bear the stamp of authorial sanction.

Figure 1: Major Collections of Elegies in Seventeenth-Century Artifacts

| | III | | | | IV | | A-III | A-III | | | u | u | A-III | u | A-III | A-III | A-III | u | A-III u | u | u | II | I | | | II | | | | Prints | | | |
	B46	H5	C9	H6	NY3	NY1 VA2	B13 C1	H3	O21	Y3	B47	C5	H7	H8	HH4	HH5	Y2	F4	HH1	O16	O34	WN1	B32 C2 C8 O20 SP1	B7 CT1 H4	DT1 H4	SA1	B40	TT1	TT2	A	B C D	E F	G
ElBrac	15¹	12¹	15¹	16¹	1¹	1¹	1²	1²	16²	2²	14¹	7¹	11²	6¹	1²	8²	9²	7¹	7¹	2¹	2²	10²	1²	1²	1²	1²	1²	2²	2²		10	10	10
ElComp	7	3	6¹	1	2	2	2	13	4	4	6	6	3	7	4		11		3	7	14	8²		2	3	2	3	3	3²	8	8	8	8
ElPerf	4¹	6¹	1¹	2¹	3²	3²	3²	4²	9²	11²	5¹		15²	8²	4				11²	5¹	10²		6²	3²	4²	3²	4²	3²		4	4	4	4
ElJeal	12¹	13¹	2¹	3¹	4²	4²	4²	10¹	7¹	7¹			1²	9²		2²			5¹		16²	4²	3²	12²	14²	3²			3²	1	1	1	1
ElServe	3	9	3		5	5	5	6	3	3	12	5	5	10		6		8	2		9	11	8	7	8	9	9	9	8	6	6	6	6
ElNat		10	4	5	6	6	6	3	14	16	11	3	8	11	4	7			1		13	7	11	8	9	5	6	7		7	7	7	7
ElWar	5	8	5	6	7	7	7	9	17	8	8	3	10	16	2	1,9		8	8	4	12	12	9	6	3	5	6	7	5				14
ElBed	1	4	6	7	8	8	8	5	6	6	1	9	13	16		1	4	3	8		4	7	2	10	12	6	4	5	4	3	3	3	3
ElChange	2	7	7	8	9	9	9	7	5	5	7	1	7	12				5	16	1	1,15		5	4	8	4	8	1	10	2	2	2	2
ElAnag	13	5	10	11	10	10	10	12	14	14	4	8	12	2,14▾	2	3		4	13	6	3	5	3	4		8				14	14	14	16
ElFatal	6	2	8	9	11	11	11	13	15	15	9	2	4	4		6	8	7	6	3	6	6	10	7	9					5	5	5	5
ElPict	14♦		9	10	12★	12★	12		13	10	2	4	2★	13	6	5★	5★	1	14	3	7	9	7★	14	16					5★	5	5	9
ElAut	9¹	1¹	11²	12²	14¹	14¹	13²	2¹	2²	1²	3¹		14¹	1²	3²	12²		6¹	10¹	6²	5²	2¹	13¹	6²	7²	7²	7²	8²	7²	9	9	9	13
ElProg	10²	12¹	12¹	13¹	13²	13²	14²	10¹	12¹	12¹			6¹	1²			10²		12¹		11¹		12²	7²	11²	2²			1²				
ElPart	11²	11¹	13²	14²		15	16²	15¹	15¹	17¹	10²		9¹	15¹	7¹			2²	15²		8²			10²		10²	10²	9²		11	11	11	11
ElExpost	8¹	11¹	14¹	15¹				8²	7²	9²	13¹			5¹	8²★				4¹											11	12	12	12
ElVar			15¹		15										5																	15	17
Sappho		16	16	17	16	16	15	11	13	13			3	6	7			1						11	13	8				10	13	13	15

Ms. classifications: roman numerals = traditional ms. groups; A-III = mss. Associated with Group III; u = unclassified mss.

Normal/boldface font changes = other poems intervene to break the sequence

Superscripts: ¹ = original version; ² = revised version

♦ = the funeral elegy *Sorrow* immediately precedes this poem

★ = *Sorrow* immediately follows this poem as part of the sequence

▾2 = ll. 29–56 only; **14** = ll. 1–28 only

Figure 2: The Elegies in the Seventeenth-Century Printed Editions

Group I (B32 C2 C8 O20 SP1) — Heading

- Elegye. (ElBrac) (E)
- Elegye: (ElBed) (E)
- Elegye: (ElJeal)
- Elegye: (ElAnag)
- Elegye (ElChange)
- Elegye: (ElPerf)
- Elegye: (ElPict)
- Elegye: (Sorrow)
- Elegye: (ElServe)
- Elegye: (ElWar) (E)
- Elegye: (ElFatal) (E)
- Elegye: (ElNat)
- Elegye. On loves Progresse (ElProg) (E)
- · · · · · · · ·
- [untitled] (Image)
- · · · · · · · ·
- Elegye. Autumnall: (ElAut)

A (1633) — Heading

- om
- om
- ELEGIE I. (ElJeal)
- Elegie II. (ElAnag)
- Elegie III. (ElChange)
- Elegie IV. (ElPerf)
- Elegie V. (ElPict)
- Elegie VI. (Sorrow)
- Elegie VII. (ElServe)
- om
- om
- Elegie VIII. (ElNat)
- · · · · · · · ·
- * Elegie. (ElComp)
- * Elegie. The Autumnall. (ElAut)
- Elegie. (Image)
- · · · · · · · ·
- * Sapho to Philænis.
- · · · · · · · ·
- * Elegie. (ElExpost)

B (1635) — Heading

- ELEGIE I. Iealosie. (ElJeal)
- Eleg. II. The Anagram. (ElAnag)
- Eleg. III. Change. (ElChange)
- Eleg. IV. The Perfume. (ElPerf)
- Eleg. V. His Picture. (ElPict)
- Eleg. VI. (ElServe)
- Eleg. VII. (ElNat)
- Eleg. VIII. The Comparison. (ElComp)
- Eleg. IX. The Autumnall. (ElAut)
- Eleg. X. The Dreame. (Image)
- Eleg. XI. Death. (BoulNar)
- Eleg. XII. The Bracelet. Vpon … (ElBrac)
- ❖ Eleg. XIII. "Come, Fates"
- Eleg. XIIII. His parting from her. (ElPart)
- * Eleg. XV. Julia.
- * Eleg. XVI. A Tale of a Citizen and His Wife. (Citizen)
- Eleg. XVII. The Expostulation. (ElExpost)
- · · · · · · · ·
- Sapho to Philænis.
- · · · · · · · ·
- Elegie on his Mistris. (ElFatal)
- · · · · · · · ·
- Elegie on the L. C. (Sorrow)

G (1669) — Heading

- ELEGIE I. (ElJeal)
- ELEGIE II. (ElAnag)
- ELEGIE III. (ElChange)
- ELEGIE IV. (ElPerf)
- ELEGIE V. (ElPict)
- ELEGIE VI. (ElServe)
- ELEGIE VII. (ElNat)
- ELEGIE VIII. (ElComp)
- ELEGIE IX. (ElAut)
- ELEGIE X. (Image)
- ELEGIE XI. (BoulNar)
- ELEGIE XII. (ElBrac)
- ❖ ELEGIE XIII. "Come, Fates"
- ELEGIE XIIII. (ElPart)
- * ELEGIE XV. (Julia)
- * ELEGIE XVI. (Citizen)
- ELEGIE XVII. (ElExpost)
- ELEGIE XVIII. (ElProg)
- To his Mistress going to bed. (ElBed)
- · · · · · · · ·
- Sapho to Philænis.
- · · · · · · · ·
- Elegie. (ElFatal)
- · · · · · · · ·
- Elegie on the L.C. (Sorrow)
- · · · · · · · ·
- † [untitled] (ElVar)

(E) = "excepted" in the Stationers' Register in 1632.

· · · · · = breaks in sequence   * = supplied from a Group II ms.

❖ = noncanonical   * = dubia   † = first printed in E (1650)

Figure 3: Major Sequences of Elegies in Seventeenth-Century Manuscripts

Source → / Sequence Poem ↓	C9 Heading (variant)	H6 Heading (variant)	NY3 Heading (variant)	B13 Heading (variant)	NY1-VA2 Heading (variant)	B32 C2-C8 O20-SP1 Heading (variant)	B7-CT1 Heading (variant)	DT1-H4 Heading (variant)
ElBrac	15 Elegye. … (11: taint)	16 Elegy. … (11: taint)	1 Elegia .1.ª| (11: taint)	1 Elegia:i (11: fault)	1 Elegia 1ma … (11: taint)	1 Elegye. (11: fault)		1 Elegie.|.| (11: fault)
ElComp	[blank pages]	1 ELEGIES. (6: coronets)	2 Eleg: 2ª| (6: carcanets)	2 Elegya. 2. (6: carcanets)	2 Elegia 2ua (6: carcanets)		2 Elegie (6: Coronettes)	3 Elegie.| (6: Coronettes)
ElPerf	1 Elegy. 2. (29: dandled)	2 Elegy. 2. (29: dandled)	3 Eleg: 3ª| (29: ingled)	3 Elegya. 3. (29: ingled)	3 Elegia 3ia (29: ingled)	6 Elegye:: (29: Ingled)	3 Elegie (29: Ingled)	4 Elegie. (29: ingled)
ElJeal	2 Elegy .3. (21: high fare)	3 Elegy. 3. (21: high fare)	4 Eleg: 4ª| (21: great fare)	4 Elegya. 4. (21: great fare)	4 Elegia 4ia (21: great fare)	3 Elegye:: (21: great fare)	12 Elegie (21: greate fare)	14 Elegie. (21: great ffare)
ElServe	3 Elegy:4.	4 Elegy. 4.|	5 Eleg: 5ª|	5 Elegya. 5.	5 Elegia 5ia	8 Elegye::	7 Elegie	8 Elegie.|
ElNat	4 Elegye:5.	5 Elegie. 5.|	6 Eleg: 6ª|	6 Elegya. 6.	6 Elegia 6ia	11 Elegye::	5 Elegie	6 Elegie.|
ElWar	5 Elegie. 6. (6: Peeres)	6 Elegie. 6. (6: peeres)	7 Eleg: 7ª| (6: press)	7 Elegya. 7. (6: press)	7 Elegia 7ma (6: press)	9 Elegye:: (6: presse)	8 Elegie (6: press)	9 Elegie.| (6: presse)
ElBed	6 Elegye.7. (46: due to)	7 Elegie. 7. (46: due to)	8 Eleg: 8ª| (46: much less)	8 Elegya. 8. (46: much less)	8 Elegia 8ua (46: due to)	2 Elegye:: (46: much less)	10 Elegie.|. (46: much lesse)	12 Elegie (46: much lesse)
ElChange	7 Elegye.8.	8 Elegie. 8.	9 Eleg: 9ª|	9 Elegya. 9.	9 Elegia 9na	5 Elegye::	4 Elegie.|	5 Elegie.|
ElAnag	10 Elegye:11: (18: wordes)	11 Elegie. 11ª (18: wordes)	10 Eleg: 10ª| (18: letters)	10 Elegya. 10. (18: words)	10 Elegia 10ma (18: words)	4 Elegye:: (18: letters)	1 Elegie.|. (18: words)	2 Elegie.| (18: words)
ElFatal	8 Elegye:9 … (46: greatest)	9 Elegie. 9. … (46: greatest)	11 Eleg: 11ª| (46: great)	11 Elegya. 11. (46: great)	11 Elegia 11ma (46: great)	10 Elegye:: (46: greate)	13 Elegie (46: greate)	15 Elegie. (46: great)
ElPict	9 Elegye.10. (8: hoarinesse)	10 Elegie. 10. (8: hoarinesse)	12 Eleg: 12ª|★ (8: horines)	12 Elegya. 12. (8: woarinesse]	12 Elegia 12ma★ (8: horinesse)	7 Elegye::★ (8: stormes)	14 Elegie| (8: stormes)	16 Elegie.| (8: stormes)
ElAut	11 Elegye:12: …	12 Elegie. 12. …		13 [no heading]	14 Elegie Autumnall·	13 Elegye. Autumnall:·	6 Elegie	7 Elegie.|
ElProg	12 Elegye:13.	13 Elegie 13.		14 Elegye of loues progresse	13 An Elegie on Loues Progresse	12 Elegye. On loues Progresse	9 Elegie	11 Elegie.|
ElPart	Loues …	Loues …		16 At hir departure				
ElExpost	13 Elegy:14:	14 Elegy. 14		15 [no heading]	15 Elegia 17ma			10 Elegie. [H4] ✠
ElVar	14 Elegye:17:	15 Elegie			16 Eleg. 18th			
Sappho	16 Sappho to Philænis	17 Sappho to Philænis					11 Sapho to Philænis|	13 Sapho to Philænis.|

Normal/boldface font changes = other poems intervene to break the sequence

★ = the funeral elegy *Sorrow* immediately follows this poem as part of the sequence

… = heading editorially elided

✠ = leaf missing from DT1

Figure 4: Discrepancies Between C9-H6 and NY3

ElPerf 29

early version (C9-H6): And kis't & **dandled** on thy fathers knee
revised version (NY3): And kist and **ingled** on thy fathers knee

ElJeal 21

early version (C9-H6): Nor, when he, swolne & pamperd with **high** fare
revised version (NY3): Nor when he swolne and pamperd w^t **great** fare

ElComp 6

correct (NY3):   They seeme no sweat drops but pearle **carcanetts.**
corrupt (H6):   They seeme no sweate drops but pearle **Coronets**

ElWar 5-6

correct (NY3):   To any one: In Flanders, who [c]an tell
                  Whether ye Maister **pres** or men rebell?
corrupt (C9-H6): To any one in Flanders. who can tell
                  whether the Master **Peeres**, or Men rebell?

ElAnag 17-18

corrupt (NY3):   If we might put the Letters but one way
                  In y^t leane dearth of **Letters**, what could we say?
correct (C9-H6): If we might putt ye Letters but one way
                  In the leane dearth of **wordes** what could we say?

Figure 5: Order of Elegies in NY3, Group I, Group II

NY3	Group I	Group II (DT1)
(1) *ElBrac*	(1) *ElBrac*	*ElBrac*
(2) *ElComp*	(2) *ElBed*	· · · · · · ·
(3) *ElPerf*	(3) *ElJeal*	*ElAnag*
(4) *ElJeal*	(4) *ElAnag*	· · · · · · ·
(5) *ElServe*	(5) *ElChange*	*ElComp*
(6) *ElNat*	(6) *ElPerf*	*ElPerf*
(7) *ElWar*	(7) *ElPict*	*ElChange*
(8) *ElBed*	(8) *Sorrow*	*ElNat*
(9) *ElChange*	(9) *ElServe*	*ElAut*
(10) *ElAnag*	(10) *ElWar*	· · · · · · ·
(11) *ElFatal*	(11) *ElFatal*	*ElServe*
(12) *ElPict*	(12) *ElNat*	· · · · · · ·
(13) *Sorrow*	(13) *ElProg*	*ElWar*
	· · · · · · ·	· · · · · · ·
	(14) *ElAut*	*ElExpost*
		· · · · · · ·
		ElProg
		· · · · · · ·
		ElBed
		· · · · · · ·
		Sappho
		ElJeal
		ElFatal
		ElPict

· · · · · = other poems intervene to break the sequence

The Early Censorship
of John Donne's Elegies
and "Sapho to Philaenis"
in Manuscript and Print

TED–LARRY PEBWORTH

L ATE IN THE YEAR 1600, John Donne sent to his longtime friend Henry
Wotton—apparently at Wotton's insistence—copies of some of his
prose paradoxes. Donne sent them, he protests, "Only in obedience,"
explaining that "I love you and them to[o] well to send them willingly
for they carry with them a confession of there [i.e., their] lightnes
and your trouble and my shame."[1] After dismissing the enclosed
compositions as "nothings" that were "made rather to deceave tyme
then her daughth[e]r truth," Donne implores Wotton to promise him,
"upon the religion of your frendship that no coppy shalbee taken for
any respect of these or any other my compositions sent to you." He
expresses his anxiety about the circulation of his work in terms of fear
and again of shame, telling Wotton that "I meane to acquaint you with
all myne: and to my satyrs there belongs some feare and to some elegies and these [i.e., the enclosed paradoxes] perhaps shame." Donne's
fear that circulation of the elegies might bring some shame upon him

---

[1] All quotations from this letter are transcribed from the Burley Ms., ff. 308v–309.
The letter is printed in full, with a few minor errors in transcription, as no. 11 in Evelyn
Simpson, *A Study of the Prose Works of John Donne* (Oxford: Clarendon P, 1924; 2nd ed.,
rev., 1948), 316–17. For the context of this letter, see Claude J. Summers and Ted–Larry
Pebworth, "Donne's Correspondence with Wotton," *John Donne Journal* 10 (1991),
26–27.

seems to have been justified. During his lifetime, several collectors of Donne's verse—either offended by the sexual explicitness of some of the elegies or, after he was in holy orders, desirous of guarding his reputation—silently censored passages in the elegies, either by omitting lines or by rewriting them; and five of the elegies so offended the official licenser in 1632 that they were "excepted" from the first edition of Donne's *Poems* (1633; STC 7045) and achieved print only in later editions. Significantly, too, one of the elegies that was permitted in the 1633 publication had an offending couplet silently excised, perhaps struck out of the printer's copy by the licenser, a common practice; and when "His Parting from Her" was added to the elegies in the second edition (1635; STC 7046), the publisher John Marriot printed a version that had been scribally censored by the excision of 62 of its 104 lines.

This early censorship of Donne's elegies has never been fully studied. Indeed, until the textual editors of *The Variorum Edition of the Poetry of John Donne* examined all the surviving manuscript and early printed copies of the elegies, its extent was only imperfectly realized. The format of the Variorum *Elegies* volume (due out in 2000) does not allow for a comprehensive discussion of the subject of censorship, however. Instead, the details of such tamperings with Donne's texts are scattered among the textual introductions to the individual poems. My textual colleagues on the project, Gary Stringer and Ernie Sullivan, have generously allowed me to pillage the textual introductions and apparatuses that they prepared for the volume, as well as those I myself prepared; and what I wish to present here is a preliminary study of the early censorship, both official and unofficial, of Donne's love elegies and of "Sapho to Philaenis."

I would like to consider first the official prepublication censorship of the elegies in the first edition of Donne's *Poems* (1633). On 13 September 1632, the publisher of that posthumous collection, John Marriot, had "Entred for his Copy" in the Stationers' Register, "vnder the handes of Sir Henry Herbert and both the Wardens *a booke of verses and Poems* ... written by Doctor John Dunn," but with the proviso that "the five *satires*" and "the first, second, Tenth, Eleaventh, and Thirteenth *Elegies*" were "excepted,"[2] that is, refused a license. Those five excepted elegies were "The Bracelet," "To his Mistress going to bed," "Love's War," "On his Mistris" (the elegy beginning "By our first strange and fatal interview"), and "Loues Progresse." The last four of these were no doubt refused a license because of what was perceived

2 Edward Arber, ed., *A Transcript of the Registers of the Company of Stationers of London; 1554–1640 A.D.* 5 vols. (London: privately printed, 1875–77), 4: 285 (actually 249).

as licentiousness or sexually explicit language, about which I will have more to say later; but on that score, "The Bracelet" is innocent enough to have passed muster.

Instead, "The Bracelet" seems to have been refused a license because, as Gary Stringer has proposed, it "trafficked in politico–theological contraband."[3] Indeed, to that elegy obviously belonged the same "feare" that Donne felt for his satires. Throughout the poem, Donne plays on the word "Angels" as both coins and heavenly beings, and in lines 9–12, he stresses in theologically suspect language the purity of the coins that he must now have melted down to replace his mistress's lost bracelet:

> Oh shall twelve righteous Angels which as yet
> No leauen of vile sodder did admitt;
> Nor yet by any **taint** haue stray'd or gone
> From the first State of their Creation. . . .

The word "taint" can be seen to imply that the heavenly angels that fell might have been created in a flawed condition, which ultimately would put the onus for their apostasy on God himself. This original reading of "taint" appears in the authoritative Westmoreland manuscript, as well as in the manuscripts of Group III and some of those associated with Group III. Early on in the manuscript circulation of "The Bracelet," however, the blasphemous implication of "taint" must have been brought to Donne's attention, for—seeking to make clear that the angels fell because of their own self-generated perversity—he changed "taint" to read "fault" and reissued the poem, as revised, into the stream of transmission. From this revised holograph descend the copies of the poem in the Group I and Group II manuscripts, as well as in several unclassified manuscripts. It was in this revised version that Marriot sought to have "The Bracelet" licensed in 1632, but the licensers evidently found even the word "fault" objectionable. Significantly, when the poem was first published two years later in the second edition of Donne's *Poems* (1635)—without official authorization, it should be noted—Donne's own placatory revision of "taint" to "fault" was silently emended by Marriot or the editor/compositor of the volume to the even more innocuous reading "way." Before leaving "The Bracelet," it is worth observing that late in the manuscript transmission of the poem, there are silent scribal omissions of passages that can be interpreted as having theological and political import, beginning with the excision of lines 75–76 ("And they are still bad Angels, myne are none / For forme giues beeing, and their forme is gone") in the

---

3 "Filiating Scribal Manuscripts: The Example of Donne's Elegies," *John Donne Journal* 17 (1998), 176.

Skipworth and Edward Smyth manuscripts (Variorum sigla B13 and C1, respectively) and ultimately resulting in the truncation of Donne's 114 lines into 88 in a miscellany now in the Folger Shakespeare Library (F9).

As noted earlier, the four remaining elegies that were excised from the first edition of Donne's *Poems* were probably excluded for their explicit sexual content, and their respective fates were various. Without license, Marriot quietly slipped "On his Mistris" into the second edition of Donne's *Poems*, as he had "The Bracelet." It was not until the final seventeenth-century edition of the *Poems* (Wing D1871), published in 1669 by Marriot's successor Henry Herringman, however, that "Loues Progress" and "To his Mistress going to bed" were included among Donne's elegies. "Love's War" did not achieve print until 1802, when it was included in F. G. Waldron's *A Collection of Miscellaneous Poetry;* and it was first included among Donne's elegies, ironically enough, in the 1872–73 edition of Donne's poetry by the Reverend Canon Alexander B. Grosart.

The licensers of 1632 allowed the publication of "The Anagram"; but they, or Marriot acting from his own sense of self-preservation, silently excised one of its couplets. As Donne wrote it, the conclusion of the elegy builds to a crescendo of outrageous claims that the ugliness of the friend's mistress would keep her chaste, at least in reputation, and culminates in the accusation that even inanimate devices of masturbation are loath to touch her:

> She whose face like clowds turns the day to night   45
> Who mightier then the Sea makes Moores seeme whight,
> Who though seauen yeares she in the stews had layd
> A Nunnery durst receive, and thinke a Mayd,
> And though in Childbirths Labor she did ly
> Midwifes would sweare, t'weare but a timpany,   50
> Whom, yf sh'accuse her selfe, I credit lesse
> Then Witches which impossibles confesse,
> Whom dildoes, bedstaves, and her velvett glas
> Would be as loth to touch as Ioseph was:
> One like none and likd of none fittest weare   55
> For things in fashion euery man will weare.

The couplet excised in 1633 is the penultimate one, the catalogue of masturbatory tools; and it was not until the final seventeenth-century edition of Donne's *Poems* (1669) that the couplet appeared in print. We know that the printer's copy that Marriot used for most of the elegies had the readings of the surviving Group I manuscripts, all of which have the couplet in question. Helen Gardner is wrong, however, in her assertion that this couplet is "present in all manuscripts."[4] Six surviving manuscripts of "The Anagram" that otherwise have the complete poem silently omit the offending couplet: the Group II Dolau Cothi manuscript (WN1) and five unclassified manuscripts (AU1, F14, F15, O23, and P4). Six other manuscript copies of the poem (B24, B43, C1, CE1, F3, and TM1) silently omit the couplet, but they omit additional lines as well. Thus we have in the case of "The Anagram" both print and scribal censorship of offending lines.

In the case of "His Parting from her," we have the first seventeenth-century printing of a Donne elegy set from a scribally censored text. As Donne wrote it, the elegy is explicitly set in an adulterous context. The speaker specifically calls attention to his mistress's husband, whose "towred eyes ... flam'd with oyly sweat of Iealousye" (ll. 42–43); and it is the presence of a husband that requires the subterfuges that he and his mistress must use in their wouldbe secret courtship:

> Yet went we not still on with constancye?
> Haue wee not kept our gards like spy on spy?   45
> Had correspondence when the foe stood by?
> Stolne (more to sweeten them) our many blisses
> Of meetings, Conference, embracements, kisses.
> Shadow'd with negligence our most respects
> Vary'd our language through all Dialects,   50
> Of Becks, winkes, lookes, and often vnderboards
> Spoke Dialogues with our feet farre from our wordes.
> Haue we prou'd all the secretts of our Art
> Yea thy pale colours inward as thy heart?
> And after all this passed Purgatorye   55
> Shall sad Diuorce make vs the vulgar story?

At one point during the manuscript transmission of the elegy, an unknown collector/scribe, obviously distressed by the adulterous nature of the affair, excised lines 5-44, thereby cutting out the reference to the husband (l. 42) and allowing the reader to suppose that the obstacle to the courtship might be the lady's overly protective father, a situation such as one finds in "The Perfume." Indeed, this scribe cut Donne's poem from 104 to 42 lines, and his or her redaction entered the stream of manuscript transmission and served as the progenitor of a surviving family of manuscript copies of the poem.[5] The editor/compiler of the

---

4 Gardner, ed., *John Donne: The Elegies and The Songs and Sonnets* (Oxford: Clarendon P, 1965), 137.

5 These include two manuscripts associated with Group III (B13 and HH1) and four unclassified manuscripts (F4, F17, O34, and Y7). The first printing of the poem, in 1635, was set from a lost exemplum of this family. An even more drastically truncated version of the poem, cut to only twenty lines and attributed to Richard Corbett, can be found in five surviving manuscripts (B16, F3, F9, F11, and P6).

1635 *Poems* had access to the complete poem; it is present in the Group III manuscripts (B46, C9, and H6), a lost exemplum of which we know he consulted, as well as in one Group I manuscript (B30) and one manuscript associated with Group III (HH4). Nevertheless, he chose to base his text on the scribally censored truncation, which thereby became the social text of "His Parting from her" until the complete version of the elegy was printed in the 1669 *Poems*.

The scribal censorship of Donne's most popular erotic elegy, "To his Mistress going to bed," was more subtle, effected not by excising lines, but by repositioning a couplet. The final twenty-four lines of the elegy as Donne wrote them are as follows, transcribed from the Westmoreland manuscript:

> Licence my roving hands, and let them go   25
> Behind, before, above, betweene, below.
> Oh my America, my newfound land,
> My kingdome, safelyest when with one man man'd.
> My Myne of pretious stones; my empiree;
> How blest ame I in this discouering thee!   30
> **To enter in these bonds, is to be free,**
> **Then where my hand is sett, my seale shalbee.**
> Full nakednes, all ioyes are due to thee;
> As Soules vnbodied, bodyes vncloth'd must bee,
> To tast whole ioyes. Gems which you women vse   35
> Are as Atlantas balls cast in mens views,
> That when a fooles ey lighteth on a gem
> His earthly Soule may covet theirs not them.
> Like pictures, or like bookes gay coverings, made
> For lay men, are all women thus arayd,   40
> Themselues are mistique bookes, which only wee
> Whom their imputed grace will dignify
> Must see reuealed. Then since I may know,
> As liberally as to a Midwife show
> Thy selfe. Cast all, yea this whight linnen hence,   45
> Ther is no penance, much lesse innocence.
> To teach thee I ame naked first: Why than
> What needst thou haue more covering then a man?

In this authorial version, the boldfaced couplet is placed between the lines trumpeting the speaker's discovery of his "Myne of pretious stones" (l. 29) and his celebration of "Full nakednes" (l. 33). This positioning of the couplet allows such critics as Doniphan Louthan to see the couplet as a "quibble on legalistic terms":

In entering the bonds of physical love (if not of matrimony), the speaker paradoxically becomes free ("Licence my roving hands," he has begged). "Then where my hand is set, my seal shall be." I pledge to fulfill my debts to the specific place where my hand is set. In turn I am entitled to a seal of exclusive ownership:

PRIVATE PARTS

NO TRESPASSING.[6]

Seventeen of the surviving sixty-seven seventeenth-century manuscripts of the elegy, however, move the couplet in question to stand before the final couplet,[7] as in this example transcribed from Harvard Ms. Eng. 686:

Licence my Roving handes, and let them goe	25
Behind, beefore, above, between, belowe.	
O my America! o my new found land!	
my kingdome's safest when with one man man'd	
my Myne of precious stones my Empery!	
How blest am I in this discovering thee?	30
[ll. 31–32 moved to stand after line 46]	
ffull nakednes, all eyes are due to thee	
As soules vnbodied, bodies vncloath'd must bee	
To tast whose ioyes, gemmes that you women vse	35
are as Atlantlas balles, cast in mens viewes,	
That when a fooles eye lighteth on a gemme	
His greedy eye might court theirs, & not them,	
Like vnto books with gawdy coveringes made	
ffor Lay-men. Are all women thus arrayd?	40
Themselves are Musick books, which onely wee	
(whom their imputed grace will dignify)	
Must see reveald: Then, sweet, that I may know	
As liberally as to a Midwife shew	
Thy self, cast all, yea this white linnen hence	45
There is noe pennance due to Innocence	46
To enter into these bonds is to bee free	31
There where my hand is sett my seale shalbe.	32
To teach thee, I am naked first, why than	47
What needst thou have more covering then a man?	48

Before this couplet was moved, the text had already been corrupted (as in, for example, the reading "Musick books" for the authorial "mistique bookes" in l. 41); and the most significant corruption was the scribally sanitized "There is noe pennance due to Innocence" for the more difficult authorial reading "Ther is no penance, much lesse innocence" in line 46. When the couplet in question was then moved

---

[6] *The Poetry of John Donne: A Study in Explication* (New York: Bookman Associates, 1951), 72.

[7] The seventeen manuscripts that move the couplet include three manuscripts associated with Group III (H3 and the cognates O21 and Y3) and fourteen unclassified manuscripts: AU1, B16, B44, F3, F6, F9, H2, LA1, O3, O38, PM1, WA1, WC1, and Y1.

to the penultimate position in the poem, we find that its repositioning reinforces the innocence ascribed to the lovers in that scribally revised "due to" version of line 46 by suggesting that the lovers have recently entered into the bonds of marriage. Indeed, the repositioning of the couplet that names "these bonds" allows the reader to see the poem as an abbreviated epithalamion, that form of celebratory poetry that characteristically permits passages on the undressing and bedding of the bride. Placed in an epithalamic context, "To his Mistress going to bed" loses much of its licentious character and is thereby redeemed. It is worth remembering here that the copy of this elegy in the Bridgewater manuscript (HH1), while it does not move the couplet in question, effects this same sanitization of its eroticism in a marginal note keyed to the phrase "enter in theise bonds": "why may not a man write his owne Epithalamion if he can doe it so modestly" (f. 106v).

Finally, while "Sapho to Philaenis" is not strictly an elegy, we have included it in the *Elegies* volume of the Variorum. Rather surprisingly, despite its lesbian and autoerotic character, it was allowed by the licensers in 1632 and was printed in full in the 1633 volume of Donne's poems and thereafter in the succeeding seventeenth-century editions. Its explicitly sexual content did offend at least one collector of Donne's poems, however, who silently excised lines 31–54, the passage that begins with Sappho's distress in imagining Philaenis playing with "some softe Boy" and concludes with her projection of the caressing of herself into the caressing of the absent Philaenis:

> Likeness begetts such strange selfe flatterie,
> That touchinge my selfe all seemes done to thee.
> My self I embrace, and myne owne hands I kisse
> And Amarously thank my selfe for this.
> (ll. 51–54)

This censored truncation of "Sapho to Philaenis," which allows the poem to be read as an expression of idealized friendship between two women, itself entered the stream of manuscript transmission and survives in seven known copies.[8]

Arthur Marotti has recently called our attention to the "large amount of bawdy and obscene verse in manuscript collections" of the earlier seventeenth century. He attributes that phenomenon to two prevailing conditions: first, that many of the miscellanies were collected in the all-male—often misogynistic—environs of the two universities and the Inns of Court, and second, that manuscript transmission was outside

---

[8] The seven surviving manuscripts that have this scribally shortened version include six manuscripts associated with Group III (B13, HH4, the cognates NY1 and VA2, and the cognates O21 and Y3) and one unclassified manuscript (B2).

the purview of official licensers and therefore could be freer in its subject matter and language than could printed works of the same period.[9] What is interesting about the fate of some of Donne's bawdier elegies is the fact that even in the relatively free environment of manuscript transmission they were in fact bowdlerized. I have only touched upon a few examples from the work of one poet, but what I have found suggests that this phenomenon may be wide spread and that it is worthy of additional study for what it can tell us of the conflicting mores of the period.

On a related topic, the study of official prepublication censorship and authorial reactions to it in the late Tudor and early Stuart periods has been devoted almost exclusively to the subjects of religious and political discourse. Such is the case with Annabel Patterson's *Censorship and Interpretation: The Conditions of Writing and Reading in Early Modern England* (1984). Moreover, putatively comprehensive works such as Fredrick Seaton Siebert's *Freedom of the Press in England 1476–1776: The Rise and Decline of Government Controls* (1952) and Donald Thomas's *A Long Time Burning: The History of Literary Censorship in England* (1969) briefly mention censorship for erotic content, but offer no detailed account of the way in which it was institutionalized and carried out. This subject, too, needs further study.

Much—perhaps too much—has been made of the famous Jack Donne / John Donne bifurcation. But what we see in the early manuscript and print treatment of his elegies and "Sapho to Philaenis" suggests that this, like most clichés, has a certain basis in fact. The rakish Jack Donne was driven to write daring and erotic poems that the more sober John Donne, his friends, and his early readers were then driven to censor and legitimate.

---

9 *Manuscript, Print, and the English Renaissance Lyric* (Ithaca and London: Cornell UP, 1995), 76–82, esp. 76.

Reading
Finnegans Wake
Genetically

SAM SLOTE

T HE IMMEDIATE CHALLENGE IN READING *Finnegans Wake* is still perhaps
the most enduring: how to wrest some semblance of sense out of
the welter of its multilinguistically polyvalent word-plays. The usual
response to this challenge is to translate the *Wake* into something a
bit more normal by mapping out the referential vectors suggested in
its Babelian puns. Much impressive research has been done on this
front: many reference works have been compiled that treat all sorts
of allusions, be they literary, musical, linguistic, or geographic, and so
on. But how important is the accumulation of such information to the
Wake? One might agree with James S. Atherton that "until all the quotations, allusions and parodies in *Finnegans Wake* have been elucidated
the complete meaning of the whole work must escape us."[1] The problem, then, would be how to delimit the myriad suggestions posited
in the *Wake* in order to articulate precisely the recondite references
and meanings.[2] Genetically informed interpretation is one means of
reining in the mass of free associations that so-often bedevils readers

---

[1] *The Books at the Wake* (Carbondale: Southern Illinois UP, 1959), 20.

[2] Clive Hart has recently characterized those early, heady days of *Wake* criticism: "we
were all working not only in a state of anxiety as to how best approach the book, but
also with assumptions deriving in large part from our experience of *Ulysses*.... The
procedure was quasi-scientific: looking at the general picture before we imagined a
possible model of how best to grasp its nature and then began to examine the detail

of the *Wake*. As early as 1963, Jack Dalton pleaded that critics turn to the drafts as a means of verifying the presence of arcane languages in the *Wake*.[3] In the introduction to his *Annotations to "Finnegans Wake,"* Roland McHugh endorses this view: "All readings that can be confirmed by reference to the manuscripts are acceptable."[4]

Is there more to the archive of Joyce's notes and drafts than such a Manichæan economy of verification and falsification? Are notes and drafts merely potential jurors for arbitrating annotation? Something to help "Wipe your glosses with what you know"?[5] The positivistic stance towards genetic criticism essentially maintains the proposition that *Finnegans Wake* is a denotational work, that the words, distorted as they may be, mean something. These referents can then be adequately decoded by a properly astute critic armed with the manuscripts and a very large reference library. As productive as such an approach may be, it reduces *Finnegans Wake* to the world's most elaborate Pig Latin. Denotative readings reduce *Finnegans Wake* to the level of information.

Rather than strive to decode what may turn out to be a non-existent meaning, the hermeneutic task with *Finnegans Wake* might be to describe the ways in which the language is encoded. This is where a genetic approach can be useful: rather than act as a hermeneutic arbitrator and fix reference in a positivistic manner (i.e., "this means that"), a genetic approach can illustrate the ways in which reference and denotation are corrupted beyond repair in Joyce's "ersebest idiom" (FW: 253.1). The encryption is what is important, not what may or may not lie encrypted. A genetic corollary to this proposition is: *in modifying a passage, Joyce reveals something about its sense.* To add a bit of rigor to this seemingly useless and trivial statement, one needs to define "sense" and "modification."

Ezra Pound's tripartite division of poetic sense—phanopoeia, melopoeia, and logopoeia—can be useful for this. Pound formulated these

---

to see if it could be understood in ways coherent with the theory" ("Fritz in the Early Awning," *A Collideorscape of Joyce*, ed. Ruth Frehner and Ursula Zeller, Dublin: Lilliput, 1998. 4–10.5).

3 Jack P. Dalton. "Re 'Kiswahili words in *Finnegans Wake*' by Philipp Wolff." *A Wake Newslitter*, old series, 12 (1963), 6–10. See also Roland McHugh, *The "Finnegans Wake" Experience* (Berkeley: U of California P, 1981), 71–72; and Laurent Milesi. "L'idiome babélien de *Finnegans Wake*," *Genèse de Babel*, ed. Claude Jacquet (Paris: CNRS, 1985), 155–213, esp. 171.

4 Revised edition (Baltimore: The Johns Hopkins UP, 1991), vii. See also R. J. Schork "By Jingo: Genetic Criticism of *Finnegans Wake*," *Joyce Studies Annual* 5 (1994): 104–27; and Danis Rose and John O'Hanlon, *Understanding "Finnegans Wake"* (New York: Garland, 1982), xiii–xiv.

5 James Joyce, *Finnegans Wake* (New York: Viking, 1939 and 1958), 304.F3. Hereafter abbreviated as FW.

categories as a means of discussing poetry and poetic effects without reference to denotation and semantic value. Phanopoeia is imagistic and tends towards precision in the visual evocation of an object upon the imagination (pictographic languages are thus inherently phanopoeic). Melopoeia concerns the sound or musicality of a word or phrase and thus detracts from eidetic precision in favor of subliminal sound effects.[6]

While phanopoeia and melopoeia respectively activate the visual and auditory faculties, logopoeia, in its most basic form, plays upon the conceptual or intellectual faculties. "Logopoeia, 'the dance of the intellect among words,' that is to say, it employs words not only for their direct meaning, but it takes into account in a special way of habits of usage, of the context we *expect* to find with the word, its usual concomitants, of its known acceptances, and of ironical play."[7] Logopoeia is thus not purely denotative, but rather it is connotative.[8] Pound states that logopoeia does not translate some previous writing, rather it evokes some manner of that writing (Pound 1935, 25).

So, in modifying a passage in a draft, Joyce alters either the phanopoeia, melopoeia, or logopoeia, or some combination of these three. For Joyce, modification almost invariably means addition or substitution. As a writer, he is exceedingly parsimonious and practically never deliberately excises text inherited from previous drafts.

There are three general types of modification he produces: 1) enhancing a phanopoeic, melopoeic, or logopoeic aspect of the text already present; 2) creating an entirely new effect; or 3) distorting an existing effect. The earliest portions of the *Wake* to be written were composed in something that approximates conventional English. The *Wakean* punplays were then added in subsequent drafts. As Joyce

---

[6] I have synthesized Pound's definitions of these terms from his *ABC of Reading* (New York: New Directions, 1934), 63, and "How to Read" (*Literary Essays*, ed. T. S. Eliot [New York: New Directions, 1935], 15–40, esp. 25–31). See also "How to Write," *Machine Art and Other Writings*, ed. Maria Luisa Ardizzone (Durham: Duke UP, 1996), 87–109, esp. 91–94.

[7] Pound 1935, 25; see also 33. See also Pound 1934, 63.

[8] "While his earliest theories of poetic language focused on its musical qualities (his study of Provençal poetry) and on its visual qualities (his study of Chinese poetry), logopoeia liberated him from the constricting notion that poetic language can operate only through auditory or visual representation. Reading Laforgue allowed Pound to recognize and later produce poetry constructed almost exclusively from other literary and nonliterary texts; it freed him from the fear that language which refers as much to other language as to sound or image must be necessarily arbitrary or unoriginal. His work on Laforgue and logopoeia greatly expanded the subject matter, diction, and tone he deemed admissible to poetry, and in important ways made the Cantos possible" (Jane Hoogestraat, " 'Akin to Nothing but Language': Pound, Laforgue, and Logopoeia," *ELH* 55.1 [Spring 1988], 259–85, esp. 259).

grew more proficient in his gibberish, he began to write directly in his Bellsybabble.[9] Of course, further obfuscations were introduced even in passages initially written in an obscure style.

So far, my categories of modifications omit transmission error. There are many demonstrable instances where a transmissional departure is not sanctioned by Joyce. Sometimes Joyce will enhance this inadvertent departure for some phanopoeic, melopoeic, or logopoeic effect, but this is usually not the norm. This raises questions about editing *Finnegans Wake*, and of producing, perhaps, a corrected edition. A prospective editor needs some sensitivity to logopoeia, phanopoeia, and melopoeia as well as a cogent understanding of the manuscript status. I will discuss this in more detail shortly.

Brief examples of the types of modification I have proposed follow. As an example of a phanopoeic modification, in the second draft of I.5, Joyce added the unit: "the fretful eff (used as a revise mark) stalks all over the page, broods amid the verbiage, gaunt, stands in the window margin, paces jerkily to & fro, flinging phrases here, there, or returns with some half-suggestion, dragging its shoestring."[10] The "fretful eff" describes the "F" mark which Joyce frequently, but not exclusively, used in his manuscripts as an insertion pointer. Joyce is here describing his own addition-mark. In subsequent drafts, Joyce enhanced the description of the "fretful eff" until, in the revisions of the *Criterion* pages undertaken prior to publication in *transition* 5, Joyce actually added two inverted Fs to this passage (JJA 46: 426). So, a passage that started by describing the morphology of a "fretful eff" now includes a pair of fretful effs, thereby enhancing the image.[11]

Melopoeia is a crucial component of *Wakean* writing. In a letter to his daughter Lucia, Joyce wrote: "Lord knows what my prose means. In a word, it is pleasing to the ear."[12] Joyce would often choose words for purely aural considerations. For example, the fair copy of a passage in II.1 reads: "The yenng frilles-in-pleyurs" (JJA 51: 17; FDV: 131; FW: 224.22). This line already alludes to Proust's *A l'ombre des jeunes filles*

---

9 See David Hayman, *A First-Draft Version of "Finnegans Wake"* (Austin: U of Texas P, 1963), 8–12. Hereafter abbreviated as FDV.

10 Michael Groden, general editor, *The James Joyce Archive*, eds. Hans Walter Gabler, David Hayman, A. Walton Litz, and Danis Rose (New York: Garland, 1978). Volume 46, 310. Hereafter abbreviated as JJA. In transcriptions of drafts, deletions are indicated with strike-outs and additions are placed within bold-faced pointed brackets.

11 See FW: 120.33–121.13; and see my essay, "Imposture Book Through the Ages," *Genitricksling Joyce*, ed. Sam Slote and Wim Van Mierlo (Amsterdam: Rodopi, 1999), 97–114.

12 Stuart Gilbert ed., *Letters of James Joyce* (New York: Viking, 1957), 341. For similar comments by Joyce on the phonic quality of *Finnegans Wake*, see Richard Ellmann, *James Joyce*, revised edition (Oxford: Oxford UP, 1982), 702–3.

en fleurs. On the subsequent draft, the first typescript, Joyce replaced the strident-sounding "yenng" with a more mellifluous collocation: "The ~~yenng~~ <youngly delightsome> frilles-in-pleyurs" (JJA 51: 32). Joyce thus intensifies the alliteration of the "l" sound, an alliteration present in the earlier draft but occulted under the weight of "yenng." The allusion to Proust is still present but is now enhanced through alliteration. Indeed, Joyce's pun "frilles"—by condensing the French words *filles* and *fleurs*—missed the slight alliteration of Proust's title, and his addition restores it.

In *Finnegans Wake*, melopoeic modalities are often at odds with the phanopoeic. Many puns are produced through discrepancies between how the word is written and how it is pronounced. Joyce plays with the "sound sense sympol" (FW: 612.29); indeed, on the page, the word "sympol" resembles "symbol," but spoken it is "simple."[13] As Joyce wrote in I.3, "Television kills telephony" (FW: 52.18). Usually, phonotextual puns are created when the word was initially drafted, but on occasion Joyce would distort an existing word to generate such an effect. For example, on the first set of galleys for I.3, Joyce changed the word "holidays": "zimmer ~~holidays~~ <holedigs>" (JJA 49: 93; FW: 69.32–33).[14]

Finally, as an example of logopoeia, I take the introduction to "Haveth Childers Everywhere" from III.3. As the draft history here is complex, I will focus on a very small swath of text. In notebook VI.B. 1 there is an early proto-draft for the opening of the "Haveth Childers Everywhere" passage: "Your H is not a / warlike man / I am brought up / under an old act / of EDW III" (VI.B. 1: 114).[15] The earliest actual draft of "Haveth Childers Everywhere"—November–December 1924—does not incorporate this text: " Sir, to you? I am known throughout the world as a cleanliving man ... " (FDV: 245; JJA 57: 55). The redrafted version of this passage does include a modified version of the VI.B. 1 entry: "—Sir, to you! I am brought under an old act of Edward the First, but I am known throughout the world wherever good English is spoken as a cleanliving man" (FDV: 245; JJA 57: 76–77). To go upstream through the archive is also, apparently, to go downstream through the Edwardian lineage, from Edward the Third to Edward the First.

---

[13] See Peter Myers, *The Sound of "Finnegans Wake"* (London: Macmillan, 1992), 20–44; and Garrett Stewart, *Reading Voices: Literature and the Phonotext* (Berkeley: U of California P, 1990), 232–58.

[14] This would also be an example of a trans-linguistic pun since "dag" is Dutch for "day," so the distortion "rearrives" at its original sense.

[15] I am grateful to David Hayman for providing a preliminary transcription of this notebook.

In the third draft, the Edwardian reference is excised: "Sir to you. I am brought up under an ~~old~~ <camel> act of ~~Edward the First~~ <Sitric Silkenbeard and of his dynasty now out of print> but I am known throughout the world wherever good English is spoken" (JJA 58: 95). Sitric Silkenbeard led the Danes to an ignominious defeat at the battle of Clontarf in 1014. But the passage has not just been invaded by a Dane, it has also been invaded by the Danish language: gammel is Danish for "old." The word "camel" is thus a logopoeic enhancement of this freshly installed Danish occupation.

So far, Joyce has retained the phrase "wherever good English is spoken"; this made sense in conjunction with the English Edward but is at odds with the Danish Sitric. On the second typescript, Joyce replaced "English" with "Allenglisch" (JJA 58: 267). And on a later typescript, he expanded this to "Allenglisches Angleslachsen" (JJA 58: 394), that is, Anglo-Saxon, the language preparatory to English. English is named Germanically—a germane effect for a Danish invader such as Sitric. So the logopoeic effect of suggesting a Danish word is here enhanced by this Saxonate terminology. This example is also melopoeic since the heavy guttural sounds of "Allenglisches Angleslachsen" suggest an Anglo-Saxon phrase.

Having elaborated my criteria, I would now like to turn to the introduction of II.1 (FW: 219.1-222.21) as a fuller illustration of these principles. This opening section is a dramatis personæ of various characters involved with a production at the "Feenichts Playhouse" (FW: 219.2). This was a late addition to II.1 and was one of the last components of this chapter to be drafted. The first draft is quite short: a brief elaboration of nine characters followed by a paragraph concerning the staff involved with the technical aspects of the theatrical production. The section ends with the line "An argument follows" (JJA 51: 8; FDV: 130; FW: 222.21), an appropriate segue into the children's games of this chapter.

Glug	: the bad <black> boy of the storybook who has been sent into disgrace by	Mr Shemus Pannem
The Floras	: a bunch of pretty maidens who form a the guard of honour of ~~the beautiful bl~~	(S. Bride's Girl Scouts School)
Izod	a beautiful blonde (approached in loveliness only by her <sister> reflection in a mirror), who having jilted Glugg is now fascinated by	Miss Herself
Chuff	, the fairhaired who wrestles with the bad black boy about caps or something till the shadows make a pattern of somebody or other after which they they are both <well> scrubbed by	
Ann	, their poor little old mother-in-lieu who is the wife of	

Hump	, the cause of all the trouble at present engaged in entertaining <in his customhouse>
The Customers	, a bunch of representatives who are served by
Saunderson	, a spoilcurate, butt of
Kate	, cook-and-general.

with battlepictures worked up by Messrs Blood and Thunder, costumes designed by Madame Delamonde, dances arranged by Harley Quin and Coulmn Bin, songs, jokes and properties for the wake supplied by Mr Timothy Finnegan, the whole to be wound up with a wound up with [sic] a magnificent transformation scene showing the Wedding of Night and Morning and the Dawn of Peace waking the Weary of the World. An argument follows. (JJA 51: 6–8; FDV: 129–30; FW: 219.1–222.21)

By the time Joyce wrote this passage, he had his cast of characters well established and so was able to produce such a list with minimal effort. This first draft is almost completely untainted by corrections and revisions and, except for the terminal paragraph (also bereft of revision), it is written in ink in a hand almost as neat as a fair copy (the final paragraph is written in pencil). Also atypical for first drafts at this late stage (1931–32), this draft is written for the most part in English. This looks like something written quickly in the knowledge that it would be revised extensively. At the first draft level, there is nothing remarkable about this passage, save for some motival references which help to graft this episode into the chapter and into the *Wake* as a whole.

This passage is quite literally the set-up for a dramatic situation. The list of characters, inherently a paratactic form, is made hypotactic through the consistent use of prepositions such as "by," "of," and "for." This is not just a simple list of characters, but an indication of how they interact. The list is made to seem dynamic through the use of hypotaxis. This account of their interactions is compatible with the action of this chapter at this stage of its drafting. The passage suggests the taunting and victimization of Glugg by the pretty maidens who are led by Izod. The girls have rebuffed Glugg in favor of Chuff, but these games end when they are all called in by their mother. This action is expressed through a delineation of the characters' roles and functions.

Four years before Joyce began writing II.1, he wrote a one page plan of Book II, with II.1 receiving the most emphasis (JJA 51: 3). On this page he had conceived of Book II as evolving out of the interactions of various combinations of sigla, the extended "Doodles family" (FW: 299.F4). The sigla had become by this time relatively discrete entities— a convenient shorthand for notes and drafts—which could be combined and manipulated to generate new narrational possibilities.[16]

---

[16] Jean–Michel Rabaté notes that Joyce continued to experiment with the sigla, pro-

Chapter II.1 had begun life as a product of the interrelation of *Wakean* characters and now, with the introduction, this dynamic is explicitly reinserted back into the text with the cast of characters. Daniel Ferrer calls this phenomenon "contextual memory": a text bears some trace of or reference to some element that had existed in a previous draft but which has since been excised.[17] This would be a subset of logopoeia: an allusion to something within the text's archive that is not directly present in the text itself.

Further notable about this first draft is the mention of "songs, jokes and properties for the *Wake* supplied by Mr Timothy Finnegan." This obviously alludes to the title of Joyce's work derived from the Irish-American ballad "Finnegan's *Wake*." At this time, Joyce kept the title secret to all except for Nora. In 1927 he set up a little contest to guess the title of his Work in Progress, but no one figured out the actual title until August 1938, by which time Joyce had dropped so many hints to his friends as to make their ascertaining the correct answer all but inevitable.[18] This was not the first reference to the title to be worked into the text; the first to be entered was "Fillagain's chrissormiss wake" (FW: 6.14–15), added in October–November 1926 to the text of I.1 (JJA 44: 51).[19]

The following draft stage, the Fair Copy, is missing, but the two successive drafts, both typescripts, survive. The changes Joyce had made on the Fair Copy are inferable from the first typescript. For example, Joyce added parenthetical names after every character's name, thereby more closely approximating the style of a theater program—a logopoeic effect. Most of the names Joyce had given to the characters in the first draft are recognizable as *Wakean* personæ, such as Hump (HCE), Ann (Anna Livia Plurabelle), Izod, Saunderson, and Kate. However, Glugg and Chuff are not immediately identifiable on the basis of their names. To be sure, they must be Shem and Shaun, but which is which? So, on the Fair Copy, expanding on the marginal note in the first draft, Joyce assigned "Mr Seumas Quillad"— i.e., Shem the Penman—to Glugg and "Mr Sean O'Mailey"—i.e., Shaun the Postman—to Chuff (JJA 51: 9). Shem and Shaun's names appear

---

ducing all sorts of iconic variations, even after they had become relatively systemized. *Joyce Upon the Void* (New York: St. Martin's Press, 1991), 85–88.

[17] "Clementis' Cap," trans. Marlena G. Corcoran, *Drafts, Yale French Studies* 89, ed. Michel Contat, Denis Hollier, and Jacques Neefs (1996), 223–36, esp. 231–36.

[18] See Ellmann, 543, 597, and 708.

[19] In the paper "Mapping Echoland," delivered at the conference "Genetic Networks" (University of Antwerp, 10–11 December, 1998), Finn Fordham listed the allusions to the title in chronological order of their draft insertion. Although he missed this example, he lists five instances that had entered the text before this passage was written in 1931/32.

as actors, whereas the other figures' names appear as the characters they play.

On this draft Glug is not just "sent into disgrace"; instead, he is "divorced into the disgrace court." The scenario of Glugg's shame is now more specific and humorous than it had been in the first draft.

The name of the actor assigned to Hump is "Mr Makeall Gonne." This name, suggesting universal disappearance, is appropriate to the character HCE, who is, as we are told here, "the cause of all the confusion." This name thus neatly encapsulates what David Hayman calls the "male plot" of *Finnegans Wake*, the crime and disappearance of HCE.[20]

However, not everything has gone: recognizable within the name "Makeall Gonne" is Michael Gunn, the manager of the Gaiety Theatre in Dublin in the late nineteenth century. Gunn is mentioned frequently in *Finnegans Wake*, usually in consociation with HCE, and occasionally with Maud Gonne.[21] His citation here is appropriate because of his theatrical background. His conflation with HCE throughout the book suggests the difficulties attendant upon the male plot: HCE may be *all gone*, but his disappearance is variously re-enacted by different characters under different names. The fact that Michael Gunn's name, too, is mixed with others suggests the perpetual difficulty of reference: Hump is not Michael Gunn, and within the name they are both gone: "Pastimes are past times. Now let bygones be bei Gunne's" (FW: 263.17–18).

So, with the addition of this name, Joyce has installed a motival link to a broader scene of *Wakean* action (or inaction). This broadening of reference is also evinced by the addition of the phrase "a recent impeachment <due to egg everlasting>." This egg impeachment enhances the association between HCE/Hump and Humpty Dumpty— Lewis Carroll's progenitor of "portmanteau priamed full potatowards" (FW: 240.36-241.1)—an association made elsewhere in the text.

This broadening of reference is also present in the elaborations given to the other characters. Ann is played by Miss Corrie Correndo, a name that suggests the Spanish word corriente, running—an appropriate name for a river such as ALP. Joyce fills in his description of the Floras by adding a reference to the fact that they number 28; they are now "a <month's> bunch of pretty maidens." He also reinforced his account of Issy's bifurcation; her rival is not just her reflection, it is her "sister reflection." Note that Joyce omitted the marginal description of Izod from the first draft as "Miss Herself," a name which would imply both an auto-equivalent identity (she is Miss, that is Mlle., Herself) as well as inequality (she *misses*, that is, loses, herself).

20 David Hayman, *The "Wake" in Transit* (Ithaca: Cornell UP, 1990), 109–10.

21 Adaline Glasheen, *Third Census of "Finnegans Wake"* (Berkeley: U of California P, 1977), 113.

There are numerous interesting modifications wrought at this level. While the passage is still mostly written in standard expository English, Joyce is slowly introducing some rudimentary *Wakean* wordplay. The phrase "Blood and Thunder" becomes "Thud and Blunder." Also, the phrase "until their shadows make" has now become the more evocative "until they shadowshow." Joyce also adds the word "geminally"—a condensation of generally and Gemini—an appropriate portmanteau for the description of the fraternal couple Shem and Shaun.

The concluding paragraph has now more clearly taken on the tone of a hyperbolic theatrical advertisement or promotion. The first draft was too brief and prosaically expository to sustain such a tone. But here the rampant capitalization as well the subtle but telling substitution of "Dresses tastefully designed" for "Costumes specially designed" all suggest that we are decamped in the province of hype. This hyperbole tends to ironically deflate the semblance of action fostered through the hypotactic interactions of the character list, especially since we are promised, for the grand finale, "a Magnificent Transformation Scene showing the Radium Wedding of Night and Morning <, arranged as the daughter of Tyre and the son of Ausonius,> and the Dawn of Peace, Pure, Perfect and Perpetual Waking the Weary of the World."

This typescript is also marked by error. The typist was apparently quite clumsy and, even in the absence of a Fair Copy, there are numerous small, demonstrable mistakes. The typist failed to consistently capitalize the characters' names and mistyped Kate's role: "Varianoekeand" instead of "Varian)cook and." However, in the absence of the preceding draft, there are a few departures that are impossible to unequivocally gauge. Joyce's "approached" from the first draft now appears as "appreached," certainly a plausible pun but also a possible typo. In any case, the typist for the next typescript, which also contains numerous departures, missed this word (JJA 51: 11) and so it remained as "approached" through the final text.

GLUG; (Mr Seumas <Mac>Quillad), the <bold> bad black boy of the storybooks, who has been ~~sent~~ <disgraced> into <the> disgrace <court> by

THE FLORAS; (Girl Scouts from ~~S. bride's~~ <St Bride's> Finishing Establishment), a <month's> bunch of pretty maidens who <while they pick at her> form the guard for

~~Izod~~ <IZOD>; (Miss Butys Pott), a bewitching blonde <who dimples delightfully and is> approached in loveliness only by her grateful <sister> reflection in a mirror, <the pearl of the opal,> who, having jilted ~~g~~<G>lug, is being fatally fascinated by

Chuff; (Mr Sean O'Mailey), the <fine> fairhaired fellow <of the fairy tales> who wrestles with the <bad> bold black boy<,> Glug<,> ~~all the time~~ <geminally> about caps or something until their~~r~~<y> ~~shadows make~~

<shadowshow> a pattern of somebody ~~or other~~ <elseorother>, after which they are both brought home <with their polls apart> to be ~~well scrubbed~~ <soundly> <soaped, sponged and scrubbed again> by

ANN; (Miss Corrie Correndo), their poor old mother-in-lieu, who is woman of the house to

HUMP; (Mr Makeall Gonne), the cause of all the confusion, who, having partially recovered from a recent impeachment, <due to egg everlasting,> is engaged in entertaining in his customhouse

THE CUSTOMERS; (Components of the Afterhours Courses at S. Laurence O'Toole's Academy for GRownup [sic] Gentlemen) ~~a~~ <a dronghahoarse> bundle of ~~representatives~~ <civics, each of whom in a jacktitative,> who are sloppily served by

Saunderson; (Mr Knut Oelsvinger), a spoilcurate and butt of

KATE; (Miss Rachel Lea Varian~~oke~~<) cook->and-general.

With battle pictures and the Pageant of History worked up by Messrs ~~Blood~~ <Thud> and ~~Thunder~~ <Blunder>. ~~Costumes specially~~ <Dresses tastefully> designed by Madame <Berthe> Delamode<,> Dances arranged by Harley Quinn and Coldlimbeina. Jests, jokes, songs and music for the *Wake* < > lent from the properties of Mr Timothy Finnegan R.I.P. The whole whirligig to be wound up by a Magnificent Transformation Scene showing the Radium Wedding of Night and Morning <, arranged as the daughter of Tyre and the son of Ausonius,> and the Dawn of Peace, Pure, Perfect and Perpetual Waking the Weary of the World.

An argument follows. (JJA 51: 9-10; slightly simplified)

A more interesting variant is the epithet ascribed to Glug. Twice in the first draft he is called "the bad black boy." On the typescript he is called, first, "the bad black boy," but at the second instance the typist entered "the bold black boy." In the absence of the Fair Copy, it is impossible to determine if Joyce had changed this or if this was a typist's error. However this discrepancy was caused, Joyce works with it by adding in overlay "bold" to the first epithet and "bad" to the second. However, after Joyce's corrections, the epithets are still unmatched: the first now reads "the bold bad black boy" and the second "the bad bold black boy." This may be deliberate or the result of carelessness on Joyce's part. In either case, the typist for the second typescript still missed Joyce's correction and rendered both epithets as "the bold black boy," neither of which were corrected by Joyce at that level (JJA 51: 11). However, Joyce did correct them at a later stage. In *transition* 22, where the chapter was first published in serial form in February 1933, both epithets are identical: "the bold bad black boy."[22] In its first draft form, "bad black boy" suggests William Blake's poem "The Little Black

---

[22] James Joyce, "Continuation of a Work in Progress," *transition* 22 (February 1933): 49–76, esp. 50; hereafter abbreviated as *t*.

Boy" from *Songs of Innocence*. This allusion is buttressed by a late modification made when Joyce prepared this chapter for the galleys.[23] Both epithets were changed to "bold bad bleak boy" (JJA 51: 284). The name "Blake" is thus suggested through the vocalic difference between "bleak" and "black" (bleak, Blake, black).

The second typescript contains only four modifications by Joyce as well as one small proofreading correction. It is notable primarily for the number of mistakes it contains. Several of Joyce's corrections on the preceding typescript were missed. Except for the "bold bad black boy," almost all the other errors were missed entirely by Joyce in preparing subsequent drafts. Except for "appreached," all the errors at this level involve a failure to decipher Joyce's overlaid additions on the first typescript. Usually these involve omitting Joyce's additions, but in one case the typist actually adds a word. On the first typescript, Chuff is described as "the <fine> fairhaired fellow" (JJA 51: 9); the second typescript reads "the fine frank fairhaired fellow" (JJA 51: 11)—the word "frank" appears without prompting and without further comment or correction by Joyce. Although this word may have been gratuitously inserted, it enhances the melopoeic alliteration already present.

This raises the question of "correcting" these transmissional errors. Applying Hans Walter Gabler's rule of invariant context, the precorrupted reading should be restored unless a passage containing a transmissional departure was subsequently modified by Joyce in a substantial way.[24] Here is an example of an error that should not be corrected, following from Gabler's rule: on the first typescript, Joyce added the following qualification to the Customers: "representatives <civics, each of whom is a jacktitative>" (JJA 51: 9). The second typist entered "civics" but left out the rest of this addition, so, at the second typescript level, the phrase reads simply "representative civics." On multiple subsequent drafts, Joyce modified this line through several discrete additions, so that it ultimately reads "representative locomotive civics, each inn quest of outings" (FW: 221.3–4).[25] Clearly, restor-

---

23 The second round of corrections to the pages of *The Mime of Mick, Nick and the Maggies*.

24 "Afterword," James Joyce, *Ulysses: A Critical and Synoptic Edition*, ed. Hans Walter Gabler with Wolfhard Steppe and Claus Melchior (New York: Garland, 1984, 1986), 1858–1911, esp. 1895–1900. This is obviously one of the more contentious aspects of Gabler's editorial procedure.

25 When this passage appeared in *transition*, it read "representative locomotive civics inn quest of outings" (*t:* 51). On an overlay to the first set of marked pages of *The Mime of Mick, Nick and the Maggies*, Joyce added "each": "representative locomotive civics inn <each> quest of outings" (JJA 51: 204; the comma after "civics" was added on the typed set of corrections to these pages, JJA 51: 288–89). This word recalls the earlier,

ing the phrase lost on the second typescript would be unacceptable since it would now no longer fit into the sentence.

Another example from the second typescript: the first typescript overlay "with their polls apart" was omitted from the following sentence: "they are both brought home <with their polls apart>." Since the rest of this sentence was unchanged through the final text (FW: 220.17), one could make a case that the omitted phrase should be restored in some "corrected text."

A more complex example: on the first typescript, Joyce added an interesting qualification to "the Radium Wedding of Night and Morning <arranged as the daughter of Tyre and the son of Ausonius> and the Dawn of Peace, Pure, Perfect and Perpetual, Waking the Weary of the World" (JJA 51: 10). This overlay was completely overlooked by the typist for the second typescript. This neglected addition subtly reinforces the pretensions of this universal "Pageant of History" by invoking a union between two great rival sea-ports in the Classical world, Tyre and Ausonia. With the exception of two minor melopoeic modifications—"Night" became "Neid" and "Morning" "Moorning"[26] —this passage was unchanged through the final text (FW: 222.17–20).

Strictly speaking, Gabler's rule of invariant context would prescribe restoring the missing phrase. But, the context is not invariant here. The missing phrase actually modifies the context in which it was supposed to have appeared. Without this phrase, the passage invokes historical grandeur in the most abstract of terms: "the Dawn of Peace, Pure, Perfect and Perpetual, Waking the Weary of the World." Although the missing phrase builds upon the pretensions of this phrase, it does so by compromising the generality with historical specificity. Because this phrase changes the logopoeic effect of this passage, restoring it becomes questionable.

After the second typescript, Joyce left this passage alone until he prepared the chapter as a whole for publication in *transition* 22 (February 1933). After *transition* 22 was published in early 1934, Joyce marked up the *transition* pages to prepare chapter 1 of Book II for separate publication as *The Mime of Mick, Nick and the Maggies*. Unfortunately, neither set of revisions—pre- or post-*transition*—survives. Collating the second typescript with the published texts of *transition* and *The Mime of Mick, Nick and the Maggies*, one can see that Joyce had considerably expanded the introduction for *transition* but made very few revisions prior to the publication of *The Mime of Mick, Nick and the Maggies*.

---

lapsed unit "each of whom is a jacktitative." The interpolated word "each" makes the pun on "inn quest" and "inquest" less readily apparent.

[26] These changes must have been made on the revised transition pages since they do not appear in *transition* (*t*: 51), but do appear in the set pages for *The Mime of Mick, Nick and the Maggies* (JJA 51: 206).

Fortunately, a great deal of extradraft material survives. These notes are contemporaneous with passages first found in *transition* and thus must have been used to prepare for the 1933 publication. The notes vary in length and quality: some are just individual words, others are discretely drafted entries. Generally, notes on any given page wind up inserted into roughly the same area of text, but there are numerous exceptions, and any random page contains apparently unrelated and diverse matter. A good number of these notes are flagged by sigla. This is an interesting and atypical procedure for Joyce at such a late stage. It also recalls the early genesis of this chapter when Joyce prepared his scheme for Book II using sigla (another example of Ferrer's "contextual memory"). Usually, in these extradraft notes, the siglum announces the appurtenance of the note to the text; for example the word "purdah," entered next to the Kate siglum (JJA 51: 147) was inserted into the text in the description of Kate in the introduction (*t:* 51; FW: 221.13). Curiously, many notes for passages outside the introductory cast of characters are likewise flagged by sigla. For example, why would the phrase "The swayful pathways of the dragonfly spider stay still in reedery"—which was inserted into a description of nightfall much later in the chapter (*t:* 66; FW: 244.27–28)—be tagged by the siglum for the Twelve (JJA 51: 148)? Not all the sigla-markers are accurate when compared with the final text. The entry "ask the attendantess for a leaflet" appears next to the HCE siglum (JJA 51: 146) but was inserted into the description of Izod in the cast of characters (*t:* 50; FW: 220.7). Usually though, the notes destined for the cast of characters are flagged by the appropriate sigla.

For publication in *transition*, Joyce made several types of modification to the introduction. He enhanced the *Wakean* feel of the passage's language by inserting more puns and further distorting the overly English feel of the early drafts. In terms of the cast, Joyce elaborated on the parenthetical actors' names. The parenthesis no longer includes merely a name but also some aside seemingly appropriate to that name. For example: "(Mr Seumas McQuillad, hear the riddles between the robot in his dress circular and the gagster in the rogues' gallery)" (*t:* 50).[27] Apart from this type of parenthetical addition, most characters' descriptions were not expanded substantially. The exceptions are the Customers, Saunderson, and Kate, each of whom received only a paltry account in the earlier drafts (their descriptions were also expanded further in subsequent drafts). Another exception is Hump: while his description by the second typescript was already generous, it has been expanded greatly here. In the drafts made after *transition*, Hump's

---

[27] This addition was derived from one of the extra-draft notes: "his riddles between the gagster in the rogues' gallery and the robot in the dress circular" (JJA 51: 145). This note is flagged by a "P."

is the only description to be further expanded substantially. Here he is identified as a "cap-a-pipe with watch and topper" (*t:* 50), which recalls, inevitably, the pipe-wielding cad in I.2 (FW: 35.1–36.34). HCE is again conflated with his accusers.

The concluding paragraph was also substantially augmented. Most importantly, Joyce added an introductory paragraph, rather than starting off immediately with the cast-list. This opening helps set the stage, in more ways than several, for this chapter, and, by extension, to Book II.

> Every evening at lighting up o'clock sharp and until further notice in Feenichts Playhouse. (Bar and conveniences always open.) With redistribution of parts and players and daily dubbing of ghosters under the distinguished patronage of their Elserships the Oldens from the four coroners of Findrias, Murias, Gorias and Falias. Messoirs the Coarb, Clive Sollis, Galorius Kettle, Pobiedo Lancey and Pierre Dusort, while the Caesar-in-Chief looks. On. Sennet. The mime of Mick, Nick and the Maggies, featuring: . . . (*t:* 50)

Like the concluding paragraph of this section, the tone of this paragraph is akin to a theatrical promotion. Here is the earliest drafted instance of the title that this chapter was given: The Mime of Mick, Nick and the Maggies. To anticipate this title, Joyce separately installed references to this title in two chapters in Book I very late, during the corrections to the galleys of Book I.[28] This is an odd title since in this chapter Mick, Nick, and the Maggies are called, respectively, Glugg, Chuff, and the Floras. However, such onomastic deviation is only appropriate for a "redistribution of parts and players." In preparing this passage for publication as *The Mime*, Joyce added the word "nightly redistribution of parts and players" (JJA 51: 201). This addition balances the "*daily* dubbing of ghosters" already in the passage, but it also enhances several global references to the *Wake* as a whole. This qualification explicitly announces an interchangeability between the characters included in the list and characters mentioned elsewhere in the *Wake*. Indeed, this is not the first such list to appear: chapter I.6 is a list of twelve characters—all of which were flagged by sigla in the first draft (April 1926), although these sigla were removed in subsequent drafts. This introductory paragraph in II.1 thus announces a kind of repetition of the "action" thus far elaborated, but through a redistribution of parts and players. The action may be the same, but the names are different. The eternal recurrence of the same is here

---

[28] These are in I.3, "the mime mumming the mick and his nick miming their maggies" (FW: 048.10–11) and in I.5, "*The Mimic of Meg Neg and the Mackeys*" (FW: 106.10–11). The first was inserted on the third set of corrections to the Book I galleys (JJA 50: 68), and the second was added on the first set of galleys (JJA 49: 146–47).

phrased as continual performance. "The Vico road goes round and round to meet where terms begin" (FW: 452.21–22).

This idea of perpetual iteration had already been suggested by the concluding line of this section, the "Perpetual Waking of the Weary of the World." This is reinforced by the new opening line, "Every evening at lighting up o'clock sharp and until further notice in Feenichts Playhouse." Obviously the suggestion of a Phoenix is important here: every night a theatrical performance is born again, born out of the ashes and thunderous applause of the night before.[29] Furthermore, the pretense to chronological accuracy so important for a theater program is belied by the vagueness of "o'clock sharp." This sentence establishes a nondescript performative recurrence.

The opening collocation "Every evening" implies a continual or imperfective action. The imperfectiveness of "Every evening" stands in contrast to the terminal, or perfective, "Night!" (FW: 216.5), at the end of I.8. Book I closed with the final action of nightfall and Book II opens with the account of a process that is ongoing through the nightly redistribution of parts and players. The slow build-up in the drafts to this phrase "nightly redistribution of parts" is another example of contextual memory as it recalls Joyce's 1926 plan for Book II which begins with "a night!" (JJA 51: 3). ALP's final night is now itself a nightly redistributed role. Indeed, since the earliest drafts of II.1, that chapter itself closes with its own variation of ALP's terminal Night: "Mummum" (JJA 51: 140–41; FDV: 141; FW: 259.10). Even the ending is repeated, a *fin* again is pantomimed again. "Hohohoho, Mister Finn, you're going to be Mister Finnagain! Comeday morm and, O, you're vine! Sendday's eve and, ah, you're vinegar!" (FW: 6.9–11).

The introductory matter has thus been further revised to thematically link with motifs developed elsewhere in the *Wake* by expanding upon the logopoeic associations that stem from the style of a theatrical programme. Joyce expanded this historical synchronicity on the corrections to the corrected pages of *The Mime of Mick, Nick and the Maggies:*

    <Time: the pressant>
With <futurist> battle pictures and the Pageant of <Past> History worked up by Messrs
    Thud and blunder [sic] (JJA 51: 204).

Actually, adiachronicity is a more accurate term here than synchronicity. Joyce brings in present, future, and past into a temporally flattened perspective of present performance. By this point in the draft history,

---

29 The phrase "Feenichts Playhouse" occurs on one of the extra-draft notes for this chapter (JJA 51: 147).

any inchoate action or dynamic that had been suggested in the first draft has been buried under the pressure of the pressant.[30] The newly installed contextualizing matter has flattened out the "action" into the semblance of a show. As Joyce wrote, in a line inserted at this stage immediately before the passage I have just quoted: "the show must go on" (JJA 51: 204; FW: 221.16). Rather than action, this is a play of stasis.

It was also at this draft level of the corrected *Mime* page that Joyce inserted a line announcing the specific context of the "pressant" performance in this chapter, children's games: "Newly billed for each wickeday perfumance. Somndoze massinees. By arraignment, childream's hours, expercatered" (JJA 51: 201; FW: 219.4–6). History is flattened out to a children's game.[31]

On the corrected pages of *The Mime*, Joyce further expanded the introductory and concluding paragraphs of this section, enhancing both the theatrical and the historical references, thereby eliciting a conflation of the two. He made further similar additions on the galleys, but made only one change (and a few corrections) on the final draft stage, the page proofs. The expanded contextualizing matter transforms the cast of characters into a series of archetypes indistinguishable from performers and characters. In the profusion of information, the characters become even less distinct. Their clearest iteration remains limited, for the most part, to the first draft. By the final draft we have more words but less, even less, action; more qualification and less left to qualify. Through the draft evolution of this section, Joyce adds all sorts of references, but, typically, rather than serve as concrete denotational markers (i.e., "HCE is Michael Gunn"), they distort what little reference the passage had to begin with. The references are not important for what they are, for what they refer to, but rather, more simply, for the fact that they are there to perplex us in any number of ways.

In sum, a genetic reading need not be purely fixated on glossing the denotational aspects of Joyce's language. Rather, by examining the text three-dimensionally through its archive, one can see just how unstable and labile reference is in *Finnegans Wake*. In terms of promoting accessibility to Joyce's text without resorting to crass simplifications

---

[30] "Le temps de *Finnegans Wake* sera donc très précisément le 'pressant' (FW: 221.17), non pas un simple présent mais un présent qui se presse, toujours déjà creusé par la marque de ce qui n'est pas lui, le temps de l'espacement des traces dans le mouvement infini des uns aux autres"; Stephen Heath, " 'Ambiviolences' 2," *Tel Quel* 51 (Fall 1972), 64–76, esp. 66.

[31] The contextualization of historical recurrence through children's games had already been present in the fair copy of the second section (FW: 222.22–236.32)—the earliest extant draft of that passage (October–November 1930)—with the Quinet passage.

and generalizations, I think that a genetic edition—something like a hypertext variorum—would be far superior to a series of annotations. Such an edition should not promise to offer a "corrected text," but rather record the various strata of textual accretion: the verso side of Gabler's synoptic edition, not the recto. In seeing the evolution of the text, one can see how reference is always subordinated to melopoeic, phanopoeic, and logopoeic effects. *Finnegans Wake* is text. It is not information.

The Wake's Progress:
Toward a Genetic Edition

DIRK Van HULLE

I N COMPARISON WITH THE LONG CONTROVERSY regarding the editions of *Ulysses*, there has been remarkably little debate over the edition of *Finnegans Wake*. Nevertheless, as several scholars have noted, it is not so evident that what we refer to as *Finnegans Wake* is "the" text of Joyce's last work. This is an attempt to give a short survey of the suggestions for a scholarly edition that have been made by two generations of scholars. The first generation could be referred to as the Theobalds, advocating a thorough restoration of the text in the form of a critical variorum edition;[1] the second generation prefers a complete account of the textual history in the form of an electronic archive or documentary edition without a critically edited text. At first sight, the approaches of these editorial Ondts and Gracehopers are diametrically opposed, but the aspects on which they focus (respectively, the product and its production) are interdependent and complementary. Therefore, this paper is an attempt to focus not on either the product or the production separately, but on the tension between them, emphasizing the temporal dimension of the work's

---

[1] As early as 1972, Fred H. Higginson suggested what he called "a developmental variorum, to the end of a final text more chronologically eclectic than Scholes's or Anderson's editions of the earlier works" ("The Text of *Finnegans Wake,*" *New Light on Joyce from the Dublin Symposium*, ed. Fritz Senn [Bloomington and London: Indiana UP, 1972], 128).

genesis, without neglecting the fact that Joyce eventually did publish a more or less finished product, which in turn made its own progress.

The problem at issue can be illustrated by means of Jan Vermeer's painting "Lady Writing a Letter with Her Maid." Vermeer did not paint many works, because he took his time; Joyce needed seventeen years to create his last work. A hole in the lady's left eye in Vermeer's painting marks the trace of the tools used by the painter to determine the vanishing point, that is, the point at which receding parallel lines seem to meet. This hole is also the spatial mark of the temporal dimension underlying Vermeer's painting. A similar vanishing point in James Joyce's *Finnegans Wake* is the Letter, written by ALP. In order to show this microscopic hole in the *avant-texte* it is useful to take a closer look at the material first. But it is perfectly possible to keep a distance and jump immediately to section *ii*, below.

i.

As the loving wife of HCE, ALP tries to counter the rumours about her husband's alleged crime in the park. By emphasizing his innocence, however, she only seems to confirm the rumours. The first versions of this Letter were drafted in December 1923 and January 1924, and they served as a kind of scaffolding for several other sections, such as the Delivery of the Letter and the two philological discussions concerning the Envelope and other aspects of the Letter. While drafting these sections, Joyce eventually decided to remove the Letter from its original context (Chapter I.5). It remained unused for fifteen years and was only re-inserted in 1938 in the final chapter of the *Wake*.

The so-called "red-backed notebook,"[2] in which the Letter was first drafted, is the result of one of the most intensive creative periods in the writing process of *Finnegans Wake*. It contains first and second drafts of parts of Chapters I.2, I.3, I.4, I.5, I.7 and I.8, as well as three drafts of ALP's letter and an early version of its delivery (which eventually became Book III).[3] All these passages were composed in about five months' time, between November 1923 and March 1924. Unlike most of Joyce's *Finnegans Wake* notebooks, the "red-backed notebook" does not contain loose paradigmatic excerpts, notes, and jottings, but whole sections of text or syntagmatic textual entities. The fact that these texts—as opposed to the majority of later manuscripts— are preserved in the form of a copy book, allows us to establish the relative chronology of the separate texts more accurately.

---

2 Preserved in the British Library: BL 47471b.

3 The first elaborations of this Book of Shaun are composed in a hard backed note-book, between March and June 1924. At that time the first and second Chapters of Book III were still conceived of as one entity.

The Letter was first drafted in December 1923. At that stage in the writing process, Joyce had written about twenty-nine pages in the red-backed notebook. The last section preceding the Letter is about HCE who appears as a fox and is hunted. After having drafted this section, Joyce apparently decided that he would write a letter, although he did not start with the opening. He left open two blank pages for the body of the letter and only wrote the closing formula, with the signature of ALP (at that time still called "Lara Prudence Earwicker") and a short post-script. This ten-line passage contains elements that ended up in three different sections, so that in a teleological classification, it has to be reproduced three times; and that is what the editors of the *James Joyce Archive* (the Garland facsimile edition) have done.[4]

Joyce subsequently started writing the Letter, not on the two pages he had left blank, however, but on the next pages: BL 47471b–31, 32, and 33. A brief survey gives an idea of the complex nature of the material. After the first draft of the Letter, Joyce made a second draft of the Foxhunt-episode as well as a second draft of the Letter (from page 34 to 42). These sections were apparently closely related at that time. This second draft of the Letter is followed by a passage concerning the Delivery of the Letter (continued on pages 35v and 34v, in retrograde direction); a first draft of the philological discussion of the Letter (33v to 25v, written in retrograde direction on verso pages wherever Joyce found some blank space); a second draft of this section (43 to 49); a first draft of the section on the Book of Kells (41v to 43v); and finally, Joyce found some blank space on the versos of pages at the beginning of the notebook (14v to 23v) to make a third draft of the Letter.

Because this intermingling of sections became so complicated, Joyce started numbering the pages. The first numbering[5] indicates that

---

4 *The James Joyce Archive*, eds. Michael Groden, Hans Walter Gabler, David Hayman, A. Walton Litz, and Danis Rose (New York & London: Garland Publishing, 1978). Hereafter abbreviated as *JJA*, followed by volume and page number. Page BL 47471b–30 is reproduced once under Chapter I.4 (*JJA*, 46: 56) and twice under I.5 (*JJA*, 46: 233 and 294), for the first two-thirds of the page contain a passage from I.5§1.*0 (*JJA*, 46: 233), which stops in the middle of a sentence and continues on page 29, indicating that it was written after the remarkable "Lara Prudence" passage with the first signature of the Letter at the bottom of the page. Apart from this first signature, the passage also contains the first draft of a sentence that ended up in the final paragraph of the "Foxhunt" section (I.4§2), as well as the first draft of a paragraph which was redrafted on page BL 47476a–42 and classified in the *JJA* under the heading "The Delivery of the Letter" (together with passages from pages 47471b–35v and 34v). In an electronic edition this document could be approached from different perspectives—without having to be duplicated—on the basis of Ted Nelson's principle of transclusion; see Yuri Rubinsky and Murray Maloney, *SGML on the Web: Small Steps Beyond HTML* (New Jersey: Prentice Hall PTR, 1997), 432.

5 The bold numeral indicates Joyce's numbering, followed by the page of the red-backed notebook: **1–3** = pp. 34–36 (= section I.4§2.*1); **3–12** = pp. 36, 37, 14v, 15v, 16v, 18v, 19v, 20v, 22v, 23v (= section I.5§2.*2).

the second draft of the Foxhunt-section is followed by the third draft of the Letter. At that stage, these two sections apparently still belonged together. But a breach was imminent. Joyce renumbered the sections[6] so that the Letter was preceded by its Philological Discussion and the section on the Book of Kells, until finally the letter was completely removed from Chapter 5 and recovered in 1938 at the very end of the writing process. The breach between the Foxhunt-section and the Letter seems to be indicated by an addition between these two sections on page 36/35v:

> Would we vision her ˏ(subconscious editor)ˏ with stereoptican relief

The addition "(subconscious editor)" refers to a paragraph on page 25v that was eventually omitted:

> Wonderfully well this explains the double nature of this gryphonic script and while its ingredients stand out with stereoptican relief we can speep ˏtourˏ beyond the figure of the scriptor into the subconscious editor's mind. (47471b–25v)[7]

It is not clear why Joyce omitted this paragraph. Possibly he judged that it was not good enough; but Joyce was generally quite reluctant to abandon any of his creations of more than a few lines. Although this sentence did not make it into the published text of *Finnegans Wake*, its content is not irrelevant. What follows is a history of the "subconscious editor's mind," starting in the fifties, when the first Joyceans drew attention to the "corruptions" of the text of *Finnegans Wake*, which led most scholars at that time to conclude that the text had to be restored.

ii.

Perhaps the best-known call for a critical edition is Jack P. Dalton's article "Advertisement for the Restoration," published in 1966, in which he reports on some interesting discoveries on the basis of manuscript analysis.[8] But Dalton was not the first scholar to collate versions of

---

[6] Joyce's second numbering: **1–3** = pp. 34–36 (= section I.4§2.*1); **4–10** = pp. 43, 44, 45, 46, 47, 48, 49 (= section I.5§1.*1); **11–13** = pp. 41v, 42v, 43v (= section I.5§4.*0); **[1]4–22** = 37, 14v, 15v, 16v, 18v, 19v, 20v, 22v, 23v (= section I.5§2.*2). I wish to thank Bill Cadbury for the stimulating exchange of ideas both during and after the "Genetic Networks" conference in Antwerp (December 1998), when we discovered that we had come to quite similar conclusions about the implications of this page-numbering.

[7] Transcription code: deletion: crossed out; addition: between carets; substitution (written over original text): bold.

[8] "Advertisement for the Restoration," *Twelve and a Tilly,* ed. Jack P. Dalton and Clive Hart (London: Faber & Faber, 1966), 119–37.

Finnegans Wake. In 1955, Theodore Dolmatch published his "Notes and Queries Concerning the Revisions of *Finnegans Wake*,"[9] a genetic study based only on published texts. Dolmatch compared three prepublications[10] of *Anna Livia Plurabelle* and concluded that most of the revisions "increase the incomprehensibility of the prose without increasing its quality," suggesting that *Anna Livia Plurabelle* existed in its "best form" ten years before the publication of *Finnegans Wake* and "that [Joyce] should have stopped his rewriting somewhere between the versions which appeared in *Le Navire d'Argent* and *transition*" (147–48). In 1956, Higginson drew up a list of twenty-nine emendations based on a collation of the prepublications of *Finnegans Wake* as *A Work in Progress*.[11] Since Higginson did not take into account the manuscript versions that followed the prepublications, Hart discovered that six of the omissions quoted by Higginson were deleted by Joyce himself.[12] Hart's approach suggests that the prepublications should be treated as versions rather than as editions, which illustrates the haziness of the twilight zone between *avant-texte* and text.

Higginson's initial approach (1956) serves as an illustration of the then prevalent idea of a publication as a "frozen" moment. In 1972, Higginson apologized with a "mea culpa"[13] for his neglect of the manuscripts. In this article he quotes an anecdote by Eugene Jolas about the remarkable insertion of the fable of "The Mookse and Gripes" in *transition* 6 after the first four-hundred copies of this journal had already been stitched. They were ripped apart, and the addition was incorporated.[14] Higginson concluded that "Joyce did not himself understand editing."[15]

---

9 *Modern Language Quarterly* 16 (1955), 142–48.

10 Most of the chapters of *Finnegans Wake* were prepublished as *Work in Progress*, mainly in Eugene Jolas's journal *transition*. Before the first edition of *Finnegans Wake* came out, different versions of *Anna Livia Plurabelle* had already been published in *Le Navire d'Argent* 11 (1925), 59–74; *transition* 8 (1927), 17–35; *Work in Progress* vol.1 (New York: Donald Friede, 1928); *Anna Livia Plurabelle* (New York: Crosby Gaige, 1928); and *Anna Livia Plurabelle: Fragment of Work in Progress* (London: Faber and Faber, 1930).

11 "Notes on the Text of *Finnegans Wake*," *Journal of English and Germanic Philology* 55.3 (July 1956), 451–56.

12 "Notes on the Text of *Finnegans Wake*," *Journal of English and Germanic Philology* 59.2 (April 1960), 229–39.

13 "The Text of *Finnegans Wake*," 122.

14 The addition was inserted between pages 106 and 107, and numbered 106a to 106f. For a more detailed account of this textual event, see Eugene Jolas's "Homage to James Joyce," *transition* 21 (March 1932), 250–53.

15 "The Text of *Finnegans Wake*," 120.

Perhaps this anecdote indeed shows that Joyce did not always realize the problems involved in editing, but it also elucidates how Joyce conceived his *Work in Progress*. Joyce apparently regarded his insertions in *transition* very literally as transitory stages, judging by the numerous additions to the *transition* pages of Book III (*JJA*, 61). The same *Archive* volume shows that prepublications in book form, however, were regarded as more or less finished. The marked pages of "The Ondt and the Gracehoper" show considerably fewer additions than the first set of *transition* pages in which this section was inserted.[16] The reason is that Joyce had already published this fable in *Tales Told of Shem and Shaun* and *Two Tales Told of Shem and Shaun*.

But until the very last moment before publication in book form, anything could happen to the text. Richard Ellmann mentions an anecdote about the first book publication of "The Ondt and the Gracehoper" in *Tales Told of Shem and Shaun*, published by the Black Sun Press. Because the last page contained only two lines, the printer suggested to the publisher, Mrs. Crosby, to ask Joyce to write eight more lines. The publisher "indignantly refused this preposterous idea,"[17] but the printer secretly told Joyce what the problem was, and Joyce immediately added a few lines.

None of the proofs for *Tales Told of Shem and Shaun* that are preserved contains either two or ten lines on the last page, and since some sets of proofs are missing or incomplete, it is difficult to reconstruct this remarkable story on the basis of the material in the *James Joyce Archive*. The only addition that could qualify for the "eight lines" mentioned in Ellmann's account, is an addition to the third set of proofs (III§1C.7). Joyce added six lines to the Gracehoper's poem and a few sentences based on the Egyptian *Book of the Dead*, to be inserted just before the poem.[18]

Joyce's susceptibility to a printer's call for extra text is yet another illustration of his awareness of and sensitivity to the sociological aspects of literary production. According to Sisley Huddleston, Joyce explained his attitude towards the serial prepublications of *Work in Progress* as follows:

> These sections serve to indicate what I am doing, but what I am doing should not be judged until it is completed. They are, if you like, serial

---

[16] *James Joyce Archive*, vol.61: 10–18; BL 47486b–306–312.

[17] *James Joyce*, rev. ed. (Oxford: Oxford UP, 1983), 614–15.

[18] The six extra lines for the poem were drafted first in a notebook (VI.B.27, p. 122) which Joyce happened to be compiling at that time (May–July 1929); they were added to the third set of page proofs of *Tales Told* (III.1C7; *JJA*, 57: 371; Texas-25).

contributions, which will eventually take their place in the whole. They have also a certain independent life of their own.[19]

This ambiguous attitude towards the status of his prepublications raises the question how definitive his "final" text is. Joyce's corrected copy of *Finnegans Wake* and his list of errata, preserved in the Buffalo collection (VI.H.4), show how relative the concept of a "final" text is. On the other hand, the fact that these errata were published as *Corrections of Misprints* implies that Joyce's disputed "love of accidentals"[20] was not unconditional.

Higginson's contention that "Joyce did not himself understand editing" perhaps only means that Joyce understood editing in a different way. According to Higginson, "[a] Theobald is required,"[21] which is a clear position statement. The theoretical debate between Alexander Pope and Lewis Theobald as editors of Shakespeare serves as a very early illustration of the dispute between supporters and opponents of restoration.[22] In this still ongoing debate—as reflected in the different views regarding critical and documentary editing—Higginson's position was shared by A. Walton Litz. In 1966, Litz remarked that "the published texts of *Finnegans Wake* are corrupt in many places,"[23] and concluded: "Of course, any editor must be cautious when he goes beyond Joyce's own corrections and emends from the manuscripts;

---

[19] Sisley Huddleston, "Back to Montparnasse" (Philadelphia, 1931), 195–96; quoted from Ellmann, *James Joyce*, 653.

[20] A. Walton Litz, "Uses of the *Finnegans Wake* Manuscripts," *Twelve and a Tilly*, 100.

[21] "The Text of *Finnegans Wake*," 129.

[22] In "The Fluid Text and the Orientations of Editing" Marcus Walsh summarizes this theoretical confrontation as follows: "Almost from the beginning of the eighteenth century Shakespeare was perceived as a writer of canonical authority. In the 1725 Preface to his edition of the plays, Alexander Pope insisted that he had piously observed the sanctity of the Shakespearian text: 'I have discharg'd the dull duty of an Editor . . . with a religious abhorrence of all Innovation, and without any indulgence to my private sense or conjecture.' [*Works of Shakespeare*, ed. Alexander Pope (6 vols., 1723–25), I: xxii]. Lewis Theobald, in *Shakespeare Restored* (1726)—the response to Pope's edition that would make him the hero of the *Dunciad*, questioned what he took to be Pope's unthinking use of the metaphor: 'what he is pleased to call a *religious Abhorrence of Innovation*, is downright superstition: . . . the writings of Shakespeare are [not] so venerable, as that we should be excommunicated for daring to innovate properly' (iv)" (Marcus Walsh, "The Fluid Text and the Orientations of Editing," *The Politics of the Electronic Text*, ed. Warren Chernaik, Caroline Davis, and Marilyn Deegan [Oxford: Office for Humanities Communication, 1993], 32).

[23] "Some of the changes made in typescript and proof never reached the printing stage; other errors were not noticed by Joyce when he prepared the *Corrections of Misprints;* and new mistakes were introduced when the *Corrections of Misprints* were incorporated into later editions" ("Uses of the *Finnegans Wake* Manuscripts," 100).

Joyce's 'love of accidentals' is well known, and some of the apparent errors may have received his silent sanction. But there is no reason why a good critical text of *Finnegans Wake* should not ultimately be produced, based upon judicious use of the manuscripts" (100).

In Vincent Deane's "Editorial" of the first issue of *A Finnegans Wake Circular*, the first objective of the new journal was defined as: "The establishment of an accurate text. At present a synoptic version of *FW* is being prepared according to the same principles as the Gabler *Ulysses*, and a discussion of work in progress by its compiler, Danis Rose, will be included in the next issue of the *Circular*" (1). But after this announcement in 1985, no account of Danis Rose's editorial work was published. Apparently the critical edition is ready but the publication is delayed because of copy-right problems, and so is the "establishment of an accurate text."

iii.

The opposite approach is represented by scholars such as Hart, who has probably discovered as many "corruptions" or transmissional departures as Dalton and Higginson. But whereas the latter come to the conclusion that the text ought to be restored, Hart argues that the corruptions are an integral part of the *Wake*. They are not only due to the author's near-blindness, but also due to a kind of "slovenliness" and the chaotic living circumstances which were largely created by himself: "In practice Joyce was often far from meticulous, nor can all the inaccuracies in his text, as Mr. Dalton is well aware, be attributed to the poor workmanship of typists and printers."[24] The transmissional departures are an inherent aspect of Joyce's writing method. If Joyce had been a different person, these so-called "corruptions" might not have found their way into *Finnegans Wake*; but then again, if Joyce had been a different person, he might not have written *Finnegans Wake* in the first place. Therefore, Hart questions the legitimacy of "taking over an author's responsibilities for him" (79) and concludes that in his opinion the unbound copy of the first edition, preserved in Buffalo (to which Joyce, together with Paul Léon, introduced several corrections) provides the text of *Finnegans Wake*.

This view corresponds with the approach suggested by Alice Kaplan and Philippe Roussin,[25] according to whom the editor's task is no longer to be compared with that of a restorer of paintings, since

---

[24] "The Hound and the Type-bed: Further Notes on the Text of *Finnegans Wake*," *A Wake Newslitter* III.4 (Aug. 1966), 78.

[25] "A Changing Idea of Literature: The Bibliothèque de la Pléiade," *Yale French Studies* 89 (1996), 261.

restoration tends to obscure the hesitations during the writing process. Bill Cadbury, who is preparing an XML-based genetic representation of the textual history inspired by the model of Gabler's synoptic
edition of *Ulysses*, remarks:

> Especially if a critical edition is accompanied by a reading text, the
> tempting notion that the presentation of chronological changes is mainly
> for the purpose of giving the evidence for decisions about the final
> product will—we have seen it happen before—obscure the fact that
> Joyce's intentions have a chronological dimension which can't be flat-
> tened out.[26]

The consequence is a tendency away from critical editions. As a result of the current interest in textual instability, and thanks to the
expandability of electronic editions, editors increasingly conceive their
edition as an archive, in an attempt to reduce the editor's interference.
Whereas in 1966, Litz carefully argued in favor of a critical edition,
he recently advocated an electronic archive with as little editorial
intervention as possible. In the "Afterword" of *The Literary Text in the
Digital Age* (published in 1996), Litz wrote:

> I think the key to making an electronic archive that will be of great use to
> the student, but not place restrictions on the student's freedom to seek
> new information or different interpretations, is nonintervention on the
> part of the editor.[27]

The dichotomy between documentary and critical editions, or archives
and restorations, may be somewhat exaggerated and gives the impression that only proponents of the former recognize the instability of
the text, whereas proponents of the latter would only be interested
in establishing a stable, edited text. The idea of reducing the editor's
intervention is in itself a noble objective, but no electronic archive or
documentary edition can completely dispense with value-judgments.
The impression of objectivity that electronic archives give may be
misleading, for this kind of editing also involves an enormous amount
of editorial interference. Data have to be digitized; the choice of which
data are fed into the computer and which are not, and the way in which
they will be presented are both determined by the editor.

The inevitability of interpretation becomes apparent as soon as one
tries to transcribe a few lines of Joyce's manuscripts. In this context,
David Hayman's transcription of the eventually omitted "Wonderfully
well" passage mentioned above is particularly telling:

---

[26] "The Development of the 'Eye, Ear, Nose and Throat Witness' Testimony in I.4,"
Probes: Genetic Studies in Joyce, ed. David Hayman and Sam Slote (Amsterdam: Rodopi,
1995), 246.

[27] Ed. Richard J. Finneran (Ann Arbor: U of Michigan P, 1996), 248.

> Wonderfully well this explains the double nature of this gryphonic script and while its ingredients stand out with stereoptican relief we can ~~see peep~~ **tour** beyond the figure of the scriptor into the subconscious writer's mind.[28]

The last two words of this passage are in fact "editor's mind." In 1963 Hayman transcribed them as the "writer's mind," which almost appears as a symbolic *Fehlleistung*, reflecting the editorial privileges in the sixties, when critical editions—as Jack Stillinger observes—often looked "like the realization of editors' rather than authors' intentions."[29] In 1990, however, Hayman adjusted his initial transcription in *The Wake in Transit*.[30] Both transcriptions reflect the editorial atmosphere in which they were made. In the three decades that separate the two, the emphasis has shifted from a preoccupation with "the writer's mind" and his intentions to "the editor's mind" and his increased awareness and self-critical attitude.

The textual history of *Finnegans Wake* may be approached from different perspectives. In the ideal situation, the chronology of the writing process coincides with the order of the novel's chapters. But this is seldom the case. As the shuffling and reshuffling of the Letter has shown, the essence of any literary work's progress is precisely the tension between the chronological course of the writing process and the final narrative structure. In order to render this tension, a genetic edition of *Finnegans Wake* could offer its users the opportunity to start reading from different starting points, so that they can study the draft stages in view of their eventual place in the published text, but also the displacement of passages at a time when the author was not yet sure what their final destination would be.

iv.

The French genetic critic Pierre–Marc de Biasi notes that in order to study a work's genesis it is often necessary to reshuffle the material as it has been arranged by archivists.[31] The Garland facsimile edition of *The James Joyce Archive* is the first attempt to organize all the *Finnegans Wake* manuscripts, and its classification corresponds with what de Biasi calls "le rangement" of the manuscripts. This teleological arrange-

---

[28] *A First Draft Version of "Finnegans Wake"* (Austin: U of Texas P, 1963), 87.

[29] "Multiple Authorship and the Question of Authority," *TEXT* 5 (1991), 290.

[30] *The* Wake *in Transit* (Ithaca, NY: Cornell UP, 1990), 175.

[31] "Vers une science de la littérature: L'analyse des manuscrits et la genèse de l'oeuvre," *Symposium, Encyclopaedia Universalis* (Paris: Encyclopaedia Universalis, 1993), 924–37.

ment, however, is only the first phase of the organization of the *avant-texte*.[32] The second phase is what de Biasi calls the "classement," that is, the chronological or genetic classification of the manuscripts. With reference to *Finnegans Wake*, this second, chronological arrangement is all but finished.

The teleological approach is not ideal with regard to a peregrinating section such as the Letter. In a classification according to the final narrative structure, the work's genesis is approached counterclockwise. This approach may give the impression that Joyce knew from the start where he was writing toward, and would thus confirm what Ellmann contends in his biography:

> Since the earliest passages to be written were from different parts of the book, it is clear that, in spite of his disclaimers, Joyce had a general notion of how to proceed in the later sections, but had not yet worked them out in detail.[33]

A chronological approach, on the other hand, shows that Ellmann's statement should at least be nuanced, for this "notion of how to proceed" was indeed rather "general," and as soon as one takes a closer look at the manuscripts, one discovers a lot of side-paths and blind alleys which should be mapped as well.

From a genetic perspective it seems important that every change is clearly marked, for example by using Bill Cadbury's system to indicate an omission at a certain level. This constant emphasis on changes vis-à-vis preceding versions might enhance the reader's awareness of the inevitability of transmissional variation and render visible a unique feature of *Finnegans Wake*—what James S. Atherton called "its awareness of itself as a 'work in progress.' "[34]

This self-reflective nature of Joyce's work was compared to Igor Stravinsky's "music about music" by Theodor Adorno;[35] and because

---

[32] De Biasi emphasizes the artificial nature of this first classification: "Il est évident que, dans de nombreux cas, ce principe téléologique faussera la perspective: un auteur peut ne trouver l'objet propre de son texte définitif que très tard dans la rédaction et avoir longtemps travaillé à des développements qui ne trouveront plus leur place dans le projet final. Un tel problème ne peut être résolu à ce niveau de l'analyse et doit être renvoyé au classement génétique." ("Vers une science de la littérature," 930). ["In numerous instances, it becomes apparent that this teleological principle will falsify the perspective: an author can only discover the definitive text's true object late in the editing process and after having worked at length on some developments which will not even appear in the final project. Such a problem cannot be solved at this level of analysis and should be referred to the genetic classification."]

[33] *James Joyce*, rev. ed., 555.

[34] *The Books at the Wake* (London: Faber and Faber, 1959), 59.

[35] *Philosophie der neuen Musik* (Tübingen: J.C.B. Mohr/Paul Siebeck, 1949), 120.

of this self-awareness, the pre-text becomes an inseparable part of the work, which Daniel Ferrer compared to a shadow.[36] Therefore, the *Wake* without account of its progress would be like Tom Rakewell without Nick Shadow in Stravinsky's opera *The Rake's Progress;* on the other hand, the same applies to the progress without *Wake:* the recent genetic focus should not obscure the fact that Joyce's last book is both a "Work in Progress" **and** *Finnegans Wake.* Perhaps, therefore, in addition to the full genetic representation, the reader could be provided with the text of the unbound copy (that is, the text Joyce chose to present to the public, the *Fassung letzter Hand*) as well as the text of the first edition, in order to emphasize that, from the date of its publication on 4 May 1939, *Finnegans Wake* led its own public life.

But the emphasis in a genetic edition is on the fact that this moment between pre- and postpublication is less of a borderline than it seems and that even as *Wake* the work continued to be in progress. The change of titles gives the impression that the transition from pre-text to text took place at a very precise moment, but as Joyce's list of errata and the large number of prepublications imply, this transition was a gradual process. By applying the same system of marking changes between draft stages to the first and subsequent editions, all the published texts could be treated as any other version in the textual history.

A sentence such as the "Wonderfully well" passage quoted above is a trace comparable to the vanishing point on Vermeer's painting. Probably nobody would suggest we fill up the hole in the lady's eye; similarly, it seems preferable not to restore the traces of textual vanishing points, certainly not without commentary. Evidently, the analogy is only partially valid. As opposed to Vermeer's vanishing point, the textual vanishing points are *not* visible in the currently published text of *Finnegans Wake.* But that does not mean that they are not there. Perhaps the main task of the editor is not to restore, but to indicate and draw the reader's attention to these textual vanishing points in order to understand "the double nature of this gryphonic script," and to increase the awareness that a literary product not only bears the traces of its production, but that these traces are an essential part of the literary work.

---

[36] "Téléologie négative: la génétique comme art d'accomoder les restes," lecture given during the conference "Genèses: Deuxième congrès international de critique génétique" on 9 September 1998, organized by the ITEM–CNRS in Paris.

No Marriage In Heaven: Editorial Resurrection in *Djuna Barnes's* Nightwood

CATHERINE HOLLIS

Sometimes the author objects and sometimes not, sometimes he is pleased, sometimes he acquiesces, and sometimes he does not notice what has happened. The work of art is thus always tending toward a collaborative status . . . .

James Thorpe, *Principles of Textual Criticism*

O N APRIL 28, 1936, Emily Coleman met with T. S. Eliot in his office at Faber and Faber in order to discuss the publication of Djuna Barnes's *Nightwood*. This meeting marked the culmination of Coleman's campaign on behalf of her friend's book: convinced that Barnes possessed the "gifts of [a] prophet," Coleman vowed "if human art can draw blood out of a stone, I will draw interest from Eliot for this book."[1] Barnes's novel had already been rejected by five publishers,

[1] Coleman to Barnes, 27 Aug., 1935, and 5 Nov., 1935. Coleman's unpublished letters to Barnes are located in The Djuna Barnes Papers, Special Collections, University of Maryland at College Park Libraries, College Park, Maryland; Barnes's letters to Coleman are located in the Emily Holmes Coleman Papers, Special Collections, University of Delaware, Newark, Delaware. I am grateful to the Author's League Fund and to Joseph Geraci, executors for Djuna Barnes and Emily Coleman respectively, for permission to quote from unpublished material. I am also grateful to Rebecca Johnson Melvin, Associate Librarian at the University of Delaware, and to Beth Alvarez, Curator of Literary

and Coleman reasoned that she would need the stature of T. S. Eliot, who combined his fame as a poet and critic with the more prosaic work of an editor, to back Barnes's novel and to see it into print. At this meeting, Coleman assured Eliot that Barnes would be "amenable to small ... omissions": if Eliot felt that the book required editorial pruning in order to be published, Coleman felt comfortable giving Barnes's assent to such changes for her.[2] This meeting between Coleman and Eliot is remarkable not only because it signals a change in the fortunes of *Nightwood*, but also because it brings together the two principal players involved in the editing and publication of that novel, neither of whom was the author. The composition and publication history of Djuna Barnes's *Nightwood* is thus very much embedded in what Jerome McGann has called "socialized authorship":[3] the text comes to existence through a collaboration between producers of literature (editors, publishers), patrons of literature, and the author herself. Whether we choose to read a version of the 1936 edition of *Nightwood*, or the text of the recent Dalkey Archive edition (1995), we are reading a novel shaped by producers of literature apart from, or in addition to, the text's nominal author.

In his biography of Djuna Barnes, Phillip Herring says of Barnes's editorial collaborators: "if one were to award laurels for the greatest contribution made to the artistic career of Djuna Barnes, it would have to go to Emily Coleman (second prize would go to T. S. Eliot)."[4] Indeed, as Cheryl Plumb, editor of the Dalkey Archive edition, argues, "*Nightwood* might never have seen print without [Coleman]."[5] This recognition of Coleman's contribution towards the publication of Barnes's novel comes rather belatedly, for Eliot's influence on *Nightwood* has overshadowed Coleman's throughout much of the novel's reception history. Eliot's preface, appended to the first American edition of 1937, functioned as an imprimatur for the novel, leading many early reviewers to respond as much to Eliot's introduction as to the novel itself.[6] Although Emily Coleman was herself a writer, publishing one novel, *The Shutter of Snow* (1930), and several poems in the

---

Manuscripts at the University of Maryland at College Park, for access to and help with the Coleman and Barnes collections. Thanks are also due to the anonymous readers at *TEXT*, whose comments were useful in the revision of this essay.

2 Coleman's diary, 28 April, 1936; University of Delaware.

3 *A Critique of Modern Textual Criticism* (Chicago: U of Chicago P, 1983).

4 *Djuna: The Life and Work of Djuna Barnes* (New York: Viking, 1995), 190.

5 "Revising *Nightwood*: 'a kind of glee of despair,' " *Review of Contemporary Fiction* 13.3 (1993), 150.

6 See Jane Marcus, "Mousemeat: Contemporary Reviews of *Nightwood*," in *Silence and Power: A Reevaluation of Djuna Barnes*, ed. Mary Lynn Broe (Carbondale and Edwardsville: Southern Illinois UP, 1991), 195–206.

little magazine *transition*, her work on *Nightwood* is what she is best known for. Coleman heard Barnes read portions of an early version of *Nightwood*, then called "Bow Down," at Peggy Guggenheim's Hayford Hall in the summer of 1932. There, Coleman functioned, along with Guggenheim's lover John Holms, as one of the manuscript's earliest critics. Later, Coleman became intensely involved with the text's revision, particularly in the years 1934 and 1935, as Barnes completed a third version of her beleaguered manuscript. Coleman's editorial suggestions helped reduce the manuscript's word count from 190,000 to 65,000 and her wild enthusiasm for the novel helped sustain Barnes through its multiple rejections.[7] Finally, Coleman pursued Eliot's support for the novel, sending him excerpts and two strongly worded letters late in 1935, badgering him until he agreed to meet with her and "do something" about the novel in April 1936.

Cheryl Plumb's recent edition of *Nightwood* continues the process of editorial collaboration by correcting the balance of influence between Coleman and Eliot. As Eliot's editorial position at Faber (coupled with his institutional prestige) gave him the authority to make the final decision concerning the body of the 1936 text, so Cheryl Plumb's role as textual editor allowed her to create what the dustjacket calls "the original version" of *Nightwood*, a pre-Eliot but post-Coleman version of the text. Plumb's edition effectively removes Eliot from the editorial realm by dispensing with his preface and reinstating the "small omissions" Coleman guaranteed Barnes would be amenable to making in order to publish with Faber and Faber.[8] The 1995 edition of *Nightwood* restores the explicit language and homosexual content that Eliot felt necessary to omit; by doing so, Plumb's edition succeeds in clarifying the political energy of this novel by placing its characters and events firmly in the context of 1920s' gay culture in Paris and Berlin. The Dalkey Archive *Nightwood* is therefore the product of a collaboration between Coleman and Barnes, with assistance sixty years on from its textual editor. However, despite the claim on its dust jacket, this is not the "original version" of *Nightwood*, since Plumb's

---

7 Barnes's estimate of the word count can be found in two letters written to Coleman following the completion of the third revision in July 1935: Barnes to Coleman, 11 July and 24 July, 1935. Coleman Papers, University of Delaware. As Cheryl Plumb points out, Barnes's word count is an approximation based on the first version of her novel. Introduction, Djuna Barnes, *Nightwood: The Original Version and Related Drafts*, ed. Cheryl Plumb (Normal, Illinois: Dalkey Archive Press, 1995), xv–xvi.

8 These omissions were primarily explicit references to homosexuality that Eliot, in his position at Faber, felt necessary to omit given the threat of censorship. See Leigh Gilmore, "Obscenity, Modernity, Identity: Legalizing *The Well of Loneliness* and *Nightwood*," *Journal of the History of Sexuality* 4.4 (1994), 603–24. Gilmore discusses the link between the 1928 obscenity trial of Radclyffe Hall's novel and Eliot's editorial strategy aimed at avoiding a similar situation with *Nightwood*.

edition reconstructs *Nightwood* as it stood at the end of 1935, after Coleman's substantial assistance in the revision of a third version of Barnes's text. An editor could, if she wanted, reconstruct an even earlier version of *Nightwood* from the fragments of its first and second versions, fragments which are published as an appendix to the Dalkey Archive edition (although to do so would be rather like building Dr. Frankenstein's monster). The Dalkey Archive *Nightwood*, like any critical edition, is a product of the culture in which its editing takes place, and it reflects recent developments in the historical documentation of homosexuality, as well as in the ongoing revision of modernism to acknowledge the figures at its margins. *Nightwood* has been revised for the 1990s, both through the restoration of its explicitly "queer" content,[9] and also through its privileging of Coleman's collaboration over Eliot's.

The text of the Dalkey Archive *Nightwood* reflects Plumb's argument that Coleman's editorial input represents a "genuine collaboration" with Barnes, as opposed to Eliot's suggestions, which Barnes acquiesced to in order to have her novel published.[10] According to Plumb, Coleman's suggestions were offered to and freely accepted or rejected by Barnes; these suggestions further Barnes's own intentions for her work and are therefore retained in the Dalkey Archive *Nightwood*. Eliot's excisions, on the other hand, were designed to make the work more publishable (which, in this case, means less subject to censorship), and therefore reflect "an altered intention" (144). Plumb distinguishes between two kinds of editorial collaborations: those that occur between writer and editor acting as equals and those that follow a more hierarchical model, where an editor imposes unwanted changes upon an author's text.[11] As Plumb acknowledges, in 1936 "T. S. Eliot was T. S. Eliot" (xxv). A "genuine" collaboration, according to Plumb, is a voluntary collaboration between equals, like that between Coleman and Barnes. Plumb's rationale for including Coleman's suggestions accepted by Barnes is accounted for by traditional editorial theory, if one assumes "traditional" to mean a theory developed to create critical editions purged of non-authorial influence. As articulated by

---

9 Joseph Boone suggests that the very contemporary term "queer" best evokes *Nightwood*'s "realm of polymorphous desire that circulates among [its] wandering community of outsiders, outcasts, and orphans" (234). See his *Libidinal Currents: Sexuality and the Shaping of Modernism* (Chicago: U of Chicago P, 1998).

10 Plumb makes this argument in her introduction to the textual apparatus accompanying her edition of *Nightwood* (144–45). All quotations taken from the novel and from its textual apparatus are taken from this edition and are cited parenthetically.

11 Lisa Ede and Andrea Lunsford characterize these two general models of collaboration as "dialogic" and "hierarchical," respectively. See their co-authored *Singular Texts / Plural Authors* (Carbondale: Southern Illinois UP, 1991).

G. Thomas Tanselle, this theory suggests that editorial changes made by a non-authorial agent may be accepted by a textual editor if "the two can be regarded as voluntary collaborators."[12] Because Barnes could and did reject many of Coleman's suggestions, it is reasonable to assume, as Plumb does, that those suggestions of Coleman's that Barnes incorporates into her text are compatible with Barnes's final intentions for it. Nonetheless, there were significant differences of opinion between Barnes and Coleman regarding the meaning of Barnes's text, and Coleman's editorial advice was influenced by her interpretation of what she read. In what follows, I will first demonstrate the extent of this difference in opinion between Barnes and Coleman, in order to confront the "significant problem" (Plumb, 147) of the ordering of the middle chapters of *Nightwood*. This is one case, I suggest, where Barnes "acquiesced" to a suggestion of Coleman's that does not necessarily improve the text. This editorial problem complicates Plumb's construction of the "genuine collaboration" between Barnes and Coleman, demonstrating as well the complex inter-relationship between textual editing and literary interpretation.

i. "No Marriage in Heaven": Coleman's Editing of Barnes

Emily Coleman read *Nightwood* as a confirmation of her own religious beliefs. Throughout the process of editorial revision, Coleman frequently invoked the biblical phrase, "no marriage in Heaven," in order to link Barnes's portrayal of homosexuality with Coleman's own ideas about Christian resurrection. In an infamous letter to T. S. Eliot, written to convince him to publish Barnes's novel, Coleman emphasized her friend's approach to the mysteries of sexuality: "The passage on the 'invert boy or girl,' can you read that and not see that something new has been said about the very heart of sex?— going beyond sex, to that world where there is no marriage or giving in marriage—*where no modern writer ever goes?*"[13] Coleman refers here to the Gospel of Matthew, and to an episode where Jesus is confronted with a riddle about resurrection. A woman has married seven brothers sequentially, after each brother dies "without issue": in the resurrection, the Sadducees ask, whose wife shall she be? Jesus replies: "in the resurrection, they neither marry, nor are given in marriage, but are like angels in Heaven" (Matthew 22:30). The similar phrase—"no marriage in Heaven, nor giving in marriage"—reappears

---

[12] See "The Editorial Problem of Final Authorial Intention," in his *Textual Criticism and Scholarly Editing* (Charlottesville and London: The UP of Virginia, 1990), 50.

[13] Coleman to Eliot, 1 Nov., 1935; Coleman Papers, University of Delaware. Quoted by Plumb, xxi.

consistently in Coleman's diary and in her letters written during the years of *Nightwood*'s revision. In April 1934, after Barnes complained that "Bow Down" was at its fifth potential publisher and likely to be rejected again, Coleman wrote Barnes that the novel was "much better than we know": "It contains mysteries one must think over . . . We have to get through sex in this life. . . . sex is this world. I'm sure of this. 'There is no marriage in Heaven.' And the love of the boy–girl and of the girl–boy is our passionate attempt to have that other life. 'The girl lost, what is she but the prince found?' "[14] Here, Coleman links Barnes's portrayal of the invert—the boy–girl or the girl–boy—to an eschatological condition: through loving a girl–boy or boy–girl, we are afforded a glimpse of that "other world." When Coleman says that "sex is this world," she refers to heterosexuality, which can be overcome in Heaven (where there is no marriage) or through inversion ("our passionate attempt to have that other life"). Coleman's conjunction of inversion and resurrection is based on a dualism between body and soul that structures both Christian resurrection and the idea of inversion itself.[15] Significantly, Barnes herself neither uses this phrase in the novel, nor in her letters to Coleman.

Coleman's emphasis on the metaphysical dimensions of Barnes's treatment of the themes of jealousy, suffering, and inversion can certainly be read as an attempt to pitch the novel in such a way as to appeal to Eliot's own critical preoccupations, or at least to Coleman's idea of them.[16] However, as Cheryl Plumb notes, Barnes's own idea of resurrection was fully secular and aesthetic; it concerned her ability to use writing as a means of transforming the immediate pain of loss into the more immortal form of art.[17] We can see the complex intertwining of both readings in a passage Coleman cites as the heart of Barnes's novel, and of the "mysteries one must think over." Robin Vote, the character based on Barnes's lost lover Thelma Wood, comes "from a

---

14 Coleman to Barnes, 30 April, 1934; Barnes Papers, University of Maryland at College Park.

15 The use of the term "inversion" to describe homosexuality originated in nineteenth-century sexology and was still current at the time of *Nightwood*'s composition. Inversion's dualistic formula—"the soul of a woman imprisoned in the body of a man"—constructs homosexuality as a metaphysical problem, as a gendered conflict between one's body and soul.

16 In her essay cited above (n. 8), Leigh Gilmore suggests that Eliot also focuses on the metaphysics of inversion in his preface as a means of deflecting the censor's eye from the homosexuality of Barnes's characters.

17 Plumb reads Barnesian resurrection specifically as it concerns Barnes's "lost life" with Thelma Wood, the real-life model for *Nightwood*'s Robin Vote character ("Revising *Nightwood*," 158–59). Plumb also distinguishes between Coleman's view of resurrection and Barnes's in her introduction to the Dalkey Archive *Nightwood*, xix.

world to which she would return," a quality that inspires her somnam-
bulistic peregrinations apart from her bereft lover, Nora Wood. Nora,
watching Robin's preparations for leave-taking, assuages her grief with
thoughts of love beyond the grave.

> 'In the resurrection, when we come up looking backward at each other,
> I shall know you only of all that company. My ear shall turn in the socket
> of my head; my eyeballs loosened where I am the whirlwind about that
> cashed expense, my foot stubborn on the cast of your grave.' In the
> doorway Robin stood. 'Don't wait for me,' she said. (52)

In this passage, Nora's passion threatens to outlive her body's death,
as her "stubborn" foot resists the centrifugal force that would whirl
away and disperse her eyes and ears, anchoring her to the "cast" of
Robin's grave. But Robin, the girl–boy who stands in the "doorway,"
is already half-way to another world, existing in a state of permanent
departure exemplified by her warning to Nora, "Don't wait for me."
Literally, Robin disappears into the night-world of bars and pissoirs,
into the lesbian social world of 1920s Paris; metaphorically, Robin's
"other world" is an inverted world where, as Emily Coleman claims,
there is no marriage. But Nora's stubborn attachment to Robin's body
paradoxically keeps her from joining Robin there—she will cling to
the abandoned grave, the body of the beloved, rather than succumb
to the forces of dispersal and entropy.

Coleman's editing of Barnes's text reflects her sense that *Nightwood*
should be "the woman's Othello,"[18] and that Barnes should focus on
the emotional drama played out between Nora and Robin, and on
the subsequent dark night of the soul Nora enters after Robin leaves
her for the "squatter" Jenny. Accordingly, Coleman asks Barnes to
remove or reduce the presence of other characters in the novel—Felix,
Robin's husband, and Guido, Robin's unwanted child, for example—
in order to focus the narrative on Nora and Robin. Although Coleman
suggested that Barnes cut the first chapter entirely, which focuses
on Felix and his obsession with the aristocracy, Barnes retained it,
indicating that Felix was, for his author at least, an intrinsic part of
the narrative. Coleman also believed that Dr. O'Connor's stories made
the narrative too diffuse, obscuring the central romantic plot with his
monologues on inversion and the night. While Coleman's editorial
opinion parallels T. S. Eliot's own initial opinion that the multiple
characters of *Nightwood*, situated in diverse dramatic situations, do
not cohere into a unified whole, Eliot read the transvestite Doctor
O'Connor as the novel's moral center, and accordingly asked for the

---

[18] Coleman to Barnes, 27 Aug., 1935; Barnes Papers, University of Maryland at College
Park.

excision of *Nightwood*'s final chapter, the notorious encounter between Robin and Nora's dog. Although Eliot was eventually convinced that the novel's focus must be the "whole pattern" of the characters' intersecting lives,[19] Coleman never accepted this, and continued to argue, even after the novel's publication, that its lack of focus was the novel's failure.

Barnes's artistic "failure" was exacerbated, for Coleman, by Barnes's inability or unwillingness to use conventional markers of plot and structure. Much of Coleman's editorial work on *Nightwood* involved encouraging Barnes to create a more reader-friendly text by including such markers—mainly setting and dialogue—in order to help situate the abstractions of the prose. Unlike Eliot, whose editorial work on the text was limited to the question of excisions necessary for publication, Coleman worked consistently with the text from its earliest drafts, suggesting major compositional changes (reordering chapters, eliminating excessive characters) over the course of the novel's three major versions prior to publication. Barnes, who freely admitted her inability to structure and shape her prose, accepted many of Coleman's suggestions, particularly those designed to help readers orient themselves within the novel. This created a collaborative dynamic where Coleman, as an opinionated reader and as an editor, pushed Barnes to provide a more structured, coherent, and unified plot to ground the abstractions of her prose.

Eventually, Barnes came to understand Coleman's criticism by taking the metaphor of resurrection that Coleman was using to interpret the novel and applying it to the editing of the text. Envisioning an etching of William Blake's, an image of spirits leaping out of dead bodies left abandoned on the ground, Barnes associates Blakean resurrection with the structural flaws in her own work. She writes Coleman: "like a clap of thunder I got what you ... must have been meaning all this time ... that in my writing I have striven ... to give that soul, that essence, but without the bodies below it ... and in the omission, evidently I have been wrong." Leaving out plot and structure is like leaving out the corpses, or as Barnes goes on to say, "I have gone on fighting over terms, as over the idea that for me plot, structure, etc, seem wrong. They did seem wrong, because I was aiming at the soul as in Blake's picture, not realizing that in leaving out the body of the death ... I was bewildering the onlooker."[20] The body of the death is the narrative structure, the structure Coleman's suggestions sought to give this text; significantly, Barnes's recognition of the accuracy of Coleman's advice is deferred until the completion of the third version

---

[19] See Eliot's Introduction to *Nightwood* (New York: New Directions, 1961), xv.

[20] Barnes to Coleman, 30 Oct., 1935; Coleman Papers, University of Delaware.

of *Nightwood*. It is as if the changes had to be instantiated before their logical necessity became apparent to Barnes, as though there were a lag time between her acceptance of the suggestions and a subsequent comprehension of them. For Barnes, souls precede bodies, as abstract colloquy precedes narrative; as Coleman's suggestions, ex post facto, precede Barnes's recognition of their accuracy. This dynamic will be at stake in the question of the ordering of *Nightwood*'s middle chapters.

Although it is clear from Barnes's own commentary that writing was, for her, a means of resurrecting and possessing the past,[21] it can also be said that *Nightwood*'s editorial history embodies the idea of resurrection through the text's subsequent versions or "lives." The manuscript that began as "Bow Down" suffered the rejections of multiple publishers, and many years of revision and rewriting, before its rebirth as *Nightwood*. In her letter to Coleman, Barnes treats resurrection as a metaphor applied to the process of revision, of learning to include the body, plot or structure, in her narrative. Paradoxically, editorial resurrection moves from Heaven to earth, from the author's idea of the work to its material manifestation as text. We can understand *Nightwood*'s editorial process by thinking of the distinction between "work" and "text" drawn by contemporary textual theory. Again, using G. Thomas Tanselle's traditional definition of the terms, the "work" is a theoretical construct, an ideal text that exists only in the author's mind, while the "text" is its material or social incarnation, a manifestation of the work in readable form. Returning to Blake's resurrection as envisioned by Barnes, the rising souls function as the author's ideal conception of her work, while the abandoned bodies are the text itself. Nora Wood's perverse attachment to the body of death—her "stubborn" foot anchored to Robin's grave—is an image of writing as revision, of Barnes's struggle to capture the soul or "essence" of loss within the material of language. But this is also an image of editorial revision: Coleman encouraged Barnes to scratch up the corpse, to connect the essence to the material, in order not to "bewilder the onlooker." Although plot and structure "seem wrong" to Barnes, they are a necessary compromise, a means for her readers to apprehend the significance of the "rising souls."

ii. "A Woman's Othello"

There is a fine line between editorial suggestions influenced by an editor's reading of the text and suggestions that impose an interpretation upon it. Despite Coleman's wish to cut *Nightwood*'s first chapter

---

[21] Plumb reads Barnes's image of Blakean resurrection primarily as a metaphor for connecting the present to the past through writing ("Revising *Nightwood*," 158).

and Eliot's wish to cut its last, Barnes held firm to her own sense of the novel's structure. This vexes the question of the re-ordering of *Nightwood*'s three central chapters. "Night Watch," "The Squatter," and "Watchman, What of the Night?" are given in this order in both the 1936 and 1995 editions of *Nightwood*. Nonetheless, this was not the order Djuna Barnes originally gave them or indeed preferred. At first, "The Squatter" chapter, a portrait of Jenny Petherbridge and her pursuit of Robin Vote, came last in this sequence. But after Barnes sent a typescript of the third version of the text to Coleman in July 1935, Coleman switched the chapters before sending the typescript to T. S. Eliot, before telling Barnes what she had done. The reordering of these chapters constitutes a case of "silent acquiescence" on Barnes's part to an editorial suggestion made by Coleman in order to bring Barnes's text more in line with Coleman's own reading of it. This was not a change that necessarily improves the novel; in fact, as with some of Eliot's revisions that mar the surface of the 1936 text,[22] this change leaves behind ragged edges and lost hermeneutic possibilities. In order to analyze the impact this editorial change has upon the text, I want briefly to review the narrative components of the "woman's Othello."

Nora Wood's love for Robin is predicated upon mourning, as if Nora recognizes a lost object found in Robin.[23] Nora begins losing Robin almost as soon as she finds her: soon after the women meet at a circus, Nora has already psychologically incorporated Robin's image: "In Nora's heart lay the fossil of Robin, intaglio of her identity, and about it for its maintenance ran Nora's blood" (50).[24] During the course of their love affair, while Robin wanders through the night-streets of Paris, Nora remains at home, nursing her image of Robin

---

[22] In the first chapter, "Bow Down," Eliot, following Coleman's suggestion, cuts several of the Doctor's stories, leaving gaps such as occur when the Doctor proposes to tell of the "mad Wittelsbach," then appears to change his mind: " 'Listen ... I don't want to talk of the Wittelsbach' " (New Directions, 27). We only get the joke in the Dalkey Archive edition, which restores the Doctor's long story of the Wittelsbach; he has been talking on the theme for three pages when he claims not to want to do so!

[23] For a recent discussion of the defining presence of loss and unspeakability in *Nightwood*, see Victoria L. Smith, "A Story beside(s) Itself: The Language of Loss in Djuna Barnes's *Nightwood*," *PMLA* 114 (1999), 194–206. Carolyn Allen reads the Nora/Robin relationship through a maternal trope, and argues that Nora's retrospective narration of Robin's loss produces its own value as a narrative of "lesbian desire and power" in her *Following Djuna: Women Lovers and the Erotics of Loss* (Bloomington: Indiana UP, 1996), 24.

[24] "Intaglio" refers to the process of carving on a hard object: Thelma Wood, the model for Robin, was a silver-point artist who etched her designs in silver. In the following quote, the "stitches" left on the grass by the absence of the corpse resemble the pin-prick designs done in silver-point.

and taking that image with her into her dreams, "as the ground things take the corpse, with minute persistence, down into the earth, leaving a pattern of it on the grass, as if they stitched as they descended" (51). Robin's "fossil" or "corpse" are all that Nora has to cling to, the remains of her abandoned body, a somewhat over-determined image for a love affair that has only recently begun. In fact, Nora's love for Robin, a love immediately and always structured by loss, reawakens Nora to the previous loss of her grandmother. As the worms take the corpse into the ground, so Nora takes Robin's image down into a dream of her grandmother, a dream where she tries to invite Robin into her grandmother's room, "yet knowing that this was impossible because the room was taboo" (55). Like Robin, her grandmother "seemed in the continual process of leaving [the room]," and saturates the room with the sense of imminent departure and "lost presence" (56). Finally, the dream "disfigures" Robin, turning her into an image of Nora's grandmother "dressed as a man ... ridiculous and plump in tight trousers and a red waistcoat, her arms spread saying with a leer of love, 'My little sweetheart!' " (56). Grandmother wears drag, the costume of the "girl–boy" or invert, to connect Nora's love for Robin with the desires of infancy, desires that are "taboo." The grief Nora feels at Robin's constant leave-taking corresponds to the grief of an earlier maternal repudiation, a grief that Nora acknowledges by loving a figure who reawakens the world of infantile desire.[25] Nora "draws upon" her grandmother, as an archaeologist would a "prehistoric ruin," in order to create the composite image of Robin and grandmother in her dreams.

The composite imagery of Nora's unconscious doesn't stop here, although the reordering of the chapters slows the process somewhat. Barnes originally structured Nora's night so that the disfigurement of Robin and Grandmother in her dream immediately precedes the vision of Robin with Jenny, both of which prompt Nora to visit the Doctor at 3 o'clock in the morning. These three events all occur in the same night, with a chapter break occurring between the vision of Robin and Jenny that concludes "Night Watch," and Nora's visit to the Doctor in "Watchman, What of the Night?" Coleman had already helped Barnes make a dramatic change to the "Watchman" chapter, where Nora, racked with jealousy, finds the Doctor in bed wearing full makeup, a blonde wig, and a "woman's flannel night gown" (69). At first, Barnes had "given" this scene to Felix, but Coleman convinced Barnes to add it to Nora's dialogue with the Doctor, in order to ground their

---

[25] Judith Butler's theory of "gender melancholy" haunts my description of Nora's attachment to Robin. Following Freud, Butler posits that gender is produced through the child's repudiation of homosexual attachments, an ungrievable because unacknowledged loss. See Butler, *The Psychic Life of Power* (Stanford: Stanford UP, 1997), 132–66.

discourse of "the night" with concrete setting and character detail. Nonetheless, when Barnes follows Coleman's advice and gives realistic detail to this scene, these details are associated with the vestments of transvestism, ironically functioning as markers of "realism," as the Doctor's nightgown and wig parody the female "soul" trapped within his body. Barnes's incorporation of this suggestion of Coleman's is paradigmatic of the dynamics of their editorial collaboration: recognizing that she was a bad editor of her own work, Barnes learned to trust (some) of Coleman's advice, particularly advice aimed at creating a more audience-friendly text.

However, when Coleman reordered the chapters, she did so in order to reflect her belief that Barnes should focus on the tragedy of Nora and Robin, and that this focus was disrupted by the appearance of the Doctor. Specifically (and mistakenly) Coleman claimed that the "Watchman" chapter let down the "action" and the "emotion" of Nora's jealous night.[26] Coleman's change, which explains Nora's vision of Robin's betrayal by placing "The Squatter" immediately thereafter, reflects Coleman's sense that Barnes needed to "compromise" with her audience, to make changes that would explain the often confusing action of the novel. Unlike the earlier change to the "Watchman" chapter, this was not a suggested revision, but rather a "fait accompli" (Plumb, xxiii). Barnes indicated her disappointment in this change— she wrote Coleman: "its [sic] such a letdown (I think) from the 'Ah' in the last chapter, the 'Nightwatch' [sic] however"[27] —in terms that indicate that the "Watchman" chapter was, for Barnes, a dramatic and emotional continuation of Nora's "Night Watch." The altered typescript had already been sent to Eliot when Barnes made this comment. Barnes partially incorporated Coleman's suggestion on her own copy of the typescript, indicating her ambivalent acceptance of it.

By partial incorporation, I mean that Barnes did not physically shuffle the chapters or repaginate the text, as Coleman did with her copy of the typescript (TSC1); Barnes's copy (TSC2) retains her preferred chapter order with a note indicating Coleman's switch on its table of contents.[28] Plumb argues that this note constitutes Barnes's

---

26 Coleman to Barnes, 27 Aug. 1935; Barnes Papers, University of Maryland.

27 Barnes to Coleman, 8 Nov. 1935; Coleman Papers, University of Delaware.

28 My recent physical examination of the typescripts of *Nightwood* reveals that Barnes's copy (TSC2) only notes the reordered chapters on its table of contents and in the numbering of its chapters; the body of the typescript retains Barnes's original chapter order and pagination. I am grateful to Beth Alvarez, Curator of Literary Manuscripts at the University of Maryland, for confirming my observation. Both TSC1 (Coleman and Eliot's copy) and TSC2 (Barnes's copy) are housed at the University of Maryland. Plumb's 1995 edition uses TSC2 as a copy-text (unlike the 1936 edition, based on TSC1), but her textual apparatus, as far as I can tell, doesn't reveal the actual physical order of the central chapters.

acceptance of Coleman's change—"it would have been very easy for [Barnes] to return the chapter to its original position" (147)—and therefore retains Coleman's order. Although it is true that Barnes could have, later on, returned the chapters to their original order, the fact that she never took them out of order in her own copy of the typescript is a compelling piece of evidence in support of her original chapter order. Against Plumb's rationale I suggest that Barnes "accepts" this change as she has accepted many of Coleman's suggestions, out of a sense that Coleman's editing provides a needed narrative structure. The partial incorporation of Coleman's change in Barnes's own copy of the manuscript opens room for doubt.

I would suggest that at this point in *Nightwood*'s composition history, Barnes was quite willing to make any change that might lead to publication (shortly thereafter Barnes began to consider privately publishing her novel).[29] Although Coleman's sense of logical narrative progression improved Barnes's manuscript in many ways, this was not one of them. Coleman's chapter sequence was predicated upon her assertion that Barnes needed to compromise with her audience by interrupting the hallucinatory progression of Nora's dream and her visit to the Doctor with the more explanatory and realist "Squatter." Coleman's wish to have Barnes focus on the "woman's Othello" and the romantic triangle of Nora, Robin, and Jenny led her to think of the Doctor's appearance as a distraction from this theme. In short, Coleman's readerly biases influenced this editorial decision. Both the chronology and the emotional arc of Barnes's pairing of "Night Watch" and "Watchman, What of the Night" are disrupted by Coleman's chapter switch. The break in continuity between Nora's dream of her grandmother and her visit to the Doctor means that these events no longer occur in the same night: we lose the conjunction of Nora's and the Doctor's symbolic night, the night world of inversion. Given Barnes's chapter order, there is a distinct connection between the Doctor's appearance—"rouged" and "painted," wearing a wig and a flannel nightgown—and the grandmother in drag: Doctor and grandmother both are distorted by the night, their apparent sex at odds with the clothes they wear. Nora's first thought at seeing the Doctor in bed—" 'God, children know something they can't tell, they like Red Riding Hood and the wolf in bed!' "(69)—explicitly connects grandmother and Doctor through the figure of the wolf, the beast who wears grandmother's nightgown. The implicit connection links childhood sexuality with the adult experience of inversion: Nora's night takes her from a dream to a "fairy" tale, from the violent dream-logic that "impales" Robin onto the image of Nora's grandmother to the fantastic appearance of the Doctor wearing grandmother's nightgown.

---

[29] Barnes to Coleman, 22 Nov. 1935; Coleman Papers, University of Delaware.

One of Coleman's minor excisions to this scene involved cutting lines referring to the flannel nightgown, lines which originally read "with what cunning had his brain directed not only the womanly, but the incestuous garment, for a flannel nightgown is our mother"; Coleman's rationale was that the lines were a bit "smarty," and perhaps meaningless, given her sense of the chapter order.[30] The omission of this "incestuous" nightgown is very intriguing, especially when viewed as an element that Barnes voluntarily suppresses from the text. Through the signifier of the gown, we approach the region of childhood, when desire was undifferentiated and profuse; this nightgown is both feral and incestuous; children like it, but they can't tell. The night—when the daytime logic of two sexes is abandoned, when the Doctor "goes back" into his dress and adults become wolves— is play-time, "children's hour," a means of approaching the "other world," where what we lost as children lies waiting for us, disfigured in grandmother's clothing. Robin's "other world" is only accessible to Nora through her dreams, at night, when she discovers her lover in her grandmother's room; in the daytime, the logic connecting Robin and grandmother is broken by repression.

Both chapters, the "Watchman" and the "Squatter," tell the same story, the meeting of Robin and Jenny at the opera and the carriage-ride they take with the Doctor and a child that culminates in Jenny's physical assault on Robin. When read in the original order—from "Night Watch," to "Watchman, What of the Night," to "The Squatter"—the Doctor is the one who tells Nora, as well as the reader, of Robin's involvement with Jenny. The Doctor's description of Jenny as a "looter" and a "thief" (82–83) thereby introduces the character who will be described in the following chapter as a "squatter." The Doctor's subjective report of Robin and Jenny's affair makes more sense in Barnes's original chapter order: Nora wakes up from the dream, sees the vision of Robin and Jenny's murderous embrace, runs to the Doctor's house, and asks him "to tell me everything you know about the night" (69). That "certain night" (82), which all of the Doctor's digressions lead up to, is the explanation of the night at the opera and its climactic carriage ride. When the story is retold by the narrator in "The Squatter," it is told by a more objective, or distanced, source, and the Doctor is himself a character in the tableau. "The Squatter" ends by reporting the tragic consequences of this sordid and petty evening: "It was not long after this that Nora and Robin separated; a little later Jenny and Robin sailed for America" (67). The narrator of "The Squatter" continues to speak in the next chapter, "Where the Tree Falls," which tells of Felix's troubled life with Guido, Robin's child, after Robin's abandonment of

---

30 Excised lines given in Plumb's textual apparatus to *Nightwood*, 165.

them. Barnes's original structure pairs "Night Watch" and "Watchman" as subjective representations of Nora's "dark night," and follows with a transition to a more objective narration of the events of that night and of its repercussions. The essence or "soul" of Nora's pain precedes the "body" or its objective narration.

Nora's Shakespearean despair precedes and exceeds the objective events themselves. Barnes's chapter order gives Nora's subjective experience priority over the mundane details of the betrayal itself. Further, these chapters create a composite figure—the grandmother in drag—who links Nora, Robin, and the Doctor as fellow dwellers in the night of inversion. Although this composite figure is still there in the reordered chapters, the direct and visceral connection is broken, and broken deliberately because Coleman thought that the Doctor would distract readers from the "woman's Othello." This is indeed a significant problem for *Nightwood*'s textual editor, as well as for its readers, because Barnes never did, as Coleman suggested she could, reverse the chapters after Coleman's switch.

The simplest explanation for this is the most obvious: Barnes was exhausted, and Coleman had been right before about structural changes designed to serve as guideposts for Barnes's confused readers. One could argue that Barnes was willing to abandon her preferred chronology of the night because it was not something to which she was attached; after all, the Doctor's appearance in drag to Nora was a late development in the text's composition history, as well as a previous suggestion of Coleman's. Nonetheless, the deeply autobiographical nature of the textual material in question (as it pertains to Barnes's own relation to her grandmother, and to Thelma Wood, who resembled her[31]) may have been subject to the same repression which prevents Nora from reaching Robin's "other world" of the night. Barnes may have been willing to break the connection between grandmother

---

[31] One of the central mysteries of Barnes's biography involves her relationship with her grandmother, Zadel Barnes, radical thinker and journalist. Up until the age of fifteen, Barnes shared a bed with her grandmother, and the letters exchanged between them are notorious for their sexual language and innuendo. This relationship has been interpreted as everything from "nanophilia" to incest. See Mary Lynn Broe, "My Art Belongs to Daddy: Incest as Exile, The Textual Economics of Hayford Hall," *Women's Writing in Exile*, ed. Mary Lynn Broe and Angela Ingram (Chapel Hill: U of North Carolina P, 1989), 41–86. The dynamics of the Barnes household—Zadel's son Wald Barnes was a polygamist and Djuna was the oldest of ten children from two wives—in combination with Zadel and Wald's theories of spiritualism and free love suggest that this was a family where traditional boundaries between grandmother and granddaughter would not hold. A reader of Barnes's biography, as well as of her personal papers, letters, etc., will find a wealth of material that may plausibly be related to *Nightwood*, but we should remember that connections that seem perfectly clear retrospectively—to us—may not have been as obvious to the actual subject of that life.

and Doctor in bed precisely *because* this material was so personally volcanic. The psychobiographical evidence that connects Robin, Nora, and the grandmother in drag to Thelma Wood, Djuna Barnes, and Zadel Barnes is so powerful, and has been of such interest to scholars of Barnes, that it seems reasonable to suggest that we can find traces of it on a textual level. Of course, Barnes's motives for granting Coleman's change are unavailable to us, except through conjecture. But that this is a case where Coleman's editing overwhelmed Barnes's authority can be seen from the material evidence.

There is a difference between editorial advice and editorial fiat. When she switched the chapters, Coleman assumed an authority that prioritizes her own interpretive agenda over and against Barnes's authorial intentions for her text. While I am not suggesting that Coleman's editorial hand ultimately imposed an unwanted shape on Barnes's text—Barnes's resistance to Coleman's desire to cut out Felix proves this—I am claiming that this question of chapter order complicates Cheryl Plumb's portrayal of the "genuine" collaboration between Barnes and Coleman. Given Barnes's self-proclaimed inability to structure her work and the text's own history of rejection at the hands of publishers, it is likely that Barnes simply ceded certain points to Coleman. In their collaboration, Barnes provided raw emotional material; Coleman provided structure. Barnes may have concurred once too often in an editorial collaboration that was otherwise beneficial for her text. In the excerpt that serves as epigraph to this essay, James Thorpe remarks: "sometimes [the author] is pleased, sometimes he acquiesces, and sometimes he does not notice what has happened."[32]

In her collaboration with Coleman, Barnes ran the full range of authorial response to editorial suggestion. She could have resisted this change but did not. Who can say whether she was pleased with it, acquiesced to it, or did not notice, consciously, what had happened?

iii. No Editions in Heaven

The metaphor of resurrection haunts the content and context of *Nightwood*. Never permanently fixed on the page, the author's text is subject to a secular resurrection as a critical edition. The Dalkey Archive *Nightwood* is the latest manifestation of Barnes's work in textual form: it is a "bodily" resurrection, if you will. The biography of Barnes's work doesn't end with this edition: the beauty of its textual apparatus, painstakingly assembled by Plumb, is that it provides incentive for further readerly, or editorial, collaboration by giving textual variants,

---

[32] *Principles of Textual Criticism* (San Marino, CA: The Huntington Library, 1972), 48.

as well as the surviving pieces of the first and second versions of *Nightwood*. We collaborate with the text when we notice that changes to its body affect the way that we read and interpret it. Coleman was perhaps Barnes's most privileged "collaborative reader" (Plumb, viii), for she was able to attempt to shape the text in accordance with her interpretation of it. In the end, I am not sure that Coleman's collaboration was any more or less "genuine" than Eliot's or, indeed, Plumb's. Although Coleman certainly deserves the "laurels" for her contribution to Barnes's career, as well as recognition for her own work, not all of her editorial suggestions were and are worth incorporating into Barnes's text. Although there are arguments for and against the question of *Nightwood*'s chapter-order, I think that Barnes scholars ought to consider the implications of reordering the text's middle chapters: Barnes's sense of structure may not have been reader-friendly, but she did have one, and it is present in the chapter sequence she originally gave. There are no editions in Heaven, because there are no texts in Heaven, only a perfectly shared vision of the work. In our sublunary world, however, we must collaborate, however imperfectly, when establishing the body of the text.

4

Reviews

Reviews

The Critical Editing of Music: History, Method, and Practice.
James Grier, Cambridge University Press, 1996. xiv + 267 pp.
$20.95 (paper).

'CRITICAL THINKING' is one of those phrases that university teachers are used to trotting out in assessment exercises. 'What do you hope students will gain from your course?' 'I hope that they will learn to think critically'. But what does this mean? And what does 'critical thinking' mean for someone engaged in trying to work out how best to represent a musical work in an edition?

Grier takes us through the process step by step. Thinking critically, in general terms, involves evaluating the available evidence rather than accepting things at face value. It involves the recognition and assessment of different viewpoints, and it involves thinking laterally about how to solve problems. In order to create a good edition, Grier maintains, it is necessary to engage with the relevant musical sources, to discover their relationship to each other and to the composer, and to find out as much of the historical background to the work as possible. It is then necessary to evaluate the sources, deciding what significance any variants have, and to decide upon the text of the edition based on a growing sense of the style of the work. Finally, it is necessary to present the edition in such a way that the editor's decisions, interventions and thought processes are transparent to the reader.

This seems like common sense. Would anyone create an edition that did not take account of the surviving sources and of their relative merit? Would anyone create an edition in which the editorial process was not explained and documented? It is because the answer to these questions is too often 'yes' that a book like Grier's needed writing.

Music publishing as an academic exercise is relatively young. Grier rehearses the narrative from the canon-forming editions of the Bach–Gesellschaft in the nineteenth century through the accretion-filled performing editions of the early twentieth century and the post-war urtext school of publishing to more recent editorial trends. As has so often been the case in the history of music theory, Grier's ideas, while they purport to be prescriptive, are to a large extent descriptive. Critical editions of music have been in existence for some time, as is evidenced by the Norton Critical Scores, to cite only the most obvious example. But little has been written about the philosophy behind critical editing. Technical guides such as those by Walter Emery, Howard Mayer Brown, and John Caldwell provide firm foundations for making critical editions, but they do not probe the theory. Arthur Mendel and Philip Brett have examined critical matters and their work forms a point of departure for Grier.

Mendel writes chiefly about the relationship between the performer and the editor, pleading for the performer to be allowed more responsibility for deciding about the details of performance. 'If editors really want to help the performer, what they should do is not provide him with ready-made answers to questions that have no definitive answers, but encourage him in every way possible (including frequent references in the score to the critical report) to think out answers for himself.' A recurring theme in Grier's book is indeed that editors should make it easy for users of an edition to identify variant readings in different sources, to see which the editor has chosen for the edition and on what grounds (see especially 172–76). He emphasises the fact that the score is a set of written instructions for the performer rather than comprising the work of art in itself. 'Many details are realized or determined only in performance, and this flexibility of interpretation is built into the construction of the work. The composer understands and even requires that performers seek their own solutions' (44). The editor's responsibility is to provide performers with sufficient information to perform the work, guiding interpretation rather than prescribing how it should be done. To this end, the editor has to decide how the meaning that the notational symbols had at the time the sources were produced can best be conveyed now (27).

Brett's article outlines the history of music editing and the preconceptions and attitudes that have shaped it. Like Mendel, he asserts that 'what the performer needs from the editor is surely an open discussion of the possibilities and a measured judgement as to which courses of action are preferable.' Brett's vision underpins so much of the spirit of Grier's book that the crux of the argument is quoted in full on page 4: 'But editing is principally a critical act; moreover it is one (like musical analysis) that begins from critically based assumptions and perceptions that usually go unacknowledged. If these assumptions were to be openly stated, if we began to recognise and allow for legitimate differences in editorial orientation, and if we ceased to use the word "definitive" in relation to any edited text, then much of the polemics surrounding editing might subside.'

The most extensive work in this field is Georg Feder's *Musikphilologie*. Grier sees his work as an improvement on Feder's in two ways (14–15). Feder identifies levels of editorial work—lower (bibliographic and mechanical) and higher (interpretative and critical)—while Grier emphasises instead that the editor's critical faculties should be engaged at all stages of the editing process. Feder also implies that the goal of editing is to determine the final compositional intentions, whereas Grier argues that this is often unattainable and that the work of art is instead a social artefact, affected by its external circumstances.

Grier's message to editors may be summarised in one sentence: obtain and use as much information as possible about the musical and historical context, engage your brain in making editorial decisions, and then clearly tell the users of the edition what you have done and why. This book is essentially an illustrative account of how such an attitude shapes all aspects of the editorial process.

Chapter 2 examines the nature of musical sources and the importance of understanding them in their historical context. Grier goes into some detail about the processes of locating, inspecting, describing and transcribing sources (50–60). The next chapter is about the adaptation of stemmatic filiation techniques to music. The introduction to Lachmann's common-error method, its history, its value and its limitations is extremely helpful for non-specialists. Grier writes that in many musical repertories, stemmata are a useful tool for illuminating the processes of transmission rather than the means for discovering a lost (and probably hypothetical) archetype. Grier's examples of various stemmatic layouts and their problems (82–89) show the strengths and weaknesses of stemmata in defining routes of transmission.

The fourth chapter, 'Errors, variants and editorial judgement: the establishment of the text', examines how critical thinking is essential when an editor is deciding which readings to reproduce in the edition, and draws together elements from the previous two chapters. Grier shows how an understanding of the historical context of the sources is essential when evaluating variants (109–21). This is followed by a set of examples illustrating the use of stemmata in the evaluation of sources and in the establishment of the text (121–29).

The following chapter deals with the presentation of the text, and fits less comfortably into the general scheme of the book. Grier acknowledges in several places that issues of text presentation have been widely explored by others, and his debt to Caldwell's work is particularly clear from the footnotes. Why re-plough the same furrow? Grier maintains that he wishes to show how the critical approach can be applied also at this stage of editing. The description of four different types of editions that begins the chapter—photographic facsimiles, edited prints that replicate the original notation, critical editions and interpretative editions—displays Grier's usual common sense, but the remainder of the chapter is highly derivative, drawing on the themes of the 'how-to' books mentioned earlier. Grier gives extended descriptions of the layout of parts within a score, the question of bar-lines in early music, and how to present the parts of transposing instruments (to name but a few) to illustrate how critical thinking can affect the presentational stage of the editorial process. Too much previous scholarship is repeated here.

This chapter might have been more successful if Grier had given a brief admonition to editors to use their critical faculties in aspiring to clear presentation (including his current section on apparatus, commentary and appendices, which shows how Grier thinks the editor can attain the required clarity), followed by illustrative examples of good and bad editing. This, in fact, is exactly what is offered in the beautifully presented epilogue. It begins with a description of Grier's own edition of the music of Adémar of Chabannes (184–99), an inspired demonstration of the editorial procedures he advocates, and a fine example of leading from the front. This is followed (200–205) by a critique of *Mozart's Symphony in C Major No. 36 K. 425 'Linz'*, ed. Cliff Eisen (London, 1992). Grier's chief criticism is that Eisen put his explanations in an article in the *Journal of the Royal Musical Association* rather than in the edition, making them inaccessible to many users. Further, Eisen does not spot the changes that seem to have been made (especially to the bassoon parts) because of the personnel available for early performances. This clearly demonstrates a) the confusion and frustration that result from an editor failing to state his procedures and b) the importance of lateral historical thinking when working out why different versions of a work are as they are. The last example (206–13) is of *Verdi's Don Carlos*, 2 vols., ed. Ursula Günther (Milan, 1980). The chief problem with this edition is that although Günther has identified the four main versions of Don Carlos that were performed during Verdi's lifetime, she does not signal clearly enough in the edition how to disentangle the material. 'A relatively minor problem in the mechanics of the presentation obscures the great accomplishment of its editor' (213). Vivid examples are used to great effect elsewhere in this book. Using these examples of well and poorly presented editions as a basis for chapter 5 would have been more in keeping with the spirit of the rest of the book than exploring practical issues of text presentation.

The chapter ends with an odd excursus (177–79) on how nice it would be if editions were presented on computers with different windows for the different versions (and presumably users would be able to double click on a bar or note to display the relevant commentary). Electronic presentation of music editions is an attractive and probably inevitable prospect, and one that would solve some existing problems of presenting an edition, while creating a host of new ones. It is not clear how this relates to the main thrust of the argument, however. Is Grier suggesting that electronic editions will solve all our presentational problems? Or is it a warning that there will be new issues to be addressed in the coming years?

The concluding chapter offers some pieces of wisdom that give a focus to Grier's project. His vision is that 'critical editions of the kind I advocate could largely replace descriptive writings as an introduction to the repertoire for students in a historical context' (182). University (and school) teachers spend their working lives trying to persuade students to put the textbooks of Hoppin, Grout et al. aside, and examine the music and recent scholarship themselves. Critical editions are undoubtedly an excellent stepping stone in this process, as they offer 'guidance from a scholar who has devoted a considerable amount of time, energy and imagination to the problems of the piece and whose opinion is therefore worth considering' (181).

Although Grier's argument is generally coherent and persuasive, the extent to which well-known material is repeated in chapters 3 and 5 is disappointing. The four appendices, which are a concise guide to source studies based on the areas of work identified in chapter 2 (location, inspection, description and transcription), are an unexpected inclusion. The second includes a beautifully clear introduction to the dense terminology of source work, from 'hair side' to 'gatherings', and in all, these practical appendices will be valuable resources for those beginning source studies. Would they not have fitted more naturally in a practically focussed book?

Despite these minor reservations, Grier's defence of critical music editing is a laudable crusade. It is too easy for musicians to enjoy good editions without fully appreciating them, and without aspiring to produce others like them. If this book, based on well-expressed and sound common sense, encourages editors to set themselves higher standards, Grier will have achieved much. Sending students to read this book should encourage them to think more critically, not only about the editions they use, but also about the editions they make, the sources they encounter, and the historical endeavours that permeate the study and practice of music.

Emma Hornby

The Iconic Page in Manuscript, Print, and Digital Culture. George Bornstein and Theresa Tinkle, eds. Ann Arbor: University of Michigan Press, 1998. x + 294 pp. $49.50.

MAYBE, JUST MAYBE, textual studies are slowly escaping their often bemoaned marginal status. Textual issues and questions now sometimes generate almost widespread interest. Recent conferences have explored the book, the page, and other textual matters; universities have established centers on the history of the book and on scholarly editing; some PhD programs have added bibliography and textual studies to their qualifying examination areas. Is it possible that for some people—and not just readers of journals like *TEXT*, for whom this attitude is nothing new—textual studies now seem almost central to whatever literary study might mean, even (gasp) "trendy"?

For journals like *TEXT*, organizations such as the Society for Textual Scholarship, and such textual critics and theorists as Jerome J. McGann, D.F. McKenzie, and Peter L. Shillingsburg, textual studies are not limited to analytical, descriptive, and enumerative bibliography and to textual criticism and scholarly editing. Without leaving these traditional areas behind, textual studies now encompass such seemingly diverse areas as relationships between writing and technology, including the different ones in oral, manuscript, print, and digital cultures; studies of the history of the book; and various ways in which the documents that have always attracted traditional textual scholars can be used for purposes other than bibliography and editing (as in the work of the French genetic critics). No doubt much of this renewed interest is fueled by our awareness of living in what Jay David Bolter has called the "late age of print": as one age transmutes into a new one before our eyes, interest grows in the technologies involved in these two ages as well as in past ones, and this interest extends to the hard data that have been both the core of traditional textual study and also the reason why so many literary scholars over several generations have shunned the entire textual enterprise.

The Iconic Page in Manuscript, Print, and Digital Culture, essays reworked from papers given at a University of Michigan conference in October 1996, wants to locate itself at the heart of the new discipline. According to its editors, George Bornstein and Theresa Tinkle, the book aims to "affect the basic methods and paradigms of textual construction and transmission by arguing for integration of the iconic or semantic features of the physical text with more traditional and purely linguistic considerations" (3). As such, it follows from two aspects of the textual enterprise that Jerome McGann started calling for in the 1980s: making bibliography and textual studies central to a general conception of literary study, and extending literary studies out from the text's words alone—what McGann calls the "linguistic code"—to also include what the editors describe as "the material features of the text such as layout, illustration, size and kind of lettering, use of space, binding, cost, and the like" (1)—McGann's "bibliographic code." One of the volume's contributors, McGann rests behind the entire enterprise more than any other individual, his two codes being cited early in the editors' introduction and in many of the book's essays.

The twelve essays are arranged chronologically by topic, and they cover a wide range of texts from the medieval period, Renaissance, nineteenth century, and twentieth century. The first three deal with medieval texts. In "Alfred the Great's Burnt Boethius," Kevin S. Kiernan considers the extant manuscript of Alfred's translation of Boethius's *Consolation of Philosophy*. This prose and verse manuscript, Kiernan argues, has been edited improperly as either all prose or all verse. The manuscript was partially destroyed and supposedly lost in a 1731 fire, then rediscovered and restored in the nineteenth century, and its iconic details tell an unintentional but unavoidable story of the fire it survived. Kiernan describes the extant document is "an iconic page of a restored medieval manuscript" (16), "no longer a medieval manuscript but a nineteenth-century facsimile edition of a medieval manuscript" (29). Second, in "Sensations of the Page: Imaging Technologies and Medieval Illuminated Manuscripts," Michael Camille studies late-thirteenth-century Latin manuscripts made for the Universities of Oxford and Paris and shows how their iconography appeals to all five senses. The manuscripts are reminders of a major difference between the medieval age and the modern, with its orientation towards the visual, and every manuscript book, each a "relic of bodily pain, desire, and death" (42), serves as a witness to the bodies as well as minds that have read and handled it. Third, Theresa Tinkle's "The Wife of Bath's Textual/Sexual Lives" looks at Chaucer's "Wife of Bath's Prologue" and contrasts the attitudes expressed by Chaucer within his text with its dissemination and publication history. Chaucer "desired to produce stable, canonical poems" (57), but the work's transmission and reception have been much more varied and unsystematic. Tinkle argues that "medieval graphic language evidences relations of conspicuous hybridity as well as relations of binary opposition" and that, in refusing to fall consistently into expected patterns, "medieval and other material cultures should be allowed to vex modern linguistic and hermeneutic theories" (67). Tinkle's headnote from Paul Zumthor, "To insert a text into history does not exhaust its potential for meaning" (55), could stand for the entire volume, since, like all the essays, hers insists that a return to history need not be reductive, deterministic, or simplistic.

The next two essays are concerned with Renaissance works. In "Icons among Iconoclasts in the Renaissance," Rudi Paul Lindner explores Pietro Della Valle's searches for Muslim manuscripts in early-1600s Istanbul and his unsuccessful attempts to publish them. Lindner discusses the cultural forces that brought about a clash between the manuscripts and print and delayed the introduction of moveable-type print in Istanbul until three centuries after it began in Europe. Second, in "The Peopled Page: Polemic, Confutation, and Foxe's *Book of Martyrs*," Evelyn B. Tribble studies the print layout of John Foxe's *Acts and Monuments*, in particular his notes in response to the documents in the book, notes which appear at the sides of the pages rather than at the bottom. She considers ways that the layout of the noisy, messy, and cacophonous "peopled" pages shape reading experiences, especially given the lack of obvious hierarchy that modern footnotes convey.

In a third group, four essays deal with the nineteenth century. In "Rossetti's Iconic Page," Jerome J. McGann considers ways in which bibliographic codes affect a reading of the linguistic features of Dante Gabriel Rossetti's poems. Interpreting several poems, including the sonnet "A Superscription," in light of what he calls "the graphical and bibliographical urgencies" in Rossetti's work (129), McGann argues that "interpretation would do well to turn to the inventors rather than the philosophers when seeking to learn how to explicate poetical work" (138). Second, in "The Faces of Victorian Fiction," Peter L. Shillingsburg tries to imagine how a typical reader in 1862 would respond to both the linguistic and bibliographic codes of two quite different Victorian novels, George Eliot's *Mill on the Floss* and M.E. Braddon's *Lady Audley's Secret*. Concluding that the iconic page focuses attention at least as much on reception as on intention, Shillingsburg argues that we can't know how anyone responded; we can merely create an interpretation of how the iconic details might have functioned. Third, in "Iconic Indeterminacy and Human Creativity in C.S. Peirce's Manuscripts," Mary Keeler looks at the writings of Charles Sanders Peirce. Most of Peirce's philosophical writings exist only in manuscript, and the documents are complex semantically as well as linguistically. Peirce is the one author in the book who explicitly wrote about "icon": his tripartite semiotic system of index/icon/symbol considers icon as relation by "resemblance" (index is "indication or interaction" and symbol is "relation by habit, rule, or convention"; 176). For Keeler, Peirce's semiotic supports claims that meaning is carried by both linguistic and bibliographic codes. Fourth, Martha Nell Smith's "Corporealizations of Dickinson and Interpretive Machines" studies the physicality of Emily Dickinson's manuscript poems in order to investigate "the location of the object 'Dickinson poem'" (195). Smith contrasts the assumption of authors and editors that manuscript pages must lead to print with Dickinson, whose "iconic page became her manuscript page" (196). Smith documents ways in which all editions of Dickinson's poems, including editions of the manuscripts, have distorted the poems because of their editors' assumptions that the manuscripts were stages on the way to print and not, either linguistically or bibliographically, the poems in themselves.

Finally, three essays look at twentieth-century works. In "Yeats and Textual Reincarnation: 'When You Are Old' and 'September 1913,'" George Bornstein looks at successive printings of two of William Butler Yeats's poems and considers the effects of the bibliographic and what he calls the contextual codes on readers' responses and interpretations. He argues that printings in Yeats's various collections of his poetry, scholarly editions after Yeats's death, and especially commercially-driven anthologies have obscured the personal or political implications of the poems, implications that the bibliographic codes of the poem's first appearances highlight. Second, in "The Open Space of the Draft Page: James Joyce and Modern Manuscripts," Daniel Ferrer examines one of Joyce's notebook drafts for *Ulysses* and argues that a draft is both "toposensitive" (since the spatial layout is significant) and "chronosensitive" (since it is part of a temporal succession; 262–63). The draft represents a dialogue between the writer and his or her later self, whereas the scholarly investigator is an intruder who "reads the page in order to find there something that was not its primary purpose" (260). Finally, James L.W. West III's "The Iconic Dust Jacket: Fitzgerald and Styron" considers the effect of the jacket for William Styron's *Confessions of Nat Turner* on the novel's reception. With a design based on nineteenth-century runaway slave posters, the jacket in both its image and typeface created an impression at odds with Styron's own stated intentions "to distance himself from the tradition of the standard historical novel" (273). Because the climate of expectations for the novel has been created by the jacket as well as by the text, West argues that a scholarly edition should include a full-color reproduction of the jacket along with the novel's words.

A chronological arrangement suits a collection that aims, as in Tinkle's headnote from Zumthor, "to insert texts into history," and the arrangement succeeds in many ways. The essays convincingly demonstrate that the "iconic page" can speak across periods: scholars dealing with the physicality of pages from specific periods have much to say to specialists who work in other periods, and the conclusions drawn from particular documents can be much more generally relevant. The essays are invariably fresh, clearly written, free of jargon, and free of polemics. The essays all proceed outward from evidence to generalizations, and several explicitly pit their evidence against what they see as prevailing theoretical trends. They tend to place themselves, however, against linguistically based theory, mostly structuralism and the various poststructuralisms. They don't mention new historicism, postcolonialism, gender studies, queer theory, cultural studies—all prominent theoretical and critical developments in the 1990s. It would have been interesting to see how some of the authors of these essays placed their enterprises within the contexts of those more recent models.

If the chronological arrangement demonstrates the significance of studying the "iconic page" historically, it nevertheless de-emphasizes some other patterns that become evident only when the collection is read as a whole. (And digital cultures enter the book only indirectly. Several essays, especially those by Kiernan, Camille, Keeler, Smith, and Bornstein, look in intriguing ways to the possibilities of digital representation and argue that digital presentations might reduce some of the problems that have plagued print representations. None of the essays studies digital culture directly, however.) For example, the essays divide almost in half into studies of the iconicity of manuscript pages and of print pages. Three of the manuscript essays are the medieval ones, but four deal with authors from the age of print (Della Valle, Peirce, Dickinson, Joyce). The medievalists naturally concern themselves with the differences between a manuscript culture and later print and digital cultures, and in various ways Kiernan, Camille, and Tinkle all convincingly stress the otherness of medieval culture. But the essays on more modern authors suggest that, at least when seen through the lens of the iconic page, this otherness might be less a matter of culture than of medium. By contrasting a culture in Italy that had moved into the age of print with one in Istanbul that had not, Lindner can show how manuscript and print cultures existing at the same time were alien to each other. And as Smith and Ferrer present and comment on their evidence, Dickinson's manuscript poems and Joyce's notebook drafts can, in Tinkle's word, "vex" modern theories of literature and interpretation as much as can the medieval manuscripts.

Keeler's essay on Peirce is somewhat an odd-essay-out in the collection. Because most of Peirce's philosophical writings were never published, she necessarily analyzes handwritten manuscripts, and she claims that the manuscripts, with their many marginalia and diagrams and in their general layout, show that "Peirce himself recognized the limitations of the traditional theory of text in terms of 'linguistic code' (although he did not refer to it as such)" (160). Nevertheless, the main part of her essay is an explication of the linguistic codes of Peirce's texts that does not seem to concern itself with the bibliographic codes.

In the essays focusing on printed texts, the chronological organization somewhat obscures another issue. Four essays emphasize the text's reception more than its production (a feature signalled in the editors' introduction): the ways in which the arrangement of text and commentary on the printed page can shape the reader's experience (Tribble on Foxe), the possible ways a reader responded to the bibliographic as well as linguistic elements of a printed book (Shillingsburg on Victorian novels), the importance of all the bibliographic and contextual elements to responses to and interpretations of poems (Bornstein on Yeats), and the ways in which a dust jacket can affect a book's reception (West on Styron). McGann's essay on Rossetti more explicitly links production with reception and interpretation: McGann argues that an awareness of Rossetti's deep concern with bibliographic codes needs to inform an interpretation of the words of Rossetti's poems.

Interestingly, even though nine of the twelve essays are concerned with the age of print, four of these essays—nearly half—study manuscripts within print culture, and perhaps this is related to questions of the extent to which the iconic page is a matter of production or of reception. Studies of reception always face the dilemma of whether they are describing a generalized, potential response or actual, particular responses. Several of the essays fit into the first category, but Shillingsburg's essay on Victorian novels sounds a note of caution: "any assessment of an iconography that *might have been* is, really, a new construction and a new interpretation of the iconic effects of books" (153). He concludes that, if "the study of the iconic page is at least as much a 'reception' study as it is an 'intention' study," then "such studies are . . . more individual than social; they are multifaceted rather than universal or singular" (153). Tribble's depiction of the ways in which Foxe's page layout shaped reading experiences, Bornstein's treatments of the contextual codes of various publications of Yeats's poems, and West's argument for the importance of the dust jacket for Styron's *Confessions* are important arguments for the significance of bibliographic elements, although they necessarily generalize their posited readers into a homogeneous group, all presumably responding alike.

But a Shillingsburg-ian pull from the social to the individual seems to slide into a pull from the receiver to the author. This tendency seems clearest in Bornstein's essay on Yeats, an essay I will critique in some detail as an example of the complexities involved in studying the iconic page. Bornstein argues that a handwritten version of "When You Are Old," copied by Yeats along with six other poems and bound privately for Maud Gonne, and the poem's first publication in the Cuala Press volume, *The Countess Kathleen and Various Legends and Lyrics*, reflected an aristocratic idea of love that later printings, especially in those from after Yeats's death, de-emphasized. Even more dramatically, the first printing of "September 1913" (under the title "Romance in Ireland") in the *Irish Times* and the first book publication, where the poem was accompanied by a long note from Yeats discussing it in relation to several recent controversial Irish political and cultural events, highlighted a political context that later printings weakened and eventually eliminated. Bornstein is undoubtedly correct that the poems *are* different in each of their printings, and his evidence supports his opening claim that "a Yeats poem is not always the same but varies according to where and when we encounter it. This means that there is no 'the' text of such a poem but only a series of texts, incarnated in various documents" (223). This statement, however, leads to two questions. Can the various incarnations of a Yeats poem "be grouped as the metatext, or 'work,' which can be known only through such incarnations," as Bornstein goes on to say (223)? If each incarnation is an "utterance," as he calls it, using Peter Shillingsburg's account of John Searle's concept (225–26), then Bornstein seems to describe something closer to a unique "version" in Hans Zeller's sense than to a subtext of a "metatext, or 'work,'" Second, even if all the incarnations can be grouped together as a work, are they equal? Bornstein says that " 'September 1913' exhibits a strong political pull in its early incarnations, a pull increasingly weakened as later reprintings drop or thin out the original bibliographic codes" (227), and his evidence supports the claim that the political implications were lessened by the changes in typeface and positioning and by the alterations in content, location, and typeface size of Yeats's explanatory note. His analysis strongly implies that he regards such diminishment as a loss, but it is not clear why. Because his own aesthetic demands a "political pull"? Because the political implications are truer to Yeats's intentions? Bornstein's essay is permeated by a sense of loss—"we are left with a sense of our own belatedness, of our inadequacy to recuperate the lost codes of lost locations in time and space" (246)—and the essay seems drawn back to origins, to the earliest appearances of the poems where the poet was most in control of the bibliographic codes that supply part of the context for interpretation. (A side note: "The lost locations in time and space" refers to the concept of "aura" in Walter Benjamin's 1936 essay "The Work of Art in the Age of Mechanical Reproduction," where it is defined as the work of art's "presence in time and space, its unique existence at the place where it happens to be" [quoted on 224–25]. Bornstein links Benjamin's aura to McGann's bibliographic codes in what seems to me a problematic way. For Benjamin, talking exclusively about visual arts, much is lost as the aura "withers" in an age of mechanical reproduction, but much is gained as well, and, written during the rise of Hitler, his analysis of the aura is highly political as well as aesthetic. Oddly, given Bornstein's charges that later printings of Yeats depoliticize and aestheticize his poems, he does just this with Benjamin's term as he removes its political implications and uses it to describe publishing contexts that we can't fully recover. The points that Bornstein makes effectively with his evidence would have been even stronger without the attempt to link the bibliographic codes to Benjamin's aura.)

The editors express the hope that *The Iconic Page* will become a "foundational text catalyzing further work in the iconic aspects of textual construction and cultural transmission" (6). It is too soon to tell if the book will become foundational, but the essays will surely inspire further work in the area. This valuable and richly provocative volume will certainly enjoy an important place on the textual-studies shelf.

Michael Groden

Berliner Beiträge zur Editionswissenschaft [Berlin Contributions to Scholarly Editing]. Ed. Hans–Gert Roloff. Berlin: Weidler Buchverlag Berlin (paper):

Vol. 1: Siegfried Scheibe, *Kleine Schriften zur Editionswissenschaft* [*Short Papers in Scholarly Editing*] Ed. Hans–Gert Roloff. (BBE 1), 1997. 318 pp. DM 84.00;

Vol. 2: *Wissenschaftliche Briefeditionen und ihre Probleme* [*Scholarly Editions of Letters and their Problems*]. Editionswissenschaftliches Symposion. Ed. Hans–Gert Roloff (BBE 2), 1998. 168 pp. DM 54.00;

Vol. 3: *Die Funktion von Editionen in Wissenschaft und Gesellschaft* [*The Function of Editions in Scholarship and Society*]. Ringvorlesung des Studiengebiets Editionswissenschaft an der Freien Universität Berlin. Ed. Hans–Gert Roloff (BBE 3), 1998. 369 pp. DM 89.00.

ALTHOUGH THE EDITING OF TEXTS IS a learned activity with a long tradition, the academic discipline of scholarly editing is extremely young. In spite of a great deal of practical editorial work, continuous discourse on practical and theoretical questions in the field did not begin in the German-speaking world until 1971 with the publication of *Texte und Varianten* [*Texts and Variants*],[1] a collection of papers edited by Gunter Martens and Hans Zeller. Since the mid-1980s, scholarly editing has established itself in the German-language academic community as an independent discipline. A telling sign of this development is the foundation of several scholarly journals and series. *editio. Internationales Jahrbuch für Editionswissenschaft* [*editio. International Yearbook of Scholarly Editing*] (ed. Winfried Woesler; since 1998 edited by Bodo Plachta and Winfried Woesler) and the accompanying series *Beihefte zu editio* [*Supplements to editio*] have appeared since 1987 and 1991 respectively. *Beihefte zu editio*, in particular, documents conferences on questions in scholarly editing in many different fields, such as literary criticism, philosophy, and musicology. Since 1995 various topical volumes of the journal *Text. Kritische Beiträge* [*Text. Critical Contributions*], edited by Roland Reuß, Wolfram Groddeck, and Walter Morgenthaler, have been published. In 1988 the first volume in the series *Arbeiten zur Editionswissenschaft* [*Papers in Scholarly Editing*], edited by Winfried Woesler appeared. Finally, in 1997 Hans–Gert Roloff founded *Berliner Beiträge zur Editionswissenschaft* [*Berlin Contributions to Scholarly Editing*], the series under consideration here. During the same period four introductions to the

---

[1] *Texte und Varianten. Probleme ihrer Edition und Interpretation*. Ed. Gunter Martens and Hans Zeller. München: C.H. Becksche Verlagsbuchhandlung 1971.

field, with varying emphases, were published.[2] An overview and a collection of papers detailing the history of German-language scholarly editing have appeared in English.[3]

The intensity of the academic discussion in the field thus constituted, and the degree of specialization achieved, would lead one to believe that the discipline has developed a terminology with a solid theoretical foundation. This is not the case. Even the name of the field is in dispute. The term generally translated in this review as 'scholarly editing' is called 'Editionswissenschaft' (literally: 'science of editing') in German. Other competing terms are: 'Editionstechnik' ('technique of editing'), 'Editionslehre' ('methods of editing'), 'Editionsphilologie' ('philology of editing') and 'Textologie' ('textology'). These terms betray the underlying attitudes toward the field on the part of those who use them. Is the editor's task considered a practical craft ('Editionstechnik') that can be taught ('Editionslehre')? Or is the field regarded as an immanent part of philology ('Editionsphilologie') or as an independent discipline with the specific task of preparing textual material editorially and making it accessible ('Textologie', 'Editionswissenschaft'). Likewise, the courses of studies in this field offered at several different universities bear different names. The advanced studies course at the University of Osnabrück and the course held jointly by the Free University and the Humboldt University in Berlin are called 'Editionswissenschaft'; a similiar course at the University of Munich, however, is in 'Textkritik' ('Textual Criticism'). This confusion in the name of the field carries over into its terminology. What, to mention a simple example, should that item containing the text of a work be called: 'Zeuge' ('witness'), 'Überlieferungsträger' ('carrier of transmission'), 'Textträger' ('text carrier')? Each of these terms contains nuances lacking in the others, indeed, at times deliberately excluded by the others. Further, what title denotes that part of the apparatus in a critical edition containing the deviations from the edited text found in other extant versions: 'Varianten' ('variants'), 'Lesarten' ('readings'), 'Mitteilungen zum Text' ('information about the text'), 'Änderungen' ('changes')? What is at the center of the editor's efforts, the 'authorized text' or the 'authentic text'? And what

[2] Siegfried Scheibe (Leitung), Waltraud Hagen, Christel Laufer, Uta Motschmann, *Vom Umgang mit Editionen. Eine Einführung in Verfahrensweisen und Methoden der Textologie.* Berlin: Akademie-Verlag 1988; Herbert Kraft, *Editionsphilologie.* Mit Beiträgen von Jürgen Gregolin, Wilhelm Ott und Gert Vonhoff. Unter Mitarbeit von Michael Billmann. Darmstadt: Wissenschaftliche Buchgesellschaft 1990; Klaus Kanzog, *Einführung in die Editionsphilologie der neueren deutschen Literatur.* Berlin: Erich Schmidt Verlag 1991 (Grundlagen der Germanistik. Vol. 31); Bodo Plachta, *Editionswissenschaft. Eine Einführung in Methode und Praxis der Edition neuerer Texte.* Stuttgart: Philipp Reclam jun. 1997 (Literaturstudium).

[3] Bodo Plachta, "German Literature." *Scholarly Editing: A Guide to Research.* Ed. D.C. Greetham. New York: The Modern Language Association of America 1995, 504–29; *Contemporary German Editorial Theory.* Ed. Hans Walter Gabler, George Bornstein, and Gillian Borland Pierce. Ann Arbor: The University of Michigan Press 1995 (Editorial Theory and Literary Criticism).

differences do these various terms entail? The list of examples could be extended considerably.

The fact that the new series *Berlin Contributions to Scholarly Editing* opens with a collection of Siegfried Scheibe's most important papers in scholarly editing takes into account the dilemma of a newly established discipline with undifferentiated terminology, as Scheibe is the scholar who, in addition to his practical work on editions of the works of Goethe,[4] Georg Forster[5] and Christoph Martin Wieland,[6] has been the most active in the efforts of the last four decades to develop a universally valid terminology within the field of scholarly editing. The collection of his papers in Volume 1 of the *BBE* demonstrates the persistence of this endeavor once again. At the same time this collection can be read as a partial history of German-language scholarly editing. By publishing the renowned *Grundlagen der Goethe-Ausgabe* [*Basic Principles of the Goethe-Edition*] (245–72), which were established between 1959 and 1961 by the collaborators on the *Goethe Academy Edition* (1952–66, not completed) during its reconception at the Academy of Sciences in (then) East Berlin, these guidelines have been made accessible to the rest of the academic community for the first time. In the 1960s they were available to scholars outside of the GDR only secretly. Nevertheless, they soon became an important standard in German-language scholarly editing. Their publication here makes it evident that these guidelines formed the foundation for Scheibe's work on universalizing procedures and standards for critical editions and on the definitions of editorial terms that he presented in 1971 in *Zu einigen Grundprinzipien einer historisch–kritischen Ausgabe* [*On Several Basic Principles of a Historical–critical Edition*; 9–44] in *Texte und Varianten* (see note 1, above). Since then, scholarly editors have not been able to ignore this terminological classification system. Nevertheless, with the possible exception of the reactions of Hans Zeller and Herbert Kraft, a discussion of the content of Scheibe's proposals has been largely lacking because most editors have been primarily concerned with their own practical work. For this reason, Scheibe presented his definitions with a few small changes twenty years later and supplemented them with an extensive section on models for denoting variants (*Editorische Grundmodelle*; *Basic Editorial Models*; 102–27). With the models of the simplified lemmatized apparatus, the integrated apparatus, the genetic apparatus in 'stair-step' form and the synoptic apparatus Scheibe presents four basic types of denotation of variants. Armed with this knowledge users of critical editions can orient themselves much more quickly to the

---

4 *Werke Goethes*. Ed. Deutsche Akademie der Wissenschaften zu Berlin. 23 vols. Berlin: Akademie-Verlag 1952–66 (not completed); a few additional volumes were published as separate editions.

5 *Georg Forsters Werke. Sämtliche Schriften, Tagebücher, Briefe*. Ed. Deutsche Akademie der Wissenschaften zu Berlin. Berlin: Akademie-Verlag 1958–.

6 *Wielands Briefwechsel*. Ed. Deutsche Akademie der Wissenschaften zu Berlin. Berlin: Akademie-Verlag 1963–.

widely differing forms of editions found in the German-speaking world. A model for a system of sigla has been added to the *Basic Editorial Models* as a step towards standardizing the various systems of sigla in use presently.

Scheibe's goal in all these endeavors has been not only to develop a stringent, precise and thus genuinely scholarly terminology for the discipline, but also, in particular, to help bridge the chasm between scholarly editors and the users of the editions they produce. The much decried dilemma in modern, German-language scholarly editing that every editor seems to find it necessary to develop his own editorial system for his edition and 'his' author, thus forcing each user to reorient himself to each edition, is far from being solved. Indeed the situation appears to be growing even more complicated because of the completely differing forms taken by new editions in the 1990s.[7] Of course, each editor considers his own form to be the most effective and appropriate to the conditions under which he works. Nevertheless, Scheibe's suggested *Basic Editorial Models* should be standard knowledge for every student of scholarly editing and, it goes without saying, for every editor. Naturally, new forms and methods can be developed on the basis of these suggestions. For example, every German-language editor must live up to Scheibe's standard for the constitution of the text (109–10) or be accused of unscholarly work. This standard contains the sum of the new orientation that has crystallized over the course of decades allowing only one version as the basis for the edited text and strictly rejecting any contamination of versions. On the other hand, many editors do not follow Scheibe's principle of making the fair copy presented to the publisher the basis for the edited text if the author did not see the page proofs before publication. These editors favor basing the edited text on the published version, even if the conventions of the publisher's type-setters and his in-house orthography cause minor variations in the published text in comparison with the author's fair copy. Such editors emphasize the reception of the text and argue that the published version is no less valid as an authorized version than the fair copy since the author knew of and accepted the contemporary publisher's and type-setters' conventions. (Of course, genuine faults in the published text are corrected.) In spite of these endeavors towards universal rules, Scheibe cannot deny the background of his own editorial experience which serves as the point of departure for his *Basic Principles*. The *Goethe Academy Edition* can claim historical credit for presenting Goethe's texts in the form of their first publication, thus ending the tradition of the *Ausgabe*

---

7 See, e.g., Georg Heym, *Gedichte 1910–1912. Historisch–kritische Ausgabe aller Texte in genetischer Darstellung.* Ed. Günter Dammann, Gunter Martens and Karl Ludwig Schneider. 2 vols. Tübingen: Max Niemeyer Verlag 1993; Georg Trakl, *Sämtliche Werke und Briefwechsel. Innsbrucker Ausgabe. Historisch–kritische Ausgabe mit Faksimiles der handschriftlichen Texte Trakls.* Ed. Eberhard Sauermann and Hermann Zwerschina. Basel, Frankfurt/Main: Stroemfeld/Roter Stern 1995–; Franz Kafka, *Historisch–Kritische Ausgabe sämtlicher Handschriften, Drukke und Typoskripte.* Ed. Roland Reuß and Peter Staengle. Basel, Frankfurt/Main: Stroemfeld/Roter Stern 1995–.

letzter Hand (final revised edition). Goethe's own edition (1827–30)[8] under this name of his own coinage, and then the monumental *Weimar Edition* (1887–1919),[9] attempted to make Goethe's view of his work as an elderly man the conclusive perspective on his oeuvre. Scheibe's proposal in his rules on the constitution of texts to base the edited text on the first published edition or whenever possible the manuscript fair copy for this edition follows the principles of the *Goethe Academy Edition* (250). For other authors and other authorial methods of composition the last authorized version might be the most representative, and arguments could be found for making it the edited text. Thus, in individual cases the universality of Scheibe's procedures and definitions must be carefully considered.

Almost all of Scheibe's other papers published in this volume can be read as further refinements, more exact arguments and more precise examples of his definitions, procedures and basic models, whether these are on the problems of text in general (54–67), of authorization (68–81), on the constitution of texts (82–90) or on the way to denote the transmission of the text (128–39). A further emphasis is on the nature of scholarly editing (Scheibe's term is 'textology') Scheibe advocates as an independent academic discipline oriented toward the user, for example in his papers on the relationship of the field to the 'Gesellschaftswissenschaften' (literally: 'sciences of society', 'social sciences'; GDR-term for 'liberal arts'; 45–53), on the unity of textology (188–98), on the standardization of editions (219–29) and on the question which edition is adapted to which kind of user (210–18). With the example of a synoptic variant apparatus for complicated prose transmission (140–87), Scheibe introduces a form of presentation for prose texts that—after Zeller's proposal two years before[10]—breaks new ground, in that all other models of variant apparatus in German-language scholarly editing have been developed for poetry, whose genetic units are naturally easier to recognize, and in that prose texts have been largely ignored in German-language scholarly editing. As an editor of letters Scheibe makes a contribution on the topic of lost letters whose existence must be inferred and recorded in an edition (199–209). The editorial principles Scheibe developed with others for the *Edition of Wieland's Correspondence* are reproduced in the Appendix (273–315) and will be relevant as a practical example for every editor of letters.[11]

---

8 *Goethes Werke. Vollständige Ausgabe letzter Hand*. 40 vols. Stuttgart, Tübingen: J.G. Cottasche Buchhandlung 1827–30.

9 *Goethes Werke*. Ed. im Auftrage der Großherzogin Sophie von Sachsen. 133 (in 143) vols. Weimar: Hermann Böhlau, 1887–1919.

10 Hans Zeller, "Die Typen des germanistischen Varianten–Apparats und ein Vorschlag zu einem Apparat für Prosa." *Zeitschrift für deutsche Philologie* 105 (1986), special issue: *Editionsprobleme der Literaturwissenschaft*. Ed. Norbert Oellers and Hartmut Steinecke, pp. 42–69.

11 The following papers have been translated into English: Siegfried Scheibe, "Some Notes on Letter Editions: With Special Reference to German Writers." *Studies in Bibliog-*

Re-reading Scheibe's collected papers in scholarly editing makes his decade-long endeavor to develop precise terminology and to standardize the field especially evident. Of necessity, Scheibe's insistence entails considerable redundancy. The reader who tolerates these redundancies will have the benefit of being presented with a segment of the history of the field. Other readers should read first—and thoroughly—the *Basic Editorial Models*. The discussion of these principles, definitions, and models is far from over. Now more than ever an important discussion is likely to ensue within the framework of the 'Lexicon of Philology of Editing', a project initiated by Gunter Martens.

As to problems of editions of letters, Scheibe illustrates some of these in Volume 2 of the *BBE* using examples from the *Wieland Edition* (73–86). Winfried Woesler adds the guidelines for commentary on letters that he developed in the course of his work on the *Droste–Hülshoff Edition*[12] (87–96). These guidelines can then be compared with those for the *Wieland Edition* in *BBE* 1 and together become important instruments for future editors of letters. In addition to contributions on individual authors and problems, this volume contains an overview of problems and a bibliography of titles pertaining to editions of letters by Renaissance and Baroque writers (19–42) and a selected bibliography on general topics regarding scholarly letter editions (147–67).

Volume 3 of the *BBE*, *Die Funktion von Editionen in Wissenschaft und Gesellschaft* [*The Function of Editions in Scholarship and Society*] is weightier than Volume 2. We are used to judging an edition for its scholarly qualities, and indeed this remains the most important criterion. At the same time, in spite of their apparent objectivity, editions transport intended influences on reception or are subject to socio-political situations that can have far-reaching effects on the edition. Walter Jaeschke shows how a divergence between intention and function resulting from the politics of ideas can occur (11–25). In the Renaissance and Baroque period editions often had polemical functions, as Roloff shows using Erasmus's edition of the *New Testament* in 1518 or Hutten's edition of Lorenzo Valla's proof of the forgery of the donation of Constantine, also in 1518 (27–41). Referring both to the reception of Tacitus's *Germania* in the fifteenth and sixteenth centuries and to editions in both parts of divided Germany in the twentieth century, Ferdinand van Ingen demonstrates how editions can serve to legitimatize and rehabilitate writers (103–22). Jürgen Rojahn gives an extensive and detailed overview of the Marx–Engels editions with their various political dependencies (133–204). Falk Wagner illustrates how politics in theology can be manifest by editions (227–76). Using examples from ancient times up until the present, Bodo

---

raphy 41 (1988), 136–48; Siegfried Scheibe, "Theoretical Problems of the Authorization and Constitution of Texts." *Contemporary German Editorial Theory* (see note 3), 171–91; Siegfried Scheibe, "On the Editorial Problem of the Text." *Contemporary German Editorial Theory* (see note 3), 193–208.

12 Annette von Droste–Hülshoff, *Historisch–kritische Ausgabe. Werke, Briefwechsel*. Ed. Winfried Woesler. Tübingen: Max Niemeyer Verlag 1978–.

Plachta shows that censorship of editions was used by political rulers as a regulator, making evident the power to destabilize systems that has been attributed even to editions (303–42). Finally, H. T. M. van Vliet explains the reciprocal relationship between editor and publisher, illustrating this with the publication policy and strategy employed by the Constantijn Huygens Instituut, the center for scholarly editing in the Netherlands (343–68). This volume, with its interdisciplinary orientation (further examples are from natural science and musicology), measures the field of tension that arises between claims to scholarship on the one hand and the situation in society as a whole on the other, and shows distinctly that scholarly editions are not made in a vacuum, but are as historically bound as the objects they present.

Rüdiger Nutt-Kofoth
translated from the German
by Diane Coleman Brandt

The Editing of Old English: Papers from the 1990 Manchester Conference. Ed. D. G. Scragg and Paul E. Szarmach. With the assistance of Helene Scheck and Holly Holbrook. Cambridge: D. S. Brewer, 1994. x + 317 pp. $71.00/£39.50.

I T HAS BEEN FIVE YEARS since the publication of *The Editing of Old English,* and the volume comprises papers that in earlier versions had been delivered in 1990; its immediacy has, thus, been lost to us. Nevertheless, many of the essays in this collection remain timely, which testifies to its overall excellence.

Like the conference that is its precursor, this collection takes Helmut Gneuss's "Guide to the Editing and Preparation of Texts for the *Dictionary of Old English,*" first published in 1973, as its point of departure. Gneuss's 1993 preface to his "Guide" re-asserts the need for "editions that do not leave it to the reader—or the lexicographer—to solve difficult problems of language and interpretation that should have been properly treated by the editor of the respective text" (7). While reiterating his original appeal for "adequately annotated editions of texts," Gneuss judiciously indicates where his views have changed in the twenty years since the publication of the "Guide": he now looks more favorably upon those arguments for preserving manuscript readings in some matters of modern capitalization, punctuation, and reproduction of manuscript accents (8). However, if the "Guide" remains an important definition of the goals of editing Old English texts, in 1999 at least one troubling lacuna seems more pronounced. Specifically, nowhere in the "Guide" do we find adequate recognition of the need for editors to examine critically their operative assumptions about Old English texts and textuality.

Certainly, we all realize that editions of Old English works result from critical assessments of the relations between written texts and Anglo-Saxon social practices, editorial notions of authorship and intention, and the needs of specialist and non-specialist readers who will use such editions. Editors therefore need to be up-front about both these assessments and their bases. How and to what extent does the editor apply judgments about features of Anglo-Saxon literacy and orality? How and to what extent does the editor employ concepts of individual or collaborative authorship as well as intention? How and to what extent does the editor remediate the formal and stylistic elements of the manuscript to meet the expectations and interests of the edition's projected readers? By not calling attention to the significance of the editor's theoretical disposition, the "Guide" fosters and remains locked into a limited (and limiting) perspective of editing as "not interpreting." Yet, because this disposition helps editors identify and resolve "difficult problems of language and interpretation," it cannot justifiably be passed over in any discussion of editorial practice; editors thus need to be aware that their "theories" of the text must make up part of the edition's significant content.

To a different degree, Marilyn Deegan and Peter Robinson's "The Electronic Edition" sidesteps the same issue, preferring instead to focus on the convenience of computer-aided editing tasks. Deegan and Robinson talk about using the computer to facilitate the preparation of scholarly editions; they suggest as well "new means of presenting editions in electronic form" (27). Deegan and Robinson eagerly anticipate more widespread application of computer technologies to the transcription and preparation of texts, encoding texts into machine-readable form, enhancement of damaged and obscured readings, collation of variants and management of large manuscript traditions, preparation of glossaries and linguistic studies, and finding sources and parallels. More importantly, the authors call for "the electronic hypertext edition," which, they assert, "would not be a substitute for the traditional scholarly edition, rather it would be a supplement to it, allowing the editor to present not only the edited text but also all the materials which were used in the preparation of the edition and upon which editorial decisions were based" (36). In fact, Kevin Kiernan's *Electronic Beowulf*, which is slated to appear very soon (before, perhaps, this review comes into print), promises to do just this, providing a high resolution image for each page of the manuscript with enhancements to those images where we need help seeing faded words or covered letters. What Deegan and Robinson imagine in 1994, Kiernan, Robinson himself, and other scholars are building today; ultimately, the response to these projects from scholars, students, and specialists will speak to the practical validity of the electronic hypertext edition. In turn this practical validity will emerge through a recognition that an electronic hypertext edition constitutes not only another kind of edition but also another kind of textuality, and as such it must provide very clear signposts to readers and users wishing to navigate the edition seriously. Unfortunately, the problems and potential problems to be faced by the electronic hypertext edition's readers—specialists and non-specialists alike—do not receive sufficient treatment by Deegan and Robinson.

Some of the most instructive essays in the collection do indeed concern the interests and needs of readers of editions. David N. Dumville's "Editing Old English Texts for Historians and Other Troublemakers" sketches out the needs of historians in editions of Old English texts, and lists "easy readability" and "[n]ecessary emendations" as two of the foremost (46). Dumville does a service to remind us that modern editions of Old English texts—even literary ones—need to speak across disciplines. In "The Search for Meaning" Antonette diPaolo Healey highlights the interests of lexicographers, for whom "the single most important feature in an edition" is the accurate transcription of the manuscript (86). Healey favors a conservative approach to editing that shows "a tolerance for possible [word] forms and an unwillingness to emend them out of existence" (87). With a survey of the lexical problems concerning the combined prefix *gebe-*, Healey convincingly supports the case for preserving manuscript readings and so to this extent overpowers Dumville's appeals for more fully modernized 'just the facts' texts.

Hugh Magennis's "Old English Texts for Student Use" urges editors to tailor editions specifically for students' objectives at various levels of study. The main features of the student-oriented edition include complete manuscript facsimiles, judiciously limited amounts of critical and interpretive commentary, and extensive bibliographies. Magennis also suggests that translations as well as detailed and well-signposted glossaries round out the edition, a suggestion that has much merit, despite its rather glib assumption that all students need or use translations to work through their own. Taken together, these three papers on audience reveal that all of us who work with Old English texts are scholars, specialists, and students. Moreover, they gesture toward the one glaring shortcoming of this book as a whole; that is, the lack of a coherent role for editions of Old English texts in a broader and rapidly changing academic culture. No longer can we publish editions that take for granted their own value in the larger academic market. Editions of Old English texts need now to account for and answer to a culture that increasingly demands—and yet is predisposed to dismiss—the practical benefits of studying cultures, languages, and texts of the past. This rather millenarian sentiment underwrites much of the collection without receiving any direct treatment.

Nevertheless, Clare Lees, Kathryn Sutherland, J. R. Hall, and Richard Dammery's essays quite profitably look back on the history of Anglo-Saxon studies. In "Whose Text is it Anyway?" Lees examines the role of textbooks in structuring our perceptions and judgments of both Old English literature and Anglo-Saxon culture. By giving a narrow range of prose works, Old English textbooks today present a canon to beginning students that fails to "hint that there may be more to Anglo-Saxon" than what the textbooks offer (103). Since Old English textbooks reflect the style of the discipline, what the discipline considers to be important, we need to examine again our conceptions of Anglo-Saxon author, text, textual contexts, and textual contents. Lees thus asks us to give more voice to Anglo-Saxon processes of creating intellectual and social culture so that we may invite students to invest themselves in Anglo-Saxon textuality.

Kathryn Sutherland's "Editing for a New Century: Elizabeth Elstob's Anglo-Saxon Manifesto and Ælfric's St Gregory Homily" discusses the way that Elstob's 1709 edition of the homily constructs "a consciously personalized editing space, which forces the reader to consider how the interpretation of the text relates to the conditions of its reproduction, not only in terms of the scholarly and non-scholarly apparatus for its recovery, but also through the typographical boundaries set for its reconstitution in the present" (235). Elstob's edition thus provides a useful lesson for editors today with different sorts of readers and readerly interests at stake, and Sutherland's essay reminds us that we may continue learning about the feminist dimensions of texts and textuality.

J. R. Hall's "The First Two Editions of *Beowulf*: Thorkelin's (1815) and Kemble's (1833)" provides a neat chronicle of the drama that helped center *Beowulf* in the canon of Old English linguistic and literary scholarship. This sort of historical treatment aids scholarship tremendously by re-introducing the contexts that express and support our assumptions about literature, literary texts, and serious literary study. In "Editing the Anglo-Saxon Laws: Felix Liebermann and Beyond," Richard Dammery examines "three fundamental flaws in Liebermann's treatment of the manuscript sources" for *Die Gesetze der Angelsachsen* (252). Dammery gives an engaging analysis, and his challenge to scholars to re-examine clause division and numeration in the Law Codes certainly raises important concerns. His closing point is, however, fairly predictable: the primary objective for editors of the Law Codes is to equal Liebermann's "enviable accuracy, while presenting new texts and translations, for general use, in a more accessible form" (261). By looking back on the history of Anglo-Saxon studies, all of these projects aid in the development of an integrated theory of text suitable for the discipline and for the works we wish to present and understand. Like many other disciplines, Anglo-Saxon studies have vested interests in not only addressing the semantic and situational contexts enjoined by oral, manuscript, printed, and digital texts, but also contributing to a general theory of culture. The need for vigorous pursuit of such a theory constitutes the most salient lesson and implicit promise of this collection as a whole, for it provides the clearest opportunity to reconceive, reestablish, and reiterate the practical benefits of historical and linguistic studies.

One particularly noteworthy paper that looks back on the history of Anglo-Saxon studies is Michael Lapidge's "On the Emendation of Old English Texts." Here, Lapidge traces changes in the scholarly climate that have made the editorial practice of conjectural emendation all but taboo. Jane Roberts's edition of the *Guthlac* poems and A. N. Doane's edition of *Genesis A* exemplify the emendation-unfriendly climate. Lapidge notes that early nineteenth century editors of scholarly editions of Old English verse recognized *emendatio* in the same way that editors of classical texts, such as A. E. Housman, did: as "an indispensable part of editing a text" (54). After reviewing the tradition of textual criticism established from work on *Beowulf* by scholars from Thorkelin to Trautmann, Lapidge decries "the present climate of conservatism" and pleads for a more interventionalist approach (ironically enough, the antidote to conservatism is to re-claim an approach established long before it). Despite its logical validity, Lapidge's reasoning ultimately suffers from rather amorphous premises. Clearly, editors need to recognize their ability and limited responsibility to use emendation. However, to argue that "the editor's first duty ... [is to] the author" (67) is to tie the editor unnecessarily to an elusive, vague, and ultimately untenable concept.

This is Joyce Hill's thesis in "Ælfric, Authorial Identity and the Changing Text," where she is correct in her assertion "that modern concepts of authorship and textual integrity are not applicable to the Anglo-Saxon period, *even when they appear to be present*" (179). For an "author" such as Ælfric, the primary interest lies in creating and guaranteeing "theological responsibility" in a context where much is seen as "inadequate, unreliable, and outside the tradition" (180). The difference in notions of authorship, textual accuracy, and textual integrity from Ælfric's scholarly milieu to our own challenges "some of the customary principles of modern editorial practice" (183). Part of this challenge, I take it, includes recognizing the 'damage control' goals of Old English texts: what uses of the text were undesirable and so to be avoided? Hill's paper invites us to consider the matter further and to investigate the mutual responsibilities of writers and readers in theological discourse. As mentioned before, we reside past the point of allowing only one disciplinary context—historian, lexicographer, student, literary scholar, and so on—to govern editorial procedure, so perhaps the answer to Lapidge's concerns consists not in primary and exclusive allegiance to 'the Anglo-Saxon author' but rather in judicious interrogation of Old English textuality's multiple and interrelated contexts.

Like Hill, Theodore H. Leinbaugh draws on the work of Ælfric. In "Ælfric's *Lives of Saints* I and the Boulogne Sermon: Editorial, Authorial and Textual Problems," Leinbaugh argues that Ælfric intended *Lives of Saints* I, a liturgical homily that has been titled *Nativitas Domini Nostri Iesu Christi* (or *In Natali Domini* in A. O. Belfour's edition), to open the *Lives of Saints*. This claim runs counter to the prevailing view that *LS* XVI begins Ælfric's plans for the *Lives of Saints*. Although this essay has little to offer in terms of editorial practice, Leinbaugh's argument that the *Sermo in Natale Domini et de Ratione Anime* found in Boulogne-sur-Mer 63 "provides Ælfric's direct source" (202) for *Lives of Saints* I complicates our theory of texts in an interesting way by making the text of sources no less an issue. More generally, this paper is productive for the light it sheds on compositional practice in Old English texts.

Perhaps less illuminating is D. R. Howlett's "New Criteria for Editing *Beowulf*." Howlett claims that the *Beowulf* poet knew and understood the rules of mathematical composition or Biblical style (on which he elaborates in his book, *British Books in Biblical Style*). Howlett's illustrations for this mode of composition begin with the opening lines of the

Gospel of John from both the Greek New Testament and the Latin Vulgate. Since the *Beowulf* poet "knew the Vulgate," Howlett's argument runs, the *Beowulf* poet also knew its style, which was reproduced "from both Hebrew Old Testament and Greek New Testament in minute particulars" (81). Maybe. The syllogism that yokes knowing the Vulgate to knowing its style to reproducing this style has strong aesthetic and intellectual appeal, but it also raises more questions than it answers. If Howlett's arguments are to gain wider acceptance, they will have to account for other sorts of phenomena in Anglo-Saxon language, reading, and textual practices. For example, one point of contact for elaboration might be the relationship between mathematical composition and "transitional literacy."

Of course, Katherine O'Brien O'Keeffe's *Visible Song* has provided the most useful treatment of this phenomenon. In "Editing and the Material Text" O'Brien O'Keeffe takes *Solomon and Saturn* I as one work preserving a transitional literacy, and she uses it to illustrate the editorial implications of transitional literacy generally. Thus, the editor's task becomes one of representing as much information as possible about not only the linguistic text but also the medium supporting the linguistic text. Accordingly, the editor should include "manuscript format, spacing, capitalization and punctuation" (150), as well as other sorts of information provided by manuscript contexts of Old English work. Since a poem like *Solomon and Saturn* I "is not a unitary phenomenon at all but rather a complex composed of all its individual manifestations in manuscript form" (151), it requires an editor to possess a more open-ended conception of a text and its materiality in the context of a manuscript. Such an idea illuminates the real problem with Howlett's concept of text, which is closed to interpretation and, indeed, to reading. Whether such closure represents the Old English author's desire remains to be studied.

Graham D. Caie's "Text and Context in Editing Old English: The Case of the Poetry in Cambridge, Corpus Christi College 201" opens the text to interpretation and reading by reading five poems in CCCC 201 together: *Judgment Day* II, *An Exhortation to Christian Living*, *Summons to Prayer*, *Lord's Prayer* II, and *Gloria* I. Using the manuscript context, Caie argues that these poems function together as a group. What the manuscript compiler has done, he asserts, is put "together a collection of devotional exercises with a clear, chronological purpose—from worldly sin to final absolution" (162). In terms of editing, Caie's reading hints at the important but under-appreciated function of the manuscript compiler, who acts both as author and as editor. The implications of the compiler-function for contemporary approaches to Old English manuscripts and texts deserve further attention.

This concept of the compiler's intention neighbors, theoretically speaking, the editor's intention, and in "Palaeography and the Editing of Old English Texts" Alexander Rumble deals with the editor's intention in communicating palaeographical data in editions of Old English texts. Rumble argues that accurate editing of Old English texts depends on "[a] sound knowledge and appreciation of palaeography" (39). Furthermore, he links the appreciation of Old English texts with awareness "of what texts look like in the original manuscript" (42). To illustrate, he discusses the conventional replacement of the Anglo-Saxon letter *wynn* with the letter "w," and argues that "it should be returned to its rightful place in the alphabet used for Old English texts" (42). While Rumble is not unpersuasive in going after the 'editorial intention' incumbent on modernization of letter forms in editions, he nevertheless leaves us with the impression that palaeography has little else to offer editors and teachers than the modeling of typefaces.

A. N. Doane's "Editing Old English Oral/Written Texts: Problems of Method (With an Illustrative Edition of Charm 4, *Wiþ Færstice*)" seeks an editorial practice that renders visible the vocality, by which is meant the condition of allowing (and sometimes demanding) vocal expression in Old English texts. Doane understands a text as "a record not only of a phonemic string (the 'text') but also of certain *performative factors*" (131). Thus Doane's illustrative edition of the metrical charm *Wiþ Færstice* seeks to translate vocality into the print medium. His is a radically conservative text that is valuable as a rationalization of all of the manuscript forms we have received, even if it is finally not successful as an edition. The lesson of this edition is clear: theories of the text have to be supported in praxis.

In "Editing Old English and the Problem of Alfred's *Boethius*" M. R. Godden argues for the "pressing need" for a new edition of King Alfred's poetic version of Boethius's *Consolation of Philosophy*, preserved in Cotton Otho A.vi (as opposed to the prose version of Bodley 180). If one objects to Godden's appeals to retrieve "what Alfred the *poet* wrote" (see the discussion of Lapidge's paper above), one will nevertheless take well Godden's sensible defense for "reconstructing original structures and accidentals" (172). His verse and prose version of the opening section of Alfred's *Boethius* persuades us not to consider a text as wholly unassailable.

J. D. Pheifer's "How Not to Edit Glossaries" is a meticulous argument for the integrity of the glossary. As he asserts, "each glossary is a text in its own right, and all its idiosyncrasies, even of spelling and punctuation, should be accurately represented," for "even errors can be instructive" (295). Glossaries preserve the connections of hundreds of years of Anglo-Saxon intertextuality. Our knowledge of them is important but hampered by the difficulty of editing them in a way that will adequately abstract both the text and the context, preserving both the content and the history.

In sum, *The Editing of Old English* creates an important foundation upon which editing and Old English studies can build in the next millennium. D. G. Scragg and Paul E. Szarmach frame the collection by ably establishing the context for the papers (Szarmach) and by neatly boiling down the complex of concerns, issues, and positions into a series of four questions for editors to ask when confronting difficult passages in Old English manuscripts (Scragg). Five years after its publication, *The Editing of Old English* now speaks to the challenging tasks of establishing the larger cultural context in which to access edited Old English works and inviting readers to investigate the potential relations between contemporary and medieval issues of language, culture, and technology.

Jonathan S. Myerov

A Guide to Editing Middle English. Ed. Vincent McCarren and Douglas Moffat. University of Michigan Press, 1998. x + 338 pp. $49.50.

T HIS COLLECTION OF ESSAYS opens with a stern preface. The editors claim to be responding to a problem: "many who have undertaken the editing of Middle English texts in the past have been unable or unwilling to shoulder all of the many burdens that fell to them" (v). Addressing an audience of those "contemplating editing for the first time" (v), they wish to "raise the standard of scholarly editing for Middle English texts" (v). Or, "at the very least [they] hope this volume will provide prospective editors with an indication of the magnitude of the work they would undertake" (v). McCarren and Moffat, it seems, are looking for a few good men.

But new recruits to the legion of editors can relax. What threatens in its opening paragraph to be a kind of editing bootcamp turns out to be a remarkably open and rich group of essays. The editors claim to provide "practical advice about how to get this job done expediently and well," and this advice certainly abounds in the book. But they also provide distractions and complications along the way. If they make the point that editing is hard work, they also give hints of the pleasures, controversies, paradoxes, and intellectual liveliness of the enterprise as it stands in a post-modern, computer-dominated world. The nineteen essays by sixteen authors refuse to array themselves in straight lines and march in formation. The bootcamp, in some very interesting ways, has rebelled.

What the prospective editor will discover in this volume is not a set of directions for "doing it right," but a carnival of voices talking about the many knowledges, skills, practices, prejudices, and goals that make up editing. The scholars behind these voices are formidable in their talents and accomplishments: Peter Baker, Richard Beadle, N. F. Blake, Helen Cooper, A. S. G. Edwards, Jennifer Fellows, David Greetham, Mary Hamel, Constance Hieatt, Nicolas Jacobs, George Keiser, Peter Lucas, Vincent McCarren, Maldwyn Mills, Douglas Moffat, Linne Mooney, Peter Robinson. In this review I will undertake not a seriatim evaluation of their individual efforts, but a description and reflection on the overall effect of the conversation. What, taken as a whole, might this collection of essays communicate to a new editor? and what would be the implications if the editor took the book to heart?

The editors have divided the book into seven sections: "Author, Scribe, and Editor"; "Perspectives on the Editing of Literary Texts"; "Editing Works of a Technical Nature"; "Elements of an Edition"; "Editing and the Computer"; "Postduction"; and "Appendices." This review, however, will address three recurring topics which are distributed more or less throughout the volume. These topics explore the various commitments and responsibilities that an editor has: the editor's relationship to an author (the source of the text), to an audience (those who will read and rely on the edition), and to fellow editors (the guild of editing practitioners).

With respect to an editor's obligations to an author, the reader of the *Guide to Editing Middle English* will understand clearly that readers and reviewers will be keenly interested in the edition's attitude toward and treatment of authorial intent. After opening with Jacobs's conservative argument that "deprivileging of the authorial text is in principle unsatisfactory" (6) and Fellows's converse plea that "we should accord [scribal] rewritings the same editorial respect as we do … any other single named author's" (16), Moffat, with acknowledgment of McCarren's help, lays out his own position in a bibliographical essay: that "the attempt to recover an authorial text continues to be a legitimate aim of Middle English editors" (52). The moderation and careful wording of that statement (along with the balance of the opening statements) is characteristic of the collection's approach to a topic which sometimes invites immoderate polemic. Nearly every contributor who weighs in on the subject refuses to make orthodoxy on the subject a litmus test for editorial excellence. Echoes of the debate recur in various essays even though it is not their focus. For example, McCarren's essay on editing glossographical texts offers biting illustrations of the sheer nonsense that scribes, medieval and modern, can make of perfectly sensible texts, scribal interferences that could only ludicrously be called "acts of re-creation" (154). On the other hand, Keiser's essay on editing scientific writings notes sensibly that "as interesting as what may have come from the compiler's pen is what has happened to a text during the history of its transmission and dissemination" (113). A respectful tension on the issue seems to be the editors' goal.

Someone setting out to edit a text, of course, unlike a collection of essays, will not be able to maintain a plurality of inconsistent positions with respect to the possibility and desirability of recovering authorial intent. Whatever their ultimate commitments, neophyte editors will find the very brief history of editing in Moffat's "Bibliographical Essay" to be useful in leading them to an informed context for explaining their commitments (or lack of them) to an authorial text. Beginning with Lachmannian recension and ending with the work of Tim William Machan, Moffat gives a balanced and sympathetic account of the motives of the move away from authorial intention, even though he is clearly not in favor of it. As a guide, the collection has a clear bias in favor of a moderate version of recovering "what the author actually wrote," but even wayward editors who will not follow this path will find the background useful. Though not as fully developed as the section on the history of "authorial intent," the subsequent section on "scribal intent" will provide those seeking to justify the ways of scribes to authors with dozens of useful references.

Most prospective editors will have been aware of the debate between those who prefer authorial genius and those who prefer a social text. What they might not have spent a great deal of time thinking about, however, is the great variety of potential readers for edited texts of Middle English and the boggling range of types of editions necessary to serve those readers well. The debates about editorial and textual theory have been waged largely by literary scholars, and what seems to be at stake is a conception of literary talent or genius. When one looks beyond literary texts and works of imagination, the stakes change. Perhaps at the far end of the spectrum are the culinary manuscripts Hieatt discusses. Readers who wish actually to make a flaming pastry castle will resent the misglossing of "ew [eau] ardant" (distilled spirits) as "hot water" for reasons other than the insult it serves to the author's genius. Likewise, McCarren's essay on glossographical texts implicitly points out that sometimes readers will consult a medieval glossary in order to find out what a word means. The situation is perhaps different with the scientific texts Keiser treats and the astrological texts Mooney covers, but it is certainly possible to imagine readers who wish not simply to write the history of now-repudiated "science" but to reproduce accurately the practices of, say, astrological analysis. The essays covering these "works of a technical nature" are gold mines of reference for anyone who would undertake the work of such editing. But literary editors, too, would do well to imagine how their own accounts of editorial theory sound in these contexts.

It is not only in the realm of non-literary texts that *A Guide to Editing Middle English* encourages prospective editors to take a serious interest in the needs and interests of their audience. Even the editor who aims to produce classroom editions of literature for students will face some dilemmas on how best to serve them. In an essay on "Editing and the Teaching of Alliterative Verse," Edwards raises the possibility that an edition may be, paradoxically, "too good" for students. Praising Ralph Hanna's edition of the *Awntyrs of Arthur* for "brilliance" and for "extraordinary and quite dazzling editorial achievement," he goes on to "find [him]self wondering whether this is the sort of text we can safely put into student hands" (99). He worries that the success of daring editorial intervention will encourage lesser talents to make similar, though less successful attempts. Students, he claims, need a more moderate approach to editing, one that neither conservatively reproduces manuscripts nor intervenes to restore "authorial" intent but instead seeks to limit distracting uncertainty on the part of students. For instance, he praises and recommends normalizing for orthographic consistency, punctuating heavily, and annotating extensively. The success of an edition, it seems, lies in its ability to produce the "proper" understanding in the student. In this, Edwards voices anxiety— and perhaps a mistrust—over student readers' ability to make mistakes. A good edition, it seems, is one that prevents its target audience from making interpretive mistakes.

Indeed, a number of essays which take up the matter of serving an audience with an edition seem not to know what to make of their audience. Is their lack of philological background a sign of declining standards? Or are editors' assumptions that students bring such a background to their reading a sign of the overwhelmingly conservative nature of textual scholarship in Middle English? Just what might be expected of "ordinary student" users of editions varies considerably among editors and over time. In his review of notable editions of Middle English literary works, Blake notes how frequently editors have appealed to the concept of the "ordinary student" or the "general reader" in order to justify their editorial principles. He also notes how elastic both the conception and its putative implications are. In general, he takes modern editors to task for clinging too conservatively to an ideal of undergraduates "who are seen only as future scholars to be trained from the beginning in philological technique" (63) and urges that the new "standards" for editing be established keeping in mind the non-homogenous body of today's "ordinary student."

The variety of editions that might arise from a "reader-based" editing practice is the subject of Helen Cooper's essay on editing Chaucer. Looking at the editing principles of, among others, Skeat, Manly and Rickert, Shoaf, and Kolve and Olson, she surveys the various successes and distortions displayed in the long genealogy of editing Chaucer. Prospective editors looking for a case study of the actual implications of editing for specific audiences will find much to ponder here. The "standards" Cooper hopes will emerge from taking readers' needs into account turn out to be very complex. She ends her essay with a memorable example of the paradoxes of editing. What is one to make of this "edition" of the roundel from the *Parliament of Fowls*: a cardboard poster appearing in hundreds of train cars in London (part of the "Poems on the Underground" series), which, she shows, is "a conjectural reconstruction of a stanza never known in any form to most of his medieval readers" (92)?

Ultimately, the promise that practical consideration of audience might resolve some of the theoretical uncertainties of editing runs up against the realization that editors have a somewhat uncertain grasp of the nature and desires of their audiences. While it does not settle the question of who the audience for edited Middle English texts is, nor the question of what the appropriate response to such an audience might be, *A Guide to Editing Middle English* very usefully presses these questions as important for editorial practice. I'm not aware of any other treatment of editing which raises the issue in such a provocative or practical way.

Another relationship which this collection of essays raises for editors' consideration is their membership in a guild of practitioners. As already mentioned, the authors of these essays do not share a common set of assumptions, nor do they reason from them in the same way when they do hold agreement. Nevertheless, a professional ethos does shine through in these representative editors—above all an ethos of helpfulness and gratitude for help received. Whatever the "magnitude" of the task of editing, the field is filled with extraordinarily learned people offering invaluable practical help. The authors of the essays in the section titled "Elements of an Edition" lay out clearly and gently enough for beginners how to go about describing a manuscript and a text, to write a linguistic description, to make a glossary, etc. These are guides that any beginning editor would cherish; their advice is practical, wise, and knowledgeable. (Mills's essay on how to use the *Linguistic Atlas of Late Medieval English* deserves particular mention for tackling an especially difficult subject.) Each of these essays provides copious references to the relevant literature and calls attention to the variety of practices that exist in modern editions. Even the less practically oriented essays in other sections, particularly those that treat works of a technical nature, display the same cheerfulness with respect to sharing hard-earned experience and esoteric knowledge, whether it be specialist knowledge of insects, Arabic culinary writings, or paleography.

The would-be editor would be well-advised to make use of that expertise, for those willing to share their learning and insight will use it scrupulously to evaluate the finished work. (The concern for "standards" which begins the book never entirely recedes into the background.) The guild of editors does not suffer fools (or even careless mistakes) lightly. There will always be someone whose Greek is better than yours or whose eye is sharp enough to catch your seven transcriptional errors in seven lines and memorialize them in a footnote (147n21). This is an intellectual community in which "getting it right" counts—from the correct interpretation of a grapheme (174) to the typefaces used in recording textual variants (235).

It is also a community which participates deeply in the general revolution wrought by a rising computer culture. The advantages of using computers in editing are obvious, yet a number of the contributors to the volume are uneasy about their influence. Cooper, most pointedly, notes that one trend in the use of computers in editing is "to turn the very meaning of 'editing' inside out," making it "a process not of fine discrimination but of maximized accumulation" (92). The results of this accumulation might not be entirely salutary: "making the full range of manuscript readings and misreadings available to every Chaucerian critic … might also allow a process of pick-your-own-text without any of the established editorial controls, such as could invite critical anarchy" (83). Cooper diplomatically omits speculation on which sort of Chaucerian critic ought to be denied access to "the full range of manuscript readings." Other authors are more covertly skeptical. Moffat, for instance, wonders rhetorically what users of comprehensive archives of material will "want or tolerate" (48), and he questions the prevailing claim that the flexibility of computer technology will better our understanding of medieval manuscript culture (48–49).

Such resistance aside, the *Guide* offers two savvy essays on the use of computers in editing. Between them, Robinson and Baker chart the course for using computers to change both what editors do when they edit and how they present the results of their editing. Any notion of computers as labor saving devices quickly recedes out of sight; even at the apparently simple level of transcription, computers complicate the work.

Will editors wish to record the distinction between particular letter forms or not? How much explanation of their choice must they provide? It's clear that descriptions and justifications of transcriptional policies will become both more necessary and more complex. Likewise, the future of editing Middle English will require not simply an expertise in "dead" languages but a strong competence in futuristic "languages" such as SGML and TEI mark-up. The promises of return on investing this additional attention to Middle English texts are tantalizing, but such an investment is also a gamble. The stakes, of course, are worth gambling for. If Robinson is right that the logic and methods of analysis developed by biologists to solve problems in phylogenetics can be transferred to the study of manuscript affiliation, the editing of multiply attested manuscript traditions will be revolutionized. Likewise, the examples Baker gives of the presentational possibilities of carefully prepared texts show that empowering readers to negotiate on their own the full corpus of textual variants need not lead to chaos. Neither Baker nor Robinson aim to offer prospective editors a textbook on computer mark-up and presentation, but their advice effectively communicates the skills that editors will need to master. They are not, however, skills that can be learned in a summer crash course, and the implications for the training of future editors is nowhere addressed in the volume.

If the editors of the volume have succeeded in communicating the "magnitude of the task" of editing, the final essay, a "postduction" by David Greetham, virtuosically and playfully conveys what it is about editing which might attract a talented and theoretically sophisticated intellect. His main subject is the apparent clarity at which editing aims, and his main point is that this clarity, even if achieved, is itself an ambiguous deception. His account ranges playfully from literary theory to the ever-shifting circumstances peculiar to this book's genesis. In the end, the joy of editing is the joy of "guilty knowledge," a term he borrows from Ralph Hanna's description of annotation. The rewards, risks, and, frankly, pleasure of managing this guilty knowledge nicely counterbalance the "many burdens" which the book continually stresses. While it is perhaps the least practical of the essays, the notion that editing ("glossing" and "glosing," Greetham would say) is "a glorious thing" provides a fine ending for the book. (Except that it is followed by three utilitarian appendices: a practical guide for describing manuscripts, a bibliography of facsimiles, and a bibliography of dictionaries. The editor, it seems, always gets the last word.)

A Guide to Editing Middle English will indeed raise the standard of scholarly editing of Middle English—not because it breaks new theoretical ground on the standard editing controversies or deals a death blow to bad theories, but because it successfully presents the total enterprise of editing, giving voice to both kindly guides and exacting curmudgeons. The standards it promotes are high ones, but they are both explainable and attainable. Perhaps most importantly, the book gives voice to the pleasure and satisfaction available in the enterprise of editing. Doing it "right" does not mean abandoning the intellectual playfulness that characterizes modern literary theory.

Eric Eliason

The Correspondence of Jonathan Swift, D.D., Vol. I, *Letters 1690–1714 nos. 1–300*. Ed. David Woolley. Frankfurt am Main: Peter Lang, 1999. 650 pp. $82.95 (subscription price).

Very early in the morning of 5 February 1711/12, Dr. William Grahame, Dean of Wells, died. Later that day, conforming to the practice of his time, Jonathan Swift wrote to his friend and patron, Robert Harley, Earl of Oxford:

> My Lord,
> I most humbly take Leave to inform Your Lordship, that the Dean of Wells dyed this morning at one a clock; I entirely submitt my poor Fortunes to Your Lordship, and remain with greatest Respect
> My Lord Your Lordship's most obedient and most obliged humble Servt.
> J: Swift. (I, 414)

Swift misdated this note, "Jan^{ry}. 5th.," perhaps evidencing, as David Woolley speculates, his "anxiety at this moment" (I, 414) and, as I would add, his discomfort with the ghoulish rhetoric of preferment-seeking. But it is we, Swift's modern readers, whose discomfort with that rhetoric is most instructive. In a mistranscription that I think is as much a symptom as it is an accident, David Woolley's predecessor, Sir Harold Williams, caused Swift to submit to Oxford his "good Fortune" (at Grahame's death, presumably).[1] And for nearly forty years, no Swiftian who has cited this letter has interrogated Williams's transcription either by consulting Williams's predecessor, F. Elrington Ball[2] (who, following H.M.C. *Bath MSS* I, provides the correct reading) or (harder, of course) by consulting the manuscript itself among the Portland Papers at Longleat House.

Woolley knows, of course, that it is extraordinary that there should be occasion in this century for yet a third edition of Swift's letters. But, as the instance above suggests, there remained in Williams's edition a great deal for Woolley to put right at a basic textual level. Thus, in Swift's letter to

---

[1] *The Correspondence of Jonathan Swift*, ed. Harold Williams, 5 vols. (Oxford: Clarendon P, 1963), I, 288.

[2] *The Correspondence of Jonathan Swift, D.D.*, ed. F. Elrington Ball, 6 vols. (London: G. Bell and Sons, 1910–16), II, 4.

Archdeacon Walls of 2 February 1713/14, Williams prints a sentence that breaks off before completion and seems to signal a blunder by Swift:

> I shall be glad if you think it convenient, to begin paying my first-Fruits, for the sooner I am out of debt, the better, and if you paid the Bp of Dromore 100^{ll} to begin with.   (Williams, II, 9)

In fact, however, in both the surviving holograph of this letter and in the transcription of that holograph printed by Ball, the sentence continues, achieving (as it does now in Woolley) a reasonable conclusion: ". . . and if you paid the Bp of Dromore 100^{ll} to begin with I should be pleased to think I had but 200^{ll} more to pay him till next Year" (I, 586). Such corrections are a regular feature of this volume. From the very first sentence of its very first letter, one observes Woolley emending texts that are wrong in Williams and often wrong in Ball as well.

That said, Woolley's edition aspires to achieve much more than a mere correcting of Williams's texts. In 1972, on the occasion of their being reprinted, Woolley performed that service for the final two volumes of Williams's five volume edition (to the extent that the mechanics of their reprinting permitted). But Woolley's present volume (to be succeeded at eighteen month intervals by volumes 2, 3, and 4) is a full re-editing of Swift's correspondence. The distinction that I make here is easy to illustrate even at a textual level (i.e., leaving aside matters like annotation and letters newly collected in this edition). The eighth volume of George Faulkner's 1762 18° edition of Swift's works is the best source for many of Swift's letters to Archbishop William King because that source "stands closest to the manuscript printer's cop[ies]" of those letters, now mainly lost (I, 144, headnote). Nevertheless, unlike Williams, Woolley's goal is not mechanically to reproduce Faulkner's texts of Swift's letters to King because Faulkner's texts exhibit their own non-Swiftian idiosyncrasies. For example, "the 'th' termination clapped liberally onto third person singular verbs" in Faulkner's volume usually represents Faulkner's usage, not Swift's. For that reason, Woolley returns Faulkner's "th" to Swift's "s" "except where Swift's observed usage permitted that form" (I, 70). Woolley's aim is to reproduce the sound of Swift's voice as nearly as appropriate editorial restraint, combined with erudition and assiduity, permits. The effect of that aim in the case of verbs ending in "th" (and not infrequently in other cases) is to give us a voice that is less conservative linguistically than the one that we are used to. In Williams, for example, Swift's letter "reacheth" Archbishop King (Williams, I, 424). In Woolley, the same letter "reaches" him (I, 572).

Generally speaking, Woolley's editorial procedures (which are concisely described at the beginning of this volume) produce satisfying texts. Woolley does cede himself substantial authority. But I, for one, am happy to have him silently eliminate the redundancy of Swift's frequent doubled stops, for example. And I am pleased for him silently "to curb by removal some excesses of 18th century printing-house style" (I, 70). After random sampling, I am persuaded that when we *need* to be conscious of Woolley's handiwork, we are made so. For example, the following mathematically muddled sentence occurs in Faulkner's volume (mentioned above) and so also in Ball and in Williams.

> There was put into my Hands a List of your House of Commons, by some who know the Kingdom well: I desired they would (as they often do here) set a Mark on the Names of those who would be for the Ministry, who I found amounted to one hundred and forty-three, which I think comes within an Equality: Twenty Names besides they could not determine upon; so that suppose eight to be of the same Side, there would be a Majority by one . . . .
> (Williams, I, 424)

In the present edition, in editorial brackets placed immediately after the word "within," Woolley neatly emends this sentence by adding two words omitted either by Swift in his final draft or by Faulkner's compositor. The words are present, however, in Swift's now lost retain copy of his letter, and so in volume 16 of the London edition of Swift's works, published in 1765, the words are "[seven of]" (I, 573). The correction is as apparently an editorial intervention as it is an appropriate one. On the other hand, although the word "who" does not appear in Faulkner's printing of the phrase "who I found amounted to one hundred and forty-three," Woolley (like Ball, Williams, and the 1775 edition of volume 16 of the London edition) does include the word and does so without the stutter of editorial brackets. My practice would be more conservative, but, because the word "who" merely clarifies Swift's sense, I am unalarmed by Woolley's reading.

Turning to letters not collected in Williams or printed only in Williams's appendices, I count seventeen in this volume. (In his preface Woolley tells us that we shall find a total of eighty-three throughout his four volumes.) The newcomers are distinguished in this edition by the fact that their series-numbers are printed in italics both in the letters' headlines and also in the register of 1508 numbered letters at the beginning of this volume (of which the first three hundred letters are printed in volume I). Judging by the very elegant advertisement for this edition (issued perhaps two years ago), one imagines Woolley would award pride of place among the newcomers—in this volume, at least—to letter number *214*. That letter, by Swift to Charles Ford and dated "Chester. Jun. 7. 1713," is featured on four of a total of six pages of the advertisement.

214 was long known to have once existed. A brief extract from it appeared in Christie's sale catalogue of 4 June 1896. Thereafter the letter disappeared until 1989 when it was purchased by Monash University Library at Sotheby's sale of 14 December. One imagines that both Woolley (whose first Swift collection forms the core of Monash University Library's rare book collections) and Clive Probyn (Professor of English at Monash University) were aware of the circumstances of this purchase, but neither Probyn in his discussion and full transcription of the letter (*SB*, 44 [1991], 265–70) nor Woolley elucidates that matter.

The letter is, as Probyn writes, "concise and allusive," and it "brings together several of Swift's pressing social and political concerns, as well as a number of his closest friends" at the period of its writing (Probyn, 267). More striking still (and here I borrow Woolley's language), in letter *214* "Swift quotes with near accuracy lines 335–336 of *The Last Instructions to a Painter*, attributed to Andrew Marvell" (I, 507, note 5). Swift's citing of these lines draws learned commentary from both Probyn and Woolley, the former referencing Swift's *The Legion Club* "as part of the poetic 'Advice to a Painter' genre first popularized in England by Waller" (Probyn, 269), the latter observing that Lord Oxford's predicament "ominously reminded Swift of the proceedings in the Commons, 1666–1667, which heralded the downfall of Charles II's Lord Chancellor Clarendon . . ." (I, 507). To these comments I would add another. Once again, in 1731, Swift will remember Marvell's political hare and hounds—

> Blither than hare that hath escap'd the hounds;
> The House Prorogu'd, the Chancellour rebounds.
> (*The Last Instructions to a Painter*, 335–336)[3]

—in a long, elaborated passage beginning:

> A Hare, had long escap't pursuing Hounds,
> By often shifting into distant Grounds.
> (*On Mr. P——y being put out of the Council*, 17–18)[4]

In Swift's lines the hare is Robert Walpole and the principal hound is William Pultney. Swift's casting proved prescient even though his prophecy—

> So keen thy *Hunters*, and thy *Scent* so strong;
> Thy *Turns* and *Doublings* cannot save thee long. (43–44)

—is more than a decade premature.

None of the other newcomers to Swift's collected correspondence in this volume have quite the cachet of number *214*, but individually they tend to finish off stories, and collectively they lend a sense of completeness to the volume. I have wondered more than once what John Partridge, the victim of the most famous literary prank in English literature, thought at the very time of the event. Letter number *45*, John Partridge to Isaac Manley, begins thus: "Old ffriend, | I dont doubt but you are Imposed on in Ireland also by a pack of Rogues about my being dead . . ." (I, 189). Similarly, anyone who has worried (along with Swift himself and Esther Johnson) about Swift's £500 lodged with the reputedly bankrupt Francis Stratford[5] will be glad to read newly collected number *168* and, just as

---

3 *Poems on Affairs of State Augustan Satirical Verse, 1660–1714*, ed. George deF. Lord, 6 vols. (New Haven & London: Yale UP, 1963), I, 116.

4 I cite these lines from the corrected state of sheet 2D of the second volume of George Faulkner's 8° 1735 works of Swift.

5 See *Journal to Stella*, ed. Harold Williams, 2 vols. (Oxford: Clarendon P, 1948), I, 351, II, 371, 411, 463.

important, its addendum of 21 November 1711 (the latter generously communicated to Woolley by Margaret Weedon):

> I do hereby empower Mr Benjamin Tooke, to accept of five hundred Pounds Stock in the Corporation erected to carry on a Trade to the South-seas, which was this Day transferred to me by Francis Stratford Esqr. | Witness my hand | Jonathan Swift. (I, 72)

Completeness, indeed, is my abiding sense of this volume. Not that new materials which would have been proper to the volume will not surface from time to time—that always happens. But there is a fullness, one wants to say a generosity, about this volume that will cause it to be, for the foreseeable future, the standard edition of the letters that it contains. Accounting for this fullness (or even describing it) is difficult because it is the consequence of accumulated details and decisions. Among the positive results of these I would list the following three first.

1) The authority of Woolley's annotations, particularly, perhaps, those annotations based on bibliographical observations: take, for example, note 7, letter 83. Woolley annotates Swift's assertion that none of Sir William Temple's writings "ever printed in my Time was from the Originall; the first Memoirs was from my Copy, so were the second Miscellanea, so was the Introduction to the English History: so was every Volume of Letters . . . (I, 270)." Here is Woolley's commentary:

> MEMOIRS . . . LETTERS, respectively Wing STC T642, 652, 638, 641, and Teerink 472, 474. The printers 'copy' for all these, he affirms, was from *his* transcript. In the single case of the first this claim poses a problem. Swift is thought to have joined the Temple household at Sheen in the summer of 1689. There is credible testimony (surviving to the present day) that the 'first Memoirs' was in print by 1685, shortly after composition, although not in fact *published* until 30 November [Swift's birthday] 1691. (*The London Gazette*, Numb. 2718: *Memoirs of what past in Christendom . . .* Printed for Ric. Chiswell. . .). H.E. Woodbridge's copy of the first edition bears this note, in a contemporary hand, on the flyleaf: 'Chiswell the publisher affirmed to J. Harrington that the first impression of these memoirs (which is of the best paper) was printed at the end of K Ch: reign but he kept it by him till this reign, and that it was printed by the author's consent then. 22 March 92/3.' (Woodbridge, 246 n9). It is also a fact that *all* of the many copies of Wing T642 that I have examined exhibit the title leaf as a bibliographical cancel, tending to validate Chiswell's testimony; for the cancellandum must in some respect have been an anomaly. (I, 273, note 7)

Woolley's authority derives from both his learning and his restraint. Almost always, as in this long note, he asserts all that he knows and only what he knows.

2) The meticulousness of Woolley's descriptions of the textual sources of Swift's correspondence and the historicizing effects of that meticulousness: a good example of this virtue would be Woolley's headnote to letter 33, a letter written by Swift to Archbishop King on New Year's Day 1707/8:

> The impression of the seal in the red wax on this letter shows very clearly a shield with three lions rampant and the legend NOLI IRRITARE LEONES. Compare 739, Ford's holograph sealed with the same or a similar seal, by the owner. Nichol Smith puts the first meeting of Swift and Charles Ford 'probably in 1707 not long before he [Swift] left for London', and shows that Ford also left Dublin for London some time in 1708 (*Letters to Ford* ix, xii). The first extant letter of their correspondence is 59, 12 November 1708. On this new evidence (and 214 *ad fin.*) Ford was already in London and let Swift use his seal on New Year's Day, 1708; and he was in Dublin by 16 August (ibid. xii). Cf 66 *ad init.* (I, 170, headnote)

3) Woolley's care "to account for the mutual links between successive letters of individual correspondences" (I, 9): this effort produces the rewarding consequence that many of the letters in this volume may be read either as part of a discrete correspondence (e.g. the Swift/Archbishop King correspondence) or as one letter within the chronological sequence of all of Swift's correspondence.

No book is perfect, of course. Woolley concludes the prefatory matter to this volume by quoting Swift's prefatory apology in his edition of Sir William Temple's letters: "*I beg the Readers Pardon for any* Errata's *which may be in the Printing, occasioned by my Absence*" (I, 97). There are errata in Woolley's volume. I list here those that I have found in the hope that they may be corrected in a new printing some time or other or at least incorporated in an errata sheet.

> title-page missing that ornament which Woolley lovingly describes on page 72
> 204, note 3 should read "Cf. 50, penultimate paragraph"
> 223, note 4 should read "*A Short Character of His Ex. T. E. of W.*"
> 241, note 7 should read "For 'Mr Molesworth's Book of Denmark' see n1"
> 250, note 5 should read "[ibid. n5]"
> 363, note 3 should read "30 September 1713"
> 401, hyphen at line 3fb should be adjusted
> 479, note 4 should be renumbered note 2
> 554, note 2 should read "' ... that ever I saw'"
> 576, at line 5 footnote number 1 should be raised

In letter 82 (I, 267–270), Woolley emends to "Worsly" a name that in Ball appears as "Whaley" and in Williams as "Wayly." I am confident that Woolley's emendation is correct and, further, that Colonel Henry Worsley is the man that Swift is writing about in letter 82. But, following Pat Rogers,[6] Woolley also identifies this same Colonel Henry Worsley as the "honest Harry" mentioned in Swift's *In Pity to the Empty'ng Town*, an identification that he repeats in letters 69, note 7, and 235, note 4. Neither Rogers nor Woolley explains the grounds for this identification, and the grounds are not obvious. Further, although Rogers and Woolley join Harold Williams in identifying as Frances Worsely the "Worsly" mentioned in *In Pity to the Empty'ng Town*,[7] no evidence is offered for this identification by any of its asserters. Both identifications are, I think (in Woolley's pleasant abbreviation), TBR, to be researched.

I do query a few of Woolley's editorial practices. The most significant is his decision to supply no translations of foreign language letters and passages within letters. The appeal of Swift's correspondence is broader than the number of readers who are at ease in Greek, Latin, and French, and I hope that in forthcoming volumes Woolley will accommodate Swift's full readership. For the same reason I hope that he will use fewer Latin abbreviations in his headnotes and annotations. "Scil.," for example, saves only one character over the more familiar "to wit," a savings hardly worth the price of puzzling readers. Finally, even in English, Woolley might in future volumes curb his pleasure in hard words and unfamiliar jargon. Of course, an editor is permitted to be learned. Woolley's riposte to Swift's assertion that his *Miscellanies in Prose and Verse* of 1711 was published "without [his] Knoledge" is both learned and witty: "The volume ... exhibits extensive authorial revision" (I, 402, note 4). But, learned or not, the following passage verges on reader harassment: "Swift had already contacted the captain of the *Wolfe*, a naval sloop flying her Blue Peter" (I, 258, note 2). The phrase "Blue Peter" (a flag indicating that a vessel is ready to sail) is defined in most good dictionaries, of course. But still.

Emphatically, however, I do not want to conclude my review of this wonderful volume on a negative note. The letters it contains carry Swift from his twenty-third through his fifty-second year. They carry him also from the abject circumstance of being recommended to Sir Robert Southwell by Sir William Temple as "a Gentleman to waite on you or as Clarke to write under you" (I, 101) to the glory of being assured by Pope and Parnell that " ... Dew or Rain may wett us to the Shift / We'll not be slow to visit Dr Swift" (I, 647). The letters were written mainly in England, and they were written by a man who identified with England and did not dream that he was destined to become an Irish hero. They are a record of that period of Swift's life that he always regarded as its high-tide. One is pleased and grateful to see that record presented with such splendid intelligence.

John Irwin Fischer

---

[6] *Swift The Complete Poems* (Harmondsworth, Middlesex: Penguin, 1983), 107 and 635.

[7] Rogers, 635; Woolley, I, 246–247; *The Poems of Jonathan Swift*, ed. Harold Williams, 2nd ed., 3 vols. (Oxford: Clarendon P, 1958), I, 123n.

William Wordsworth, *Early Poems and Fragments, 1785–1797.*
Ed. Carol Landon and Jared Curtis. *The Cornell Wordsworth.*
Ithaca: Cornell University Press, 1997. xxiv + 891 pp. $100.00.

William Wordsworth, *Translations of Chaucer and Virgil.* Ed.
Bruce E. Graver. *The Cornell Wordsworth.* Ithaca: Cornell University Press, 1998. xxviii + 583 pp. $80.00.

S INCE ITS FIRST VOLUME, published in 1975, the Cornell Wordsworth has
aimed at restoring the early Wordsworth. Wordsworth wrote major
poems in the 1790's, revised them substantially in subsequent decades,
and published them much later in life. *The Prelude*, completed in 1805
and not published until after his death in 1850, is the prime example of a
poem substantially revised to suit Wordsworth's changing attitudes. The
Cornell Wordsworth series was designed to restore texts to their earliest
versions, partly on the grounds of their aesthetic superiority to later versions and partly on biographical and historical grounds. The arguments
in favor of the early poems are too complex to rehearse here, but when
the policy of the Cornell series began, there was general agreement that
the early versions were superior. Thus in criticism the title *The Prelude*
usually referred to the 1805 version. This policy, stated in each volume
by the general editor, Stephen Parrish, presented the "earliest finished
version" in an uncluttered "Reading Text" along with all textual variants to
the final version printed in Wordsworth's lifetime. In addition, transcripts
were printed of the manuscripts, with different typefaces and type sizes
distinguishing Wordsworth's hand from those of his amanuenses and
the original drafts from later revisions inserted on the same page. The
most complex manuscripts were reproduced photographically. This policy
was brilliantly executed by the editors of the earlier volumes, enabling
the patient critic or biographer to trace the development of the text in
astonishing detail over a period of years and sometime decades. Yet in
later volumes, the format changes somewhat to suit the poems.

Early Poems omits poems edited in earlier volumes in the series, *An
Evening Walk, Descriptive Sketches, Salisbury Plain*, and *The Borderers*,
and it omits shorter poems contained in those volumes that in one way
or another contributed to those poems. Since *Early Poems* contains few
published poems, Wordsworth authorized no single version of them.
Many of the poems were drafted in a brief time, perhaps a few weeks,
in several different notebooks, so that removing the encrustation of later
revisions is not necessary. Thus the reading texts were chosen from "the
fullest or most finished manuscript version or versions of the piece concerned, within the limits of the period covered by this edition" (6), and
the *apparatus criticus* contains all manuscript variations. "The Vale of
Esthwaite," the most important poem in the edition, the editors present
in "the earliest existing" (413) level of composition, without trying to
construct an ideal text from the fragments of composition. The presence
of drafts of a poem in different notebooks requires a change in format.
In earlier volumes the reading text with notes on variants was in one

section and the transcripts and photographs in another. Here however, the photographs of all the relevant manuscripts are presented in the first part with notes identifying the poems in each photograph. The second part contains the reading texts and headnotes immediately followed by the transcriptions of the manuscripts and is divided into three sections: 1785–91, the end of Wordsworth's years at Cambridge; Work of Uncertain Date; and 1793–1797. From 1791 to 1793 Wordsworth wrote little else but *An Evening Walk* and *Descriptive Sketches*, so no shorter poems can be dated then. Each part has adequate references to the other, so that moving from photograph to reading text and transcript is easy. The editors have devoted more space than editors of earlier volumes to identifying the sources of the poems and Wordsworth's experiments with genre, so that one can map the influences on him.

Editing early unpublished poems from notebooks written in the late eighteenth century presents other problems. One naturally asks whether the notebooks were used exclusively for drafts of Wordsworth's poems or whether the notebooks were also used as commonplace books, those in which he may have copied verses written by others. Given any verse or set of verses, how does one know that it is Wordsworth's and not lines of a poet now lost to fame? Some few lines are identified from Milton and from James Beattie, John Dyer, William Gilpin, and other obscure authors. The editors argue convincingly that Wordsworth's poems show multiple versions and careful revision, so that the question of authorship is not a problem. Still, one wonders when the fragments printed here are as brief as the following from sections titled "Miscellaneous Drafts and Jottings": "Ha, treacherous Foe" (697), or "holy bell" (700), or "The lake of the mountain" (704). When the definition of "fragment" includes phrases of two or three words, one questions the issue of authorship and at the same time stands in awe of the editors' attention to detail.

There is, however, a more serious issue of attribution and authorship here. Wordsworth not only borrowed from other writers for mottoes and models for adaptation and imitation, he worked together with Francis Wrangham on an imitation of Juvenal's "Satire VIII." The editors attribute many lines to Wordsworth, but others cannot with certainty be attributed to him rather than Wrangham. Finally, Wordsworth gave Coleridge some short poems, which Coleridge subsequently published in the *Morning Post* under a pseudonym, and the first two parts of a ballad, "The Three Graves," for which Coleridge later wrote two more parts published in *Sibylline Leaves* (1817). One great value of this edition is that it provides not only reliable and full versions of episodes Wordsworth later transformed, such as the stolen boat episode and the second example of a spot of time from *The Prelude*, it also makes clear that adaptation, imitation, and collaborative authorship were present from the very beginning of Wordsworth's poetic career, as they were in Coleridge's. The case for the study of collaborative authorship in the period is thus strengthened. The boundaries of the edition extend beyond the works of a single author.

At first glance, Bruce Graver's edition of *Translations of Chaucer and Virgil* follows more closely the earlier format of the Cornell Wordsworth.

Modernizations of Chaucer's "Prioress's Tale," "The Manciple, (from the Prologue) And his Tale," 169 lines from "Troilus and Cresida," and "The Cuckoo and the Nightingale," in the eighteenth century thought to be Chaucer's, along with the first three books of the *Aeneid* with short sections from later books are presented in clean reading texts with notes to all textual variants and a separate table of nonverbal variants. In separate sections, full transcripts of the relevant manuscripts are set in pages facing the photographs of the manuscripts for the Chaucer modernizations, and full transcripts of the manuscripts follow a continuous printing of the photographs for *The Aeneid*. Wordsworth began his modernizations of Chaucer in 1801 and finished initial work on them in April 1802. Revisions were made on "The Prioress's Tale" for publication in *The River Duddon* (1820), and that version provides Graver's copy text, because, as Graver says, it is "the earliest complete version" (33). The reading texts of "The Cuckoo and the Nightingale" and "Troilus" come from *Poems, Chiefly of Early and Late Years* (1842), although both were published in *The Poems of Geoffrey Chaucer, Modernized* (1841), edited by R. H. Horne and Thomas Powell, whom Mary Wordsworth suspected of trying to capitalize on Wordsworth's name. Wordsworth did not supervise the versions in *Chaucer, Modernized*, so Graver chose the texts that Wordsworth did supervise a year later. The reading text of "The Manciple," not published in Wordsworth's lifetime, comes from a manuscript prepared for *Chaucer, Modernized* in 1840. Thus while most of the work on modernizing Chaucer was done in 1801–1802, the reading texts of the complete versions come from 1820 and the 1840's, a slight deviation from the Cornell Wordsworth's declared intention of bringing the early Wordsworth into view.

A more interesting difference between this and earlier volumes in the series is the inclusion of commentary on literary history. Graver remarks at the outset that we know a great deal about Wordsworth's relationship to Shakespeare, Spenser, and Milton, but nothing about Wordsworth's relationship to Chaucer, in spite of the claim in a note to the 1800 Preface to *Lyrical Ballads* that Chaucer's language is "pure and universally intelligible even to this day." Graver pays close attention to the state of Chaucer modernizing in the eighteenth-century, the attempts by Dryden and William Lipscomb in *The Canterbury Tales, Complete in a Modern Version* (1795). Graver points out that Dryden's is best described as an adaptation, since it often deviates from Chaucer's text, and that Lipscomb changed Chaucer's verse forms, notwithstanding his claims of staying close to Chaucer's texts. In comparison to Dryden and Lipscomb, Wordsworth remained close to Chaucer's language and figures, changing only what was absolutely necessary. Graver includes a section of "Editor's Notes" in which he explains Wordsworth's choice of diction, taking into account his edition of Chaucer in Anderson's *The Works of the British Poets*, which in turn reprinted Thomas Tyrwhitt's edition of *The Canterbury Tales* and glossary (1775–78), a highly regarded work, and the minor poems from John Urry's 1721 edition of Chaucer. Graver also includes some important paragraphs on a revival of interest in Chaucer in 1817 and 1818. Both William Hazlitt and Leigh Hunt derided Dryden's work, and Hunt called for modernizations similar to Wordsworth's, so that when Wordsworth published "The Prioress's Tale" in 1820 he could hope for a warm reception. Graver's introduction provides essential information on Wordsworth's relationship to Chaucer, and thus provides a basis on which fuller discussions must be based. His inclusion of material from literary history in an edition has, perhaps, an unintended consequence. It widens the audience to include medievalists interested in Chaucer's reception, and after all, publishers do pay attention to the size of a potential audience for any book. A medievalist in my department bought his copy before I received my review copy.

Wordsworth's efforts at translating Virgil were less successful than his Chaucer modernizations. Wordsworth began translating Virgil in 1823 with the intention of surpassing Dryden by avoiding the rigid syntax and cadences of Dryden's couplets. Wordsworth used heroic couplets, but with a greater degree of enjambment, which came closer to Virgil's verse. Wordsworth's attempts to translate Virgilian diction produced awkward English at times. His translations were coolly received by his friends and patrons in 1824, although Wordsworth persisted in thinking them worthy and seeking experts' approval for publication, although finally only lines 901–1041 of Book I were published in the journal *The Philological Museum* (1832). In 1827 with the assistance of his nephew Christopher Wordsworth, he corrected manuscripts of 1834, which form the reading texts of Books I and II. The reading text for Book III comes from an 1824 manuscript with some additions from a later manuscript. Wordsworth borrowed from earlier translators, and Graver's "Editor's Notes" print parallel sections from Dryden, Pitt, Ogilby and Trapp where Wordsworth borrows or slightly modifies their work.

His notes to the reading text are complex and include, for Book I, Coleridge's commentary, which appears in a band beneath the reading text. The textual variants come beneath Coleridge's commentary, and beneath the variants, a third band of Graver's commentary on Wordsworth's translation. Coleridge's notes are pointed, peevish, clever, and merciless. Coleridge complains of "unenglishisms here & there in this translation of which I remember no instance in your own poems" (190), although I must add that his comments on Wordsworth are much milder than those he wrote in the margins of Southey's *Joan of Arc* (1796). On Wordsworth lines "His arts conceal'd the crime, and gave vain scope / In Dido's bosom to a trembling hope," Coleridge wrote, "You have convinced me of the *necessary* injury which a Language must sustain by rhyme translations of narrative poems of great length. What would you have said at Allfoxden or in Grasmere Cottage to giving vain scopes to trembling hopes in a bosom?" (197). From these two comments one could construct a concluding chapter in the relationship between the Wordsworth and Coleridge.

Both of these volumes are edited and annotated with care for detail and brilliance of learning one has come to expect of the Cornell Wordsworth series. From a careful reading of them, one may learn more than from a full shelf of critical opinion. Most importantly, to my mind, these two volumes widen the scope of scholarly editions from a focus on an individual author to include work of other writers, collaborators, and commentators. Perhaps some will regard this as burdensome clutter; others, however, will recognize that the inclusion of others' work gives a truer picture of the creative process.

Paul Magnuson

The Frankenstein Notebooks: A Facsimile Edition of Mary Shelley's Manuscript Novel, 1816–17 As It Survives In Draft and Fair Copy. The Manuscripts of the Younger Romantics. 2 vols. Edited by Charles E. Robinson. New York & London: Garland Publishing, 1996. cx + 827 pp. $445.00.

MANY OF THE CRITICAL CONTROVERSIES surrounding *Frankenstein* have involved the manuscript material. In particular, Mary Shelley scholars have quarrelled over the role her husband Percy played in helping to prepare the manuscript for publication. Some have claimed that he did so much to revise the text that he ought to be elevated almost to the level of co-author. Others have belittled his role and even argued that his revisions, far from improving Mary Shelley's text, actually made it worse in certain respects. Until the publication of this facsimile edition of the manuscript, the general academic public has been forced to rely on reports from the few scholars who were fortunate enough to obtain access to the *Frankenstein* manuscript material in the Bodleian Library, Oxford. Now, thanks to the editorial efforts of Charles E. Robinson, those interested in *Frankenstein* can see for themselves what Percy's contribution to the published version of the book was (with some inevitable ambiguity remaining because of handwriting and other problems). More generally, these two large volumes provide an unprecedented glimpse into Mary Shelley's workshop and thus a chance to explore the question she herself formulated in her introduction to the 1831 edition of *Frankenstein*: "How I, then a young girl, came to think of, and to dilate upon, so very hideous an idea?" No scholarly edition can ever solve the mystery of artistic creation, but the *Frankenstein* notebooks will give Mary Shelley scholars much to ponder for years to come.

To begin with, it is important to realize what this edition does and does not contain. The bulk of the two volumes is devoted to reproducing the 301 pages of the 1816–17 *Frankenstein* manuscript, largely in Mary Shelley's hand but including suggestions and changes made by Percy. Unfortunately the manuscript is not complete, but represents by Robinson's estimate roughly 87% of *Frankenstein* as first published in

1818. The edition also contains whatever remains of the Fair Copy of the text prepared for the publisher, some of it in Mary's hand, some of it in Percy's, amounting to only 12% of the 1818 *Frankenstein* edition. For both the Manuscript and the Fair Copy, Robinson's edition provides photocopies on one page and then on a double-columned facing page a transcription of the photocopied page coupled with a transcription of the corresponding portion of the 1818 text. Having a transcription helps the reader in deciphering the Manuscript and the Fair Copy (which are fairly legible to begin with) and the use of different fonts (and other graphic aids) makes it possible to sort out Percy Shelley's contributions from Mary's. Since Percy and Mary had surprisingly similar handwritings, the editor's effort to distinguish their contributions turns out to be helpful to the reader. Robinson re-assures us: "there are enough differences" in their scripts "to make me confident that in almost all cases I have properly distinguished their hands" (I, xxx). The column transcribing the 1818 text of *Frankenstein* makes it easy to compare the handwritten material with the first published version of the novel. The volumes also contain several appendices that make other significant comparisons possible, such as the Manuscript with the Fair Copy material in either Mary's or Percy's hand. In short, the editor and publisher have done everything within reason to make this edition useful to Mary Shelley scholars.

What this volume does not and cannot provide is the first draft of *Frankenstein*, which simply does not survive. But as Robinson points out, there are many signs that the manuscript we have is derived from an earlier version or versions. Above all, we have Mary Shelley's claim in her introduction to the 1831 edition of *Frankenstein* that the earliest version of the story began with the words: "It was on a dreary night of November." Since this passage does not appear in the text we now have until well into the novel (page 97 in Robinson's edition, for example), we must surmise that Mary substantially reworked her earliest version into what we today know as *Frankenstein*. Robinson speculates on what the *Urtext* of *Frankenstein* might have looked like, though he is the first to admit how hypothetical such a reconstruction must be. But he plausibly argues that the original core of *Frankenstein* was the story of Victor's creation of the creature and that Mary Shelley expanded the material into novel length by adding the frame story of the arctic explorer Robert Walton and the inner tale of Safie the Arabian maiden. In the absence of the earliest manuscript version or versions of *Frankenstein*, the full history of the novel's genesis will never be known with certainty. Another stage in the creation of *Frankenstein* as we know it is also missing; none of the page proofs have survived and it is clear that some changes and additions to the text were made during the proofreading process—in which both Percy and Mary participated (the parallel columns in Robinson's edition make it easy to identify passages in the 1818 printed text that do not appear in either the Manuscript or the Fair Copy as we have them, but under the circumstances it is very difficult if not impossible to determine whether Mary or Percy was responsible for any given change on the proof sheets). I emphasize what is missing from this edition, not to criticize it—after all,

Robinson cannot reproduce what does not exist—but to caution readers that even an edition as good as this is not going to settle all our questions about *Frankenstein*.

Still, it is remarkable how many insights this new edition offers into Mary Shelley's novel—and not only into the question of its genesis but also into the question of its meaning. As editor, Robinson is mainly concerned with making the material accessible to scholars, and he genuinely wants them to be able to draw their own conclusions. As he explains: "I have attempted to be as objective and factual as possible in editing this novel, and I do not intend to offer any extensive analysis at this point" (I, lvii). Nevertheless, in his introduction and his notes, Robinson makes many apt observations about *Frankenstein* and illustrates how useful this manuscript material can be to scholars. For example, his introduction contains a very interesting section on the problem of naming in the *Frankenstein* notebooks. Robinson deals first with the perennial question of what to call the being Frankenstein creates, but he also shows how complicated the naming of other characters is in the manuscript. The character we know as "Elizabeth Lavenza" was originally called "Myrtella" and Frankenstein's friend Henry Clerval was originally called "Carignan" (this is some of the best evidence that the manuscript we have is derived from an earlier version). As Robinson points out, the fact that Clerval's name is spelled "Clairval" at twenty places in the manuscript suggests a connection in Mary Shelley's mind between this character and the Clairmont family (her stepsister Claire Clairmont was involved in the Byron–Shelley circle at the time of the genesis of *Frankenstein*).

Perhaps the most interesting name change in the manuscript involves the Arabian maiden Safie, who was originally called "Maimouna." Robinson traces this name to a character named "Maimuna" in Robert Southey's orientalist fantasy epic *Thalaba the Destroyer* (in the one error I found in this edition Robinson unaccountably gives Southey's first name as "William" on p. lix). Robinson adds that Percy Shelley used the name "Maimuna" for one of the characters in his own orientalist fantasy, the unfinished 1814 prose romance *The Assassins*. This link to works like *Thalaba* and *The Assassins* places *Frankenstein* squarely within the realm of early nineteenth-century orientalist discourse. This observation thus serves to confirm a claim that several critics in recent years have made independently, that *Frankenstein* can be understood as an example of Romantic orientalism. The creature even has "yellow" skin—a point we can now underscore thanks to Robinson's edition because the manuscript shows that Mary Shelley originally wrote "dun skin" and changed it to "yellow" in the margin (I, 97)—as if she were reconceiving the creature on the model of an oriental (an idea further developed by the way Mary Shelley links the creature with the Arabian Safie—both strangers in a strange land, they in effect learn the French language together).

As for the main issue this facsimile edition finally allows us to examine for ourselves—the extent of Percy Shelley's role in the composition of *Frankenstein*—I confess that I am still digesting the evidence. My initial reaction is that Percy's contribution was more extensive than I had been led to believe by those who wish to minimize his role in the creation of *Frankenstein*. At the same time, though, his role seems to me to be considerably less than I was led to believe by those who wish to proclaim him the co-author of the book. By Robinson's count, Percy "actually wrote and was responsible for more than 4000 words" in the *Frankenstein* manuscript as we have it, although he quickly qualifies this statement by pointing out that it is not always possible to tell Percy's handwriting from Mary's with certainty (I, lxviii). Still, even allowing for a margin of error, 4000 words is a substantial contribution to a relatively brief work like *Frankenstein*. But, as Robinson explains, many of the revisions are very slight, sometimes involving nothing more than changing "that" to "which" or "men" to "fishermen" (I, lxviii). Occasionally Percy did propose substantive additions to the text of *Frankenstein*, for example a passage about the superiority of Swiss "republican institutions" over neighboring monarchical regimes (I, 127–29). But I have not seen evidence to convince me that Percy played a significant role in shaping the plot of *Frankenstein* or the basic conception of the novel.

On balance, I would characterize Percy Shelley's contribution to *Frankenstein* as that of a very careful and sympathetic editor, working with an author who trusted him and whose interest he genuinely took to heart. This is the view of Percy's role taken by Zachary Leader in the best account I have seen of the subject, the "Parenting *Frankenstein*" chapter of his *Revision and Romantic Authorship* (Oxford: Oxford UP, 1996). I refer readers to this volume if they wish a fuller account of the whole controversy surrounding Percy's contribution to *Frankenstein*. Leader reviews the main arguments that have been made on both sides of the dispute, including the work of James Rieger and Anne Mellor, and he illuminates the controversy by discussing parallel cases, including Mary Shelley's editorial contribution to Byron's work as one of the chief transcribers of his manuscripts for the printer, as well as her work in editing Percy's manuscripts for publication. As Leader points out, no one has proposed that Mary be regarded as the co-author of *Don Juan*, even though, as he shows, her contribution to the published form of the poem was only slightly less than Percy's to the published form of *Frankenstein*.

One of Percy's marginal comments on the *Frankenstein* manuscript perhaps best encapsulates his role in its composition. In the section describing the visit Frankenstein and Clerval make to Oxford, Mary had originally written about their activities as tourists: "We were also shown a room which the Lord Chancellor Bacon had inhabited and which, as it was predicted, would fall in when a man wiser than that philosopher should enter it" (II, 461). Realizing Mary's mistake, Percy wrote in the margin: "no sweet Pecksie—'twas *friar* Bacon the discoverer of gunpowder." This is perhaps a more intimate glimpse into the domestic relations of Percy and Mary than we really wish to have, and many might regard his comment as condescending. And yet it is difficult to deny that Percy was genuinely concerned to prevent Mary from making an error in print, and we can see that she dutifully entered her husband's corrections on the manuscript (misspelling "friar" as "frier" in the process). But the blank space staring at us in Robinson's edition in the parallel column with the transcription of the 1818 published version of *Frankenstein* informs us that for some reason this whole passage was dropped when the novel actually went into print. As fruitful and cordial as the working relationship between Percy and Mary may have been, perhaps his suggestions, however well-meaning, did produce some tension between them after all.

I suspect that the opportunity Robinson has provided to examine the *Frankenstein* notebooks will chiefly provoke Mary Shelley scholars to weigh in on the debate over Percy's role in the novel's composition. But this manuscript material can prove useful in other ways, including interpreting *Frankenstein*. Take, for example, the passage describing Frankenstein's reaction to his creature when he first animates it. The scientist is horrified when he finally sees how his ideal vision has become corrupted now that it has been embodied in material form. Ever since I started teaching *Frankenstein* in the 1960s, I have been struck by the way Mary Shelley here anticipates her husband's understanding of his poetic creativity—the fact that he felt that his poems as written down never lived up to the way he initially imagined them, or, as Percy himself explained in his *Defence of Poetry*: "when composition begins, inspiration is already on the decline, and the most glorious poetry that has ever been communicated to the world is probably a feeble shadow of the original conception of the poet." I made the parallels between Frankenstein's disappointment as a scientific creator and Percy Shelley's as a poet the centerpiece of my interpretation of *Frankenstein* in my book *Creature and Creator: Myth-making and English Romanticism* (Cambridge: Cambridge UP, 1984). Now that I am able to view a good reproduction of the manuscript of *Frankenstein*, I can see that Percy actually had a hand in the passage that has been key to my interpretation of the book. Mary originally phrased Frankenstein's description of his creature this way: "His limbs were in proportion and I had selected his features as handsome. Handsome; Great God! His dun skin scarcely covered the work of muscles and arteries beneath" (I, 97). Robinson's edition reveals that Percy changed "handsome" to "beautiful" in the margin of the manuscript and that is the way the passage has read ever since. Thus it was Percy who introduced the issue of beauty in this passage; that is, he made this scene more a matter of aesthetics than it was in Mary's original formulation. One might even conclude that Percy himself sensed the connection between Frankenstein's aesthetic disappointment in his creation and his own view of poetry as he was to go on to articulate it in the *Defence*.

The careful examination of the *Frankenstein* manuscript material Robinson's edition has made possible should lead Mary Shelley scholars to many such observations and discoveries. Certainly no one writing about *Frankenstein* can now afford to ignore Robinson's facsimile edition, and even anyone with a general interest in the book and in Mary Shelley should take a look at this manuscript evidence. And anyone interested in theoretical questions concerning the complicated nature of authorship should consider using *Frankenstein* as a case study. As Robinson and others have suggested—particularly Leader in his excellent chapter on the book—the composition history of *Frankenstein* raises all sorts of questions about the relations between authors and editors. Where does editing end and co-authorship begin? Are an editor's comments always intrusions and impositions, or might the author welcome them as a way of genuinely improving his or her work? As Leader suggests, might an editor try to craft his or her emendations in the style of the author he or she was editing? Though I myself have come to some tentative conclusions about these questions with regard to *Frankenstein*, I know that I will be pondering them for years. That is why I regard this facsimile edition of the *Frankenstein* notebooks as one of the most important editions published in decades.

Paul A. Cantor

Adventures of Huckleberry Finn. Intro. by Justin Kaplan. Foreword and Addendum by Victor Doyno. New York: Random House, 1996. xxviii + 418 pp. $25.00.

Mark Twain's Letters, Volume 5, 1872–1873. Ed. Lin Salamo and Harriet Elinor Smith. Berkeley: University of California Press, 1997. xxxv + 939 pp. $60.00. 80 b/w illus.

I T IS SOMETIMES INSTRUCTIVE, at a distance of three or four years, to look backward and assess the reception that newly available texts were accorded upon their arrival.

To take one instance, perhaps the oddest thing about the much-publicized Random House version of *Adventures of Huckleberry Finn* was the relative lack of *scholarly* debate about the unorthodox editorial principles of that notable event in Twain studies. Whereas most current Mark Twain bibliographies seem to be aflame with books and articles attacking or defending the cultural and artistic merits of Twain's most important novel, particularly in light of Twain's decision to permit Huck Finn to use an offensive racial pejorative, only a few sparks have flown over the appearance of this first edition to exploit the long-lost initial portion of Twain's manuscript. Not that the discovery of these 665 holograph sheets in 1990, their attempted sale in 1991, and the legal wrangling that ensued before they rejoined the 696-sheet second half of the novel in the Buffalo and Erie County Public Library exactly passed unnoticed. *The New York Times* and virtually every other major news organ covered these developments rather thoroughly. The successive and unprecedented occurrences were viewed as highly newsworthy footnotes in American literary history. But by the time the first fruit of this find issued from

Random House five years later, both public ardor and campus interest had apparently cooled.

The volume did of course get passing notice in both the commercial and intellectual press. Reviewing for the *Antioch Review* (54 no. 3 [Summer 1996]: 363–364), William Baker noted that "Twain couldn't have written a better detective story himself. A literary find (in an attic of all places) reveals minor changes (and some not so minor) in a classic" (364). Yet Baker merely added, noncommittally, "In either edition it is still our most notable American novel" (364). *Library Journal* diplomatically called it "the first to incorporate four previous unknown episodes discovered in 1990.... All this at a reasonable price makes Random's comprehensive edition of *Huckleberry Finn* essential for all libraries" (121 [15 April 1996]: 126). Reviewing the subsequent Fawcett/Ballantine paperback edition, *Library Journal* again opined that "considering the book's importance to American letters, this complete edition is essential for all libraries" (122 [15 April 1997]: 125).

However, the *Times Literary Supplement* was far less impressed. Joking of the first half of Mark Twain's manuscript that the "reports of its loss were clearly exaggerated," Ben Hadley in *TLS* nonetheless decreed that "this new edition is more provisional than 'comprehensive.'" Hadley felt that editor Victor Doyno had stated things "a bit defensively and not quite accurately" in assuring readers that they could easily read the original version by skipping over the "inserted sections." Still, all in all, Hadley wrote, the Random edition offers "a modestly expanded version of a well-known text, sensibly annotated and handsomely packaged" (3 January 1996: 24). Likewise, the reviewer for *Atlantic Monthly* declared that "it is a handsome book, with fine antique illustrations, but there is no need to discard one's present copy of *Huckleberry Finn*. All this edition really proves is that Twain was a careful writer who sometimes changed his mind but always knew what he was doing" (278 no. 2 [August 1996]: 94).

Less understandably, the academic sector in general basically shrugged, with only two exceptions. An essay-review by James W. Tuttleton condemned the Random House experiment altogether. What bothered Tuttleton was the reinsertion of manuscript passages that Twain had eventually omitted from the version he actually published. "The book represents a violation of the principles of textual scholarship in editing," Tuttleton concluded, insisting that it "cannot be used as the basis of any sound literary criticism." He argued that "its release to the reading public can only create a misunderstanding about *Huckleberry Finn* amongst general readers" ("Mark Twain: More 'Tears and Flapdoodle,'" *New Criterion* 15 no. 1 [1996]: 59-65). Robert H. Hirst, General Editor of the Mark Twain Project of the Bancroft Library at the University of California, Berkeley, expressed similar concerns that the book-buying public might be confused by a hastily prepared commercial edition and mistake it for the more thorough scholarly treatment being readied by Project editors. (The resurfacing of these presumably forever-vanished manuscript sheets is necessitating a drastic overhaul of the majestic 875-page edition of Twain's famous novel released by the Mark Twain Project in 1988.) Asked by reporter Josh

Getlin about the "so-called unexpurgated edition of 'Huckleberry Finn,'" Hirst contended that "by stitching together the rough first draft with the author's final version ... Random House has confused and misled the reading public." According to Hirst, "Mark Twain deleted this material for sound reasons, and to put it into a new authorized version now is to mix up two levels of textual reality." Victor Doyno disputed this dire interpretation, arguing that the glimpse Random House has afforded of Twain's artistry "shows us his strength as a critic and a comic." Getlin pondered "whether these Twain outtakes are a literary revelation or an overblown mishmash of what the author really intended" ("New Version of 'Huck' Stirs Controversy," *St. Louis Post-Dispatch*, April 25, 1996, p. 3G, also reprinted as "Revising 'Huck'/Controversy Swirls Over Adding Twain's Deleted Text to His Classic," *Newsday*, April 22, 1996, p. B3).

Doyno, increasingly recognized as the greatest living expert on Twain's masterpiece since the demise of Walter Blair in 1992, teaches at SUNY—Buffalo and has often been able to avail himself of the convenient proximity of Twain's manuscript while undertaking an assiduous study of the author's process of composition and practices of alteration. Random House allowed Doyno to produce an almost joyful edition, an exuberant tribute to Twain's writing methods that manages to capture much of the sense of discovery that Doyno obviously relished as he reconstructed Twain's habits of writing, originally summarized in Doyno's *Writing Huck Finn: Mark Twain's Creative Process* (Philadelphia: U Pennsylvania P, 1991) and now enlarged upon in his Foreword and Textual Addendum to what was advertised (on the dust jacket) as "the only comprehensive edition" of Twain's masterpiece.

Precisely what was it that antagonized the few reviewers who bothered to comment in any detail about Doyno's edition? Essentially their objections centered on his decision to provide readers with a "clear" text while reinserting various passages Twain later deleted.

The first of Doyno's decisions seemingly should not have aroused much opposition. He merely followed the lead of the Mark Twain Project/University of California Press edition of *Huckleberry Finn* in rescuing from near-oblivion the dramatic (so-called) "raftsmen" passage (in which Huck Finn surreptitiously boards a large raft on the river in an effort to eavesdrop and ascertain how far south he and Jim have drifted). This idea vastly enriches Chapter 16, where the episode formerly belonged before Twain and his publisher Charles L. Webster employed rare bad judgment by excising it in 1884. Few subsequent editions had been bold enough to overrule Twain in this matter, but the example of the respected Mark Twain Project in disobeying Twain's presumed "final intentions" in this regard has cleared the path for all future editors to make the same call. The MTP editors had defended themselves by pointing out that Twain had failed to notice that "some modification of the text was in fact needed" if this part of *Huckleberry Finn* were removed (447). In effect, their quiet reintroduction of Twain's bragging, brawling, yarning raftsmen reminds us of the degree to which purportedly objective and quasi-scientific editorial methodology can sometimes boil down to an essentially critical judgment.

As Doyno recognized, that portion of *Huckleberry Finn* virtually cries out for the return of this mistakenly jettisoned episode. But the version Doyno incorporated was, in his words, "less polite" than the raftsmen passage that Twain and Webster pried out of the novel and dumped expeditiously into the first part of Twain's *Life on the Mississippi*. So the work is thereby changed.

What other crucial differences set off the Doyno edition? There was, in particular, an account by the slave Jim of his ghoulish experiences in a dissecting room where he had been assigned by a medical student to warm up a cadaver. Doyno labels the unnerving episode an example of "burlesque gothic" and considers it to be quite possibly "Twain's best 'ghost story'" (375). The tale, told to a rapt Huck, fills more than three pages in the Random House edition, and whether or not Doyno is right about its merits (some will wince at this depiction of a black man's superstitious fears), it is rare for any such anecdote by a celebrated author, fully polished, to turn up after the passing of so many years—especially when it involves two of his best-known literary characters. Putting the passage in the rear of the volume would not have offered readers the same rush of excitement as exploring Jim's story within the larger context of Chapter 9. (And it should be noted that Doyno takes the precaution of setting off this subsequently canceled passage with horizontal bars at its beginning and end.)

Doyno also prints a harsher rendition of the King's missionary efforts at the camp meeting, producing a narrative in which a slave woman's antics at the mourner's bench draw unfavorable attention. Other, smaller variants from the first edition crop up throughout the text and are duly explicated by the editor.

These restorations aside, the information and insights provided by Victor Doyno's "Textual Addendum" are worth the price of the book itself, yielding far more knowledge than the purchasers of any trade book edition have a right to expect. There is, for example, a discussion of public education in Missouri in the 1840s, a treatment of methods of corporal punishment for children, a dissertation upon the role of graveyard "resurrectionists," a rumination on religious camp meetings, and numerous analyses of Twain's subtle revisions in language discernible in the newly found manuscript. Additionally, Doyno attaches reprintings of the first-edition versions of three passages that differed markedly from Twain's original manuscript. Then he supplies facsimile reproductions of thirty sheets from the long-missing manuscript displaying (with impressive clarity) some of Twain's most intriguing holograph revisions. In the latter, for example, we see Twain's ink superscript insertion that turned the first sentence of the novel from the stiff opening, "You will not know about me . . . " into a noticeably more informal "You don't know about me. . . . " We also see Twain, who seldom found a need to delete many words when composing, deciding to cancel nearly half a page of material when Huck is carefully devising his escape from the cabin where his father has locked him.

By contrast with the headline-grabbing discovery that set the stage for the Random House *Huckleberry Finn*, the Mark Twain Project edition of

Mark Twain's Letters arrived to a relatively familiar reception. By now nearly all reviewers appear inured to both the extremely deliberate pace of the Mark Twain Project productions as well as the mammoth textual apparatus and explanatory notes that accompany these "Cadillac" editions. Both tendencies formerly received comment, but no longer. "This volume is the fifth in the only complete edition of Mark Twain's letters ever attempted," was the routine-sounding notice in the *Virginia Quarterly Review* ([Winter 1998] 74 no. 1: 20). "The editors have thoroughly annotated and indexed the letters.... A job well done." A brief review in *Library Journal* complimented the editors: "There is not a boring letter herein. Essential for all libraries with Twain holdings" (122 no. 13 [August 1997]: 89). *American Literature* merely observed that more than half of the letters in the volume had never been published previously (69 no. 4 [December 1997]: 874). The editors of *Nineteenth-Century Literature* (52 no. 3 [December 1997]: 411) were enthusiastic. They termed the volume "a matchless research tool; a source of endless pleasure and gratification."

The most laudatory of all was Gary Scharnhorst's review in *Western American Literature* (33 no. 4 [Winter 1999]: 429–430). "A model of documentary editing.... This truest type of biography describes in inimitable detail the prosperity he enjoyed in the wake of the sales success of *Roughing It*" (429). "If there are no sensational revelations here, there are surprises aplenty. Who would have guessed (save the occasional specialist) how sentimental Twain could be in his letters to his wife, Olivia?" (430).

It could conceivably be objected by an aesthetic purist that too many of the missives are of a totally practical, utilitarian nature, frequently simply devoted to making arrangements. "Dear Sir: May I send you a brief article for acceptance or rejection" constitutes the complete text of a letter of 23 September 1873 to Shirley Brooks (442). "Can you send me a couple of copies of my Tribune letter of a few days ago concerning British liberality & the awarding of the Humane Society's gold medal to Capt. Mouland?," Twain wrote on 30 January 1873 to the staff of the New York *Tribune*. But such inclusiveness satisfies the diverse and unpredictable needs of the literary historian; besides, this was not designed to be a volume that will be read straight through for pleasure by the nonspecialist. That is *not* to say, however, that the letters assembled here from various collections are devoid of snatches of vintage Twain. Those with patience and a few hours to spend will run across such memorable nuggets as his bemoaning the mind-numbing labor of his day's writing on 17 February 1873, as the result of which his "head is thicker & muddier than ever.... I will ... go out & walk off some of this accumulating imbecility" (298). He could improvise humorously self-deprecating phrases like those without even trying. And although he would later come to question the credentials of Shakespeare, he seemed delighted on 11 September 1872 to report to Livy that he had "spent all day yesterday driving about Warwickshire in an open barouche. It is the loveliest land in its summer garb! We visited Kenilworth ruins, Warwick Castle (pronounce it *Warrick*) and the Shakespeare celebrities in & about Stratford-on-Avon" (155). Here, too, is the mildly famous letter of 15 June 1872 in which Twain facetiously implores William Dean Howells to send a copy of the dignified portrait of Howells that had appeared in *Hearth and Home*. Tongue-in-cheek, Twain claimed that Bret Harte "says his children get up in the night & yell for it. . . . I want you to send a copy to the man that shot my dog. I want to see if he is dead to every human instinct" (103). At the same time, Twain makes plans for one of his few truly profitable business ventures—Mark Twain's Self-Pasting Scrapbook (143), even sketching a picture of how the invention would look. His tenderness with his wife and daughters, his dawning awareness of the potential marketability of "Mark Twain" as an author and lecturer, his incredible energy for foreign travel, his ceaseless schemes, his nonstop correspondence with then-illustrious names on both sides of the Atlantic—Moncure D. Conway, Joaquin Miller, Petroleum V. Nasby (David Ross Locke), Whitelaw Reid, Andrew Lang, Thomas Nast, James Redpath, Frank Mayo—make us admire his industry (309 letters in the span of two years) as well as the foresight of the many recipients who prized and managed to preserve these ephemeral documents. Surely Mark Twain wrote hundreds more that did not survive, but it seems amazing that so many letters could be gathered and published after the passage of a century and a quarter. In 1872, be it noted, "Mark Twain" was not yet the household word that would guarantee the keeping of his every line of prose.

This fifth volume of *Mark Twain's Letters* has been embellished with every conceivable sort of aid for the working scholar—a facsimile reproduction of the broadside announcing Twain's first lecture series in London, a full transcription of the two journals he maintained during his visit to England in 1872, genealogical charts, thirty-six photographs, facsimile reproductions of sample letters, his book contracts, and even his preface to the English edition of *The Gilded Age*. A special section dedicated to eleven letters that somehow made their appearance *after* the preceding four volumes of letters were published by the Mark Twain Project testifies both to the editors' scrupulousness and to the amazing rate at which Twain items still keep coming to light nearly a century after his death. A twenty-eight-page "Guide to Editorial Practice" continues to defend, with persuasive logic, the "plain text" approach that was adopted from the outset of the series over the "clear text" and "genetic text" alternatives. Exhaustive "Texual Commentaries" record the copy-text, provenance, and editorial emendations connected with each letter. The voluminous "References" section and a minutely subsectioned index are luxuries that only the seasoned researcher can possibly appreciate with adequate gratitude. As usual with the Mark Twain Project volumes, then, a substantial price, a handsome if very hefty tome, more data than any single scholar could possibly ever utilize, and a sense of permanent value and invincible reliability.

Alan Gribben

Notes on Contributors

PAUL A. CANTOR is Professor of English at the University of Virginia. He has written on Mary Shelley's *The Last Man* and her "Transformation," and discusses *Frankenstein* in his *Creature and Creator: Myth-making and English Romanticism*.

ERIC ELIASON is Associate Professor and Chair of the Department of English at Gustavus Adolphus College. He is co-editor of *The Piers Plowman Electronic Archive*, Vol. 1, Corpus Christi College, Oxford MS201 (F).

JOHN IRWIN FISCHER is Professor of English at Louisiana State University. He is co-editor of the *Swift Poems Project: An Edition and Electronic Archive*.

ALAN GRIBBEN is Distinguished Research Professor and Head of the Department of English and Philosophy at Auburn University Montgomery. He writes the annual Mark Twain essay for *American Literary Scholarship*.

MICHAEL GRODEN is Professor of English at the University of Western Ontario and Artist-in-Residence at Eyebeam Atelier in New York City. He is the Director of *James Joyce's "Ulysses" in Hypermedia*, co-editor and co-translator (with Daniel Ferrer and Jed Deppman) of the forthcoming *French Genetic Criticism: Twelve Essays* and co-editor (with Martin Kreiswirth and Imre Szeman) of the forthcoming second edition of *The Johns Hopkins Guide to Literary Theory and Criticism*.

W. SPEED HILL is Emeritus Professor of English, Lehman College and The Graduate Center, CUNY. He was general editor of the *Folger Library Edition of the Works of Richard Hooker* and is current co-editor of *TEXT*.

CATHERINE HOLLIS is a Ph.D. candidate at the University of California at Berkeley, where she is finishing a dissertation called "Do-It-Yourself Modernism: Collaboration, Gender, and the Production of Books," a project that focuses on the material production of modernist texts.

EMMA HORNBY completed her doctorate (at Oxford) on the interaction between oral and written transmission in early medieval liturgical chant, using a close analysis of the eighth-mode tracts as its focus. From 1997–99 she was a Junior Research Fellow at Worcester College, Oxford. She is Lecturer in Music at Christ Church, Oxford.

KLAUS HURLEBUSCH is a member of the editorial team for the scholarly edition of the Complete Works and Letters of Friedrich Gottlob Klopstock (the *Hamburg Klopstock Edition*), in progress since 1974. He is Director of the edition's research center at the Hamburg State and University Library and the volume editor of several individual edition volumes. Together with K. L. Schneider, he also edited the study edition of the poetry, writings, and letters of the early expressionist poet Ernst Stadler (1983). The principal subjects of his scholarly and critical writing are German authors of the eighteenth and early nineteenth centuries, as well as editorial theory.

ANNEMARIE KETS–VREE is Head of the Department for Modern Literature at the Constantijn Huygens Institute for Text Editions and Intellectual History in The Hague (Holland). She has published several scholarly editions of nineteenth- and twentieth-century Dutch literature. She is currently working on a study edition of the *Studentenschetsen* of Johannes Kneppelhout (1814–85) and on the *Complete Works* of Willem Frederik Hermans (1921–1995).

TIM WILLIAM MACHAN is Professor and Chair of English at Marquette University. He has published widely on medieval literature, textual criticism, and English linguistics. He is currently completing a book entitled *Diversely They Said: Language and Society in Medieval England*.

PAUL MAGNUSON is Professor of English at New York University. His recent books include *Coleridge and Wordsworth: A Lyrical Dialogue* (1988) and *Reading Public Romanticism* (1998).

STEVEN MENTZ is a Ph.D. candidate at Yale University. He is writing a dissertation on prose romance, the book market, and popular culture in Elizabethan England, focusing on the works of Sidney, Greene, Lodge, and Nashe.

JONATHAN S. MYEROV is completing his doctorate in English at West Virginia University. His dissertation will examine early medieval English literature in the context of the possibilities and problems created by electronic editions for scholarly use.

RÜDIGER NUTT–KOFOTH worked from 1992–99 on the historical–critical edition of the works of Annette von Droste–Hülshoff and the edition of the letters of Therese Huber. He teaches scholarly editing at the University of Osnabrück and is a collaborator at the "Goethe-Dictionary" in Hamburg.

TED–LARRY PEBWORTH is William E. Stirton Professor in the Humanities and Professor of English Emeritus at the University of Michigan-Dearborn. He is the author of *Owen Felltham*, co-author of *Ben Jonson* and *Ben Jonson Revised,* and co-editor of *The Poems of Owen Felltham*, *Selected Poems of Ben Jonson*. A past president of the John Donne Society of America, he is a senior textual editor and member of the Advisory Board of *The Variorum Edition of the Poetry of John Donne*, for which he is presently editing Donne's satires.

SAM SLOTE is the scholar in residence at the Poetry/Rare Books Room, SUNY-Buffalo. He has co-edited two books on Joyce and genetic criticism: *Probes: Genetic Studies in Joyce* (1995) and *Genitricksling Joyce* (1999). He is also the author of *The Silence in Progress of Dante, Mallarmé, and Joyce* (1999).

GARY A. STRINGER is Professor of English at the University of Southern Mississippi and general editor of *The Variorum Edition of the Poetry of John Donne*, of which volumes 6 and 8 have appeared. He is currently working on volume 2 containing the elegies, due to appear in 2000.

DIRK VAN HULLE is Research Assistant at the Antwerp James Joyce Centre (University of Antwerp, UIA, Belgium), preparing a Ph.D. dissertation on the textual genesis of James Joyce's *Finnegans Wake*, Marcel Proust's *A la recherche du temps perdu*, and Thomas Mann's *Doktor Faustus*. His recent English publications on electronic editing and Proust appear in *Human IT* (1999); on Joyce and Beckett, in *Joyce Studies Annual* (1999) and *European Joyce Studies 9* (also 1999).

H. T. M. VAN VLIET is Director of the Constantijn Huygens Institute for text-editions at The Hague and visiting professor of textual scholarship at the Free University of Amsterdam. He has produced several scholarly editions of modern Dutch literature and published many essays on editing and bibliographical problems. His most recent publication is a book on the bindings and their variants of the works of Louis Couperus (1863–1923).

PAUL WERSTINE is Professor of English at King's College and in the graduate department of the University of Western Ontario. He has written widely on the editing of Shakespeare's plays and is co-general editor (with Richard Knowles) of the New Variorum Shakespeare and co-editor (with Barbara A. Mowat) of the New Folger Library Shakespeare.

The Society for Textual Scholarship

F OUNDED IN 1979, the Society for Textual Scholarship is an organization devoted to providing a forum, in its biennial conferences and its journal *TEXT*,* for the discussion of the interdisciplinary and theoretical implications of current research into various aspects of contemporary textual work: the discovery, enumeration, description, bibliographical analysis, editing, and annotation of texts in disciplines such as literature (European, American, Classical, and Oriental), history, musicology, biblical studies, philosophy, art history, legal history, history of science and technology, computer science, library science, lexicography, epigraphy, palaeography, codicology, cinema studies, theater, linguistics, as well as textual and literary theory. All these have been represented in conferences or STS publications since the first gathering in New York in 1981, and the conference is now recognized as the most wide-ranging and influential meeting of textual scholars in the world. In the first ten conferences, over 800 papers have been presented by speakers representing the disciplines listed above, with a chronological range of topics from early Egyptian and Mycenean inscriptions and pre-exilic biblical texts to computer concordances of present-day authors and the examination of governmental and foundation funding for editing and textual research.

The first nine presidents of the Society represent a similarly wide range of authority, from Anglo–American bibliography via Renaissance and neo-Latin scholarship to biblical studies and linguistics, philosophy, seventeeth-century English literature, and Italian opera: G. Thomas Tanselle (*John Simon Guggenheim Memorial Foundation*), 1981–83, Paul Oskar Kristeller (*Columbia University*), 1983–85, Fredson Bowers (*University of Virginia*), 1985–87, Eugene A. Nida (*American Bible Society*), 1987–89, Jo Ann Boydston (*Center for Dewey Studies*), 1989–91, James Thorpe (*Huntington Library*), 1991–93, Philip Gossett (*University of Chicago*), 1993–95, Bruce M. Metzger (*Princeton Theological Seminary*), 1995–97, and Jerome McGann (*University of Virginia*), 1997–99. David Greetham (*The Graduate School, CUNY*) is president for 1999–2001. The members of the Society's Advisory Board, which evaluates contributions to *TEXT*, show a parallel range of interests, with a large international component.

The range of editorial work represented by members, conferees, advisors, or officers of STS is very broad, including editors of, for example, the *Anchor Bible* and the Garland James Joyce, various Old English works, Marguerite de Navarre, Chaucer, Langland, Gower, Wycliff, Hoccleve, the Polyphonic *Kyrie*, the Towneley Plays, Wyatt, Shakespeare, G. Bellini, Richard Hooker, Donne, Milton, Dryden, Rochester, Pope, Johnson, Klopstock, Voltaire, Hume, Blake, Burns, Scott, Wordsworth, Coleridge, Byron, Shelley, Keats, James Fenimore Cooper, Rossini, Thackeray, Melville, Verdi, Flaubert, Lewis Carroll, Edison, Olmsted, Morris, Henry Adams, Conrad, D. W. Griffith, Yugoslav oral epic, Proust, Dewey, Santayana, Yeats, Pound, O'Neill, Orson Welles, Spender, Pinter, and others.

The biennial conferences, held in New York City, encourage the same interdisciplinary range. While there are usually some period or author-centered sessions (e.g., on medieval, Renaissance, or modern textual studies), most sessions address a general textual problem, with contributions from speakers in various disciplines. Such sessions have included *Feminism and Editing Texts by Women, Computerizing Critical Editions, Contemporary Literary Theory and Textual Criticism, Authorial Revision, Non-Verbal Texts, Words and Music, Editorial Ethics, Editors and the Problem of Intention, The Relations of Text and Document, The Meaning of the Text, Problems in Attribution and Provenance, Stemmatics and Contamination, Theorizing Text and Editing: European Perspectives / Anglo–American Perspectives, The Book as Construction Site*. A typical illustration of the cross-disciplinary aims of STS is a session at the 1987 conference called *Text as Performance Representation Reconstruction*, in which G. E. Bentley, Jr., spoke on Blake's verbal and visual texts as differing "performances," Stephen Orgel discussed the "representation" of a Shakespeare "score" of a play on stage, Charles E. Beveridge analyzed the relations between Olmsted's "greensward plan" for Central Park and its implementation in the park itself, and Boyd H. Davis illustrated the problems of reconstructing Saussure's *Cours* from the multilingual students' notes of lectures: four speakers from four different disciplines, each confronted with the issue of analyzing a "text" in its "performance." Complementing these general sessions, STS members may also arrange their own sessions at the conferences (for example, on specific editorial projects), in which case they are responsible for confirming speakers and topics. At each conference, the Fredson Bowers Prize is awarded for a distinguished essay in textual scholarship published in the previous two years. Past winners were James L. W. West III, Adrian Weiss, Neil Fraistat, Michael O'Gorman, Robert Clare, and Marta L. Werner. The dates for the 2001 conference are 19–21 April; inquiries should be addressed to the conference organizer, Robin G. Schulze, Department of English, Penn State University, University Park, PA 16802-6200; email: RGS3@psu.edu.

The editors welcome contributions for future volumes of *TEXT*. All submissions are read and evaluated by selected members of the STS Advisory Board. The Society also welcomes applications for membership. Enquiries regarding membership should be sent to:

Nancy Goslee, Secretary–Treasurer
Society for Textual Scholarship
Department of English
University of Tennessee
Knoxville, TN 37996-0430
E-mail: ngoslee@utk.edu

Submissions to *TEXT* (except requests about reviews or books for review) should be sent (three copies, please) to:

W. Speed Hill
Co-Editor, *TEXT*
33C Tier Street
Bronx, NY 10464-1343
Tel: 718 885-0885 (voice/fax–call first)
E-mail: WSHLC@cunyvm.cuny.edu

Inquiries about reviews, or books for review, should be sent to:

Peter L. Shillingsburg
Book Review Editor, *TEXT*
English Department
University of North Texas
Denton, TX 76203
Tel: 904 565-2050
Email: PLS1@unt.edu

The Society's web site is www.textual.org

Board of Advisors, *TEXT*

Officers

TEXT, Volumes 1–12

TEXT 1, New York: AMS P, 1984. pp. xvi + 338.
TEXT 2, New York: AMS P, 1985. pp. xii + 280.
TEXT 3, New York: AMS P, 1987. pp. xvi + 432.
TEXT 4, New York: AMS P, 1988. pp. xv + 414.
TEXT 5, New York: AMS P, 1991. pp. vii + 366.
TEXT 6, New York: AMS P, 1994. pp. xvi + 420.
TEXT 7, Ann Arbor: U of Michigan P, 1994. pp. xvi + 550.
TEXT 8, Ann Arbor: U of Michigan P, 1995. pp. xiv + 508.
TEXT 9, Ann Arbor: U of Michigan P, 1996. pp. x + 492.
TEXT 10, Ann Arbor: U of Michigan P, 1997. pp. x + 438.
TEXT 11, Ann Arbor: U of Michigan P, 1998. pp. x + 436.
TEXT 12, Ann Arbor: U of Michigan P, 1999. pp. x + 283.

To order back copies of each volume, please write to the Society for Textual Scholarship at the address above. (Volumes 1–3 and 8 are out of print.)